Medieval and
Renaissance Music on
Long-Playing Records:
Supplement, 1962-1971

D0562719

Medieval and Renaissance Music on Long-Playing Records: Supplement, 1962-1971

by James Coover
and Richard Colvig

Detroit Studies in
Music Bibliography 26

Information Coordinators, Inc.
Detroit, 1973

Copyright 1973 by James Coover and Richard Colvig
Printed and bound in the United States of America
Price $8.50 paper $7.00
Library of Congress Catalog Card Number 65-916
Standard Book Number 911772-44-8

Information Coordinators, Inc.
1435-37 Randolph Street
Detroit, Michigan 48226

CONTENTS

INTRODUCTION

Twelve years ago, to the day, in the "Introduction" to the original edition of this index (dated 1960), we remarked the effect of the first decade of the long-playing record upon our musical life, the amount of serious music, including unusual repertoire, being made available to us, and the increasingly commendable quality of the performances. That such outpourings complicate the problems of bibliographical organization and create particularly urgent needs for bibliographical control of special periods, styles, media, genre, performers and species was also noted —— not without some hope. As we laid aside the final proofs for that edition and its *Supplement,* which brought the coverage to the end of 1961, we were reasonably certain that some project or service would appear before another decade had passed which would obviate the need for this, the *Second Supplement.* But such has not been the case.

There have been discussions —— endless discussions —— among music librarians about how to provide users of recordings with access to the individual pieces contained in recorded anthologies —— whether they be jazz, rock or other popular music, folk songs, romantic piano works, organ recitals, or medieval and renaissance compositions. Out of these talks has come very little —— a surge of excitement from time to time over a new scheme for shared cataloging or photolith publication of an existing catalog, short-lived smiles over the prospects for a computerized data base to which all could have access and whose data could be infinitely, instantly and inexpensively exploited by all libraries, and guarded enthusiasm over announcements about the impending publication of new discographies (mostly abortive) which would ease the problems. But solutions stubbornly refuse to appear, and the mass of material to be organized increases at a geometric rate.

One of those bright prospects was the MARC (machine readable cataloging) project at the Library of Congress which may one day provide, on magnetic tape, information about recordings to assist libraries in cataloging them. Unfortunately, much of its promise is chimerical, especially in so far as the cataloging of difficult anthologies is concerned. Since the *Anglo-American Cataloging Rules* (with the infamous Rule 250.B.1, "Two or more works by different persons issued under a collective title are entered under the title, unless the compiler is prominently displayed on the label or other source..."), have been accepted as Holy Writ by the Library of Congress (and many other libraries!) none of the cataloging supplied by LC —— by MARC tape or in whatever fashion —— will provide access to the myriad musical works bibliographically buried on thousands of recorded anthologies existing now or in the future. That some solution must be found is obvious. The experience of the past clearly shows that the efforts of individuals, like the present compilers, can never catch up with or stay abreast of, the output of recordings throughout the world.

And so, in the final stages of completing this *Second Supplement,* the coverage of another decade, to the end of 1971, we are less hopeful than we were twelve years ago. And saddened, for if this *Second Supplement* does nothing else, it points up the wealth of material which could and should be made readily available to people —— not at ten-year intervals, but currently, as the records are issued and received in libraries.

As the product of ten years of activity some 459 anthologies are listed here. The original edition and its supplement included 387, some of them only seven-inch and ten-inch discs. The number of individual compositions has nearly doubled, the number of different composers almost trebled. One can be dismayed at the appearance of the seventeenth (!) recorded performance of Isaac's *Innsbruck, ich muss dich lassen* as well as by the innumerable worthwhile works which this index, by individual composers, shows to be unrecorded, but there has been an undeniably bounteous harvest.

Not to be overlooked in the excitement of perusing the wealth of new anthologies is the frequency with which many of the recordings listed ten years ago have been reissued and made once again available. Over a hundred reissues are noted here in the "Addenda and Corrigenda to the Original Edition and First Supplement," and this, even though we have made no special effort to search out all such reissues but have noted only those which came to us incidentally as part of our collecting.

In general we have made few changes in this supplement, and what changes we have incorporated should make the use of the book easier and quicker. So far as scope is concerned, unlike the original, 45 rpms have not been included, but the range of countries whose record production we have attempted to cover remains the same.

As before, we have tried to standardize titles of compositions, reconciling differences found among recordings of the same work, but again, we have not listened to each composition with an authentic score in hand to arrive at those reconciliations. We have worked hard for accuracy and relied heavily upon recognized and authoritative sources of information, but often have had, finally, to rely upon record jacket information, or worse, advertisements. The source of information about each anthology which we were unable personally to audition is shown in curves after the listing of the contents.

We have tried once more to indicate sources for compositions, such as e.g.

Introduction

Fitzwilliam Virginal Book, Glogauer Liederbuch but have not attempted to be thorough; were each item to have been checked for its source, another decade would have passed before publication.

We have made two small changes to assist the user. Record labels are not abbreviated as they were before but are spelled out for each entry, and the confusing separation of performers into groups in the Performer Index has been eliminated. They now appear in one alphabet.

We are indebted for assistance to more persons than before –– more than we can individually thank. A timely grant from the Faculty of Arts and Letters, State University of New York at Buffalo, was, to our great advantage, used in the early collecting stage several years ago by Mr. Michael Keller, now Reference Assistant in the Music Library, SUNY at Buffalo. Mr. David Hall, Head, Rodgers & Hammerstein Archives of Recorded Sound, New York Public Library, gave generously of time and thought to help us with some of our most intransigent problems. Mr. Lou Shafir, formerly with A&A Records in Toronto, helped in the same fashion, and another Toronto firm, Ross, Court & Company (now unfortunately closed) kept us supplied with foreign record catalogs. To Mr. Dale Good, Music Division, New York Public Library, we are grateful for making us aware of an important series of records. Genial Gerald Gibson, Record Librarian at the Eastman School of Music, was enormously helpful and straightened out many problems for us. To Ms. Elizabeth Murray, and to Ms. Regan Coover, who both helped greatly in the early stages of the indexing, we are happily indebted.

A separate expression of gratitude should go to Ms. Florence Kretzschmar, President of Information Coordinators, whose patience –– as she listened to us tell her for five years that "we're working on it" –– must have worn thin at times. We never knew.

JBC, RC
May 13, 1972

ABBREVIATIONS

adv	advertisement
arg	American Record Guide
b	born
bar	baritone
biel	Bielefelder Katalog
c	century
ca	circa
cemb	cembalo
cond	conductor
c-tnr	counter-tenor
d	died
DGG	Deutsche Grammophon Gesellschaft
dia	Diapason. Catalogue general
dir	director
ed	editor
fl	flourished
gr	Gramophone Classical Record Catalogue
gram	The Gramophone (monthly)
guit	guitar
H.M.V.	His Master's Voice
hi fi	High Fidelity magazine
hn	horn
hpsi	harpsichord
instr	instrumental
k-bd	keyboard
m-sop	mezzo-soprano

Abbreviations

Myers	"Index of Record Reviews" in issues of <u>NOTES</u>
orch	orchestra
org	organ
pf	pianoforte
rcdrs	recorders
sant	Santandrea. <u>Catalogo generale</u>
sch	<u>Schwann Record and Tape Guide</u>
sop	soprano
tnr	tenor
tromb	trombone
trpt	trumpet
va	viola
virg	virginals
/	used to separate simultaneous texts in motets of the thirteenth century

ADDENDA AND CORRIGENDA

To Original Edition and the First Supplement

PART I - ANTHOLOGIES

Anthology
   No.

5   ARCHIVE PRODUCTION: 1. Gregorian Chant. Beuron.
       The blessings and the Easter song.
          Reissued on DGA APM 14204

6   ————. *The Baptismal Promises ...*
          Reissued on DGA APM 14205

7   ————. *Easter Sunday Mass.*
          Reissued on DGA APM 14017

27-30 GREGORIAN CHANT (series). SPL 569-70, 576, 707
          Reissued on 4-12" Everest 6159; 3159

44   Polifonica Ambrosiana; Biella, dir. *Ambrosian chants.*
          Reissued on Vox DLBX 207

62   Solesmes Abbey Monks Choir; Gajard, dir. *Chant Grégorien.*
          Reissued on Italian Decca LXT 2704/8

64   ————. *Christmas Midnight Mass; Mass for the Day.*
          Reissued on Italian Decca FAT 173690 and German Decca
          AWD 9906-C

65   ————. *Easter Sunday Mass.*
          Reissued on Italian Decca FAT 173691 and German Decca
          AWD 9909-C

66   ————. *Corpus Christi Mass; Pentecost Mass.*
          Reissued on Italian Decca FAT 173693 and German Decca
          AWD 9910-C

67   ————. *Ascension & Assumption Masses.*
          Reissued on Italian Decca FAT 173692 and German Decca
          AWD 9911-C

68   ————. *Festività della S. Vergine; Immacolata Concezione.*
          Reissued on London 5595

13

Addenda and Corrigenda

Anthology
   No.

127   *Anthologie de la musique chorale allemande: Les Maîtres de la Renaissance.* Radio-Berlin Chorus; Koch, dir.
      Reissued on Monitor MC 2047 plus 19th and 20th century works and on Chant du Monde LDX 8264, as listed.

132   ANTHOLOGIE SONORE. *v.2, rec.3: The Italian Madrigal.* "Luca Marenzio" Ensemble; Saraceni, dir.
      Reissued on Everest 3179

139   ————. *v.9, rec.1: French Masters of the Renaissance.* Chanteurs traditionels de Paris; M. Honegger, cond.
      Reissued on Adès ADE 13006

140   *Anthology of Guitar Music.* Byrd (guit).
      Reissued on Orpheus 9411

141   *Anthology of Renaissance Music.* Primavera Singers; Greenberg, dir.
      Reissued on Dover HCR 5248

146   ARCHIVE PRODUCTION: III. The Early Renaissance (1350-1500). *Ser. D. (The Netherlanders to Ockeghem). Rec. 1:* DUFAY.
      5 Sacred Songs.
      Substitute in contents: Vexilla regis for In tempore passiones, and Veni Creator for In festo Pentecostes.

151   ARCHIVE PRODUCTION: IV. The High Renaissance (16th Century). *Ser. D. (Social Music in Italy). Rec. 1.*
      GESUALDO not GESAULDO

172   *Christmas Music.* Renaissance Singers; Campbell, cond.
      Add to contents: AMNER. O ye little flock. ANON. Dominus dixit (plainsong); Vox in rama (plainsong); Eya martir Stephane; Coventry carol.

178   *Danseries et fanfares de la renaissance.* Concert de l'Ensemble P. Devevey.
      Contents: FANTINI. Sonata a due tromba detta del guciardini; Prima sonata di tromba detta colloretta; Balletto detto il cadalca; Balletto primo parte detto del valzer. GERVAISE. Pavane d'Angleterre; Mamy est tant honneste et sauge; Trois allemandes; Pavane; Bransle de Bourgogne; Bransle gay; Pavane passemaize; Bransle simple; Bransle de Champagne; Bransle de Poitou. TERTRE. Pavane d'Angleterre; Deux bransles d'Ecosse. ANON. Le bon vouloir; Celle qui m'a le nom d'amy donné; Bransle double; Que je chatouille ta fossette; Bransle simple.

185   *Echoes from a 16th Century Cathedral.* Roger Wagner Chorale.
      Reissued on Angel S-36013

stopped here (handwritten)

Anthology
   No.

186   *École anglaise de clavecin.* Gerlin (hpsi).
        Contents: BULL. The Duke of Brunswick's alman; The Duchess
        of Brunswick's toye. BYRD. Wolsey's wilde; Galliarde for the
        victorie; Volte; The flute and the droome. FARNABY. The new
        sa-hoo; A toye. PEERSON. The fall of the leafe. PHILIPS.
        Galiarda dolora. Also Arne and Purcell.

187   *Elizabethan and Jacobean Music.* Deller (c-tnr); Dupré (lute),
    Leonhardt (hpsi). Consort of viols.
        Reissued on Vanguard S 306 and Amadeo AVRS 6001

190   *Elizabethan Lute Songs.* Pears (tnr), Bream (lute).
        Reissued on London LL 1532 and Decca-Eclipse ECS 545

193   *English Keyboard Music: Tudor Age to the Restoration.* Wolfe
    (hpsi).
        Reissued on Musical Heritage Society MHS 679

194   *English Lute Songs.* Deller (c-tnr).
        Reissued on Amadeo AVRS 6144
        Add to contents: ANON. Miserere, my maker.

195   *The English Madrigal School, v.1 and 2.* Deller Consort.
        Reissued on Amadeo AVRS 6071/72

199   *Evenings of Elizabethan Verse and Music.* New York Pro Musica;
    Greenberg, dir. (Auden reading)
        Reissued on Odyssey 32 16 0171

203   *Flemish Choral Music.* Ghent Oratorio Society; de Pauw, cond.
        Reissued on Counterpoint/Esoteric 5514

207   *French Chansons and Dances of the 16th Century.* Brussels Pro
    Musica Antiqua; Cape, dir.
        Reissued on Dover HCR 5221

208   *French Renaissance Music.* Vocal and Instrumental Ensemble;
    Boulanger, cond.
        Reissued (with new jacket notes -- not Boulanger's) on Decca
        DCM 3201

211   *German Songs of the Middle Ages and the Renaissance.* Cuenod
    (tnr), Leeb (lute).
        Reissued on H.M.V. CLP 1877 and Westminster 9621

219   *Italian Songs, 16th and 17th Centuries.* Cuenod (tnr), Leeb (lute).
        Reissued on Westminster 9611

220   *Italian Music in the Age of Exploration.* Fleetwood Singers.
        Also issued as monaural London LL75

Original Edition

Addenda and Corrigenda

PART II - INDEX TO ANTHOLOGIES AND INDIVIDUAL DISCOGRAPHIES BY COMPOSER

59   JANEQUIN, CLEMENT
      perf: Ensemble Vocal S. Caillat   10" Dec 133723
         Reissued (with works by LEJEUNE) on Société Française 154091

60   LASSUS, ORLAND DE
      perf: Swabian Chorus (Grischkat)   Vox DL 380
         Reissued on Dover HCR 5269; HCRST 7269
      perf: Swabian Chorus & Soloists (Grischkat)   Vox DL 400
         Reissued on Dover HCR 5268; HCRST 7268

64   MORLEY, THOMAS
      perf: Golden Age Singers (Field-Hyde)   West 18764
         Reissued on 3-Westminster no.1006 (with Tomkins, Weelkes &
         Wilbye)
      perf: Primavera Singers (Greenberg); Winogron (virg)   Eso 520
         Reissued on Counterpoint/Esoteric 5 2397 5520

66   PALESTRINA, GIOVANNI PIERLUIGI DA
      perf: Chor der St. Hedwigs-Kathedrale, Berlin (Forster)
      10" Elec E 60602
         Reissued on H.M.V. ALP 2019; ASD 569 (with Mozart)
      perf: Netherlands Chamber Choir (de Nobel)   2 records -- LC 3359
      and 3045
         The one side on each of these devoted to Palestrina have been
         combined and reissued as Philips A 00272
      perf: Vienna Akademie Kammerchor (Theuring)   West 18362
         Reissued as Westminster C 30 5454 (according to dia 70)
67   *perf:* Vienna Akademie Kammerchor (Theuring)   West 18364
         Reissued as Westminster 9605

70   ROSSI, SALOMONE
      perf: Pro Musica Antiqua (Greenberg)   ML 5204
         Reissued on Italian Angel LPA 5914

72   TALLIS, THOMAS
      perf: Deller Consort   BG 551
         Reissued on Vanguard SRV 287 SD

72   TOMKINS, THOMAS
      perf: Golden Age Singers (Field-Hyde)   West 18764
         Reissued on 3-Westminster no.1006 (with Morley, Weelkes &
         Wilbye)
      perf: In Nomine Players, Ambrosian Singers (Stevens), Sidwell (org)
      2-12" EA 0027/0028
         Volumes 1 and 2 reissued on Oryx 719 and 720, and on Musical
         Heritage Society MHS 687 and 688 with title: Music of the 16th
         and 17th Centuries, v.5 and 6

Addenda and Corrigenda

PART III - PERFORMER INDEX

FIRST SUPPLEMENT, PART I - ANTHOLOGIES

Anthology
  No.

         attribution of this performance to the Solesmes Abbey Choir is
         incorrect (see note). Other DGG numbers are APM 14164;
         SAPM 198046

332   St. Susanna Choir. MacEwan, dir.
         Add to contents: Mass of 21st Sunday after Pentecost

336   Solesmes Abbey Choir. Gajard, dir. *Good Friday.*
         Reissued on Italian Decca 173903 and German Decca AWD 9916-B;
         SAWD 9916-C

337   ————. *Septuagesima.*
         Original London number should have been 5599
         Reissued on Italian Decca 173904

344   ARCHIVE PRODUCTION: IV. The High Renaissance.
         Ser. N. (The Circle of the Venetian Style).
         Reissued also on DGA 198042 SAPM; APM 14160

349   *Elizabethan and Jacobean Ayres, Madrigals and Dances.* New York
         Pro Musica; Noah Greenberg, dir.
         Reissued on British Decca AXA 4515; SXA 4515

350   *The English Country Dancing Master.* Telemann Society Orchestra;
         Schulze, cond.
         Reissued in stereo as Vox STDL 470

352   *Flemish and German Motets from the 16th and 17th Centuries.*
         Reissued on Cantate 640215

354   *The French Ars Antiqua.* Compositions from the Montpellier Ms.
         Oberlin (c-tnr); Bressler (tnr); Price (tnr); Myers (bar); Blackman (viol).
         Reissued on Musical Heritage Society MHS 685 with same series
         title: Music of the Middle Ages, v.7

356   *The Golden Age of English Lute Music.* Bream (lute).
         Reissued by Victor on LSC 3196, on German RCA LM 2560-C;
         LSC 2560-B, and in Great Britain as SB 2150

361   *Italienische Musik der Renaissance.* Chorus and Soloists of the
         Polifonica Ambrosiana; Biella, dir.
         Reissued on Amadeo AVRS 130010

364   *Lute Songs.* P. Pears (tnr); Bream (lute).
         Reissued on German Decca AWD & SAWD 9912, and on London
         OL 5896; OS 25896

366   *Madrigals and Motets.* Budapest Madrigal Ensemble; F. Szekeres, dir.
         Reissued on Chant du Monde LDX A8259

Addenda and Corrigenda

Anthology
No.

368   *Motets a Cappella.* Ensemble Vocal Caillard; P. Caillard, dir.
Reissued on Musical Heritage Society MHS 634, Christophorus
CGLP 75803, and Erato STU 70066

370   *Music at Notre Dame, Paris, 1200.* Deller Consort.
Reissued on Harmonia Mundi (French) HMS 30823 (1-12" disc),
on 2-10" Harmonia Mundi recordings HM25143 and 25147
In contents: Dic (not Die) Christi veritas

379   *El Siglo de Oro.* Coral Antica Escolans, Barcelona; Gassuli-Duro, dir.
Add number: Harmonia Mundi 25121

383   *Spanish Music of the Renaissance.* New York Pro Musica; Greenberg,
dir.
Reissued on Decca 3209

387   *Two Thousand Years of Music.* Berlin State Academy Choir, and
others.
Reissued on Folkways FT 3700

FIRST SUPPLEMENT, PART II - INDEX

Page
No.

106   BYRD, WILLIAM
perf: King's College Choir, Cambridge (Willcocks) Lon 5725; OS 25725
Reissued on German Decca SAWD 9947
perf: In Nomine Players (Stevens) EA-37
Reissued on Musical Heritage Society MHS 689S in series: Music
of the 16th and 17th Centuries, v.7

107   DEPRES, JOSQUIN
perf: Ensemble Instrumental et Vocal Roger Blanchard MGM-7; S-7
New Music Guild numbers MG 134; S 134
perf: Dessoff Choirs (Boepple)   2 records -- Vox DL 580 and 600
Both reissued on one disc by Turnabout TV 34437 with the
elimination of a few short works

108   *perf:* New York Pro Musica, with Oberlin, Bressler, Myers and Lewis
(Greenberg) Dec 9410; 79410
Reissued on Brunswick AXTL 1095; SXA 4004
perf: Pro Musica Antiqua (Cape)   ARC 3159; 73159
Also on DGA APM 14171; SAPM 198171

108   DUNSTABLE, JOHN
perf: Ambrosian Singers, Poulter, Oberlin, Brimer (Stevens) EA-36

22

First Supplement

Page
No.

Reissued on Musical Heritage Society MHS 686 in series: Music
of the Middle Ages, v.8

109 GABRIELI, GIOVANNI
perf: Schola Cantorum Basiliensis (Wenzinger)   ARC 3154
Also on DGA ARC 73154 and APM 14160; 198042
Reissued on German Columbia STC 91108
perf: Choir and Brass Ensemble of the Gabrieli Festival (Gillesberger)
BG 611; 5037
Reissued on Amadeo AVRS 6231
perf: Brass Ensemble of the Vienna State Opera Orchestra (Stone)
WST-14081
Reissued on Westminster XWN 18887

114 OCKEGHEM, JEAN DE
perf: Ensemble Instrumental et Vocal Roger Blanchard   MGM-7; S-7
Music Guild numbers are now MG 134; S 134

114 PALESTRINA, GIOVANNI PIERLUIGI DA
perf: Chanteurs de St.-Eustache
Pastorale Musique number is 25001

116 TOMKINS, THOMAS
perf: Magdalen College Chapel Choir, Oxford (Rose)   Argo RG-249
Argo ZRG number should be 5249

116 VICTORIA, TOMAS LUIS DE
perf: Capilla et Escolania de Montserrat (Segarra)   AMS-23
Now in stereo on Lumen AMS 1523

FIRST SUPPLEMENT, PART III - PERFORMER INDEX

Page
No.

121 DESSOFF CHOIRS. Delete Victoria

122 RAVIER, not RIVIER

PART I

Anthologies of Medieval and Renaissance Music

All records are 12", 33 1/3 rpm unless otherwise indicated. In some cases two or more issues are given, separated by a semicolon; these may represent foreign and domestic issues of the same recording, monaural and stereophonic issues, or successive numbers released by the same company (in the last case, earlier issue numbers are usually given first).

The *Chant* list (nos.388-443) is arranged by a place name or by the name of an institution with which the performing group is associated. Contents are given in greater detail for most of the discs than they were in the original edition.

Medieval and Renaissance anthologies (nos.444-901) are listed by title (or by performer or performing group when no title could be determined). In general only those works on each disc dating from before approximately 1600 fall within the scope of this discography and are set out in detail. Anonymous compositions within that scope are listed by title after works by known composers. Composers whose dates are later than about 1600 are listed by name only at the end of the statement of contents.

Please note that discs devoted to the works of one or, at most, two composers are listed under the name of the composer(s) in Part II.

References: All entries for anthologies not personally consulted by the compilers or verified in the holdings of a major U.S. music library are followed by the source from which the information was taken. An explanation of the abbreviations used to indicate those is on pages 11 and 12.

ARGENTAN. Abbaye Notre-Dame. Nuns' Choir; Gajard, cond.

388. *Liturgy for the dead; Interment.*
Société Française 20,518; (It.) Decca 174049
[Dies irae; Domine Jesu; Requiem; Absolve; Agnus Dei; Lux aeterna;
Subvenite; Libera me; In paradisum; Ego sum resurrectio; Benedictus;
Placebo Domino; Dominus custodit te; Si iniquitatis; Opera manuum;
Audivi vocem; Omne quod.]

389. *Mass of St. Benedict; Mass of St. Cecelia; Antiphons from the Consecration of Virgins.*
Société Française XL 174066; SXL 20520; (It.) Decca 174066

390. *Mass and Office, of St. Michael.* Société Française SL 174146; SXL 20146

391. *Octave of Pentecost.*   (It.) Decca XSL 20224
[Veni Creator; Basta nobis gaudis; Te lucis ante terminum; Dum
complerentur; Spiritus Domini; Repleti sunt omnes; Fontes; Loquebantur; Alleluja, hodie omnes; Deus dum egredereris; Veni Sancte
Spiritus; Spiritus sanctus; Spiritus est; Spiritus eius; Dictus es; Spiritus
qui a Patre; Benedictus es; Spiritus ubi vult; Emitte Spiritum tuum;
Ultimo festivitatis die; Si quis diligit me.]

392. *Mysteries of the Rosary.*   (It.) Decca SXL 20225
[Ave Maria; Ecce Ancilla Domini; Felix es; Magnificat; Descendit de
coelis; Genuit puerpera Regem; Senex puerum portabat; Hodie beata
Virgo; Remansit puer Jesus; Fili quid fecisti; In monte Oliveti; Oppressit
me dolor; Ecce vidimus; Caligaverunt; Vadis propitiator; Ecce quomodo
moritur; Stabat Mater; Alleluja lapis, quem quaeris et noli flere; Regina
coeli; Optatus votis omnium; Beata Dei Genitrix; Assumpta est; Ave
Regina coelorum.]

BEURON, GERMANY. St. Martin (Benedictine Abbey). Monks' Choir;
Pfaff, cond.

393. *Praeconium paschale: Exultet; Alleluja, Tractus und Laudes der
Osternachtsmesse.*   10" DGA 13075 AP

394. *Mass of Pentecost.*   DGA ARC SAPM 198303

27

BUSTO ARSIZIO, ITALY. Choir of the Frati Minori; Fra Filippo Cavalleri, Fra Illuminato Colombo, conds.

395. *Third Mass for Christmas; Easter Sunday Mass; Mass for the dead.*
                                           Angelicum LPA 5997; STA 8997

CLERVAUX, LUXEMBURG. St. Maurice & St. Maur (Benedictine Abbey). Monks' Choir.

396. *Easter music.*   Philips PHC 9004; AO 2082 L; 835077 AY
[Christus resurgens; Resurrexi; Victimae paschali; Pascha nostrum; Angelus autem Domini; Et ecce terraemotus; Erat autem aspectus; Prae timore autem; Respondens autem; Ad cenam Agni; Et respicientes; Post dies octo; Regina caeli; Salve, festa dies; Alleluia, lapis revolutus est; Ave Maria; Te Deum.]

397. *Hymnodia.*   Philips AO 2092 L; 835039 AY
[Mass II (Gloria); Christe, redemptor omnium; Magnificat; Alma redemptoris Mater; Christus natus est nobis; Inviolata; Hodie nobis caelorum Rex; Quem vidistis, pastores; Genuit puerpera Regem; Angelus ad pastores; Facta est cum angelo; Parvulus filius; Dominus dixit ad me; Lux fulgebit; Puer natus est nobis; Ave Maria; Sub tuum praesidium.]

398.   Fontana 804077 ZKY
[Resurrexi; Dominus probasti me; Victimae paschale laudes; Pascha nostrum; Christus natus est nobis; Dominus dixit ad me; Quare tremuerunt gentes; Lux fulgebit; Puer natus est nobis; Cantate Domino; Asperges me; Miserere mei Deus; Kyrie XI; Gloria XI; Credo I; Sanctus XI; Agnus Dei XI; Ite missa est XI; Requiem aeternam; Te decet hymnus; Dies irae; Lux aeterna; In paradisum.]

COLLEGEVILLE, MINN. St. John's Abbey Choir; Farrell, cond.

399. *Corpus Christi.*   (no record no.)

DOURGNE, FRANCE. Saint-Benoît d'Encalcat (Benedictine Abbey). Monks' Choir.

400. *Gregorian chants.*   Music Guild 137; S 137; 25; S 25
[Qui sedes; Christe redemptor; Vox in rama; Omnes de Saba; Vidimus; Jubilate; Exsurge; Videns Dominus; Collegerunt; Ad coenam Agni; Haec dies; Quasimodo geniti; Spiritus Domini; Alleluia, veni sancte Spiritus; Dirigatur oratio; Christe redemptor; Subvenite; Sanctus IX.]

DUBUQUE, IOWA. Sisters of Charity. Novitiate Choir & Schola.

401.   Gregorian CA 2
[Alma redemptoris; Ave Regina; Regina coeli; Salve Regina; Mass I (Kyrie); Salve Mater; Victimae paschali; Ave Maria.]

FICHERMONT DOMINICAN SISTERS. Pater de Brabandere, cond.

402.   Philips PCC 212; PCC 612; SM 889878 RY
[Prelude; Gaudens gaudebo; Te lucis; Kyrie; Quem vidistis pastores; Puer
natus; In splendoribus; In pace; Media vita; Veni Sancte Spiritus; Alleluia;
Haec dies; Victimae paschali laudes; Regina coeli; Viri Galilaei; Salve
Regina; O spem miram; Finale.]

HERSTELLE an der WESER. Heilig Kreuz (Benedictine Abbey). Nuns'
Choir; Müller (org); Steinruck, cond.

403.   Psallite PSC 50/171067
[1st Vespers of Advent; Christus natus est nobis; Christe redemptor
omnium; Lessons and responsories of the 1st Nocturn; Te decet laus.]

LONDON. Carmelite Priory Choir; McCarthy, cond.

404.   Oiseau OL 50209; SOL 60040
[Tenebrae factae sunt; Jesus tradidit impius; Christus factus est; Creator
alma siderum; Iste confessor Domini; Pange lingua gloriosi; Hodie
Christus natus est; O Sapientia; In paradisum; Vos estis sal terrae; Laudes
seu acclamationes; Flores apparuerunt; Alleluia, justus germinabit;
Montes Gelboe; Ave verum; Lumen ad revelationem; Nunc dimittis; Alma
redemptoris; Ave Regina caelorum; Regina coeli; Salve Regina; Dicit
Dominus; Passer invenit.]

MARIA LAACH (Benedictine Abbey). Cantors and Choir; Heckenbach,
cond.

405. *Mass of Sexagesima Sunday* (with Merendino, org).
                                              10" Psallite PSB 18/260265

406. *Sunday Vespers* (with Merendino, org).
                                              10" Psallite PSB 25/081065

407. *Passion.*   Psallite BSC 26/091065
[Responsorium der Karmetten; Passionsbericht nach Markus.]

408. *Epiphany.*   10" Psallite PSB 27/071065

409. *Missa Mediaevalis* (with Reichling, org).   Psallite PSC 38/100267
[Puer natus est (3d Mass of Christmas); Ordinary: Mass of Barcelona (Ars
nova); organ pieces from the Robertsbridge Codex.]

MECHLIN (Malines), BELGIUM. Saint-Rombaut Cathedral Choir;
Vijverman, cond.

410. *Hymnes grégoriennes de l'année liturgique.*   10" Orphée 21.065
[Populus Sion; Dominus dixit; Puer natus est; Laetere; Viri Galilei;
Alleluias: Dies sanctificatus, Veni Sancte Spiritus, Pascha nostrum;

410. *Hymnes grégoriennes de l'année liturgique.* (Continued)
Victimae paschali laudes; Veni Sancte Spiritus; Ascendit Deus.]

MUNICH CAPELLA ANTIQUA. Schola Cantorum; Ruhland, cond.
411.   Telefunken AWT 9493; SAWT 9493
[Conditor alme siderum; Nato canunt omnia; Cum natus esset Jesus;
Lumen ad revelationem; Nunc dimittis; Mittit ad Virginem; O Redemptor,
sume carmen; Surrexit Dominus vere; Ad coenam Agni; Veni Sancte
Spiritus; Kyrie fons bonitatis; Aeterne rerum conditor; Te Deum
laudamus.]

MYSTIC, CONN. St. Edmund's Novitiate; Pierik, cond.
412.   Folkways 8954
[Kyrie XI, IX, IV; Gloria XI; Sanctus XI, IX, IV; Agnus Dei XI, IX, IV;
Rorate caeli; Puer natus est; Ecce advenit; Gaudeamus; Alleluia ecce
Virgo; In splendoribus; Beati mundo corde; Veni creator Spiritus; O
oriens; Adoro Te; Ave verum; Tota pulchra es; Salve Regina; Regina
caeli.]

ST. BENEDICT, ORE. Mt. Angel Seminary Gregorian Choir; Nicholson,
cond.
413.   Gregorian Institute MA 2
[Adoro te; Pange lingua; Alma redemptoris; Ave Regina; Regina caeli;
Salve Regina; Asperges me; Sanctorum meritis; Exsultet caelum laudibus;
Credo VII.]   (narration by Tyrone Power)

414. *Chants of the Church.*   RCA Victor LM 2786; LSC 2786; WLSM 8; 8S
                                  (also, through "Virgo Maria," on LSC 2218)
[Gaudeamus; Laeta quies; Desiderium; Fidelis servus; Oportet te; Qui
biberit aquam; Nemo te condemnavit; Lutum fecit; Videns Dominus; De
profundis; Ave verum; Virgo Dei; Sub tuum; Virgo Maria; Jesu dulcis
memoria; Attende Domine; Kyrie Fons bonitatis; Rorate caeli; Alma
redemptoris; Ave Regina; Regina caeli; Salve Regina; Alleluia lapis
revolutus est.]

ST. FRANCIS OF ASSISI PAPAL CHAPEL. Del Farraro, cond.
415.   DGG SLPM 139169
[De Missa; De lotione pedum; De solemne translatione ac repositione
sacramenti; Cantus tempore poenitentiae; In festo corporis Christi.]

ST. THOMAS ABBEY. Monks' Choir; Mowrey, cond.
416. *A Treasury of Gregorian Chant, v.1.*   Vox PL 16420; STPL 516420

417. *A Treasury of Gregorian Chant, v.2.*   Vox PL 16470; STPL 516470

418. *A Treasury of Gregorian Chant, v.3* (with Tachezi, org).
Vox PL 16480; STPL 516480
[Ad te levavi; Jesu Redemptor omnium; Jubilate Deo; Intellige clamorem
meum; Christus factus est; Victimae paschali; Veni Sancte Spiritus;
Justorum animae; Beati mundo corde; Requiem aeternam; In paradisum.]

SANTO DOMINGO de SILOS (Benedictine Abbey). Monks' Choir;
Fernández de la Cuesta, cond.

419. *Advent and Christmas.*   Discoteca Pax G 305
[Rorate; O sapientia; Christus natus est; Christe Redemptor; Quem
vidistis; Genuit puerpera; Facta est cum angelo; A solis ortus cardine;
Adeste fideles; Puer (motet); Descendit; Puer natus est; Viderunt omnes;
Alleluia, dies; O admirabile; Rubum quem viderat.]

420. *Mozarabic Mass; Liturgical chants.*   DGG SAPM 198459

SOLESMES. Saint-Pierre (Benedictine Abbey). Monks' Choir; Gajard,
cond.

421. *Canti gregoriani.*   Voce del Padrone QELP 8008

422. *Alleluia; Offertories; Tract; Communions.*   (It.) Decca FAT 173691

423. *Masses in Paschal time.*   (It.) Decca 173956
[Domenica in Albis (Low Sunday); Easter Eve; 3d Sunday after Easter.]

424. *Masses in Paschal time.*
(It.) Decca 173988; (Ger.) Decca AWD 9927-C; SAWD 9927-B
[2d, 4th and 5th Sundays after Easter.]

425. *Mass of the Annunciation; Mass of St. Joseph.*
(It.) Decca 174019; Decca 7513

426. *Holy Thursday.*   London OL 5832; OS 25832; (It.) Decca 174029;
Decca 7503; (Ger.) Decca AWD 9929-C; SAWD 9929-B
[Nos autem; Christus factus est; Dextera Domini; Dominus Jesus; Ubi
caritas et amor.]
Tenebrae responses.
[In monte Oliveti; Tristis est; Ecce vidimus; Amicus meus; Judas merca-
tor; Unus ex discipulis; Eram quasi Agnus; Una hora; Seniores populi.]

427. *Good Friday.*   (It.) Decca 174047; Decca 7504
[1st lamentation; Omnes amici mei; Velum templi; Vinea mea; Tamquam
ad latronem; Tenebrae factae sunt.]
Tenebrae responses.
[Animam meam; Tradiderunt me; Jesus tradidit; Caligaverunt; Vexilla
regis; Vadis propitiatior.]

428. *Mass of St. Peter; Mass of St. John the Baptist.*
(It.) Decca 174064; Decca 7509

429. *Mass "Gaudete" (3d Sunday of Advent); Mass "Laetare" (4th Sunday of Lent).*   (It.) Decca 174080

430. *Purification of the Blessed Virgin; Our Lady of Seven Sorrows.*
                                                                   (It.) Decca 174092

431. *Responses of Holy Saturday: Oratio Jeremiae.*   (It.) Decca 174103

432. *Dedication of a church.*   (It.) Decca 174107

433.   Musica Sacra AMS 58
    [Kyrie, Agnus Dei, Gloria, Sanctus (Lux et origo); Domine Jesu Christe;
    Christus factus est; Hoc corpus; Qui sedes; Dirigatur oratio mea; Alleluia,
    justus germinabit; Da pacem; Kyrie (Orbis factor); Spiritus Domini;
    Spiritus sanctus docebit; Spiritus a Patre; Jubilate Deo; Descendi;
    Christus resurgens; Alleluia, lapis revolutus est.]

SPENCER, MASS. St. Joseph's Abbey Choir.

434. *Cistercian Chant.*   Cambridge CRS 402; St. Joseph's 1000
    [Mass of the Assumption; Bells; Tierce; (hymns): O quam glorifica, Jesu
    salvator, Avete solitudinis; Tota pulchra es; Ascendit Christus; Magnificat.]

VARENSELL. Unserer Lieben Frau (Benedictine Abbey). Nuns' Choir;
Weiss, cond.

435. *Mass of Pentecost.*   DGG ARC 3203; 73203;
                                                       APM 14303; SAPM 198303

VENICE. S. Giorgio Maggiore Schola; Ernetti, cond.

436. *Solemn mass; Planctus Mariae.*   Cetra LPU 0043

437. *Mass of feasts of the 2d class; Mass of the Madonna.*   Cetra LPU 0044

438. *Sunday Mass; Mass of minor feasts; Missa universalis.*   Cetra LPU 0045

439. *Sunday Vespers; Vespers of the Madonna.*   Cetra LPU 0046

VIENNA. Hofburgkapelle; Schabasser, cond.

440. *Lent and Easter.*   Turnabout 4070; 34070
    [Exurge quare obdormis; Cor movisti Domine; Intellige; Improperium
    expectavit; Christus factus est; Dextera Domini; Resurrexi; Haec dies;
    Easter alleluia; Victimae paschali; Terra tremuit; Pascha nostrum; Regina
    caeli; Viri Galilaei; Ascendit; Spiritus Domini; Veni Sancte Spiritus;
    Quotiescumque.]

441. *Gregorian Chants for Christmas.*   Turnabout TV 34181 S
    [Ad te levavi; Rorate caeli; Dicite: pusillanimes; Gaudete in Domini; Ave
    Maria; Jesu redemptor omnium; Puer natus est nobis; Alleluia, dies
    sanctificatus; Video caelos apertos; Justus et palma; Jubilate Deo; Dicit

Dominus: Implete.]

442. *Gregorian Chants.*   Vox DLBX 206; SDLBS 5206
[Ad te levavi; Alleluia; Ascendit Deus; Ave Maria; Beati mundo corde;
Christus factus est; Commovisti; Dextera Domini; Dicite pusillamines;
Dignus est Agnus; Exurge; Dicit Dominus: Implete; Gaudeamus omnes;
Gaudens gaudebo; Gaudete; Haec dies; Improperium; In paradisum;
Intellige clamorum meum; Jesu redemptor omnium; Jubilate Deo;
Justosue anime; Justus et palma; Pascha nostrum; Puer natus est; Regina
caeli; Requiem aeternam; Resurrexi; Rorate caeli; Quotiescumque;
Sedebit Dominus Rex; Spiritus Domini; Terra tremuit; Veni Sancte
Spiritus; Victimae paschali; Video caelos apertos; Viri Galilaei.]

WASHINGTON, D.C. National Shrine of the Immaculate Conception;
Seiner, cond.

443.   Gregorian M 103; S 203
[Gaudens gaudebo; Benedicta es tu; Alleluia; Ave Maria. PALESTRINA.
Maria Mater gratiae.]   (Also Refice, Draconinus, Justina, Seiner)

444. *Advent mit den Regensburger Domspatzen.* Regensburger Domspatzen;
Hans Schrems, dir.   Polydor 249 182
[CROCE. Veni Domine. ECCARD. Ich lag in tiefer Todesnacht; Übers
Gebirg Maria geht. A. GABRIELI. Benedixisti. GUMPELZHAIMER.
Deutsches Magnificat; Maria durch ein'n Dornwald ging. HAMMER-
SCHMIDT. Machet die Tore weit. PALESTRINA. Macht hoch die Tür;
Missa Lauda Sion (Benedictus).] (adv)

L'âge d'or du motet anglais. See *Die Englische Motette im "Goldenen
Zeitalter"* (No.537).

445. *Ah Sweet Lady; The Romance of Medieval France.* New York Pro
Musica; John White, cond.   Decca 9431; 79431
[MACHAUT. De petit po; Nes que on porroit; Sanz cuer m'en vois-Amis,
dolens-Dame, par vous; Quant je suis mis; Je sui aussi; De Fortune me
doy pleindre; De Triste cuer-Quant vrais amans-Certes, je di; Pas de tor
en thies pais; Se je souspir; Douce dame jolie. ANON. 4 motets on "In
saeculum": 1. Bien doit avoir joie-In saeculum; 2. In saeculum viellatoris;
3. Hoquetus in saeculum; 4. Ja n'amerai autre-In saeculum; Crucifigat
omnes (conductus); Flor de lis, rose espanie / Je ne puis / Douce dame
(motet); Quant je parti de m'amie-Tuo (motet); S'on me regarde /
Prennés i garde / He! mi enfant (motet).]

446. *Airs from the Courts and Times of Henri IV and Louis XIII.* Caillat Vocal
Ensemble.   Turnabout 34316
[BALLARD. 2 arias for lute. BATAILLE. Beautés qui residés; Qui veut
chasser une migraine; Un satyre. BONNET. La vertu d'un personnage.
CERVEAU. Comme nous voyous la rose. DUFAULT. Tombeau de
Monsieur de Blancrocher. LEJEUNE. Doncques tu vas te mourant;
Qu'est devenu ce bel oeil. MAUDUIT. Eau vive, sourve d'amour; Voicy
le verd et beau may. PERICHON. Courante. PLANSON. Chambrière;
Par un matin la belle s'est levée. TESSIER. Amants qui vous plaignez.
VALLET. Variations "Les Pantalons."] (sch 1/70)

447. *Altdeutsche Weihnacht.* Vocal and instrumental ensemble; Walter Gerwig
(lute).   Harmonia Mundi HM 30609; 530609
[ECCARD. Ich steh an deiner Krippe hier. GESIUS. Christum wir sollen

447. *Altdeutsche Weihnacht.* (Continued)
loben schon / Ein Kind, geborn zu Bethlehem. GUMPELZHAIMER.
Vom Himmel hoch, da komm ich her. PRAETORIUS. A solis ortus
cardine; Ein Kind geborn zu Bethlehem; Es ist ein Ros entsprungen; In
dulci jubilo; Maria zart. WALTER. Gelobet seist du, Jesus Christ. Also
Reusner.] (biel 2/67)

448. *Alte Chormusik zur Weihnachtszeit.* Monteverdi-Chor, Hamburg; Jürgen
Jürgens, cond.   Telefunken AWT 9419-C; SAWT 9419-B
[AGRICOLA. Her, her, ich verkünd euch neue Mär. BODENSCHATZ.
Joseph lieber, Joseph mein. COSTANTINI. Pastores loquebantur.
ECCARD. Vom Himmel hoch, da komm ich her. GUERRERO. Oyd,
oyd una cosa. LASSUS. Resonet in laudibus. MORALES. Pastores,
dicite. OCKEGHEM. Alma redemptoris Mater. OSIANDER. Christum
wir sollen loben schon. PRAETORIUS. Es ist ein Ros entsprungen; In
natali Domini; Psallite. VULPIUS. Und als bald war da (motet).
PAMINGER. In dulci jubilo (quodlibet). ANON. Nous étions trois
bergerettes. Also Buxtehude and Scheidt.] (Myers 9/66)

449. *Alte französische und italienische Tanzweisen.* Ensemble de cuivres;
Jean Petit, cond.   Soc. Fr. 174093; 20093 and Decca SMD 1502
[GERVAISE. Danceries à 4 et 5 parties: 12 Bransles de Champaigne,
8 Bransles de Poictou, 6 Bransles de Bourgogne. TRABACI. 8 Galliards.
ZANETTI. 9 Tänze zu 4 Stimmen. ANON. 8e Suite Française de la
Bibliothèque de Cassel (1668).] (biel 2/67)

450. *Alte Meister der Orgelmusik aus Spanien und Italien.* Gaston Litaize
(org).   Schwann AMS 2530
[CABEZON. Tiento du I ton. A. GABRIELI. Canzone ariose; Ricercares
VII & VIII ton. Also Cabanilles, Correa, Frescobaldi, and Zipoli.]
(biel 2/69)

451. *Altspanische Musik des goldenen Zeitalters.* Montserrat Abbey Choirs;
Ireneu Segarra, cond.   Harmonia Mundi HM 30463-K; HMS 30678
[MARQUÈS. O vos omnes (motet). MORALES (motets). Andreas
Christi famulus; Ave Maria; Quanti mercenarii; Per crucem tuam; Tu es
Petrus. Also Casanoves, Cererols, Marti.] (biel 68)

452. *Altspanische Romanzen und Volkslieder.* S. Behrend (guit).
                                                       DGG 139155
[MILAN. Durandarte. MUDARRA. Isabel, perdiste la tu faxa.
NARVAEZ. Con que la lavaré. ANON. 6 Spanish romances of the 16th
century. Also Händel and later Spanish folksongs.] (biel 1/68)

453. *Am Hofe der Königin Elisabeth I.* Ambrosian Singers; Denis Stevens,
cond; Studio der frühen Musik; soloists.   DGG DGA 199001
[BYRD. The Carmans Whistle; Lord Willobies welcome Home.
DOWLAND. Can she excuse; Come, ye heavy states of night; I saw my
lady weep; Me, me and none but me; Shall I sue; Sorrow, stay. MORLEY.

Farewell; Good love; Hark jolly shepherds; The fields abroad; My lovely wanton jewel; Now is the gentle season; Sweet nymph; Stay heart; O grief even on the bud.]   (biel 2/70)

Ambrosian Singers. Denis Stevens, cond. See *Missa Salve* (No.684).
Dover HCR 5263

454. Ambrosian Singers. John McCarthy, cond.
Ace of Diamonds ADD 196; SDD 196
[BANCHIERI. Contrappunto bestiale alla mente. BYRD. Ego sum panis vivus. DE MELLE. O Jesu Christe. DEPRES. Ave vera Virginitas. ENCINA. Pues que Jamás. FORD. Almighty God who hast me brought. FORSTER. I say adieu. GOMBERT. Hors envieux! Retirez vous. GUERRERO. Hoy, José. HANDL. Orietur Stella. HASSLER. Das Herz tut mir aufspringen. LEJEUNE. Revecy venir du printans. LEMLIN. Der Gutzgauch. MARENZIO. O Rex Gloriae. MORLEY. Fire! Fire! My heart; The fields abroad. PALESTRINA. Verbum caro. PHILIPS. Regina coeli. PRAETORIUS. Psallite. VECCHI. Fa una canzone. VICTORIA. O magnum mysterium. WILBYE. Change me, O heavens.] (gr 3/69)

Die Anfänge der polnischer Musik; unbekannte Meister des 15. Jahrhunderts. See *U Zrodel Muzyki Polskiej* (No.890).

455. *Anthologie de la musique d'orgue, no.4: Maîtres des anciens Pays-Bas.* Hansen (org).   Cycnus 30 CM 019; 60 CS 519; Nonesuch 71214 [BULL. Prélude sur "Laet ons met herten Reijne." CORNET. Toccado del 3 tono. LUYTHON. Fuga suavissima. NOORDT. Psaume 6 "Heer, toon mij uw genade." SCKRONX. Echo. SPEUY. Psaume 118 "Dancket den Heer." SWEELINCK. Fantaisie en écho. Also Kerckhoven.] (dia 12/68)

Anthologie de la musique médiévale espagnole.
v.1: See under ALFONSO EL SABIO in Part II.
Orpheus OR 302 and Erato STU 70694

456. *v.2: Monodie de cour médiévale (XII-XIIIe siècles); Musique arabo-andalouse (XIIIe siècle).* C. Orihuela (sop); M. Aragon (m-sop); L. Quijano (contralto); J.-U. Eggers (tnr); J. L. Ochoa de Olza (bar); Choeur de voix blanches et Atrium Musicae; G. Paniagua, dir; Orchestre Marocain de Tetouan et musiciens de l'Atrium Musicae; A. Chkara, dir.
Erato STU 70697
[BERENGUER DE PALOU. De la iensor; Dona, la ienser. CADENAL. Un sirventés. MARTIN CODEX. Cantigas de amigo (6). GUIRAUT DE BORNELH. Reis glorios. GUIRAUT RIQUIER. Canco a la Maire de Deus; Fis e verays. MARCABRU. Pax in nomine. MONGE DE MAUTAUDO. Fort m'enoia. PONS D'ORTAFÁ. Si ay perdut. ANON. Sol eclysim patitur (Planctus for Ferdinand II of Léon; Florence, f134). Also Nubas arabo-andalouses (4 selections).]

Anthologie de la musique médiévale espagnole. (Continued)

457. *v.3: La musique en Catalogne jusqu'au XIVe siècle.* Capilla Musical y
Escolania de Santa Cruz del Valle de los Caidos; L. Lozano, dir; Atrium
Musicae; G. Paniagua, dir; J. L. Ochoa de Olza, general music dir.

Erato STU 70695 and Orpheus OR 433

Side 1

[Cantantibus hodie cunctis (Vic, CXI); Alleluia, personet nostra iocunda
(Vic, XXX); Potestati magni maris (Tarragona, Monastery Scala Dei); In
eadem quippe carnis (Gerona, Collégiale de San Feliu); Hosanna, sospitati
dedit mundum (Orfeo Catalá, Ms 1); Veri dulcis (Escorial); In gedeonis
area (Ripoll, Ms 116); Mentem meam ledit dolor (conductus, Paris, Bibl.
Natl., lat.5132); Cedit frigus hiemale (conductus, Paris, Bibl. Natl., lat.
5132); Veri floris (conductus, Tortosa, Catedral, Ms.20486).
Side 2   The "Llibre Vermell" complete:
O Virgo espendens; Cuncti simus (6); Inperayritz (9); Los set goyts de
vostre dona (5); Laudemus Virginem (3); Ad mortem festinamus (10);
Splendens ceptigera (4); Polorum Regina (7); Mariam Matrem (8); Stella
splendens in monte (2).]

458. *v.4: Manuscrit du Pape Calixte II (XIIe et XIIIe siècles); Antiphonaire
Mozarabe (IXe siècle).* Soloists and chorus of Moines de l'abbaye
bénédictine de Santo Domingo de Silos; P. I. Fernandez de la Cuesta.

Erato STU 70696

Side 1   Codex Calixtinus:
[O adiutor omnium; Alleluia in greco; Ad honorem regis; Clemens
servulorum; Ecce adest nunc Iacobus (introit); Regi perennis glorie
(benediction); Congaudeant catholici; Dum Pater familias.
Side 2   Antiphonaire Mozarabe de Silos:
Première leçon du Jeudi Saint; Deuxième leçon du Jeudi Saint; Première
leçon du Vendredi Saint; Première leçon du Samedi Saint; Prère de
Jérémie.   Also Gloria (from the Antiphonaire Mozarabe de Léon).]

459. *v.5: Le manuscrit de las Huelgas (XIIe-XIVe siècles).* Choeur de
religieuses du Monastère cistercien de Santa Maria la Real de las Huelgas;
Atrium Musicae; G. Paniagua, dir.   Erato STU 70698
[Planctus - Rex obit (169); Plange castella misera (172); Quis dabit capiti
(170); O monialis concio (171). Conductus - De castitati thalamo (145);
Omnium in te (159); Ihesu Clementissime (167). Benedicamus -
Resurgentis (43); Sane per omnia (173). Prosas - Novis cedunt vetera
(56); Flavit auster (58). Benedicamus - Catholicorum concio (31);
Virgini matri (183); Exultemus et laetemur (35). Motets - Virgo parit
puerum (100); Ex illustri nata prosapia (132). Conductus - Casta
catholica (134); Ave Maria (156). Sanctus et Agnus - Cleri caetus (14);
Christi miseration (27).]

460. *Anthologie der mehrstimmigen Volksmusik des 16. Jahrhunderts.*
Quartet Polifonic de Barcelona.   DGG ARC 198454
[ANCHIETA. O bone Jesu. CEBALLOS. Quan bienaventurado.
CEBRIÁN. Lagrimas de mi consuelo. ENCINA. Mi libertad en sosiego;
Todos los bienes del mundo. ESCOBAR. Pásame por Dios, barquero.
GUERRERO. Hermosa Catalina; Huyd, huyd, o çiegos amadores.
INFANTAS. Hodie Maria Virgo. MORALES. Parce mihi, Domine.
MORATA. Ojos que ya no veis. PASTRANA. Domine, memento mei.
RIBERA. Por unos puertos arriba. ROBLEDO. Magnificat. TORRE.
Dime, triste coraçon. TORRENTES. O sapientia. VICTORIA. Beati
immaculati. ANON. Aquella boz de Cristo tan sonora; Ay, lune que
reluces; Puse mis amores.]   (biel 2/70; gr 6/69)

461. *An Anthology of Elizabethan and Restoration Vocal Music.* Mary
Thomas (sop); John Whitworth (c-tnr); Diana Poulton (lute); Michael
Thomas (k-bd).   Saga XID 5222; STXID 5222
[ATTEY. Vain hope, adieu. BYRD. Ye sacred muses. CAMPIAN. It fell
on a summer's day. DOWLAND. Come when I call; Flow not so fast, ye
fountains. JONES. Fie what a coil is here. MORLEY. I should for grief
and anguish; It was a lover and his lass; Leave now mine eyes lamenting; Who
is it that this dark night? Also Boyce, Purcell, and Weldon.]   (gram 12/70)

Antiphonal Music from the Cathedral of San Marco. See *Musique en la
Basilique Saint-Marc de Venise* (No.774).

462. *Ars Antiqua.* Capella Antiqua, Munich; Konrad Ruhland, cond.
                              Telefunken 2-12" SAWT 9530/31
[Alleluia: Pascha nostrum immolatus est Christus (Florence, Pluteus
29.I.ff.109r/v). Alleluia: Pascha nostrum immolatus est Christus
(Florence, Pluteus 29.I.ff.23r-24v). Alle psallite cum luia (Codex
Montpellier). Ave gloriosa / Ave virgo regia / tenor: Domino (Codex
Bamberg). Ave gloriosa mater salvatoris (Harleian 978). Ave virgo
virginum (Florence, Pluteus 29.I.ff.240r/v). Belial vocatur (Las Huelgas).
Benedicamus Domino (Florence, Pluteus 29.I.ff.250r-252r). Benedicamus
Domino (Florence, Pluteus 29.I.ff.41v-42v). De se debent bigami / tenor:
Kyrie (Codex Montpellier). Deus in adiutorium (Codex Montpellier).
Flos ut rosa floruit (British Museum, Add. 27630). Homo luge / Homo
miserabilis / Brumas e mors (Darmstadt 3317). In illo tempore: Egressus
Jesus (Polling, CLm. 11764). Jube domne benedicere-Primo tempore
(Diessen CLm. 5511). Judea et Jerusalem (Florence, Pluteus 29.I.ff.46v-
47r). Kyrie magne deus potencie (Munich, Mossburg 156, Mossburger
Gradual). Kyrie virginitatis amator (Wolfenbüttel 677 [W1], ff.194r/v).
Lux vera lucis radium (Prague. Univ. Bibl. VI G IIIa). O Maria maris
stella (Wolfenbüttel 1099 [W2], ff.125r/v). Salve virgo virginum (British
Museum Arundel 248). Salve virgo virginum / tenor: Omnes (Codex
Montpellier). Sanctus (Las Huelgas). Verbum bonum et suave
(Wolfenbüttel 1099 [W2]). Vetus abit littera (Florence, Pluteus
29.I.ff.41v-42v). Victime paschale laudes (Las Huelgas).]

463. *The Ars Nova; Vocal Music of 14th-Century France and Italy.* Capella Cordina; A. Planchart, cond.

    MHS 899 and EA 83; EAS 83 (Music of the Middle Ages, v.9) [ANDREA DI GIOVANNI. Sotto candido vel. CICONIA. I cani sono fuora. DONATO DI FIRENZE. L'aspido sordo. GIOVANNI DI FIRENZE. Per larghi prati. JACOB DE SENLECHS. En ce gracieux tamps. JACOPO DA BOLOGNA. Lux purpurata / Diligite institiam; O cieco mondo. LANDINI. Giovine vagha; Sy dolce non sono. MACHAUT. S'il estoit nulz / S'amours; Se quanque amours. MAESTRO PIERO. Con dolce brama. MATHEUS DE PERUSIO. Le greygnour bien. PHILLIPPE DE VITRY. Douce plaisance / Garison selon nature; Tuba sacre fidei / In arboris. SOLAGE. Fumeux fume. ANON. Je vois douleur / Fauvel nous a fait (Roman de Fauvel); Super cathedrum / Presidentes (Roman de Fauvel).] (MHS ad)

464. *The Art of Ornamentation and Embellishment in the Renaissance and Baroque.* Devised by Denis Stevens. Various performers. (Each selection in 2 versions, original and ornamented.)   2-12" BGS 70697/8 [ARCHILEI. Dalle più alte sfere. FRANCESCO DE LAYOLLE. Lasciar il velo. HOFHAIMER. Nach willen du. MERULO. La Zambeccara. PARSONS. Pandolpho. RORE. Ancor che col partire. SANDRIN. Douce mémoire. ANON. Ay me sospiri. MONTEVERDI. Il combattimento ..., and works by later composers.]

    The Art of Suzanne Bloch - Medieval/Renaissance Music. See *Music for the Lute* (No.707).

    The Art of the Lute, v.1 (Gerwig). See *Lautenmusik aus Frankreich und England* (No.648).

    The Art of the Lute, v.2 (Gerwig). See *Italienische Lautenmusik der Renaissance* (No.633).

465. *At the Imperial Court of Maximilian I.* Concentus Musicus, Vienna; Harnoncourt, cond; Vienna Choir Boys; Chorus Viennensis.

    DGA 14323; 198323 and ARC 3223; 73223 [BRUMEL. Noe noe; Tandernac. DEPRES. Coment peult. FESTA. Quis dabit oculis nostris. HOFHAIMER. Tendernaken. ISAAC. A la bataglia; An buos; Carmen in fa; Fortuna in mi; Imperii proceres; Innsbruck, ich muss dich lassen; J'ay pris amours; La morra; Sancti spiritus assit nobis gratia. LA RUE. Fors seulement. OBRECHT. Vavilment. SENFL. Carmen in la; Carmen in re; Nasci, pati, mori. ANON. Carmen Hercules; En l'ombre du busonet; Naves pont; Si je perdu.] (Myers 9/66)

466. *Aus dem goldenen Zeitalter der englischen Musik.* Capella Fidicinia; Hans Gruss, dir.   DGA 199014 [BASSANO. Galliard. BRADE. Alman. BYRD. Ah silly soul; Who made thee hob forsake. COOPER. Fantasia in e. DOWLAND. Now, oh now I needs must part; What if I never speed. FERRABOSCO II. Fantasia on

the hexachord. HOLBORNE. The funerals; The honeysuckle. HUME.
Tobacco is like love. WARD. Fantasia in d. Also Purcell.] (biel 2/70;
gr 6/69)

Aus dem Repertoire der kaiserlichen Hofkapelle. See *At the Imperial
Court of Maximilian I* (No.465).

467. *Ave Virgo Virginum; Mariengesänge aus dem 13., 15. und 17
Jahrhunderts.* Capella Antiqua, Munich; Konrad Ruhland, dir.
                                    10" Christophorus CLP 75480
[ADAM DE ANTIQUIS VENETUS. Senza te, sacre regina. DUFAY.
Alma redemptoris mater; Magnificat VIII tone. ANON. O Maria maris
stella; Veni virgo beatissima; Ave virgo virginum. Also pieces from
Psalterium Harmonicum, 1642.] (biel 2/69)

468. *Ballades, Rondeaux and Virelais, 14th-15th Centuries.* Zurich Ancient
Instrument Ensemble; Miskell, cond.
            Harmonia Mundi 30592 and Odyssey 32160177; 32160178
[BAUDE CORDIER. Tout pas compas. DE HASPRE. Ma doulce amour.
DUFAY. Franc cuer gentil; Adieu m'amour; Se la face ay pale (vocal and
instr). EBREO (?). Falla con misuras. GALLO & DE INSULIS. Je ne vis
pas. LANDINI. Va pure, amore; I' prieg amor; Per allegrezza; Gram
piant' agli occhi. MACHAUT. Nesque on porroit; Je sui aussi; Tres bonne
et belle; De petit po; Amours me fait désire. ANON. Du bist mein Hort;
Quene note; La Spagna.] (sch)

469. *Baroque Brass.* New York Brass Quintet.
                                    RCA Victor LM 2938; LSC 2938
[ADSON. Courtly masquing ayres, no.19 and 21. DEPRES. Vive le roy.
FINCK. Greiner Zanner. G. GABRIELI. Canzona per sonare no.2.
HOLBORNE. Honie-suckle; My Linda; Night watch; Pavan; Galliard.
SENFL. Carmen in la. SUSATO. Pavan; Rondeau; Saltarelle (all from Het
derde Musyck Boexken). ANON. Als ich anschau das fröhlich Gsicht
(St. Gall Ms.462); Ich sag ade. Also Bach, Monteverdi, Pezel, Purcell.]

470. *Bauern-, Tanz- und Strassenlieder in Deutschland um 1500.* Studio der
frühen Musik, Munich.   Telefunken AWT 9486-A
[MAHU. Es gieng ein wilgezogner knecht. SENFL. Es hett ein biderman
ein weib; Es taget vor dem Wald; Es taget / Es warb (Quodlibet); Ich arme
megdlein klag mich ser; Ich stund an einem Morgen; Ich weiss nit; Im Bad
wöl wir recht frölich sein. SENFL (?). Es wolt ein meydlin wasser holn.
STOLTZER. Entlawbet ist der walde. ANON. Es ist ein schnee gefallen;
Es warb ein schöner jüngling; Es wolt ein fraw zum Weine gan; Ich het
mir ein endlein fürgenommen; Ich trau keinm alten / Ach guter gsel; Ich
weet een Vrauken amorues; Im maien; Ein meidlein tet mir klagen; Den
meinen sack; Nun zu disen zeyten; Ein pauer gab sein son ein weib; Die
prunle die da fliessen.]

Bavarian Court Chapel in the 16th Century. See *Die bayerische Hofkapelle im 16. Jahrhundert* (No.471).

471. *Die bayerische Hofkapelle im 16. Jahrhundert.* Capella Antiqua, Munich; Konrad Ruhland, dir.   Telefunken SAWT 9431
[DASER. Fratres, sobrii estote. ISAAC. Christe, qui lux es et dies (hymn); Ecco virgo concipiet (Communio); Rorate coeli (introit). LASSUS. Ave verum corpus; De profundis (Busspsalm VI); Domine, labia mea aperies; Exaudi Deus orationem meam; Gloria patri; Justorum animae; Tui sunt coeli. SENFL. Asperges me; Carmen in re; Carmen Lamentatio; Missa ferialis; Magnificat V. toni.]   (Myers 9/66)

472. *Berkshire Boys Choir.* George Guest, cond.
                                                   Berkshire Boys Choir, N.Y.C. (unn.)
[BYRD. Make ye joy to God. GIBBONS. The silver swan. MORLEY. My bonny lass. TALLIS. O nata lux de lumine. VICTORIA. Requiem mass. Also Bartok, Poulenc, Bruckner.]   (arg 5/68)

473. *The Birth of Christ.* Netherlands Chamber Choir; Felix de Nobel, cond.
                                                                      Epic LC 3614
[CROCE. Dies Sanctificatus. CLEMENT. Pastores, quidnam vidistis? GABRIELI. O Jesu mi dulcissime. HANDL. Jerusalem, gaude; Omnes de Saba. HASSLER. Angelus ad pastores ait. LASSUS. Exspectans exspectavi; Jubilate Deo; Resonet in laudibus. PALESTRINA. Alma Redemptoris Mater; Hodie Christus natus est. PRAETORIUS. Enatus est Emanuel; Puer natus in Bethlehem. SWELINCK. Ecce, Virgo concipiet; Hodie Christus natus est. VICTORIA. Ave Maria. WILLAERT. O magnum mysterium.]

Bläsermusik am Hof King James I. See *The Royal Brass Music of James I* (No.834).

474. *Bourne Singers.*   Ace of Diamonds ADD 163; SDD 163
[BENNET. Weep, o mine eyes. BYRD. Ave verum corpus. CERTON. Je ne l'ose dir. CLEMENT. Adoramus te. FARRANT. Call to remembrance. HANDL. Resonet in laudibus. HASSLER. Tanzen und Springen. LASSUS. Bonjour, mon coeur. MONTEVERDI. Lasciatemi morire. PALESTRINA. Dies sanctificatus. PASSEREAU. Il est bel et bon. SCANDELLO. Ein Hennlein weiss. SERMISY. Au joly bois. Also Carissimi and Pitoni.]
(gr 12/69)

Brass Music of James I. See *The Royal Brass Music of James I* (No.834).

475. *Brass Music of the Late Renaissance.* Eastman Brass Quintet.
                                    Vox STGBY 619 and Candide CE 31004
[FERRABOSCO II. Four-note pavan. GIBBONS. In Nomine. HOLBORNE. Galliard. OKEOVER. Fantasie. SIMMES. Fantasie. WEELKES. As wanton birds; Death has deprived me; In pride of May; O care thou wilt despatch me; Sit down and sing. Also Scheidt.]   (sch 1/69)

Byrd and His Contemporaries. See *William Byrd and Master of His Time* (No.900).

476. *Cancioneiro musical e poetico.* Choeurs de la Fondation Gulbenkian; O. Violante, cond. (Anonymous compositions from Ms of the Bibliothèque Públia Horténsia de Elvas.)   Philips 837.913 LY
[A la villa voy (no.63); Mas deveis a quie os sirve (no.15); Mil vezes llamo la muerte (no.45); Ojuelos graciosos (no.61); Poq me não vees Ioãña (no. 20); Que he o q vejo (no.32); Se do mal q me qreis (no.37); Todo plazer me desplaze (no.53); Las tristas lagrimas mias (no.25); Venid a sospirar al verde prado (no.65). Also CARDOSO. Missa Tui sunt coeli. (Portugaliae Musica, v.8)

477. *El Cancionero.* Ensemble Polyphonique Paris R.T.F.; Charles Ravier, cond.   Valois MB 431; 931
[ENCINA. Guarda no lo seas tu; Pues que jamas; Te do los; Triste Espana; Una sanosa porfia; Vuestros amores. ESCOBAR. Las mis penas. GABRIEL (or MENA). De la dulce mi enemiga. MUNOZ. Pues bien para esta. PONCE. Alla de me ponga el sol; Como esta sola; Alegria. ANON. Ay que non era; Entra mayo; Aquel caballero; En Avila; Yo me soy; Ya mi despodato.]   (dia 64)

Las Cantigas de Santa Maria. See under ALFONSO X, EL SABIO in individual composer index.

478. *Cantilènes et chansons de troubadours.* Ochoa and Rondeleux (vocalists); Lepaun (vièle); Depannemaker (tambourin).
                                      Harmonia Mundi HM; HMO 30566
[ALPHONSO X, EL SABIO. Cantigas: Assi pod' a Virgen (226); Fazer pode d'outri vivel-os seus (118); Gran dereit'é que mal venna (244); Macar ome per folia (11); Marovillosos / et piadosos (139); O ffondo do mar tan chão (383); Santa Maria leva (320); Virgen, Madre groriosa (340). BERNARD DE VENTADOUR. Quan vei la laudets mover. FAYDIT. Fort chausa aujatz. FOLQUET DE MARSELHA. En cantan m'aven a membrar. GUIRAUT RIQUIER. Jhesu Crist, filh de Diu viu. JAUFRÉ RUDEL. Lanquam li jorn son lonc en mai. MONGE DE MONTAUDON. Mout m'enoja s'o auzes dire. MARCABRU. L'autrier jost' una sebissa. NOVELLA. Bella donna cara. RAIMON DE MIRAVAL. Selh que no vol auzir cansas. VIDAL. Pois tornatz sui en Proensa.]   (dia 67)

479. *Capella Lipsiensis.* Fritz Seidemann (lute); Dietrich Knothe, dir.
                                                      Eterna 820290
[JANEQUIN. Le chant du rossignol. LECHNER. Das Hohelied Salomonis; Deutsche Sprüche von Leben und Tod (1606). LEJEUNE and JANEQUIN. Le chant du rossignol. MONTEVERDI. Lamento d'Arianna.]
(Eterna ad)

480. *Carmina Burana: Aus Handschriften des 13. Jahrhunderts.* Capella
Antiqua, Munich; K. Ruhland, dir.   Christophorus SCGLP 75939
[Axe Phebus aureo (71); Crucifigat omnes (47); Exiit diliculo (90);
Homo quo vigeas vide (22); Nomen a solemnibus (147a); Procurans
odium (12); Vite perdite (31).]   (adv)

481. *Carmina Burana; 20 Lieder aus der Originalhandschrift um 1300.* Studio
der frühen Musik; A. von Ramm (m-sop); W. Cobb (tnr); S. Jones (fidel
and rebec); T. Binkley (lute and pommer).   Telefunken SAWT 9455-A
[Procurans (12); Fas et nefas (19); Dum iuventus floruit (30); Vite
perdite (31); In Gedeonis area (37); Estivali sub fervore (79); Veris
dulcis in tempore (85); Iove cum Mercurio (88a); Exiit diluculo (90);
Conspexit (90); Chramer gip diu varwe mier (107); Chramer gip (107:
rebec solo); Sic mea fata canendo solor (116); Dulce solum (119); Dic
Christi veritas (131); Nomen a solemnibus (147a); Sage, saz ih dirs (147a);
Tempus transit gelidum (153); Fulget dies celebris (153); Diu werlt frovt
sih uberal (161); Planctus Mariae Virgine (Gottfried von Breteuil).]

482. *Carmina Burana (II); 13 Songs from the Benedikt-Beuren Manuscript.*
Studio der frühen Musik.   Telefunken SAWT 9522-A
[NEIDHARDT VON REUENTHAL. Nu gruonet aver diu heide (168a).
PETER VON BLOIS. Dum iuventus (30); Vite perdite (31). WALTHER
VON CHATILLON. Ecce torpet (3). ANON. Homo quo vigeas (22);
Licet eger cum egrotis (8); Crucifigat omnes (47); O varium Fortuna (14);
Celum non animum (15); Axe Phebus aureo (71); Ecce gratum (143);
Tellus flore (146); Tempus est iocundum (179).]

483. *Carols and Motets for the Nativity of Medieval and Tudor England.*
Deller Consort; Musica Antiqua, Vienna; R. Clemencic, dir.
Bach Guild BG 654; BGS 5066
[DUNSTABLE. Kyrie (instr); Quam pulchra est. PYGOTT. Quid petis o
fili. ROY HENRY (HENRY VIII?). Sanctus (instr). SMERT. In die
Nativitatis. ANON. Angelus ad Virginem (instr); Blessed be thou,
Heavenly Queen; Carol with burden (instr); Fauxbourdon and Gymel
(from Ms of Guilelmus Monachus); Hail, Mary, full of grace; I saw (instr);
Nova, nova; Nowell, nowell: Out of your sleep; Nowell, nowell: Tidings
true; Qui natus est; There is no rose of such virtue.]

484. *Célébration chorale en l'ancienne Église St., Philibert de Dijon.* Joseph
Samson Ensemble (Dijon Mixed Chorus); J. F. Samson, dir.
Pathé-France CVC 2084
[AICHINGER. Ubi est Abel. BERNIER. Cantique de Paques. CAPON.
Ad te levavi. CROCE. O sacrum convivium. DEPRES. Ave verum.
JOHN (JOÃO). Crux fidelis. MAUDUIT. Psalm 150. PALESTRINA.
Ego sum panis vivus. VICTORIA. Vere languores.]   (Peters Int. catalog)

485. *Ceremonial Music of the Renaissance.* Capella Antiqua, Munich; Konrad
Ruhland, cond.   Telefunken SAWT 9524-B
[CICONIA. O Pauda sidus praeclarum; Venetia mundi splendor. DUFAY.

Nuper rosarum flores; Supremum est mortalibus. FERAGUT. Excelsa
civitas Vincentia. ISAAC. Imperii proceres; Quis dabit capiti meo aquam.
ENCINA. Triste España. MOUTON. Non nobis domine, non nobis.
ANON. Advenit nobis desiderabilis (Trent Codices).] (gram 12/70)
N.B.: Another disc by this group cited frequently with this same title is
entered here under Staatsmusik der Renaissance, q.v.

486. *Chamber Music for Voices.* Klagenfurter Madrigalchor; Mittergradnegger,
cond.   Mace 9078; S9078
[DEPRES. Tulerunt Dominum meum. HANDL. Jerusalem gaudes.
JANEQUIN. Cocu. VECCHI. Tridola, non dormire. WIDMANN.
Wohlauf, ihr Gäste. WILBYE. Adieu, sweet Amaryllis. Also Bruckner,
Burkhart, David, Distler, Haselböck, Heiller, Hindemith, Lotti.]
(Myers 3/69)

487 *Chansons amoureuses et guerrières de la Renaissance.* Ensemble Vocal
Caillard.   Erato EFM 8026
[BONNET. Francion vint l'autre jour. CADEAC. Je suis déshéritée.
CERTON. La, la, la, je n'ose le dire. DEPRES. Milles regrets.
JANEQUIN. La bataille de Marignan; Le chant des oiseaux; Le chant de
l'alouette. LASSUS. Matona mia cara; Mon coeur se recommande; Le
rossignol; Un jeune moine. LEJEUNE. Qu'est devenu ce bel oeil; Voici
du gai printemps; Perdre le sens devant nous; Las! où vas-tu sans moi?
MAUDUIT. Vous me tuez si doucement; Voici le vert et le beau mai.
PASSEREAU. Il est bel et bon.] (dia 67)

488. *Chansons d'amour du XVe siècle.* Ensemble Gaston Soublette.
                                              Bôite à Musique BAM C 109
[BINCHOIS. Adieu mes très belles amours; Amour et souvenir de celle;
Je loe amours; Seule esgarée de tout joyeulx plaisir; Toutes mes joyes
sont éteintes. FONTAINE. Fontaine à vous dire. GHIZEGHEM. De
quatre nuys; Pour ce que j'ai joui. GRENON. La plus joilie et la plus
belle. JOYE. Non pas que le veuille penser. MORTON. Est temps;
N'araige jamais mieulx que j'ay; Pièce instr. VIDE. Las j'ay perdu mon
espincel. ANON. C'est à ce joly mois de may; Chappeau de saulge; Je
suis trop jeunette.] (dia 70)

489. *Chansons der Troubadours.* Studio der frühen Musik; T. Binkley, cond.
                                                     Telefunken SAWT 9567
[BERNARD DE VENTADOUR. Can vei la lauzata mover. COMTESSA
DE DIA. A chanter m'er de so qu'eu no volria. GUIRAT DE BORNELH.
Leu chansonet'e vil. RAIMBAUT DE VAQUEIRAS. Kalenda maia.
VIDAL. Baron de mon dan covit. ANON. A l'entrada del temps clar;
Saltarello; Veris ad imperia.] (sch 9/71)

490. *Chansons galantes de la Renaissance.* Ensemble Vocal Passaquet.
                                              10" Harmonia Mundi HM 25304
[BATAILLE. Ma bergère non légère. BONNET. Voulez-vous donc

490. *Chansons galantes de la Renaissance.* (Continued)
toujours Madame. CLEMENT. Une fillette bien gorriere. COSTELEY.
Mignonne allons voir si la rose. JANEQUIN. Petite nymphe folâstre.
LASSUS. Un doux neny; Il était une religieuse; Fleure de quinze ans.
ANON. Vray dieu d'amours.] (dia 64)

491. *Chansons galantes et à danser.* Ensemble Vocal Philippe Caillard du
Mouvement "A Coeur Joie"; P. Caillard, dir.   10" Erato EFM 42066
[BONNET. Francion vint l'autre jour. CADÉAC. Je suis déshéritée.
CERTON. La, la, la, je ne l'ose dire. COSTELEY. Allons au vert bocage.
DU CAURROY. Deliette, mignonette, pucelette. GERVAISE. Trois
danses. GUEDRON. C'est une demoiselle. LASSUS. Mon coeur se
recommande. MAUDUIT. Vous me tuez si doucement. PLANCON.
Chamberière. SERMISY. Contentez-vous, ami. TESSIER. Au joli bois.]
(Erato catalog)   Compare with EFM 8026, no.487, above.

492. *Chansons und Madrigale der Renaissance.* NCRV Vocal Ensemble,
Hilversum; Camerata Vocale, Bremen; Ensemble Vocal Ph. Caillard;
Niedersächsischer Singkreis; W. Träder, cond.   Camerata CMS 30033 LP
[*English:* BENNET. All creatures now. DOWLAND. Say, love; Shall I
sue. MORLEY. Sing we and chant it. PILKINGTON. Rest, sweet
nymphs. WEELKES. Hark all ye lovely saints. *Flemish:* BELLE. O
amoureusich mondeken root. BENEDICTUS. Mijn liefkens bruin oghen.
CLEMENT. De lustelijcke mey. SOULIAERT. Een costerken op sijn
clocken clanc. VERDONC. Alle mijn ghepeys. ANON. Ic truere.
French: BONNET. Francion vont l'autre jour. COSTELEY. Je vois des
glissantes eaux; Quand le berger; Que de passions. LLANSON. Chamberière. PASSEREAU. Il est bel et bon. *Italian:* ARCADELT. O feliche
occhi miei; Voi ve n'andate; Sapet' amanti. FESTA. Se'l pensier. RORE.
Da le belle contrade.] (biel 2/70)

493. *Chants Judéo-espagnols du XVIe siècle.* Gorby (m-sop).
                                                    Philips PHI 832581
[A la una yo naci; Avre tu puerta cerrada; Buenas noches; Durme durme;
Hija mia, mi querida; Mi coracon; Morena me llaman; Nani-nani; Noches;
Porque lloras blanca mia; La sirena; Ven querida; Yo m'enamori d'un
aire.] (dia 67)

494. *Chapels of the Princes.* Roger Blanchard Ensemble; P. Froidebise (org).
                                          Music Guild M 15; S 15; 105; S 105
[GASCOGNE. Christus vincit; Missa Pourquoy non. SERMISY. Agnus
Dei; Dulcis amica Dei; Si bona suscepimus (2 versions). VERMONT
L'AINE. Ave virgo gloriosa. ANON. Prelude (org. Attaingnant).]
(Myers 6/63)

495. *Choral Masterworks Through the Centuries.* McGill University Martlets;
Whyte, cond.   Bärenreiter 1877; 2877
[BYRD. While the bright sun. COSTELEY. Mignonne. ENCINA.
Gasajémonos de Husía. FORD. Since first I saw your face. LASSUS. O

bella fusa. MORALES. Ecce Virgo concipiet. PALESTRINA. Agnus Dei.
TESSIER. Au joli bois. VECCHI. Fa una canzona. ANON. Je me leve un
bel maitin. Also Schütz, Brahms, Händel and others.]   (sch 8/67)

496. *Choral Music by Morales, Victoria and Byrd; Madrigals and Dialogues by*
Giovanni Gabrieli. The Ambrosian Singers and Consort; Denis Stevens,
cond.   Dover HCR-ST-7271
[G. GABRIELI. Vagh' amorosi; Ahi, senza te; Dormiva dolcemente; S'al
discoprir; Alma cortes'e bella; O che felice giorno; Dolce care parole; Se
cantano gl'augelli. BYRD. Domine, praestolamur adventum tuum.
MORALES. Missus est Gabriel angelus. VICTORIA. Magnificat primi
toni.]

Choral Music of the Middle Ages. See *Missa Tournai - Motets, ca.1320*
(No.685).

497. *Choral Music of the Renaissance.* Ensemble Vocal Philippe Caillard.
Erato EFM 42075 and Musical Heritage Society MHS 617
[DEPRES. Missa Pange lingua [Side 1]. LEJEUNE (chansons). Fuyons
tous d'amour le jeu; Las, où vas tu sans moi; Notre Vicaire; Perdre le sens
devant vous; Qu'est devenu ce bel oeil; Voici du gai printemps; Psalm 45
in the third mode (verse 1,4,5,7).]

498. *Choral Tapestry.* The Ambrosian Singers; McCarthy, cond.
2-12" Avant-Garde AVS 128/129
[BENNET. Weep o mine eyes. BYRD. Ave verum corpus. CERTON. I
cannot conceal it. CLEMENT. Adoramus te. FARRANT. Call to
remembrance. HANDL. Resonet in laudibus. HASSLER. Dancing and
springing. LASSUS. Good-day, my dear. MONTEVERDI. Lasciatemi
morire. PALESTRINA. Dies sanctificatus. PASSEREAU. Il est bel et
bon. SCANDELLO. A little white hen. SERMISY. To yon fair grove.

BANCHIERI. Counterpoint of the animals. BYRD. Ego sum panis vivus.
DEPRES. Ave vera virginitas. ENCINA. Since I cannot forget. FORD.
Almighty God who hast me brought. FORSTER. I say adieu.
GOMBERT. Go jealousy. GUERRERO. On this day Saint Joseph brought
us. HANDL. Orietur stella. HASSLER. My heart with love is springing.
LEJEUNE. The return of springtime. LEMLIN. The cuckoo. MAREN-
ZIO. O rex gloriae. DE MELLE. O Jesu Christe. MORLEY. The fields
abroad; Fire, fire in my heart. PALESTRINA. Verbum caro. PHILIPS.
Regina coeli. PRAETORIUS. Psallite. VECCHI. Sing, sing a song for me.
VICTORIA. O magnum mysterium. WILBYE. Change me, o heavens.]

499. *[Chorale Music Madrigals.]* The State Ensemble Chorus of Tîrgu-Mureş;
Szalmán Loránt, cond. (Sung in Hungarian)   Electrecord ECD 1052
[ARCADELT. Madrigal a hattyuhoz. COSTELEY. O nézd mily szép a
rózsa. GASTOLDI. Csolnakos ének. HASSLER. Gagliarda. LASSUS.
Vágyodás. SENFL. Fü, fa. Also works by later composer.]
(Electrecord catalog)

500. *Christmas Carols and Motets of Medieval Europe.* Deller Consort;
Musica Antiqua of Vienna (R. Clemencic, dir); A. Deller, dir.
Bach Guild BG 680; 70680 and Amadeo AVRS 5056
[BYTTERING. Nesciens Mater (motet). CICONIA. Et in terra pax
(instr). DUNSTABLE. Sancta Maria. ESCOBAR. In Nativitate Domini.
FOGLIANO. Ave Maria (laude). ISAAC. Puer natus (introit). JAN OF
JENSTEJN. Decet huius cunctis horis (monody). PALESTRINA. Hodie
Christus natus est (motet). POWER. Beata Progenies (motet). ST.
GODRIC. Crist and Sainte Marie. SENFL. Maria zart. STOLTZER.
Foeno iacere (instr). ANON. Alleluya Psallat (Engl., 14th c.); Gloria
(Engl., 14th c.); De Nativitate Domini (Czech motet, 15th c.); O Maria
Virgo (instr, isorhythmic motet); O Regina, Lux Divina (Czech, 15th c.).]

501. *Christmas Festival.* Roger Wagner Chorale.   Angel S 36016
[A. GABRIELI. Magnificat. G. GABRIELI. Beata est Virgo Maria;
Jubilate Deo. PALESTRINA. Hodie Christus natus est. REGNART.
Puer natus est. Also Peeters, Pinkham.]   (Myers 6/68)

502. *Christmas Music.* The Clerkes of Oxenford.   Abbey S 603
[PYGOTT. Quid petis, o fili? SOPHRONIOS. Pro tis genniseos.
WRIGHT. Nesciens mater. ANON. Angelus ad Virginem; I come from
heaven high to tell; Nova, nova, Ave fit ex Eva; Nowell, owt of your
slepe; Guadete, gaudete, Christus est natus; Quem pastores laudavere.]

Christmas Music of the Middle Ages and the Renaissance. See
Weihnachtsmusik aus Mittelalter und Renaissance (No.898).

503. *Cinq siècles de joyeuse musique.* Ensemble Syntagma Musicum; Otten,
cond.   2-12" Voix de son Maître SME 191761/2
(Not examined, but may be the same as Music of the Middle Ages and
Renaissance (HMV HQS 1195/6) and similar to Seraphim Guide to
Renaissance Music (SIC 6052), q.v.)   (dia 70)

504. *Cinq siècles de musique dans la Cathédrale de Reims.* Maîtrise de la
Cathédrale de Reims; Paillard Chamber Orch; A. Muzerelle (org); J. F.
Paillard, cond.
Erato LDE 3377; STE 50277 and Musical Heritage Society MHS 894
[BAUDE CORDIER. Gloria. DEPRES. Vive le Roy. MACHAUT. Felix
Virgo (motet). Also Cosset, Grigny, Hardouin.]

Colección de música antigua española. See *Anthologie de la musique
médiévale espagnole* (Nos.456-459).

505. *Complesso "Madrigale" di Mosca.*   Chant du Monde LDX-A 78424
[ENCINA. 3 Villancicos. FUENLLANA. Duelete de mi, señora.
MORALES. Motet [unspecified]. ORTIZ. Ricercada: O, le bonheur
de mes yeux. VICTORIA. O magnum mysterium. ANON. La hija del
Rey; 3 Chants de Nöel; Pastorcito no te aduermas; Pequeñe flor; Si la
noche es oscura; 3 Villancicos.]   (sant 5-6/71)

Composers of the Chapel Royal. See *Music of the Court Homes and Cities of England, v.1* (No.727).

506. *Concert à Notre-Dame de Paris.* Chanteurs de Saint-Eustache; Quintette cuivres Paris; Cochereau (org); Martin, cond.   Philips 835792 LY
[A. GABRIELI. 2 canzonas (instr); Imploration pour un temps de détresse. PALESTRINA. Messe du Pape Marcel (Agnus Dei I et II). VICTORIA. O vos omnes. Also Lotti and Monteverdi.]   (dia 67)

507. *Concert Renaissance au château de Chenonceaux.* Ensemble Vocal Philippe Caillard; Mildred Clary (lute).   Erato LDE 3316; STE 50216
[BERTRAND. Je ne suis seulement amoreux de Marie; Certes mon oeil fut trop aventureux. CERTON. J'ai le rebours; Que n'est-elle auprès de moi? COSTELEY. Mignonne, allons voir si la rose; Allons gai, bergères; Que de passions et douleurs; Je vois des glissantes eaux. DALZA. Piva (lute). DOWLAND. King of Denmark galliard; Orlando sleepeth (lute). JANEQUIN. Au joli jeu du pousse avant; Il s'en va tard; Ce mois de mai; Je ne connais femme en cette contrée; Voici le bois; Ma peine n'est pas grande. MILAN. Pavane (lute). SERMISY. Tant que vivrai; Vous perdez temps; C'est une dure départie. ANON. Spagnoletta (lute); Je demeure seule égarée.]

Concerts from the Renaissance. See *From the Renaissance (Concerts of Great Music)* (No.582).

508. *Concert sacré en la Cathédrale de Chartres.* Chorale Stephane Caillat; Orch. de Chambre Jean-François Paillard; S. Caillat, cond. ("Collection Chateaux et Cathédrales")   Erato LDE 3348; STE 50248
[BRUMEL (motets). Ecce panis angelorum; Mater Patris et Filia. DU CAURROY. Te Deum. Also Jullien and Pierre Robert.]

509. *Concerts pour deux princes au château de Blois.* Paris Polyphonic Ensemble; ORTF Instrumental Ensemble; Charles Ravier, cond.
Erato STU 70-367 and Musical Heritage Society MHS 955
[ATTAINGNANT. Basse-danse variée; Mon coeur avez. BOESSET. N'espérez plus, mes yeux. CONSEIL. L'aultre iour, iouer m'aloie; De nuyt et jour. GERVAISE. Gaillarde variée. JANEQUIN. Ville de Bloys. MOUTON. La, la, la l'oysillon du boys. ANON. A qui dir'elle sa pensée (canti B); Hor vedi, Amor; Reuelis vous, Picars et Bourguignons (Odhecaton); Ils sont bien pelz (Canti C?).]

Consortiana. See *English, French and Italian Madrigals and Songs* (No.542).

510. Coro di Conservatorio Verdi, Milan; Bortone, cond.
10" Orphée ORP 21030
[ARCADELT. Il bianco e dolce cigno. BROCCHUS. Alma svegliate ormai. CARA. Pieta cara signora. MARENZIO. Scendi dal paradiso. PALESTRINA. La cruda mia nemica. TROMBONCINO. Arbor victorioso; Ave Maria. VECCHI. Il bianco e dolce cigno.]   (dia 67)

511. *Court and Ceremonial Music of the Early 16th Century.* Roger
Blanchard Ensemble; Poulteau Consort.   Nonesuch H 1012; 71012
[BRUMEL. Mater Patris et Filia. COMPERE. Un franc archer; Nous
somme de l'ordre de Saint-Babouyn. DEPRES. Allégez-moy; Adieu mes
amours; Vive le roi. FEVIN. Gaude Francorum regia corona.
LONGUEVAL. Passio Domini nostri Jesu Christi. MOUTON. Quis dabit
oculis nostris. ANON. Il était un bonhomme; On a dit mal de mon ami;
Si j'ay perdu mon ami.]

512. *The Cries of London: Music in Honor of Queen Elizabeth.* Ambrosian
Singers and Players; D. Stevens, cond.
          Expériences Anonymes EA 81; Eas 81 D and reissue on Penn State
          Music Series PSMS 100; 100-S and AVRS 6149 and ORYX EXP 31
[Cries of London: DEERING. The cries of London. MORLEY. Blow,
shepherds, blow; Will you buy a fine dog? RAVENSCROFT. Maids to
bed; Where are you, fair maids? TYE. In nomine "Crye." WHYTHORNE.
Buy new broom.
In Honor of Queen Elizabeth: BENNETT. All creatures now are merry-
minded; Eliza, her name gives honour. BYRD. The Queen's alman; This
sweet and merry month (à 4 and à 6). HILTON. Fair Oriana. JOHNSON.
Eliza is the fairest queen. YOULL. Each day of thine.]   (Myers 9/66)

513. *Cuivres et violes de la Renaissance.* Devevey, cond.
                                        Counterpoint MC 20145
[BANCHIERI. Fantasia in eco. DU CAURROY. 2ème Fantaisie; 5ème
Fantaisie. FANTINI. Prima sonata a due tromba detta del Carsi; Sonata
a due tromba detta del Ricaseli; Sonata a due tromba detta del
Piccolomini; Entrate imperiale per sonare in concerto; Baletto detta il
Gischeri; Sonata del Gonzague; Sonata a due tromba detta del
Castaldi; Sonata a due tromba detta del Corsini; Capriccio detta del
Gardi. G. GABRIELI. Canzon per sonare, primi toni. LUZZASCHI.
Canzon à 4. MACQUE. Toccata a modo di trompette. MASCHERA.
Canzon da sonare. PALESTRINA. Ricercare du 3e ton; Ricercare du 5e
ton. PHILIPS. Allemande. ANON. Doulce amye; Gentille fillette; Mari
ie songeois laultre jour; Par fin d'esprit; Vous aurez tout ce qui est myeu.]
(biel 1/64)

514. *Danby, Nicholas.* Organ Recital.   ORYX 511
[BULL. In nomine IX. GIBBONS. Fancy for double organ. TOMKINS.
A short verse; Voluntary in C major. Also Blow, Purcell, Boyce, Wesley,
Walond.]   (gr 10/67)

Dance Music of Four Centuries. See *Tanzmusik aus vier Jahrhunderten*
(No.868).

Dance Music of the Renaissance. See *Tanzmusik der Renaissance* (No.
870).

515. *Dance Music of the Renaissance and the Baroque.* Jaye Consort of
Viols; Philip Jones Brass Ensemble; Canzona Ensemble; Accademia
Monteverdiana; Baroque Trio; H. Lester (hpsi); D. Stevens, cond.
                                                            Orpheus OR 352/3/4
[AMMERBACH. Gagliarda; Passamezzo; La Riprese. ARBEAU. Pavane
"Belle qui tiens ma vie." ASTON. Hornpipe. ATTAINGNANT.
Gagliarda; Gagliarda "Belfiore." BASSANO. Galliard. BRADE. Alman;
Coranto; Galliard. BYRD. Gagliarda. DALZA. Pavana alla Ferrarese.
FERRABOSCO. Pavan "Dovehouse." GERVAISE. Allemande; Basse
dance; Bransle; Pavane & Gaillarde; Pavane & Gaillarde de l'Angleterre;
Tourdion. GESUALDO. Gagliarda. HAUSSMANN. German dances I,
II, III. HOLBORNE. 2 Galliards; The Honiesuckle; Pavan & Galliard;
The Wanton. NAU. Ballet music. PEERSON. Alman; Piper's Pavan.
PESENTI. Balletti IV, V; Correntes I, XVI; Gagliardi II, VI, X, XI, XXV.
PHALESE. Passamezzo. SUSATO. Basse danse "San Roch"; Pavane &
Gaillarde "La Bataille." TOMKINS. Pavan. TORRE. Alta. ANON. A la
mode de France & Nonesuch; Coranto; Heartsease; Istampita "Ghaeta";
2 Saltarelli; Staines Morris Dance; Tickle my toe; La Traditore; Watkins
Ale. Also Blow, Frescobaldi, Locke, Purcell, Scheidt.]

516. *Danceries du XVIe pour orgue d'après la tablature de Jan de Lublin,
1540.* H. Schoonbroodt (org).
                    Charlin CL 25 and Schwann VMS 2002 and Musica M 2002
(Includes some works, unidentified on the recording, by Janequin, Depres,
Willaert, Nicolas de Cracovie, and others.)

Danses de la Renaissance. See *Tanzmusik der Renaissance* (No.870).

Danze di 4 secoli. See *Tanzmusik aus vier Jahrhunderten* (No.868).

517. *De Josquin des Prés à Igor Stravinsky.* Maîtrise R.T.F.; Besson and
Jouineau, dirs.   Plaisir Musical PLM 30308
[COSTELEY. Que vaut catin, cette fuite frivolle; Allons gay bergères.
DEPRES. Milles regrets de vous abandonner. R. GODARD. Hault le
boys! M'amye Margot. JANEQUIN. Chantons, sonnons, trompettes;
La bataille de Marignan. LASSUS. Fuyons tous d'amour le jeu.
PALESTRINA. Exercices sur la gamme. PASSEREAU. Hé, gentil
mareschal. SERMISY. Hau, hau, hau le boys. SERVIN. La piafe
guerrière. Also Mozart, Beethoven, Schubert, Kodaly, Stravinsky.]
(dia 64)

De Noël à la Chandeleur. See *Nativity to Candlemas* (No.783).

518. *Demantius-Passion.* Stuttgarter Kantatenchor; A. Langenbeck.
                                                        Harmonia Mundi HM 30836
[BRUCK. O du armer Judas. BURGK. Der Herr mit seinen Jüngern.
DEMANTIUS. Deutsche Passion nach dem Evang. St. Johannes.
LECHNER. Allein zu dir, Herr Jesus Christ. PRAETORIUS. O vos
omnes. Also Schütz.]   (biel 2/67)

519. *Das deutsche Chorlied.* Various German choruses.   DGG 136 340
[FRANCK. Das Bergwerk wolln wir preisen. FRIDERICI. Drei schöne
Dinge. HASSLER. Feinslieb, du hast mich gfangen; Das Herz tut mir
aufspringen; Jungfrau, dein schön Gestalt. ISAAC. Innsbruck, ich muss
dich lassen. LASSUS. Audite nova; Baur, was trägst im Sacke; Tritt auf
den rigel. LECHNER. O Lieb, wie süss und bitter. SENFL. Es taget vor
dem Walde. WIDMANN. Schneiderlied.]   (adv)

520. *Das deutsche Chorlied I: Madrigale aus dem 16. und 17. Jahrhundert.*
Solistenvereinigung des Berliner Rundfunks; Helmut Koch, cond.
                                                      Eterna 830007
[ALBERT. Du mein einzig Licht. ECCARD. Nun schürz dich. FINCK.
Wach auf, wach auf. FRANCK. Kommt, ihr G'spielen. FRIDERICI. Wir
lieben sehr im Herzen. HASSLER. Das Herz tut mir aufspringen; Ihr
Musici, frisch auf; Mein G'müt ist mir verwirret; Nun fanget an, ein gutes
Liedlein. HOFHAIMER. Herzliebstes Bild. ISAAC. Ich stund an einem
Morgen. JACOBI. Sichres Deutschland. LASSUS. Ein guter Wein is
lobenswert. OTHMAYR. Mir ist ein feins brauns Maidelein; Wie schön
blüht uns der Maie. PRAETORIUS. Wach auf, wach auf mit heller Stimm.
SENFL. Ach Elslein; Es taget vor dem Walde; Mit Lust tät' ich ausreiten;
Quodlibet. STOLTZER. Entlaubet is der Wald. Also Schein and Schütz.]
(Eterna catalog, 1965)

521. *Deutsche, englische und italienische Madrigale. (Lieder der Völker, XIII).*
Soloistenvereinigung des Berliner Rundfunks; Helmut Koch, cond.
                                                      Eterna 830004
[BENNET. Fliesset dahin, ihr Tränen. DONATO. Wenn wir hinausziehn.
DOWLAND. O süsses Lieb, komm zurück. GASTOLDI. An hellen Tagen.
GESUALDO. Ecco, mirirò dunque; Hai, già mi discoloro. HAGIUS.
Herzlich tut mich erfreuen. HASSLER. Jungfrau, dein schön Gestalt.
ISAAC. Innsbruck, ich muss dich lassen; Schöne Maruschka. LASSUS.
Audite nova; Ich liebe dich. LEMLIN. Der Gutzgauch. MONTEVERDI.
Quel Augellin, che canta; Se nel partir da voi. MORLEY. Tanzlied im
Maien. SCANDELLUS. Ein Hennlein weiss. VECCHI. Es sang ein
Vöglein. ANON. Ach herzig's Herz; Ich sag ade. Also Schein.]
(Eterna catalog 1965)

522. *Deutsche Lautenmusik der Renaissance.* Walter Gerwig (lute).
                                                 Harmonia Mundi HM 30460
[CRAUS. Pavan Fuchs beiss mich nicht. FABRICIUS. Es ist ein Bauer
in Brunnen; Gut Gsell und du musst wandern; Polnischer Tanz;
Studentenlob; Studententanz. GINTZLER. Recercar quarto. JUDEN-
KÜNIG. Niederländischer Rundtanz; Welscher Tanz "Rossina"; Wo soll
ich mich hinkehren. KARGEL. Fantasia. MERTEL. Ballett; Praeludium;
So wünsch ich ihr eine gute Nacht. H. NEUSIEDLER. Bettlertanz; Ein
guter welscher Tanz; Ich sag adieu; Welscher Tanz "Wascha mesa." M.
NEUSIEDLER. Der Fuggerin Tanz. OCHSENKUHN. Innsbruck, ich muss
dich lassen. SENFL. Ach Elslein, liebes Elselein. Also Schlick.] (biel 2/70)

523. *Deutsche Messe zur Osterzeit.* Collegium Musicum St. Martini, Bremen;
L. Ströbel, cond.   10" Psallite PSB 32/190226
[ECCARD. Zu diser österlichen Zeit. FRANCK. Galliarda. HAUSS-
MANN. Deutscher Tanz. KUGELMANN. Wir loben. RASELIUS. Wir
glauben an den Heil'gen Geist. RESINARIUS. Wir glauben auch an Jesus
Christ. SCHRÖTER. O Jesu Christ. SIGEFRID. Kyrie. WALTER. Wir
glauben all'.]   (biel 2/67)

524. *Deutsche Volkslieder, II: Liedsätze aus älterer und neuerer Zeit ... z.T.*
mit historischen Instrumenten. Various performers.
                                      2-12" Camerata CM 30004/5 K
[BRANDT. Es wurb ein's Königs Sohn; Frisch auf, in Gottes Namen.
BRUCK. So trinken wir alle. ECCARD. Nun schürz dich, Gretlein.
FINCK. In Gottes Namen fahren wir. HAUSSMANN. Tanz mir nicht
mit meiner Jungfer Käthen. ISAAC. Dich, Mutter Gottes; Es hätt ein
Baur ein Töchterlein; Innsbruck, ich muss dich lassen; Mein Mütterlein.
LECHNER. Christ ist erstanden. LEMLIN. Der Gutzgauch. OTHMAYR.
Ach Gott, wie weh tut Scheiden; Es liegt ein Schloss in Österreich.
PAMINGER. Hüt's Feur. PRAETORIUS. Ach Herr, du allerhöchster
Gott; Es ist ein Ros entsprungen; Quem pastores laudavere. SENFL. Ach
Elslein; Es taget; Im Maien; Mir ist ein rot Goldfingerlein; Wann ich des
Morgens. WALTHER. Wach auf, du Deutsches Land. ANON. Ich hab
durchwandert Städt und Land; Nun bitten wir den heiligen Geist; St.
Michael; Wir zogen in das Feld.]   (biel 1/64)

525. *Deutsche Volkslieder in Sätzen des 16. Jahrhunderts.* RIAS Kammerchor;
Berlin Ensemble für alte Musik; G. Arndt, cond.   Columbia SMC 80891
[HOFHAIMER. Greiner Zanner, Schnöpfitzer. ISAAC. Zwischen Berg
und tiefem Tal. SENFL. Ach Elslein, liebes Elselein. STOLTZER.
Entlaubet ist der Walde. STOLTZER (or ISAAC). Ich stund an einem
Morgen. ANON? Ich schell mein Horn; Mit Lust tät ich ausreiten.]
(biel 2/70)
N.B.: This record was unavailable for audition and catalogues do not give
composers' names. Attributions above are speculative.

Divertissement courtois. See *French Dances of the Renaissance* (No.577).

Dix chants de Noël. See *Ten Christmas Songs from the Time of Praetorius*
(No.874).

526. *Doppelchörige Motetten alter Meister.* Windsbacher Knabenchor; Hans
Thamm, dir. Columbia C 91308; STC 91308 and Mace M 9054; SM 9054
[DULICHIUS. Ich hebe meine Augen auf (Ps. 121). HANDL. Pater
Noster. HASSLER. Herzlich lieb hab ich, O Herr. SCHRÖTER. Wo der
Herr nicht das Haus bauet (Ps. 127). STADEN. Beati omnes qui timent
Dominum. Also Bach and Pachelbel.]   (biel 1/64)

527. *Dresdner Kreuzchor.* Mauersberger, cond.   Pelikan PSR 40503
[BRUCK. Aus tiefer Not schrei ich zu dir. ECCARD. Ein feste Burg ist
unser Gott. GESIUS. Verleih uns Frieden gnädiglich. PRAETORIUS.
Ein neues Lied wir haben an; Wir glauben all an einen Gott (instr).
SCHRÖTER. Allein Gott in der Höh sei Ehr (instr). VULPIUS. Jesaja
dem Propheten das geschah. WALTHER. Wär Gott nicht mit uns diese
Zeit; Wach auf, du deutsches Land; Mit Fried' und Freud'. Also Bach,
Scheidt, Buxtehude, Weckmann, Tunder.]   (dia 2/68)

528. *Duets for Countertenors.* A. and M. Deller.
                    Columbia C 10022 and Philips Vanguard VSL 11047
[DEERING. Gaudent in coelis; O bone Jesu. JONES. Sweet Kate.
MONTEVERDI. Angelus ad pastores ait; Currite populi (solo); Fugge,
fugge, anima mea; Salve Regina. MORLEY. Sweet nymph; I go before,
my darling; Miraculous love's wounding. ANON. Ah, my dear son. Also
Purcell, Schütz, Blow.]   (gram 12/70)

529. *The Dulcet Pipes.* Taylor Recorder Consort; S. Taylor, cond.
                    Bach Guild BG 645; BGS 5057 and Amadeo AVRS 6295
[BYRD. The bells; Callino casturame; Earle of Oxford's marche.
FARNABY. Rosasolis; Wooddy cock. HOLBORNE. Suite.
PALESTRINA. Ricercar del 1º tuono. Also Händel, Schmelzer, Warlock.]
(Myers 6/64)

Dutch and German Motets of the 16th and 17th Centuries. See
Niederländische und Deutsche Motetten ... (No.785).

Early and Late 15th Century Music. See *Historical Anthology of Music
in Performance, v.2* (No.609).

Early Music of England, Flanders, Germany and Spain. See *Frühe
Musik in England ...* (No.585).

Early Music of Italy, France and Burgundy. See *Frühe Musik in
Italien ...* (No.586).

530. *Early Scottish Keyboard Music and Dances from the Dublin Virginal
Manuscript.* Alan Cuckston (hpsi).   HQS 1150 and Waverly LLP 1037
[from DUBLIN VIRGINAL MANUSCRIPT. Alman Bruynsmedelijn;
Alman le pied de cheval; Alman Prince; Reprise of the Alman Prince;
Branle; Branle Hoboken; Chi passa per questa strada; Galliard; Master
Taylor's Pavan and Galliard; Pavan and Galliard; Pavan and Galliard on
the Passamezzo Antico; Variations on the Romanesca. BURNETT.
Pavan. JOHNSTON (arr. Kinloch). Pavan - Jhonstounis Delyt.
KINLOCH. Kinloche His Fantasie; Galliarde of the lang paven. ANON.
Allmayne and Coranto; Galliard.]   (gram 10/68)

531. *Elizabethan Lute Songs.* Peter Pears with Julian Bream (lute).
                    RCA Victor LSC 3131 and English Victor SB 6835
[DOWLAND. Can she excuse? Come, heavy sleep; Dear, if you change;

I saw my lady weep; Shall I sue? Stay, time; Sweet, stay awhile; Weep you no more. FORD. Come, Phyllis; Fair, sweet, cruel. MORLEY. Absence; It was a lover and his lass; Who is it? ROSSETER. If she forsake me; What then is love but mourning? When Laura smiles.] (gram 12/70)

Elizabethan Music (Bream Consort). See *An Evening of Elizabethan Music* (No.559).

532. *An Elizabethan Panorama in Sound; City Gulls and Country Swains.* The Singers; Elizabethan Consort of Viols; Layton Ring Recorder Consort.
H.M.V. CLP 1920
[DEERING. Country cries. DOWLAND. Sir John Gouch His Galliard. GIBBONS. London cries. ANON. Beggar boy; La Bergomesca; The Carman's whistle; Cuckoo; Malts come down; Nobody's jig; Watkins ale. Also readings by John Neville from Dekker, Breton, Howard and Marlowe.] (gr 1/66)

533. *Elizabethan Songs.* Austin Miskell (tnr) with ensemble of viols; Nesbitt, cond. H.M.V. HQS 1113
[BENNET. The hunt is up. BYRD. O mistress mine; Sellenger's Round. HENRY VIII. Pastime with good company. MORLEY. It was a lover and his lass. SAVILE. Here's a health unto his Majesty. ANON. Agincourt song; Barley brake; Coventry carol; Gathering peasecods; Go from my window; Greensleeves; John, come kiss me now; Lachrimae; Lilliburlero; Mall ser gather ye rosebuds; Summer is a coming-in; Watkins ale.] (gram 12/69)
N.B.: This record was unavailable for audition and catalogues do not give composers' names. Attributions given above are speculative.

534. *Elizabethan Words and Music.* Purcell Consort of Voices; Robert Spencer (lute); Grayston Burgess, dir. Argo ZRG 652
[DOWLAND. My Lady Rich's Galliard; My Lord Willobye's welcome home. GIBBONS. Ah, dear heart. HOLBORNE. See what a maze of error. MORLEY. I love, alas. PILKINGTON. O softly singing lute. TOMKINS. Come, shepherds. VAUTOR. Lock up, fair lids; Never did any more delight. WARD. Hope of my heart. WEELKES. Lady, your eye my love enforced; My Phyllis bids me pack away; Sing we at pleasure. WILBYE. Lady, when I behold. ANON. Loth to depart; Sir Philip Sidney's lamentation.] (gr 1/70)

535. *En Retrouvant le Moyen Age.* Ensemble Polyphonique de Paris; Charles Ravier, cond. Bôite à musique BAM LD 5100
[BINCHOIS. Seule esgaree. BORLET. He! Tres doulx roussignol. FONTAINE. Pastourelle. GACE BRULÉ. Au renouviau de la douçor d'este (Paris. Bibl. de l'Arsenal, 60); De Bone Amor (Arsenal 88); Les Oisellons de mon pais (Arsenal 77). LANDINO. El mie sospir (Squarcialupi Codex). R. MORTON. Chanson. RAIMBAUT DE VAQUEIRAS. Kalenda maya. THIBAUT DE CHAMPAGNE. Aussi

535. *En Retrouvant le Moyen Age.* (Continued)
comme unicorne sui (Arsenal 32). VIDE. Il m'est si grief. ZACHARIA
DE TERAMO. Madrigale (Codex Faenza). ANON. Motet quadruple
maniere (Montpellier, 33); Motet quadruple viderunt (Montpellier, 26);
Lauda (Laudario 91 di Cortona); Lo que demanda el romero; Epitaphe
de l'amant vert.]

536. *Englische Consort-Musik.* Leonhardt Consort; Veronika Hampe (gamba);
G. Leonhardt, dir.   Telefunken AWT 9481; SAWT 9481
[BYRD. Fantasia no.2; Fantasia no.3; Miserer "Gloria tibi trinitatis";
Pavan and Galliard. TOMKINS. A sad pavan for these distracted times,
1649. Also Lawes suites.]

English Madrigale und Tänze der Spätrenaissance. See *English Secular
Music of the Late Renaissance* (No.553).

537. *Die Englische Motette im "Goldenen Zeitalter."* Choir of St. John's
College, Cambridge; George Guest, cond.   Musica Sacra AMS 37; 37 STE
[BLITHEMAN. In pace. BYRD. Haec dies; Justorum animae; Laudibus
in sanctis; Miserere mei. DEERING. Gaudent in coelis; O bone Jesu;
Quem vidistis pastores. PHILIPS. Cantantibus organis; Ne reminiscaris.
TALLIS. O nata lux; Salvator mundi. TAVERNER. Christe Jesu, pastor
bone; Kyrie "le roy." TYE. Ad te clamamus.]

Englische Musik für Blockflöten und Gamben-Consort. See *English
Music for Recorders and Consort of Viols* (No.551).

538. *Englische Virginalisten.* G. Leonhardt (on Ruckers, 1640 cemb).
                                    Harmonia Mundi HM 492 K
[BULL. English toy; Fantasia in d; the King's hunt. BYRD. Pavan and
galliard of Mr. Peter. CUTTING. Walsingham variations. FARNABY.
Maske in g. GIBBONS. Fancy in d; Fantasia in d; Fantasia in d (no.6);
Pavane in g (no.16). TOMKINS. Barafostus' dream.]   (biel 2/70)

539. *Englische Virginalmusik.* Gustav Leonhardt (virg and cemb).
                                    Telefunken AWT 9491; SAWT 9491
[BULL. The Duchesse of Brunswick's toye; Hexachord fantasia. BYRD.
Pavana and Galiarda. FARNABY. Fantasia. GIBBONS. Pavana.
MORLEY. Fantasia; Nancie. RANDALL (?). Dowland's Lachrimae and
Galliard; Can she excuse my wrongs. TISDALL. Pavana chromatica:
Mrs. Katherin. ANON. A toye.]

540. *English Cembalo Music.* A. B. Speckner and Kurt Wittmayer (cemb).
                                    Harmonia Mundi HMS 30824
[BYRD. Alman; The batell; The bells; Coranto; Galliards; Pavan.
JOHNSON. Alman. PEERSON. Fall of the leafe. ANON. Irish Ho-
hoane; Watkins Ale; Why ask you.]   (biel 2/67)

English Consort Music (Leonhardt Consort). See *Englische Consort-
Musik* (No.536).

541. *English Consort of Viols.*   Turnabout 34443
[BULL. In nomine. BYRD. Fantasy no.2 "Browning"; Come to me grief
forever. CAMPION. Turn back you wanton flyer. COOPER. Fantasy in
F; Fantasy "Io Piango". FERRABOSCO. Almaine in F; The dovehouse
pavan; Fantasy in G. HOLBORNE. He, ho, holiday; Prelude; The tears
of the muses. JENKINS. Fantasy in C; Pavan in G. JOHNSON. Away
delight. JONES. What if I seek for love of thee. PEARSON. Look up,
fair lids. WIGTHORPE. I am not, of such belief.]   (sch 11/71)

542. *English, French and Italian Madrigals and Songs.* Deller Consort; soloists;
A. Deller, dir.
          Harmonia Mundi DR 204 and HM 30702 and Victrola VICS 1428
[CORNYSHE. Ah Robin; Hoyda jolly Rutterkin. GENTIAN. Je suis
Robert. GIBBONS. Cries of London. JOHNSON. Care charming sleep.
MONTEVERDI. Baci soavi e cari; Lamento della Ninfa. SERMISY.
Tant que vivray. VAUTOR. Mother I will have a husband. WEELKES.
Cease sorrows now. WILBYE. Lady when I behold.]   (biel 2/70)

543. *English Harpsichord Music.* Igor Kipnis (hpsi).
                    Epic LC 3898; BC 1298 and Columbia SCX 6159
[BYRD. Earl of Salisbury; Galiardo; A gigg: F. Tregian; Pavana; Queene's
Alman; Wolsey's wilde. BULL. Prince's galliard; Queen Elizabeth's pavin.
FARNABY. Fantasia; Loath to depart; Tower hill. Also Clarke, Handel,
Purcell.]   (sch 6/65)

English Madrigal School (Deller Consort, SRV 157). See under MORLEY
and WILBYE in individual composer index.

544. *English Madrigals.* Ambrosian Singers; D. Stevens, dir.
                                      H.M.V. HQM 1080; HQS 1080
[BATESON. Down from above. BENNETT. O sleep, fond fancy. BYRD.
This sweet and merry month. FARMER. A little pretty bonny lass.
FARNABY. Ay me, poor heart. GIBBONS. Now each flowery bank of
May. MORLEY. April is in my mistress face; False love did me inveigle.
MUNDY. My prime of youth; Were I a king. PILKINGTON. Why should
I grieve? TOMKINS. To the shady woods. VAUTOR. Ah sweet, whose
beauty. WEELKES. Cold winter's ice is fled; Sing we at pleasure.
WILBYE. Adieu sweet Amaryllis; Flora gave me fairest flowers.] (gr 2/68)

545. *English Madrigals and Folk Songs.* Deller Consort. Odyssey 32160017;
                    32160018 and Harmonia Mundi HMO and HMS 30593
Side 1
[CAVENDISH. Sly thief, if so you will believe. FARMER. A little pretty
bonny lass. MORLEY. My bonny lass. PILKINGTON. Sweet Phillida.
TOMKINS. See, see, the shepherd's queen; Weep no more, thou sorry
boy. VAUTOR. Shepherds and nymphs. WEELKES. Hark, all ye lovely
saints; Say, dear, when will your frowning leave,
Side 2
English folk songs.]

546. *English Madrigals from the Courts of Elizabeth I and James I.* Purcell
   Consort of Voices; G. Burgess, cond.   Turnabout TV 34202
   [ALISON. Shall I abide this jesting. BATESON. Sister, awake.
   BENNETT. All creatures now are merry-minded. BYRD. Lullaby, my
   sweet little baby; This sweet and merry month; Though Amaryllis dance
   in green. FARMER. Fair nymphs I heard one telling. FARNABY.
   Construe my meaning. GIBBONS. The silver swan. GREAVES. Come
   away sweet love. KIRBYE. Sorrow consumes me. MORLEY. Now is
   the month of Maying; Whither away so fast? TOMKINS. Too much I
   once lamented. VAUTOR. Sweet Suffolk owl. WARD. Retire, my
   troubled soul. WEELKES. Say, dear, when will your frowning leave?
   WILBYE. Sweet honey-sucking bees.]

547. *English Madrigals of Weelkes, Bateson, Wilbye, Tomkins, Morley.* The
   Randolph Singers; The Golden Age Singers; Field-Hyde, cond.
                                                          Westminster WM 1006
   [BATESON. Camilla fair tripped o'er the plain; Come follow me; Come,
   sorrow, help me to lament; Cupid in a bed of roses; Cytherea smiling
   said; I heard a noise; She with a cruel frown; When to the gloomy woods.
   MORLEY. Arise, get up, my dear; Fire! Fire!; Hark, jolly shepherds; I
   go before my darling; In dew of roses; In every place; Lady, if I through
   grief; Leave now, mine eyes, lamenting; My bonny lass she smileth; Now
   is the month of Maying; O grief even on the bud. TOMKINS. Fusca, in
   thy starry eyes. Phyllis, now cease to move me; See, see the shepherds'
   queen; Too much I once lamented; Weep no more thou sorry boy; When
   David heard; Yet again, as soon revived. WEELKES. The Andalusian
   merchant; As wanton birds; Cease sorrows now; Death hath deprived me;
   Hence care, thou art too cruel; Lord, when I think; O care, thou wilt
   despatch me; Thule, the period of cosmography. WILBYE. Adieu, sweet
   Amaryllis; All pleasure is of this condition; And though my love
   abounding; As fair as morn; Flora gave me fairest flowers; Fly not so
   swift, my dear; Happy, o happy he; Hard destinies are love; I fall, O
   stay me; O what shall I do?; Oft have I vowed; Sweet honey-sucking
   bees; Thus saith my Cloris bright; Weep, O mine eyes; Weep, weep mine
   eyes; Ye that do live in pleasures; Yet sweet, take heed.]

548. *English Medieval Christmas Carols.* New York Pro Musica Antiqua; Noah
   Greenberg, dir.
                           Everest LPBR 6145/7 (side 5 of 6) and Esoteric ES 521
   [Nowell sing we; Ave Maria; Gloria and Alleluja; Lullay lullow; What
   tidings bringest thou; Marvel not, Joseph; Alma redemptoris mater; Make
   we joy now; Nowell, nowell, tidings true; Sancta Maria; Hail Mary, full of
   grace; Ave Rex Angelorum; Tibi laus, tibi gloria; Beata progenies; Nova,
   nova.]

   English Medieval Songs. See *Medieval English Lyrics* (No.675).

549. *English Music.* Siegfried Behrend (guit).   DGG 2530079
[BATCHELOR. Monsiers almaine. CUTTING. Galliard; Greensleeves.
DOWLAND. Captaine Digori Piper's galliard; Galliard; King of Denmark's
galliard. Lachrimae antiquae; Melancholie galliard; Queen Elizabeth her
galliard. ROBINSON. Almaine; Galliard; Merry melancholie. Also
Camidge, Duarte, McCabe, Musgrave.]   (sch 2/71)

550. *English Music.* Zusana Ruzickova (hpsi).   Supraphon SUAST 50787
[BULL. Dr. Bull's juell; In nomine; King's hunt; Walsingham. BYRD.
Galliardas passamezzo. DOWLAND. Melancholy galliard; My Lady
Hunsdon's puffe; Shoemaker's wife. FARNABY. Nobodyes gigge.
MORLEY. Alman. MUNDY. Bonny sweet Robin. PEERSON. Fall of
the leafe. RICHARDSON. Pavane. ANON. Almande. Also Purcell and
Croft.]   (gr)

English Music. See also *The Treasury of English Church Music, v.1,
1100-1545* (No.882).

551. *English Music for Recorders and Consort of Viols.* Brüggen-Consort;
F. Brüggen, dir.   Telefunken AWT 9511; SAWT 9511
[BEVIN. "Browning" a 3. BYRD. "Browning" a 5; In nomine (no.3) a 5.
GIBBONS. In nomine a 4. HOLBORNE. Galliard; Heigh-ho holiday;
Honie suckle; Night watch; Pavan; Sighes. MORLEY. La caccia; La
Girandola; Il lamento. SIMPSON. Bonny sweet Robin a 4. TAVERNER.
In nomine a 4. TYE. In nomine (Crye) a 5. Also Jeffreys and Purcell.]

552. *English Polyphonic Church Music.* Choir of Magdalen College, Oxford;
Bernard Rose, cond; Bernard Rose and David Wulstan (org).
     Saga XID 5287; STXID 5287 and Audiovision developments AVM 009
[BYRD. Hodie beata Virgo Maria. CARLTON. A verse (for two to play
on one virginal or organ). DEERING. Jesu, dulcis memoria. GIBBONS.
Fantasia in a; O clap your hands together. MUDD. Let thy merciful ears,
O Lord. NICOLSON. O pray for the peace of Jerusalem. SHEPPARD.
Reges Tharsis et insulae. TALLIS. Ex more docti mistico (org).
TOMKINS. Almighty God, the fountain of all wisdom; Pavan (org).
ANON. Rejoice in the Lord alway.]

553. *English Secular Music of the Late Renaissance.* Purcell Consort of
Voices; Jaye Consort of Viols; G. Burgess, cond.
                    Vox STGBY 624 and Candide CE 31005
[DEERING. Country cries. GIBBONS. Do not repine fair sun.
PEERSON. Sing, love is blind. RAVENSCROFT. Rustic lovers.
TOMKINS. Alman a 4 for viols. VAUTOR. Weep, weep mine eyes.
WEELKES. The cryes of London; Since Robin Hood; Thule, the period
of cosmography. ANON. Hey down a down down; Take heed of time,
tune and ear.]   (sch 1/69)

English Songs. See *An Anthology of Elizabethan and Restoration Vocal
Music* (No.461).

554. *English Tone Paintings, Toccatas and Dances for Harpsichord.* Sylvia
Kind (hpsi).   Turnabout TV 34200 (gram 12/70 says TV 34205)
[BULL. The King's hunt. BYRD. The battell; The bells; The carman's
whistle. MUNDY. Fantasia. PEERSON. The fall of the leafe; The
primerose. ANON. Muscadin.]   (gr 5/69)

English Virginal Music (Leonhardt). See *Englische Virginalmusik*
(No.539).

555. *Ensemble Stephane Caillat.*   Amadeo AVRS 6326
[COSTELEY. Que de passions et douleurs. DEPRES. Mille regrets.
GALLUS. Jerusalem gaude. LASSUS. Mon coeur se recommande a vous.
PASSEREAU. Il est bel et bon. VECCHI. Tiridola.   Also Durante,
Haydn, Heiller, Lukacic, Zganec.]   (biel 2/65)

556. *Ergetzlich Tanntzereyen.* Franz Haselböck (org).
                                        Da Camera Magna SM 93216
[AMMERBACH. Herzog-Moritz-Tanz mit proportio. ASTON. A
hornepype. ATTAINGNANT. Basse dance; Branle gay; Gaillardes (2);
Pavenne. BYRD. Alman; Coranto; A gigg; La Volta. FACOLI. Aria
della Signora Lucilla; Tedesco dita l'Austria; Tedesca dita la Proficia.
JAN DE LUBLIN. Conradus; Hayduczky; Hispaniarum; Italica;
Poznanie. KOTTER. Spaniol Kochersberg. NÖRMIGER. Intrada; Der
Mohren Auftzugh. PAIX. Schirazula Marazula; Ungarescha und
Saltarello. SCHMID. Alemando novelle-ein guter neuer Dantz-Proportz
darauf; Le corante de Roy; Ein schöner englischer Dantz; Der hupfauf.
VALENTE. Le ballo dell'intorcia. ANON. 2 Corantos; Dalling alman;
Daunce; Nowel's galliard (all from Fitzwilliam Virginal Book); Le forze
d'hercole; Fusi Pavana piana; Passemezzo antico; Saltarello del Re;
Venetiana gagliarda.]

557. *Estampies, Basses Dances, Pavanes.* Ensemble d'instruments Ancienne de
Zurich; Lionel Rogg (positiv).   Harmonia Mundi HMO 30573
                    and Oryx 1509 and Odyssey 32160035; 32160036
[AMMERBACH. Passametzo. ATTAINGNANT. Gaillarde. ASTON.
Hornepype. BENDUSI. Cortesana Padoano. BUCHNER. Ach hülf mich
Leid und sehnlich Klag. FONTAINE. Sans faire de vous départie.
GÖTZ. Vil lieber zit. NEUSIEDLER. Judentantz; Der Zeuner Tantz.
SCHMID. Wie schön blüht uns der Maie. ANON. Estampie and Estampie
Rétrové; 2 Ductiae; Boumgartner; La fille Guillemin; La Spagna; Suite
(Pavane-Bergerette-Gaillarde "Saint-Roch"-Ronde "Mon Amy"-Ballo
Milanese); Bassa imperiale; Suite (Pavane "La garde"-Gaillarde "Au joly
boys"-Branle de Poictou-Premier branle de Gay); Suite (Basse danse
"Mon désir"-Gaillarde "La rocque"-2 bransles-Basse danse "Le cuer est
bon"-Entrée du fol).]

558. *Eton Choirbook, v.2.* Purcell Consort of Voices; All Saints Choristers;
G. Burgess, cond.   Argo RG 557; ZRG 557
[BROWNE. Stabat Mater. CORNYSH. Ave Maria. FAWKYNER. Gaude
Rosa. LAMBE. Nesciens Mater. NESBETT. Magnificat. WYLKYNSON.
Salve Regina.]   (gr 12/70)

559. *An Evening of Elizabethan Music.* Julian Bream Consort.
Victor LM 2656; LSC 2656; LSC 3195;
RB 6592 and AWR 7904; SAWR 7904-B
[ALLISON. Bachelors delight; De la tromba pavin. BYRD. Monsieurs
almaine; My Lord of Oxenford's maske; Pavin (lute). CAMPIAN. It fell
upon a summer's day. DOWLAND. Dowlands adew; Fantasie (lute);
Galliard, Can she excuse; Lachrimae pavin; Tarletons resurrection (lute).
JOHNSON. The flatt pavin. MORLEY. Fantasie, La Rondinella; The
frog galliard; Joyne hands; O mistress mine. PHILLIPS. Phillips pavin.
ANON. Le Rossignol; Kemps jig (lute).]   (Myers 6/66)

560. *Fanfares from the Sixteenth Century to the Present.* Brass Ensemble of
Paris; Trombone Quartet of the R.T.F. Orchestra; André (trpt);
Barboteu (hn); Suzan (tromb); Paillard, cond.
Music Guild MG 120 and Erato STU 70178
[DEPRES. Royal fanfares for the consecration of Louis XII. ESTIENNE
DU TERTRE. Bransle d'Escosse. FRANCK. Intrada VII. G. GABRIELI.
Sonata pian e forte. GERVAISE. [Dances]. ANON. Celle qui m'a le nom
d'amy donné. Also works by other composers from Locke to Florent
Schmitt.]

561. *Das Fest des Pierbaldo (Le Festin de Pierbaldo) nach dem Sonettenkranz
"Mundus Pacidus" des Simon d'Orvieto.* Les Menestrels.   Tudor 0501
[Works by BARTOLINO DA PADUA, CICONIA, GHERARDELLO DE
FLORENTIA, LAURENTIUS DE FLORENTIA, LANDINO, PIERO DI
FIRENZE.]   (Tudor 1971 catalog announcement)

562. *The Festive Pipes, v.2: Eight Centuries of Music for Recorders.*
Krainis Consort; Krainis Baroque Ensemble.   Kapp 9049; KC 9049-S
[BYRD. Browning. HENRY VIII. If love now reynyd. REVENTHAL
(NEIDHARDT VON REUENTHAL?). Sinc ein guldin Huon. SUSATO.
Bergerette; Bransle; Galliarde le tout; La Mourisque; Pavana; Ronde et
saltarelle. ANON. Trotto. Also Corelli, Schein and Telemann. Volume 1
of The Festive Pipes appeared as No. 351 in original volume.]   (Myers)

563. *Fifteenth Century Motets.* The Columbia University Collegium Musicum;
R. Taruskin, dir.   Collegium Stereo JE 108
[CARMEN. Pontifici decori speculi. CESARIS. A virtutis ignitio / Ergo
beata nascio / Benedicta. GRENON. Ave virtus virtutum / Prophetarum
/ Infelix. OCKEGHEM. Gaude Maria; Ut heremita solus. REGIS. O
admirabile commercium. TAPISSIER. Eya dulcis / Vale placens.]   (adv)

564. *Fitzwilliam Virginal Book.* Blanche Winogron (virg).
                                        Dover HCR 7266; HCR-ST 7015
[BULL. In Nomine; The Spanish paven. BYRD. Coranto; Galliarda;
Monsieurs alman; Pavana. FARNABY. Woody-cock. R. JOHNSON.
Alman. MUNDY. Munday's joy. PEERSON. Alman. P. PHILIPS.
Amarilli di Julio Romano; Galliardo. STROGERS. Fantasia. TISDALL.
Pavan chromatica. TOMKINS. Worster braules. ANON. Barafostus'
dreame; Pakington's pownde.]

565. *Fitzwilliam Virginal Book.* George Malcolm (hpsi).
                                   Cantate 047704 and Bärenreiter BM 30 L 1209
[BULL. In Nomine; Fantasia. BYRD. Courante, Pavan & Allemande.
FARNABY. A toye; Loth to depart. GIBBONS. Pavane. ANON. Why
aske you; Nowel's galliard. Also Purcell.]   (sch 4/64)

566. *Fitzwilliam Virginal Book, A Comprehensive Selection from.* Joseph
Payne (org and hpsi).   Vox VBX 72; SVBX 572
[BULL. The Duchesse of Brunswick's toye; The Duke of Brunswick's
alman; In Nomine (2). BYRD. Alman; The Carman's whistle; Fantasia
(2); A gigg; Miserere; Monsieurs alman; Pavana; Pavana & galliarda; La
volta; A Wolsey's wilde. FARNABY. Bonny sweet Robin; Fantasia;
Farnabye's conceit; Giles Farnaby's dream; His rest; Loth to depart;
Tower Hill; A toye. R. FARNABY. Fayne would I wed. GIBBONS.
Pavana. R. JOHNSON. 3 almans. MUNDAY. Goe from my window;
Munday's joy. PEERSON. The fall of the leafe. P. PHILIPS. Pavana;
Pavana dolorosa. ANON. Alman; Barafostus' dream; Can shee; Coranto;
Watkin's ale; Why aske you; Muscadin.]

Five Centuries of Music in the Great Reims Cathedral. See *Cinq siècles
de musique dans la Cathédrale de Reims* (No.504).

567. *Five Centuries of Song.* Abbey Singers.
                     Decca 10073; 710073 and Brunswick AXA 4518; SXA 4518
[BYRD. Lullaby my sweet little baby. COSTELEY. Mignonne.
FARMER. Fair Phyllis I saw. LASSUS. O vin en vigne. PASSEREAU.
Il est bel et bon. RIVAFLECHA. Salve Regina. WEELKES. Hark all ye
lovely Saints. Also Mozart, Toch, Copland, Billings and other.]
(sch 10/63)

Flemish and Burgundian Music in Honor of the Blessed Virgin Mary.
See *Music Dedicated to the Virgin Mary* (No.700).

568. *A Florentine Festival. Music for Ferdinand de Medici.* Musica
Reservata; J. Beckett, cond.   Argo ZRG 602
[CARA. Io non compro. CAVALIERI. Ballo - O che nuovo miracolo;
Godi turba mortal. FESTA. Quando ritrova. MALVEZZI. Dal vago e
bel sereno; O fortunato giorno; O qual risplende nube. MARENZIO.
Belle ne fe natura; Chi dal delfino; O figlie di Piero; Se nelle voci nostre;
Secondo intermedio; Sinfonia. MONTEVERDI. Toccata. NOLA. Tri

ciechi siamo. TROMBONCINO. Io son l'occello. ANON. Ahimè sospiri; Allemana-ripresa; Bussa la porta; E su su su quel monte; Era di Maggio; Gagliarda Giorgio; In questo ballo; Maggio valente; El marchese di Salluzzo; Noi ci vogliam' partire; Orsu, orsu car'signori; La pastorella; Pavan La cornetta; Pavana El colognese; Pavana Forze d'Ercole; Quando ritrova; Sorella mia piacente.]   (gram 1/71)

569. *Florentine Music (Ars Nova and Renaissance).* New York Pro Musica; La Noue Davenport, dir.   Decca DL 9428; 79428 and Brunswick AXA 4546; SXA 4546 and MCA MUC 121; MUCS 121 [ANDREAS DE FLORENTIA. Non più doglie ebbe Dido. DONATUS DE FLORENTIA. I' fu'già usignol. GHIRARDELLUS DE FLORENTIA. Per non far lieto; Tosto che l'alba (caccia). FESTA. Deus, venerunt gentes. ISAAC. In festo Nativitatis S. Joannis Baptistae (mass proper). ANON. Istampita Ghaetta.]

570. *Florentine Music of the 14th Century.* Early Music Consort; David Munrow, dir.   Argo ZRG 642 [GIOVANNI DA FIRENZE. Con brachi assai; Da, da, a chi avareggia. JACOPO DA BOLOGNA. Fenice fu. LANDINO. Amore (2); Biance flour; La bionda treccia; Cara mie donna; De dinmi tu; Donna'l tuo partimento; Ecco la primavera; Giunta vaga bilta; Questa fanciulla. MAGISTER PIERO. Con dolce brama. TERANO. Rosetta. ANON. Istampita Ghaetta; Lamento di Tristan; Manfredina; Quan je voy le duc; Saltarelli (2); Trotto.]   (sch 8/70)

571. *Florid-Song und Gambenmusik in England um 1610-1660.* Concentus Musicus, Wien; Studio der frühen Musik; T. Binkley, cond. Telefunken AWT 9472; SAWT 9472 [CAMPION. Come, you pretty false-eyed wanton. COOPER. Fantasia; My joy is dead. GIBBONS. Fantasia da gamba. HINGSTON. Fantazia (for one cornet, sagbutt and organ). HUME. Tobacco. JOHNSON? Care-charming sleep. WARD. Fantasia. WEELKES. Cease sorrows now. ANON. Deerest love; Nothing on earth. Also Locke, Lupo, Wilson.]

572. *Fourteen Lieder and Instrumental Pieces from the Locheimer Liederbuch,* Nuremberg Gambencollegium; Josef Ulsamer, cond; Elza Van der Ven (org); Fr. Brückner-Rüggeberg (tnr).
              DGG ARC 3222; 73222 and DGA 19322 and APM 14332
Side 1   Music from Nuremberg
[PAUMANN. Des klaffers neyden; Mit ganczen willen (from Fundamentum Organisandi). H. SACHS. Als ich, Hans Sachs, alt ware; Gloria patri: lob und er; Ich lob ein brünnlein küle; Ein Tigertier; Zu Venedig ein kaufman sass.
Side 2   Locheimer Liederbuch
All mein gedencken dy ich hab; Es fur ein pawr gen holz; Ich het mir auszerkoren; Ich spring an disem ringe; Ich var dohin; Des klaffers neyden; Mein trawt geselle; Mit ganczem willen; Möcht ich dein begeren; Der summer; Ein vrouleen edel von naturen; Der wallt hat sich enlawbet.]

573. *Französische Lautenmusik.* Michael Schäfer (lute).
                                                    Turnabout TV 4137; STV 34137
[ATTAINGNANT. Pavan, Galliard; Basse danse "La brosse"; Tordion;
Tant que vivray. MOUTON. L'amant content (canarie); La dialogue des
graces sur Iris (Allemande); La Mallasis (Sarabande). Also Bittner, Visée,
Le Sage de Richée.]   (biel 2/67)

574. *Französische Lautenmusik der Renaissance.* Walter Gerwig (lute).
                                                    10" Harmonia Mundi HM 25164
[ATTAINGNANT. Basse dance "La brosse" avec Recoupe et Tordion;
(Basse dances) La roque; Sans roche; Tous mes amys; Destre amoreux;
Galliarde; La rote de Rode; Tant que vivray (chanson). BESARD. 2
Bransles; Bransle gay; Courante; Galliarde; Prélude de 6. Bocquet;
Villanella; Volte.]
(Lautenmusik aus Frankreich und England has same contents plus works
by Bittner and Mace, q.v.)

575. *Französische Musik aus Mittelalter und Renaissance.* Studio für alte
Musik, Düsseldorf.   Da Capo SM 91702
[ADAM DE LA HALLE. Tanzlied (Robin et Marion). ATTAINGNANT.
Basse dance; Pavane; Branle gay. BINCHOIS. Plaine de plours. DUFAY.
Alma redemptoris Mater. MACHAUT. Ballade; De tour sui; Puis dure
que un. MARIE DE BOURGOGNE. Basse dances. THIBAUT DE
CHAMPAGNE. Danse.]   (biel 2/70)

576. *The French Ars Antiqua.* The Columbia University Collegium Musicum;
R. Taruskin, dir.   Collegium Stereo JE 104
[ADAM DE LA HALLE. A dieu commant; Bonnes amouretes; Fi, maris;
Fines amouretes; Je muir, je muir; Or est Baiars. MACHAUT. Hoquetus,
David. PEROTIN. Alleluia, Nativitas. PETRUS DE CRUCE. Aucun /
Lonc tans / Annuntiantes. ANON. Balaam (motet); De calamitatibus
Galliae (Pluteus 29.1); C'est Ja jus / Quia Concupivit (Chansonnier
Noailles); Chanconette / Ainc voir / A la cheminee / Veritatem (Bamberg
and Montpellier 25); Deus misertus hominis (Pluteus 29.1); Dieus! /
Dieus ! / Dieus! / Et vide; In saeculum (Hoquetus, Bamberg); Jacet
granum oppressum palea (Pluteus 29.1); Nus ne se doit / Audi filia
(Montpellier 208); Trois serrors (Montpellier 27); Vetus abit littera
(Pluteus 29.1).]   (adv)

577. *French Dances of the Renaissance.* The Ancient Instrument Ensemble of
Paris; Cotte, cond.   Nonesuch H 1036; 71036 and
                                            Discophiles Francais DF 730059; 740011
[ATTAINGNANT. Basse danse; Bransle simple - Bransle double; Bransles
(clavier); Pavane; La volunté; Vous aurez tout ce qui est mein. BESARD.
Bransle gay; Les cloches de Paris. CAROSO. Nobilità di Dame:
Spagnoletta. GERVAISE. Allemande; Bransle de Bourgogne; Bransle de
Poitou; Bransle gay; Bransles de Champagne; Pavane et gaillarde
d'Angleterre. TABOUROT. Allemande; Belle qui tiens ma vie; Gavotte;

Jouissance vous donnerai; Moresca; Tourdions; Volta. ANON. L'amour de moy; Greensleeves; Concert pour les Chevaliers; Pavane pour le retour de Pologne. Also Pasquini, Rameau, Exaudet and Visée.]

French Love Songs of the 15th Century. See *French Songs* (No.578).

French Lute Music. See *Französische Lautenmusik* (No.573).

French Lute Music of the Renaissance. See *Französische Lautenmusik der Renaissance* (No.574).

French Music of the 15th and 16th Centuries. See *Inédits: Musique française des XV et XVI siècles* (No.621).

578. *French Songs.* Austin Miskell (tnr); Elizabethan Consort; Nesbitt, cond.
H.M.V. HQM 1041; HQS 1041
[BINCHOIS. Adieu, adieu mon joileux souvenir; Mon seul et souverain desire. DEPRES. Cueurs desolez; Milles regretz. DUFAY. Adieu m'amour; Bon jour bon mois; Franc cueur gentil. FRESNEAU. J'ay la promese de m'amye. LAYOLLE. La fille qui n'a point d'ami. LA RUE. Autant en emport le vent. LEJEUNE. Doucete sucrine toue de miel; O rose, reyne des fleurs. SANDRIN. Qui voudra scavoir qui je suis.]   (gr 12/70)

579. *Freu Dich, du Himmelskönigin.* Johannes Lorenzen (org).
Christophorus CLP 73319
[DUFAY. Alma redemptoris mater. HOFHAIMER. Ave Maris stella. KOTTER. Salve Regina. SCHLICK. Maria zart. SCHROEDER. Ave Maria klare. Also Bach, Ahrens, Hornung, Hummel, Schilling.]
(biel 2/69)

580. *Freudenreiche Weihnachts-Lobgesang (from the Andernacher Gesangbuch, 1608).* Alfred Reichling (org); Capella Antiqua Stuttgart; E. Hoffman, cond.   Psallite PEU 45/170767
[ECCARD. Resonet in laudibus. ERBACH. Canzon del 6. tono; Intonatio 2. toni. FINCK. Der Tag der ist so freudenreich. PAMINGER. In dulci jubilo; Omnis mundus; Resonet in laudibus. PRAETORIUS. In dulci jubilo. SALEM. Resonet in laudibus. SICHER. Resonet in laudibus. WALTER. Josef lieber, Josef mein. ANON. A solis; Omnis mundus; Psallite; Präambulum; Veni redemptor gentium.] (biel 2/70)

581. *From Folk Dances to Blues.* Krainis Consort.
Odyssey 32160143; 32160144
[BULL. In Nomine. ENCINA. Fata la parte; Hoy comamos; Triste España. GIBBONS. Fantasia à 2. ANON. Dadme Albricias; Pase el Agoa. Also Biber, Telemann and others.]   (sch 12/67)

582. *From the Renaissance (Concerts of Great Music).* Ambrosian Singers;
Ambrosian Consort; Accademia Monteverdiana; soloists; D. Stevens, dir.
                                                    5-12" Time-Life STL 160; TL 160
Record 1
[BYRD. Lamentationes. GESUALDO. In Monte Oliveti; Jesum tradidit.
MONTEVERDI. Chiome d'oro; Zefiro torna. TALLIS. Gloria tibi
Trinitatis (antiphon); Spem in alium (motet).
Record 2
A. GABRIELI. Benedictus Dominus; O crux spendidior. G. GABRIELI.
Timor et tremor; Magnificat. MONTEVERDI. Orfeo (Acts 2 and 3).
Record 3
BULL. St. Thomas wake. BYRD. Hey ho, to the greenwood. CAMPION.
Shall I come sweet love. DOWLAND. The Right Honourable Lady Rich,
her galliard. EDWARDS. Where griping grief. HENRY VIII. Consort II;
Pastime with good company. MORLEY. Now is the month of Maying.
TOMKINS. Worcester brawls. WILBYE. Draw on sweet night. ANON.
Fortune my foe.
Record 4
Schütz, Buxtehude, Moritz von Hessen, et al.
Record 5
LASSUS. De Profundis. PALESTRINA. Missa Papae Marcelli.]

583. *From the Renaissance (The Story of Great Music).* Ambrosian Singers;
Ambrosian Consort; Accademia Monteverdiana; soloists; Denis Stevens,
cond.   4-12" Time-Life STL 150; TL 150
[BYRD. Ave verum corpus; Gigg (FVB); Haec dies; O quam gloriosam;
This sweet and lovely month. CAMPION. Oft have I sighed. DOWLAND.
Come again; Semper Dowland, semper dolens; Say love, if thou didst
find. A. GABRIELI. Gloria; Ricercar. G. GABRIELI. Buccinate in
neomenia; Canzona; In ecclesiis. GESUALDO. Languisce al fin.
LASSUS. Iustorum animae; Quand mon mari; Fuyons tous d'amour le
jeu. MONTEVERDI. Gloria; Hor che'l ciel; Il Ballo delle ingrate;
L'Incoronazione di Poppea (excerpts). MUNDY. Robin. PALESTRINA.
Stabat mater. SUSATO. Rondo and saltarello, Allemainge. TALLIS.
Ecce tempus; Jesu salvator. WEELKES. Sing we at pleasure. WILBYE.
Adieu, sweet Amaryllis. ANON. Almaine; Scot's marche; Watkin's ale;
Kemp's jig.]

Frottole. See *Italienische Frottolen der Renaissance* (No.632).

584. *Frühe Musik in England.* Studio der frühen Musik, Munich.
                                                    Telefunken AWT 8041
[BYRD. Fantasy (unspec.). DA NOLA (i.e., DEL GIOVANE). Madonna
nui sapimo (motet). DOWLAND. Flow my tears. JONES. Allemande:
Disdaine that so doth. MORLEY. Mistresse mine. PEERSON. La
primevère. ANON. Estampie; Samson dux fortissimae; Te Deum.]

585. *Frühe Musik in England, Flandern, Deutschland, Spanien.* Studio der
frühen Musik, Munich.   Telefunken AWT 9432; SAWT 9432
[ENCINA. Fata la parte (Cancionero del Palacio). LA RUE. Mijn hert.
LAURENTIUS d. Ä. Mij heeft een piperken. OBRECHT. Ic draghe de
mutze clutze. SACHS. Nachdem David war redlich. WAELRANT. Als
ic un vinde. WOLKENSTEIN. Gar wunniklaich; In suria ain praiten hal.
ANON. Estampie; El fresco ayre; Ich spring an diesem Ringe (Locheimer
Liederbuch); Mij quan eyn hope; Rodrigo Martinez; Dale si le das; Venid
a sospirar; Samson dux fortissime; Te deum.]   (Myers 9/66)

586. *Frühe Musik in Italien, Frankreich und Burgund.* Studio der frühen
Musik, Munich.   Telefunken AWT 9466; SAWT 9466
[BINCHOIS. De plus en plus; Filles à marier. BORLET. He, tres doulz
roussignol. DONATUS DE FLORENTIA. Come da lupo. FEVIN. Faulte
d'argent. FILIAMO [sic, probably FOGLIANO]. L'amor donna.
GANASSI. Ricercar. GUYARD. M'y levay par ung matin. LANDINO.
Gran piant; Ecco la primavera. LUPRANO [i.e., LURANO]. Se me
grato. LUZZASCHI. O dolcezze. NOLA. Chichilichi. VAILLANT. Par
maintes fois. VERDELOT. Madonna il tuo bel viso. ANON. Filles à
marier; He, Robinet; Il est de bonne heure; Je suis d'Alemagne; Le joli
teton; Ma, tres dol rossignol; Saltarello; Tres douce regard.]

587. *Game of Love and Other Renaissance Delights.* Oakland Symphony
Chamber Chorus; Liebling, cond.   Orion 7148
[BYRD. Non vos relinquam. DOWLAND. Fine knacks for ladies. DU-
FAY. Gloria. FARNABY. Construe my meaning. HILTON. My mistress
frowns. LAWES. Cupid detected. LEJEUNE. Reveci venir du printemps.
MONTEVERDI. Ecco mormorar l'onde; Raggi dov'el mio bene; Ah,
dolente partita. MORLEY. I go before, my charmer; Sing we and chant
it. TESSIER. Au joli bois. WEELKES. As Vesta was from Latmos Hill
descending. WHYTEHORNE. When Cupid had; Thou shalt soon see;
Such as in love. WILBYE. Thus saith my Cloris bright; Ye that do live in
pleasures plenty. ANON. Alle Psallite (12th century). Also Purcell and
Schütz.]   (sch 10/71)

588. *Geistliche Lieder und Instrumentalsätze der Lutherzeit.* Studio der
frühen Musik, Munich.   Telefunken AWT 9532; SAWT 9532-B
[BRUCK. Aus tiefer Not. HELLINCK. Capitan herrgot; Pro oemium.
HOFHAIMER. Carmen. ISAAC. Carmen in fa; Carmen in sol; Christ ist
erstanden; Suesser Vatter. KOTTER. Aus tiefer Not. KUNGSBERGER.
Urbs beata. SCHLICK. Maria zart. SENFL. Da Jacob nun das Kleid
ansach; Da Jesus an dem Kreuze hing; O du armer Judas. ANON.
Gelassen hat eyn sustergen; Mit got wöln wirs haben an; O Jesu Christ;
Urbs beata.]   (biel 2/70)

589. *Geistliche Musik um 1400.* Capella Antiqua, München; K. Ruhland, dir.
Telefunken AWT 9505; SAWT 9505
[BRASART. O flos flagrans. CICONIA. Doctorum principem; Gloria in
excelsis; Ingens alumnus Padue; Melodia suavissima; O virum, o lux, o
beata Nicolae; Ut te per omnes. DUNSTABLE. Quam pulchra es.
FOREST. Qualis est dilectus tuus. GRENON. Nova vobis gaudia.
JOHANNES DE LYMBURGIA. Salve virgo regia (laude); Surge propera
amica mea. LANTINS. Tota pulchra es amica mea. POWER. Anima me
liquefacta est. ANON. Jesu nostra redemptio (Ms. Apt); Kyrie "de
Angelis".]

German and English Music of the Late Renaissance. See *Brass Music of
the Late Renaissance* (No.475).

German Liturgical Music. See *Ich steh an deiner Krippe hier* (No.617).

590. *German Music of the Renaissance.* Ambrosian Consort; In Nomine
Players; D. Stevens, cond.   Dover HCR 5270; HCR-ST 7270
[DEMANTIUS. Hertzlich thut mich erfrewen. FINCK. Habs nun getan.
GREITER. Es hüdri hüt', gut schädri Schäfer. ISAAC. Innsbruck, ich
muss dich lassen; (mass) Magnae Deus Potentiae (Kyrie, Gloria, Sanctus,
Agnus Dei). LEMLIN. Der gutzgauch. OTHMAYR. Bauerntanz;
Quisquis requiem quaeris. PAULUS DE BRODA. Der Pfauenschwanz.
SENFL. Quodlibet. STOLTZER. Entlaubet ist der Walde. WALTER.
Wach auf.]

German Peasant Dances and Popular Street Songs. See *Bauern-, Tanz-
und Strassenlieder in Deutschland um 1500* (No.470).

German Songs and Dances of the 15th and 16th Centuries. See *Lieder
und Tänze aus Deutschland, 1460-1560* (No.652).

Gesellige Musik der Renaissance. See *Secular Music of the Renaissance*
(No.839).

Gesellige Zeit. See *Gesellschaftslieder und Villanellen* (No.591).

591. *Gesellschaftslieder und Villanellen.* Hugo-Distler-Chor und sein
Instrumentalisten; Klaus Fischer-Dieskau, cond.
10" Bärenreiter BM 25 R 613
[BRUCK. So trinken wir alle. DEPRES. In meine Sinn. ECCARD. Zeit
tut Rosen bringen. HASSLER. Feinlieb, du hast mich g'fangen; Nun
fanget an. LASSUS. Annelein, du singst fein. LECHNER. Gott b'hüte
dich. PEUERL. O Musika, du edle Kunst. SCHEIN. Der Kühle Maien.
SIES. Mich hat gross Leid umgeben. ZIRLER. Die Sonn, die ist
verblichen. ANON. Lieblich hat sich gesellet.]   (biel 1/64)

592. *Gesellschaftsmusik der Renaissance.* Kammerchor Walther von der
Vogelweide; O Costa, cond.   Amadeo 5044; S 5044 and MCS 9062
[GESUALDO. Dolcissima mia vita. LASSUS. Audite nova; L'Eccho; Ich
weiss mir ein Maidlein; Matona mia cara. LECHNER. Che più d'un
giorno è la vita mortale; Come nave ch'in mezzo all'onde sia; Gott b'hüte
dich; Die Musik g'schrieben auf Papier; Der Unfall reit mich ganz und gar.
MARENZIO. Schau ich dir in die Augen; Zefiro torna. OTHMAYR. Es
steht ein Lind in jenem Tal. PEUERL. O Musika, du edle Kunst.
PRAETORIUS. Der Morgenstern ist aufgedrungen.]   (biel 2/70)

593. Girod.   (org).   Contrepoint MC 20142
[CABEZON. Tiento du 2e ton; Tiento du 4e ton; Quatre versions pour
l'Ave maris stella; Variations sur l'air du Chevalier. CORREA DE
ARAUXO. Tiento a modo de cancion du 4e ton. HEREDIA. Tiento de
falsas du 6e ton; Plein jeu pour le "Salve Regina."ANON. Cancion "del
la Virgen que pario." Also Cabanilles and Oxinagas.]   (dia 12/70)

594. *Glanz der Renaissance aus dem Liederbuch des Arnt von Aich* (c1520).
Renaissance Ensemble; Pöhlert, dir.   Da Camera Magna 91701
[ADAM VON FULDA. Ach hülf mir leid. HOFHAIMER. Ich klag und
reu; O werder mund. ISAAC. Ich schrei und rief. NACHTIGALL. Ein
fröhlich wesen. PIPELARE. Fors seulement. SENFL. Ein meidlein tet
mir klagen. ANON. Ach was will doch; Cupido; Eim jeden gfelt; Ein
Bauer sucht; Ein weilbliches bild; Fried gib mir her; Das kalb get seiner
narung nach; Der liebe strick; Mein M. ich hab; Mit got so wöln wirs heben
an; Vil hinderlist; Der welte lauf.]

595. *Gloria in Excelsis Deo.* Domchor Münster; H. Leiwering.
                              10" Harmonia Mundi HM 25162
[G. GABRIELI. Hodie Christus natus est. HANDL. Canite tuba; Resonet
in laudibus. PALESTRINA. Ecce veniet dies illa. SCHRÖTER. In dulci
jubilo. Also Benevoli, Foggia, A. Scarlatti.]   (biel 2/65)

Golden Age of English Motets. See *Die Englische Motette im "Goldenen
Zeitalter"* (No.537).

Golden Age of English Music. See *Aus dem goldenen Zeitalter der
englischen Musik* (No.466).

596. *Golden Age of Harpsichord Music.* Rafael Puyana (hpsi).
                              Mercury MG 50304; SR 90304
[BESARD. Branle gay. BULL. Les buffons; The king's hunt. BYRD. La
volta. FRANCISQUE. Branle de Montirandé. PEERSON. The primerose;
The fall of the leaf. P. PHILIPS. Pavana dolorosa; Galiarda dolorosa.
ANON. My Lady Carey's dompe.]   (arg 3/63)

Gothic and Renaissance Dances. See *Tanzmusik der Gotik und
Renaissance* (No.869).

597. *Grand Passé Musical de Paris.* Ensemble instrumentale et solistes;
J. Chailley, dir; Ensemble Vocal Saint-Paul; Cochereau (org).
                                                              DGG 636501
[DEPRES. Mille regrets de vous abandonner. JANEQUIN. Si Dieu
voulait que je fusse arondelle. LEJEUNE. Sur la mort d'une belle.
PEROTIN. Organum "Virgo." Also Bernier, L. Couperin, Charpentier,
Racquet.] (dia 2/67)

598. *Gregorian Chants - Polyphonic Motets.* The Benedictine Monks of Saint
John's Abbey, Collegeville, Minn.; Farrell, dir.
                                          Liturgical Press (no number)
Side 1   Gregorian Chants:
[Gloria (mode 4); Christus factus est (mode 5); Jubilate Deo (Mode 1);
Hoc corpus (Mode 8); Ave Maria (Mode 8).
Side 2   Polyphonic motets:
BYRD. Sacerdotes Domini. DEPRES. Ave, verum Corpus Christi.
PALESTRINA. O bone Jesu. VIADANA. O sacrum convivium.
VICTORIA. Jesu dulcis memoria.]

599. *Grosses Quempas-Weihnachtssingen; weihnachtliche Chorsätze.* Der
Schwäbische Singkreis; H. Grischkat, cond; Kantorei Barmen-Gemarke;
H. Kahlhöfer, cond.   Bärenreiter BM 30 SL 1800
[ECCARD. Ich steh an deiner Krippe hier. GESIUS. Freut euch, ihr
lieben Christen all. GUMPELZHAIMER. Gelobet seist du, Jesus Christ.
PRAETORIUS. In dulci jubilo. WALTHER. Josef, lieber Josef mein.
And works, unspecified in secondary sources, by BODENSCHATZ,
HERMANN, LECHNER, SCHRÖTER, ZANGIUS and ANON. Also
Schein.] (biel 2/69 and 2/70)

600. *Guitar Music and Songs of the Spanish Renaissance.* R. Tarragó (guit);
Barbany (vocalist).   Everest 3197
[DAZA. Dáme acogida en tu hato; Tiento. FUENLLANA. Ojos claros
serenos; Morenica dáme un beso. MILAN. Con pavor recordo el moro;
Fantasia. MUDARRA. Tientos VII, VIII; Isabel Isabel perdiste la tu
faxa; Claros y frescos rios. NARVAEZ. Variaciones sobre el tema Conde
claros. PALERO. Himno XIV "Ave Maris Stella." PISADOR. Pavana;
Porques es dama tanto quereros; Si te vás a banar Juánica. VALDERRA-
BANO. Fantasia XIV en re menor. VASQUEZ-PISADOR. En la fuente
del rosel.] (sch 7/68)

601. *Guitare Classique.* Barna Kovats (guit).
                                    10" Erato ERA 42025; EFM 42025
[GIOVANNI DA FIRENZE. Madrigal. MILAN. 2 Pavanes.
NEUSIEDLER. Gassenhauer. POLAK. Courante. VISÉE. Suite.
ANON. Pass'e mezzo. Also Mozzani, Giuliani, Bach and Tarrega.]
(Erato catalog)

602. *Harpsichord Music on Early Instruments.* Gustàv Leonhardt (hpsi).
                                    Telefunken AWT 9512; SAWT 9512
[CACCINI. Amarilli. FARNABY. Spagnioletta. TOMKINS. Pavan and
Galliard of three parts. ANON. Daphne. Also Frescobaldi, J. C. Bach,
J. S. Bach.]

Henry VIII Court Music. See *To Entertain a King: Music for Henry VIII
and His Court* (No.877).

603. *Herod, The Play of; a medieval musical drama.* As Presented at the
Cloisters, The Metropolitan Museum of Art, New York. New York Pro
Musica; Noah Greenberg, cond.   Decca DXA 187; DXS 7187

604. *Herod.* Ensemble Polyphonique de Paris, R.T.F.; Charles Ravier, dir.
                                    Nonesuch H 1181; 71181 (gr 12/68)

605. *Der Herr ist König; Psalmen und Spruchmotetten des 16. und 17.
Jahrhunderts.* Stuttgarter Hymnus-Chorknaben; G. Wilhelm, dir.
                                    Christophorus CGLP 75856; SCGLP 75857
[DEMANTIUS. Du sollst Gott, deinen Herren lieben; Ich bin ein guter
Hirte; Es ward eine Stille. FRANCK. Lobet den Herren, alle Heiden.
GUMPELZHAIMER. Wir danken dir, Herr Gott Vater. LASSUS.
Gloria Patri. ANON. Lobe den Herren meine Seele; Lobet den Herren,
alle Heiden. Also Hammerschmidt, Pachelbel, Hartmann.]   (biel 2/67)

606. *Hill Chamber Orchestra and Chorus.*   Orion 7022
[GIBBONS. Veni Creator. MONTEVERDI. Cantate Domino; Psalms.
VICTORIA. O magnum mysterium; O vos omnes. Also Haydn.]

607. *Historic Organs of Europe.* E. Powers Biggs (org).
                                    Columbia ML 6255; MS 6855
[DALZA. Pavana alla Venetiana. KOTTER. Praeambulum in fa.
LEONINUS. Hec dies. PAUMANN. Mit ganczem Willen. PEROTINUS.
Motets for "Hec dies." TALLIS. Gloria Tibi Trinitatis; Te Deum. ANON.
Agincourt hymn; Christo psallat; Orientis partibus; Sit gloria Domini;
Estampie; Hymn to St. Magnus. Also Bach, Couperin and others.]
(sch 7/67)

608. *Historical Anthology of Music in Performance.*
v.1: Late Medieval Music (1300-1400). University of Chicago Collegium
Musicum; Howard Brown, cond; Southern Illinois University Collegium
Musicum; Morgan, cond.   Pleiades P 250
[BAUDE CORDIER. Amans ames; Belle bonne. CICONIA. Et in terra
pax. FAUVEL. Detractor est. GHERARDELLUS DE FLORENTIA. Io
son un pellegrin; Nel mezzo. GIOVANNI DA FIRENZE. Tosto che
l'alba. JACOPO DA BOLOGNA. Non al suo amante. LANDINO. Amor
c'al tuo suggetto; Sy dolce non sono. LEGRANT. Credo. MACHAUT.
Comment qu'a moy; Je puis trop bien; Plus dure; S'il estoit nulz.
SELESSES. En attendant. WOLKENSTEIN. Der May. ANON. Alleluia

608. *Historical Anthology of Music in Performance.* (Continued)
   v.1: Late Medieval Music (1300-1400). (Continued)
   psallat; Gloria in excelsis; Estampie; Lamento di Tristan with Rotta;
   Sumer is icumen in.]

609. *v.2: Early and Late 15th Century Music.* University of Chicago
   Collegium Musicum; Howard Brown, cond; Southern Illinois University
   Collegium Musicum; Morgan, cond.   Pleiades P 251
   [BINCHOIS. De plus en plus; Filles à marier. COMPERE. O vos omnes;
   Royne du ciel. DAMETT. Beata Dei genetrix. DUFAY. Adieu m'amour;
   Alma redemptoris mater; Missa L'Homme armé (Kyrie and Agnus Dei);
   Mon chier amy. DUNSTABLE. O rosa bella; Sancta Maria. FINCK.
   Veni sancte spiritus; Veni creator spiritus. A. DE LANTINS. Puisque je
   voy. H. DE LANTINS. Ce ieusse fait. OBRECHT. O beate Basili; Missa
   Sine nomine (Kyrie I and Agnus Dei II). OCKEGHEM. Ma bouche rit;
   Ma maîtresse; Missa L'Homme armé (Kyrie and Agnus Dei). POWER.
   Sanctus and Benedictus qui venit.]

610. *v.3: Late 15th- and Early 16th-Century Music.* University of Chicago
   Collegium Musicum; Howard Brown, cond; Southern Illinois University
   Collegium Musicum; Morgan, cond.   Pleiades P 252
   [D'ASCANIO. In te Domine. DALZA. Tastar de corde con il ricercar
   dietro. DEPRES. Agnus Dei; Faulte d'argent; Tu pauperum refugium.
   ENCINA. Congoxa mas que cruel; Mas vale trocar; Pues que jamás
   olvidaros. FOGLIANO. Ave Maria. HOFHAIMER. Mein's traurens ist.
   ISAAC. Zwischen Berg und tiefem Tal. LA RUE. Kyrie I & II. MILAN.
   Durandarte, Durandarte; Oh dulce. SCHLICK. Salve Regina; Maria Zart.
   SPINACCINO. Ricercar. TORRE. Alta. TROMBONCINO. Non val aqua.
   WECK. Spanyöler Tanz. ANON. O rosa bella (Glogauer); Der neue
   Bauernschwanz (Glogauer); Praembulum in G (Ileborgh); Praeambulum
   super D, A, F, et G (Ileborgh); Praeambulum super G (Buxheimer);
   Praeambulum super O (Buxheimer); Praeambulum in mi (Kleber);
   Praeambulum in re (Kleber); Praeambulum in fa (Kotter); A dew, a dew;
   I have been a foster; My Lady Carey's dompe; Tapster, drinker; Per
   scriptores (canto carnascialesco).]

611. *v.4: Late 16th-Century Music.* University of Chicago Collegium
   Musicum; Howard Brown, cond; Southern Illinois University Collegium
   Musicum; Morgan, cond.   Pleiades P 253
   [BRUCK. Aus tiefer Not. CAVAZZONI. Ricercar (org). FEVIN. Missa
   Mente tota (Agnus Dei). GANASSI. 2 Ricercars for viola da gamba.
   GOMBERT. Super flumina; Ricercar. JANEQUIN. L'Alouette.
   NEUSIEDLER. Hoftanz (lute); Der Juden Tanz (lute). SENFL. Da
   Jacob nu das Kleid ansah; Salutatio prima. STOLTZER. Christ ist
   erstanden. TAVERNER. Western wynde; Mass the Western wynde
   (Benedictus). WALTER. Aus tiefer Not. WILLAERT. Victimae paschali
   laudes. REDFORD. Veni redemptor (org).]

612. *v.5: 16th-Century Music.* University of Chicago Collegium Musicum;
H. Brown, cond; Southern Illinois University Collegium Musicum;
Kentucky University Collegium Musicum; Morgan, cond.   Pleiades P 254
[ARCADELT. Voi ve n'andat' al cielo. BOURGEOIS. Qui au conseil.
CABEZON. Diferencias Cavallero; Versos del sexto tono. CLEMENT.
Vox in Rama. FESTA. Quando ritrova. FUENLLANA. Paseábase el rey
moro. GABRIELI. Intonazione settimo tono; Ricercare del 12º tono.
GERVAISE. 3 dances. GOUDIMEL. Deba contre mes debateurs.
GUERRERO. Salve Regina. LEJEUNE. D'une coline. MILAN. Fantasia
(lute). MORALES. Emendemus in melius. NARVAEZ. Diferencias sobra
O Glorioso Domina. RORE. De le belle contrade. TALLIS. Audivi
vocem. VALDERRABANO. Diferences sobre Guardama las vacas.]
(sch 4/71)

613. *v.6: Late 16th-century Music.* University of Chicago Collegium Musicum;
H. Brown, cond; Kentucky University Collegium Musicum; Morgan, cond.
Pleiades P 255
[AMMERBACH. Passamezzo antico. BYRD. Non vos relinquam; Christ
rising again. COSTELEY. Allon, gay gay. G. GABRIELI. In ecclesiis.
HANDL. Ecce quomodo. KERLE. Exurge, Domine. LASSUS. Bon
jour, mon coeur; Penitential Psalm III. MARENZIO. Madonna mia
gentil. MERULO. Toccata. MONTE. Missa super Cara la vita. NANINI.
Hic est beatissimus. PALESTRINA. Missa Papae Marcelli (Agnus Dei I);
Alla riva del Tebro; Sicut cervus. PHILLIPS. Bon jour, mon coeur.
PICCHI. Variations. VICTORIA. O vos omnes. WERTH. Cara la vita.]

614. *Historical Keyboard Instruments at the Victoria and Albert Museum,
London.* Margaret Hodsdon (spinet); Valda Aveling (spinet); Esther
Fisher (pf); Malcolm Binns (pf).   Musica Rara MUS 70-1
[BYRD. Like as the lark; Lord Willobie's welcome home; The Queen's
alman. HOLBORNE. The Queen's gifte. MORLEY. Nancie; Pavan -
Lachrymae. ANON. Alman Prince; Branle Hoboken; I smile to see how
you devise; My Lady Carey's dompe; When griping grief. Also Frescobaldi,
Bach, etc.]

615. *History of European Music. Part 1: Music of the Early Middle Ages.*
Musical Director, D. Stevens. Soloists and Instrumentalists; Schola
Cantorum Londoniensis; E. Fleet, dir.   Orpheus 349/51
[*v.1:* ADAM DE ST. VICTOR. Jubilemus Salvatori. BERNARD DE
VENTADOUR. Be m'an perdut. GUIRAUT DE BORNELH. Reis glorios.
MARCABRU. Pax in nomine Domini. PEROTINUS. Beata viscera.
PERRIN D'AGINCOURT. Quant voi en la fin d'estey. RAIMBAULT DE
VAQUIERAS. Kalenda maya. RICHARD I, KING OF ENGLAND. Ja
nun hons pris. WIPO. Victimae paschali laudes. ANON. Aeterna Christi
munera (2 versions); Aeterne rerum conditor (3 versions); Alleluia:
Angelus Domini; C'est la fin; Christo psallat ecclesia; Christus hunc diem;
Cunctipotens genitor; Dominus in Sina; Douce dame debonnaire; E, dame

615. *History of European Music. Part 1: Music of the Early Middle Ages.*
(Continued)
v.1 (Continued): jolie; En ma dame ai mis mon cuer; Eructavit cor
meum (2 versions); Haec dies; Lauda anima mea Dominum; Laudabo
Deum meum; Libera me, Domine; Omnipotens genitor; Orientis
partibus; Pour mon cuer; Sol oritur in sydere; Vos n'aler mie.

v.2: GUILLAUME LE VINIER. Espris d'ire. NEIDHARDT VON
REUENTHAL. Der may hat meing hercze; Winder wie ist nu dein kraft.
SACHS. Lob sei Gott Vater. ST. GODRIC. Sainte Marie virgine.
SPERVOGEL. Swa eyn vriund. WALTHER VON DER VOGELWEIDE.
Nu al erst lebe ich. ANON. Angelus Domini; Aque serven todo los
celestiaes; Benedicamus Domino (5 versions); Cunctipotens genitor (2
versions); Domino (clausula); Dominator Domine; Domino fidelium
(W^2); Gloria in cielo; A Madre do que liurou; Mais nos faz Sancta Maria;
Nobilis, humilis; Nos qui vivimus; Pucelete bele et avenant (Montpellier);
Rex coeli Domine; Santo Lorenzo; Sit gloria Domini; Viderunt Hemanuel.

v.3: ADAM DE LA HALLE. Diex soit en cheste maison; Li mans
d'amer; Tant con je vivrai. PETRUS DE CRUCE. Aucun ont trouvé
chant par usage. ANON. Alle psallite cum luya; Candida virginitas;
Danse royale-Ductia; Danse royale-Estampie; Deo confitemini; Ductia
(2 versions); Estampie; Flos filius (Pluteus 29.1); Hac in anni janua (W^1);
Haec dies (W^1, 3 versions); Huic main au doz mais de mai (Montpellier);
In seculum; Je cuidoie bien metre (Montpellier); O mitissima Virgo
Maria; On parole de batre et de vanner (Montpellier); Quant revient et
foille et flor; Quant voi revenir (Montpellier); Roma gaudens jubila (W^1);
Rex virginum amator; Trop sovent me dueil (Montpellier).]

History of Spanish Music in Sound. See *Anthologie de la musique
médiévale espagnole* (Nos.456-459).

History of Spanish Music in Sound, v.8. See under CABEZON (Orpheus
OR 436) in Part II.
(N.B.: At time of compilation this volume of the Anthologie de la
musique médiévale espagnole had not yet been issued as part of that set,
but was available on the Orpheus label under title given.)

616. *Hodie Christus Natus est.* Figuralchor der Gedächtniskirche, Stuttgart;
H. Rilling, cond.   Bärenreiter-Musicaphon BM SL 1326
[ECCARD. Ich lag in tiefer Todesnacht. G. GABRIELI. Hodie Christus
natus est. GUMPELZHAIMER. Gelobet seist du, Jesu Christ. HASSLER.
Angelus ad pastores ait; Verbum caro factum est. HERMAN. Lobt Gott,
ihr Christen alle gleich. OSIANDER. Christum wir sollen loben schon.
OTHMAYR. Gelobet seist du, Jesu Christ. PRAETORIUS. Quem
pastores laudavere. SCHRÖTER. Lobt Gott, ihr Christen alle gleich.
WALTER. Gelobet seist du, Jesu Christ. Also Schildt and Schütz.]

Las Huelgas. See *Missa Salve* (No.684).

617. *Ich steh an deiner Krippe hier.* RIAS Kammerchor; Consortium Musicum;
R. Zartner (positiv); G. Arndt, cond; Altmeyer (tnr); Brennecke (org).
Columbia C 80798; STC 80798 and Mace 9022; SD 9022
[ECCARD. Von Himmel hoch, da komm ich her. HASSLER. Von
Himmel hoch, da komm ich her. ISAAC. Süsser Vater, Herre Gott.
LUTHER. Von Himmel hoch, da komm ich her. PRAETORIUS. In
dulci jubilo. RASELIUS. Gelobet seist du, Jesu Christ. STADEN.
Aufzug; Pavana. SUSATO. Allemaigne. WALTER. Gelobet seist du,
Jesu Christ; In dulci jubilo. Also Bach, Baumann, Crüger, Hensel and
others.] (Myers 9/67)

618. *Ihr Musici, frisch auf: alte Madrigale, Villanellen und Chansons.*
Monteverdi-Chor, Hamburg; J. Jürgens, dir.
Telefunken AWT 9462; SAWT 9462
[GASTOLDI. Tutti venite armati. HASSLER. Ihr musici, frisch auf; Im
kühlen Maien; Mein Lieb' will mit mir kriegen; Jungfrau, dein schön
Gestalt. ISAAC. Innsbruck, ich muss dich lassen. LASSUS. Bonjour,
mon coeur; Io ti vorria; Matona mia cara; Quand mon mari; S'io ti vedess'
una sol. MONTEVERDI. Dolci miei sospiri; Fugge il verno. OTHMAYR.
Mir ist ein fein's braun's Maidelein. SENFL. Das G'läut zu Speyer.
SERMISY. Languir me fais. VECCHI. Tiridola, non dormire. WERT. Un
jour je m'en allai. WILLAERT. O bene mio. Also Albert and Schein.]

619. *In a Medieval Garden: Instrumental and Vocal Music of the Middle Ages
and Renaissance.* Stanley Buetens Lute Ensemble.
Nonesuch H 1120; 71120
[ATTAINGNANT. Basse danse Tous mes amys. BORLET. Ma tredol
rosignol. CAPIROLA. La Spagna. DUFAY. Adieu m'amour, adieu ma
joie; Pour l'amour de ma doulce amye. OBRECHT. Ic draghe de mutse
clutse. ANON. Auf rief ein hübsches freuelein; Ave verum corpus; Dale,
si le das; En albion; In seculum artifex; In seculum viellatoris; Die
Katzenpfote; La Spagna; Trotto. All are instrumental except Dufay
works and first two anonymous works listed.]

In dulci jubilo. See *Alte Chormusik zur Weihnachtszeit* (No.448).

620. *In dulci jubilo. Der Thomanerchor singt zur Weihnachtszeit.* Der
Thomanerchor; E. Mauersberger, cond. DGG 135 051
[BODENSCHATZ. Joseph, lieber Joseph mein. FREUNDT. Wie schön
singt uns der Engel Schar. M. PRAETORIUS. Allein Gott in der Höh
sei Ehr'; Es ist ein Ros' entsprungen; Gelobet seist du, Jesus Christ;
Hosianna dem Sohne Davids; In dulci jubilo; Der Morgenstern ist
aufgedrungen; Vom Himmel hoch, da komm ich her.] (adv)

621. *Inédits: Musique française des XV et XVI siècles.* Ensemble
Polyphonique de l'O.R.T.F.; Charles Ravier, dir.   Barclay 995001
[CHARITÉ. Jusqu'à tant. DEPRES. L'homme armé; Petite camusette.
DUFAY. J'attendray tant qu'il vous plaira; Lamentation de Constanti-
nople; Mon coeur me fait tout dit penser. FONTAINE. Mon coeur
pleure; Pastourelle en un vergié. HAUCOUR. Je demande ma bien venue.
JANEQUIN. Elle mérite. LEGRANT. (J? or G?). A l'aventure; Or avant
gentils; Si vous saviez. MORTON. L'homme armé; Mon bien ma joyeuls.
SERMISY. Elle s'en va; Pour un plaisir. ANON. Bransle; Gaillarde;
Tourdion (all Attaingnant).]   (Peters Int. furnished contents)

622. *Innsbruck, ich muss dich lassen: Lieder aus der Zeit Keiser Maximilians.*
Kammerchor Walther von der Vogelweide; Othmar Costa, cond.
                                                        Amadeo AVRS 5043
[APIARIUS. Es taget vor dem Walde. DEPRES. Tu pauperum refugium.
DUNSTABLE. Quam pulchra es. HOFHAIMER. Meîns Traurens ist.
ISAAC. Ich stund an einem Morgen; Innsbruck, ich muss dich lassen;
Mein Freud allein. LECHNER. Nun schein, du Glanz; O Lieb, wie süss.
SENFL. Ach Elslein; Mag ich Unglück nit; Quis dabit oculis. SWELINCK.
De Profundis.]   (biel 2/65)

623. *Instrumental Music from the Courts of Queen Elizabeth and King James.*
New York Pro Musica; Noah Greenberg, dir.
            Decca DL 9415; 79415 and DGG 18867 LPM; 138867 SLPM
[BYRD. Lord Willobies welcome home. COPERARIO. Fantasia à 5.
GIBBONS. The Lord Salisbury his pavin. HOLBORNE. The choise; The
fairy round; Heigh ho holiday; The honie suckle; Pavan; Pavana ploravit;
Sic semper; The wanton. LUPO. Fantasia à 6; Fantasia à 3. MORLEY.
Il lamento. WARD. In nomine à 4. ANON. The mountebank's dance;
Williams his love.]

Instrumental Music in the Year 1600. See *Instrumentalmusik um 1600*
(No.625).

624. *Instrumentalmusik am Hofe Maximilians I.* Concentus Musicus.
                                                        Amadeo AVRS 6233
[BRUMEL. Fors seulement; Bicinium; Vray dieu d'amours. COMPERE.
Et dunt (instr). DEPRES. Adieu mes amours; Basies moy; De tous biens;
Vive le roy; Canon: Petrus et Johann currunt in puncto. FINCK. Greiner,
Zanner, Schnöpfitzer (instr). ISAAC. Et ie bois d'autant; Helas; Der
Hund; Innsbrucklied (instr); Jai pris amours; La la ho ho; La mi la sol;
Lombre; Maudit soyt; Palle, palle; Par ung chies de cure; Tartara; two
untitled instr. works. OBRECHT. Fors seulement; Tsat een meskin.
SENFL. Das erste K. dein bin ich; Das ander, ich sag und klag; Das
dritt M. dein bin ich; Das viert, Es taget vor dem Walde; Fortuna, ad
voces musicale. ANON. Bicinium.]

625. *Instrumentalmusik um 1600.* Concentus Musicus, Vienna.
        Amadeo AVRS 6234; AVRS 130003 and Bach Guild BG 626
[BEVIN. Browning. COOPER. Fantasia. DU CAURROY. 5 Fantasias
on "Une jeune fillette." G. GABRIELI. Canzon a 8, "Fa sol la re";
Canzon a 4. GUAMI. Canzon a 8. HOLBORNE. Pavan "The funerals."
MASSAINO. Canzon a 8. MORLEY. Fantasia "Il Grillo." POSCH.
Intrada; Couranta. SOMMER. Pavan and Galliard. TERTRE. Branle I
and II; Galliarde; Pavane. TOMKINS. Alman. Also Scheidt.]
(sch 12/62)

626. *Internationale Woche für Chormusik in Graz.* Various choirs and vocal
ensembles.   Amadeo AVRS 6326
[COSTELEY. Que de passions et douleurs. DEPRES. Mille regrets.
HANDL. Jerusalem gaude. LASSUS. Mon coeur se recommande a vous.
LUKACIC. Panis angelicum (Cantiones sacrae). MONTEVERDI. Si ch'io
vorrei. PASSEREAU. Il est bel et bon. VECCHI. Tiridola. ZGANEC.
3 Lieder aus Medjimurje. Also Chailley and Durante.]   (biel 2/67)

627. *It was a Lover and His Lass: Music of Shakespeare's Time.* New York
Pro Musica; Noah Greenberg, cond.
        Decca DL 9421; 79421 and Brunswick AXA 4524; SAXA 4524
[BARTLETT. Whither runneth my sweetheart. BYRD. Browning;
Susanna Fair sometime assaulted was. DOWLAND. Gryffith galliard;
Queen Elizabeth's galliard; Sorrow, stay. EAST. When Israel came out
of Egypt. HUME. Death and life. MORLEY. It was a lover and his lass;
What saith my dainty darling? PEERSON. Blow out the trumpet.
WEELKES. When David heard that Absalom was slain. WILBYE.
Fantasia. ANON. Kemp's jig.]   (Myers 9/66)

628. *Italian and English Church Music.* St. John's College Choir; George
Guest, cond.   Argo ZRG 621
[A. GABRIELI. Missa brevis. GESUALDO. O vos omnes. BANCHIERI.
Omnes gentes. Also Casciolini, Purcell, Howell, Britten.] (gr 10/69)

629. *Italian Madrigals.* Abbey Singers.
        Decca DL 10103; 70103 and Brunswick AXA 4538; SAXA 4538
[ARCADELT. O felici occhi. A. GABRIELI. Ecco l'aurora; Dimmi
cieco. LUZZASCHI. Quivi sospiri. RORE. Non è lasso. VERDELOT.
Madonna. WERT. Vezzosi augelli. WILLAERT. O bene mio. Also
Haydn.] (gram 12/67)

630. *Italian Madrigals of the Renaissance.* Luca Marenzio Ensemble;
Saraceni, cond.   Everest 3179
[AGAZZARI. Dimmi donna gentile. BANCHIERI. Festino.
MARENZIO. Ahi dispietata morte; A Roma; Scendi dal paradiso
venere. MARINI. O luci belle. MONTEVERDI. S'andasse amor a
caccia; Vattene pur crudel. NOLA. Tri ciechi siamo.] (sch 12/67)

631. *The Italian Trecento.* The Columbia University Collegium Musicum;
R. Taruskin, dir.   Collegium Stereo JE 105
[CICONIA. Doctorem principem / Melodia suavissima. GHIRARDEL-
LUS DE FLORENTIA. Donna, l'altrui Mirar. JACOPO DA BOLOGNA.
Aquil'altera / Creatura gentil / Ucel di Dio (instr). LANDINO. Nessun
ponga speranca; Si dolce non sono. LORENZO DI FIRENZE? A poste
messe. WOLKENSTEIN. Es fuegt sich. ANON. L'antefana de ser
Lorenco; La nobil scala.]   (adv)

632. *Italienische Frottolen der Renaissance.* Vocalists and Instrumentalists;
Monterosso, cond.   Candide-Vox CE 31017
[CARA. S'io siedo a l'ombra; Se de fede vengo a meno. FOGLIANO.
Quodlibet (fl, va and hpsi). MONTAVANO. Lirum bililirum lirum; Da
poi ch'el tuo bel viso. NEGRI. Ameni colli. PESENTI. Questa èmia,
l'ho fatta mi; L'acqua vale a mio gran foco. TROMBONCINO. Acqua
non é l'umor; Non peccando altri che'l core; Nunqua fu pena maggiore;
Ostinato vo' seguire; La pietà chiuso ha le porte; Vale diva, vale in pace.
ANON. De speranza ormai; Che debbo far, che mi consigli amore; Felice
fu quel di; Se mai per meraveglia alzando il viso; La tromba sona.]
(biel 2/70)

633. *Italienische Lautenmusik der Renaissance.* Walter Gerwig (lute).
                              Harmonia Mundi HMS 30676 and VICS 1408
[CAROSO. Forza d'amore. M. GALILEI. Correnta. V. GALILEI. Io mi
son giovinetta; Il vostro gran valore; Ricercare. GORZANIS. Passamezzo
e padoana. MILAN. Ricercare. PARMA. Aria de Gran Duca; Ballo del
Serenissimo Duca di Parma; Correnta. NEGRI. Bianca fiore; Catena
d'amore; Spagnoletta. REGGIO. Cappriccio cromatico. ANON. Danza;
Danza-Correnta; Dove son quei fiori occhi; Hor ch'io son Correnta; Io
vorrei fuggir; Mascherada; Passo mezzo moderno; Pezzo tedesco.]
(First edition as 10" Harmonia Mundi; see No.360 in original edition.
Biel 2/70 lists as HM 30462.)

634. *Italienische Lautenmusik der Spätrenaissance.* Walter Gerwig (lute).
                              10" Harmonia Mundi HM 25165
[GARSI. Ballo del Serenissimo Duca di Parma; Correnta. GORZANIS.
Passamezzo e padoana. NEGRI. Bianca fiore; Catena d'amore;
Spagnoletta. REGGIO. Cappriccio cromatico.]   (biel 2/67)
See preceding entry.

635. *The Jaye Consort.* Francis Baines, cond; London Cornett and Sackbut
Ensemble; Alan Lumsden, dir.
                              Pye Golden Guinea GGC 4102; GSGC 14102
[BANCHIERI. Fantasia sesta in eco movendo in registro; Fantasia
vigesima. A. GABRIELI. Ricercar del sesto tuono. GRILLO. Canzon
quintadecima. GUSSAGO. La fontana. HASSLER. Canzon duodecimi
toni; Canzon noni toni. MASCHERA. Canzon terza; La Mazzuola.
TAEGGIO. La Basgapera. VIADANA. Le Venetiana. Also Frescobaldi.]

636. *The Jolly Minstrels: Minstrel Tunes, Songs and Dances of the Middle Ages on Authentic Instruments.* English (tnr); Jaye Consort.
Vanguard Cardinal VCS 10049
[ADAM DE LA HALLE. Li mans d'amer. RAIMBAULD DE VAQUEIRAS. Kalenda maya. RICHARD CÖUR DE LION. Ja nun nous pris. ANON. C'est la fin; Die süss Nachtigall; Ductia (2); English dance; Estampie (3); Estampie royale; In saeculum artifex; Lamento di Tristan; Li mans d'amer; Moulin de Paris; Novus miles sequitur; Pour mon coeur; Rege mentem; Saltarello; Sol ovitur; Song of the ass; Trotto; Vierhundert Jar uff diser Erde; Worldes bliss.]   (Myers 12/70)

637. Jones, Geraint. Keyboard Recital.   H.M.V. HQS 1100
[BYRD. A gigg. FARNABY. Tell me, Daphne. GIBBONS. Pavana. MUNDY. Robin. SWELINCK. Von der fortuna werd' ich getrieben. Also Bach, Händel, Scarlatti, Rameau, and others.]   (gr 10/67)

638. *Jubilate Deo.* Regensburger Domspatzen; T. Schrems, cond.
Eurodisc 70712KK; S 70173KK and RCA Victor LM 2855;
LSC 2855 and Cetra KK 70172; SKK 70173
[AICHINGER. Factus est repente; Confirma hoc. LASSUS. Jubilate Deo. PALESTRINA. Dum complerentur; Incipit lamentatio; Tu es Petrus (mass). VICTORIA. Caligaverunt. Also Allegri and Scarlatti.]
(biel 2/70)

639. *Julian Bream in Concert.* Julian Bream (lute); Peter Pears (tnr).
Victor LM 2819; LSC 2819 and RB 6646; SB 6646
[*(instr)*: BYRD. Galliard; My Lord Willobie's welcome home; Pavan; Pavana Bray. DOWLAND. Captain Piper's galliard; Lady Clifton's spirit; Queen Elizabeth's galliard; Sir John Langton's pavan; Tarleton's resurrection.
(voice and lute): DOWLAND. In darkness let me dwell; The lowest trees have tops; Say, love, if ever thou didst find; Sorrow, stay; Time's eldest son; Wilt thou, unkind, thus reave me?]   (Myers 6/66)

640. *Kirchenmusik der Salzburger Renaissance.* Musica Antiqua, Vienna; R. Clemencic, dir.   Schwann AMS 67; 67 STE and Charlin AMS 67
[FINCK. Veni redemptor gentium. GUETFREUND. Jubilate deo; Tu es Deus (graduale). HOFHAIMER. Recordare, virgo mater (org); Salve Regina; Tristitia vestra (motet). ISAAC. Optime pastor (motet). MASSAINO. Illumina oculos (motet). SENFL. Beati omnes (motet). SICHER. Ave maris stella (org); In dulci jubilo (org); Resonet in laudibus (org); Tripellied (org). STADLMAYER. Christe redemptor omnium (hymn).]

641. *Die Kleinorgel.* Albert de Klerk (org).   Telefunken AWT 9409
[GIBBONS. A fancy in A re; The Kings juell. PALESTRINA. Ricercare primi toni. SWELINCK. Von der Fortuna werd' ich getrieben. TOMAS DE SANTA MARIA. Organ fantasias. Also Buxtehude, Casanovas, Frescobaldi, Zipoli and others.]

642. *Krainis Recorder Consort.*   Decca Ace of Clubs ACL R 271
[DOWLAND. Earl of Essex galliard; Mr. George Whithead his almand;
Lachrimae antiquae. GERVAISE. Allemande; Bransle de Bourgogne;
Bransle de Champaigne; Pavane and galliarde; Passamezzo. TORRE.
Alta. ANON. Air; Daphne; Lamento di Tristano; Manfrolina; My
Robbin; Paduana del Re; Le Quinte estampie real (2); La Rocha e'l
fuso; Saltarello (2); Stantipes; A Toye; Tickle my toe; Trumpet tune.
Also Scheidt.]   (gr 5/66)

643. *The Kynge's Muzicke: Instrumental Music of the Tudor Court from
Henry VIII to Elizabeth I.* New York Pro Musica; John White, dir.
                                                    Decca DL 79434
[BEVIN. Browning. BYRD. Fantasia; My Lord of Oxenford's march; O
mistress mine. COPERARIO. Fantasia. CORNYSH. Fantasia, Fa la sol.
DOWLAND. Frog galliard; Lachrymae triste. FARNABY. Rosasolis.
HENRY VIII. Tanndernaken. MUNDY. Tres partes in una. MASTER
NEWMAN. Pavane. TALLIS. Clarifica me pater; A point; Veni
redemptor. WARD. Ayre; Fantasia. WHYTE. In nomine. ANON. La
bonnette; La chymyse; La doun cella; Galliard.]

644. *Lamento d'Arianna (Madrigal Masterpieces, v.3).* Deller Consort.
                    Bach Guild BG 671; BGS 70671 and Amadeo AVRS 6292
[DEPRES. La déploration de Jehan Okeghem; Parfons regretz.
GESUALDO. Beltà poi che t'assenti. JANEQUIN. Le chant des oyseaux;
Le chant de l'alouette. LASSUS. La nuit froide et sombre. MARENZIO.
Cedan l'antiche tue chiare vittorie. MONTEVERDI. Lamento d'Arianna;
Ohimè il bel viso.]

645. *Laments.* Monteverdi Choir; Gardiner, cond.   Abbey 608
[MONTEVERDI. Lagrime d'amante al sepolcro. GIBBONS. What is our
life? MORLEY. O grief, even on the bud. WILBYE. Weep, weep, mine
eyes; Oft have I vowed; Draw on sweet night.]   (gram 12/70)

646. *Laudario di Cortona: Codex 91 of the Etruscan Academy of Cortona
(Thirteenth Century).* Quartetto Polifonico Italiano.
 Musical Heritage Society MHS 858 and Angelicum LPA 5976; STA 8976
[Magdalena degna da laudare (40); Peccatrice nominata (18); Laudar
voglio per amore (37); Sia laudato San Francesco (38); Ciascun che fede
sente (39); L'alto prense Arcangelo lucente (41); San Iovanni, al mond'è
nato (43); Vergene donzella da Dio amata (18); Ogn'om canti novel
canto (44); Benedicti, el laudati (46); Facciamo laude a tutt'i sancti (42);
Venite a laudare (1); Laude novella sia cantata (2); Ave, donna santissima
(3); Madonna Santa Maria (4); Ave, Regina gloriosa (6); Altissima luce
col grande splendore (8); Fami cantar l'amor di la beata (9); Regina
Sovrana de gram pietade (11); Ave, Dei genitrix (11); O Maria, d'omelia
se' fontana (10); O Maria Dei cella (13); Ave, Vergene gaudente (14);
O Divina Virgo (15); Salve, Salve, Virgo pia (16); Salutiam divotamente
(47); Da ciel venne messo novello (7); Stella nuova 'n fra la gente (21);

Cristo è nato et humanato (19); Gloria 'n cielo e pace 'n terra! (20);
Piangiam quel crudel basciare (22); Troppo perde il tempo (33); Stomme
alegro et lazioso (34); Ben è crudele e spietoso (23); Oimè lasso, e freddo
lo mio core (35); Chi vol lo mondo desprezzare (36); De la crudel morte
de Cristo (24); Onne homo ad alta voce (26); Dami conforto, Dio (25);
Jesù Cristo Glorioso (27); Laudamo la resurrectione (28); Spiritu Sancto,
dolze amore (29); Spirito Santo glorioso (30); Spirito Sancto da servire
(31); Alta Trinità beata (32); Amor dolze senza pare (45).]

647. *Laudari 91 di Cortona.* Settings by Luciano Sgrizzi. Soloists; Società
Cameristica di Lugano; Edwin Loehrer, dir.   Nonesuch H 1086; H 71086
                              and Eurodisc 707174; 707175 and Cycnus 9031
[Preludio; Lauda; Annunciazione; Natività; Adorazione dei pastori;
Contemplazione di Maria nel presepe; Adorazione delle Madri; Presenta-
tione al tempio; Adorazione dei Magi; Lauda di Maria Maddalena; Il bacio
di Giuda; Flagellazione e salita al Calvario; Crocifissione; Pianto di Maria;
Invocazione; Lauda della Croce; Resurrezione; Ascensione.]

648. *Lautenmusik aus Frankreich und England.* Walter Gerwig (lute).
                                        Harmonia Mundi HM 30180 L and
                              RCA Victrola VICS 1362 (as Art of the Lute)
[ATTAINGNANT. La brosse; Destre amoureux; Gaillard; La Roque; La
Rote de Rode; Sans roche; Tant que vivray; Tous mes amys. BESARD.
Bransle; Bransle gay; Bransle volte; Courante; Gaillarde; Prelude de 6;
Villanella. BITTNER. Suite in g minor. MACE. Suite in d minor.]
(biel 2/70)

649. *Lautenmusik der Renaissance.* Eugen Müller-Dombois (lute). SME 81033
[BALLARD. Branle de Village I - Branle II - Branle III - Branle IV;
Entrée de Luth I - Entrée II - Entrée III - Courante. MILAN. Fantasia
del quarto tono. MUDARRA. Fantasia que contrehaze la harpa.
NARVAEZ. Diferencias sobre "Guárdame las vacas." NEUSIEDLER.
Preambel - Elslein, liebstes Elslein mein; Nach Willen dein; Welscher
Tanz "Wascha mesa"; Niederlendisch Tentzlein. ANON. Kemp's jig;
Robinson's May; Watkins ale; The cobler; Currant.]   (Peters Intl.
furnished)

650. *Die Libe ist schoen: Liebeslieder aus den 15. und 16. Jahrhunderts.*
Capella Antiqua, Munich; K. Ruhland, cond.
                              10" Christophorus CLP 75495; SCLP 75496
[CLEMENT. Ich sag ade. HASSLER. Mein Gmüt ist mir verwirret.
ISAAC. O liebes Herz. LECHNER. Ach Lieb, ich muss dich lassen.
REGNART. All mein Gedanken; Wann ich gedenk. SCANDELLI. Schein
uns, du liebe Sonne. VOIT. Für all ich krön. ANON. Lieblich hat sich
gesellet; Ach reine zart (Glogauer); Es seufzt ein Frau so sehre in ihrem
Gemüte (Glogauer); Die Libe ist schoen (Glogauer).]   (biel 2/69)

651. *Lider, corali e madrigali.* Vienna Boys Choir; Grossmann, cond.
Philips 835399 LY
[CERTON, GASTOLDI, LEJEUNE, MORLEY and WIDMANN. Also
Brahms, Frescobaldi and Schubert.]   (sant 5-6/71 - no contents)

652. *Lieder und Tänze aus Deutschland, 1460-1560.* Cornelia Krumbiegel
(sop); W. Reinhold (tnr); H.-C. Polster (bass); Capella Lipsiensis;
Dietrich Knothe, dir.   DGG ARC 2533066
[FINCK. Ach herzigs Herz; Sauff aus und machs nit lang; Tanz.
HOFHAIMER. Ach Lieb mit Leid; Zucht, Ehr und Lob. HOFHAIMER-
KLEBER. Zucht, Ehr und Lob. ISAAC. Es hätt ein Baur ein Töchter-
lein; Ich stund an einem Morgen; Gross Leid muss ich jetzt tragen;
Innsbruck, ich muss dich lassen; Mein Trost ob allen Weiben.
JUDENKÜNIG. Von edler Art. KOTTER. Spaniol Kochersperg.
NEUSIEDLER. Ach Lieb mit Leid; Der Bettlertanz; Ein guter Gassen-
hauer; Entlaubet ist der Walde; Ich klag den Tag. OTHMAYR. Ein
beurisch tantz; Dem Maidlein ich mein Treu versprich; Es ist ein Schnee
gefallen. RHAW. Ach Elslein, liebes Elselein; Entlaubet ist der Walde;
Mir ist ein feins brauns Maidelein. SENFL. Das bringt mir grossen
Schmerze; Entlaubet ist der Walde; Herzog Ullrichs Jagdlied: Ich
schwing mein Horn; Ich soll und muss einen Buhlen haben; Mit Lust
tritt ich an diesen Tanz; Von edler Art. STOLTZER. Ich klag den Tag;
Ich stund an einem Morgen. WECK. Ein ander dancz / Hopper dancz.
ANON. Mir ist ein feins brauns Maidelein.]

653. *Il liuto nel rinascimento italiano.* P. Possiedi (lute).
Vedette VPC 1506; VST 6006
[CREMA. Bertoncina; Bolognese; Louetta; 2 Ricercari. GORZANIS. La
dura partita. NEGRI. Alemana d'amore; Bianco fiore; Catena d'amore;
Fedeltà d'amore. SPINACCINO. La Cara cosa; 3 Fantasie; Gagliarda;
Paduana; Pescatore che va cantando; Ricercari; Saltarello. ANON.
Italiana; Mascherada; Venetiana; Villanella.]   (sant 5-6/71)

654. *Liverpool Cathedral Choir.* N. Rawsthorne (org); Liverpool and Bootle
Constabulary Band Brass Section; R. Woan, cond.   Abbey LPB 663
[AICHINGER. Regina Coeli. BYRD. Ave Verum Corpus. G. GABRIELI.
Jubilate Deo. LASSUS. Adoramus te. PALESTRINA. Recordata.
WEELKES. Hosanna to the Son of David. Also Mathias, Bach, Leighton,
Crotch, Hadley, Bennett, Joubert and Ley.]   (gram 3/71)

Llibre Vermell. See *Anthologie de la musique médiévale espagnole, v.3*
(No.457) and *Weltliche Musik um 1300* (No.899).

655. *Lo, Country Sports.* J. Neville (speaker); Purcell Consort of Voices;
G. Burgess, cond; Elizabethan Consort of Viols; J. Tyler (lute).
Argo ZRG 658
[BATESON. Come, follow me, fair nymphs. BENNET. The hunt is up.
BOLTON. A canzon pastoral. BRETON. Shepherd and shepherdess.
CAMPION. Jack and Joan. CAVENDISH. Down in a valley. EAST.

Farewell, sweet woods and mountains; Sweet muses, nymphs and shepherds sporting; Thyrsis, sleepest thou? FARMER. O stay, sweet love. FARNABY. Pearce did dance with Petronella; Pearce did love fair Petronel. R. JOHNSON. Alman. LODGE. Corydon's song. NASHE. Spring, the sweet spring. RAVENSCROFT. Sing after fellows; Tomorrow the fox will come to town. TOMKINS. Adieu, ye city-prisoning towers. VAUTOR. Mother I will have a husband. WEELKES. Lo, country sports; Our country swains in the Morris Dance; Whilst youthful sports are lasting. YOUNG. The shepherd, Arsilius' reply. ANON. Almain; The wych.] (gram 1/71)

Locheimer Liederbuch. See *Fourteen Lieder and Instrumental Pieces from the Locheimer Liederbuch* (No.572).

656. *Love and Dalliance in Renaissance France.* Cambridge Consort; Cohen, dir.   Turnabout TV 34380
[ARCADELT. Margot labourez les vignes; Nous voyons que les hommes. BERCHEM. Jehan de Lagny. CADÉAC. Je suis désheritée. CERTON. Je ne fus jamais si aisé. DEPRES. Adieu mes amours; Allegez moy; Mille regrets; Une mousse de Biscaye. JACOTIN. Je suis désheritée. JANEQUIN. Fiez-vous-y. LE ROY. Branle de Bourgogne. MOULU. Amy souffrez. PLANÇON. Nous étions trois jeunes filles. SERMISY. Tant que vivray. ANON. Adieu mes amours; L'amour de moy; Dit le bourgignon; Filles à marier; Galliard Fortune à bien; Il me suffit; La Spagna.]   (sch 1/71)

657. *Love Songs of Long Ago.* Renaissance Quartet.   Project 3 PR 7004
[CORKINE. He that hath no mistress. DANYEL. Stay, cruel, stay. DOWLAND. Can she excuse; Come again! Sweet love doth now invite; Fortune my foe; What if I never speed. MILAN. Pavanne. MORLEY. Aria; It was a lover and his lasse; See mine own sweet jewel. SERMISY. Tant que vivray. TORRE. Danza. ANON. La bounette; Elslein, liebstes Elselein; Ich bins erfreut; La primavera; Saltarello; Si la noche; Willow song.]

658. *Ludis Paschalis.* A Liturgical Easter-play, edited by Charles Ravier from Ms.86, Saint-Quentin. Ensemble Polyphonique de Paris, RTF; Ravier, dir.   Valois MB 444; MB 944
(gr 10/64)

659. *Lute Music from the Royal Courts.* Julian Bream (lute).
                  Victor LM 2924; LSC 2924 and RB 6698; SB 6698
[BAKFARK. Fantasia. BESARD. Air de cour; Branle. DLUGORAJ. Fantasia; Finales (2); Villanellas (2). DOWLAND. Fantasia (Fancye); Queen Elizabeth's galliard. FERRABOSCO. Pavan. GUILLEMETTE. Volte. HOWETT. Fantasia. MOLINARO. Ballo detto "Il Conte Orlando"; Fantasia; Saltarellos (2). MORITZ VON HESSEN. Pavan. MUDARRA. Fantasia. NEUSIEDLER. Hie' folget ein welscher Tanz;

659. *Lute Music from the Royal Courts.* (Continued)
Ich klag' den Tag; Der Juden Tanz; Mein Herz hat sich mit Lieb verpflicht.
PHILIPS. Chromatic pavan; Galliard to the chromatic pavan.]

Lyric Songs and Poems, 1200-1320. See *Minnesang und Spruchdichtung um 1200-1300* (No.681).

660. *Madrigals.* I Madrigalisti di Roma; Domenico Cieri.
                                          Philips Fourfront 4FM 10017
[ARCADELT. Il bianco e dolce cigno. DEPRES. El grillo. LASSUS.
Matona mia cara. MARENZIO. Estote fortes. MONTEVERDI. Ecco
mormorar l'onde; Lasciatemi morire. PESENTI. Dal lecto me levava.
SERMISY. Au ioly boys. TORRE. Adoramus Te Senor. VIADANA.
Exsultate justi in Domino. VICTORIA. Duo Seraphim; Sanctus;
Benedictus. WILBYE. Adieu sweet Amaryllis. Also Kodaly, Dugan,
Klonowsky.]   (gr 2/70)

661. *Madrigals and Keyboard Music of the English Renaissance.* London
Ambrosian Singers; J. McCarthy, dir; Hans Kann (org).
                                    Musical Heritage Society MHS 1173
[BLITHEMAN. Eterne rerum alias, IV (MB 52). BYRD. Though
Amarylis dance. CARLETON. Gloria tibi Trinitas (MB 3). DOWLAND.
Say, love, if ever thou didst find. EDWARDS. When griping griefs
(MB 113). GIBBONS. The silver swan. MORLEY. Now is the month of
Maying. REDFORD. Christe qui lux est (MB 40); Eterne rex altissime
(MB 26); Glorificamus (te dei genitrix) (MB 54); Jam lucis orto sidere
(MB 75); O Lux with a meane (MB 29); Salvator with meane (MB 36);
[untitled piece] (MB 58). SHELBYE. Miserere (MB 41). TALLIS. Iste
confessor (MB 106); Per haec nos (MB 119); A point (MB 103);
Remember not, O Lord (MB 43). TOMKINS. Oft did I marle. TYE.
When that the first day was come. WEELKES. Hence Care, thou art
too cruel; O Care, thou wilt despatch me. ANON. I smile to see how you
devise (MB 88); [The Maiden's song] (MB 1); O ye happy dames (MB 0);
Since thou art false to me (MB 110).]

662. *Madrigal Masterpieces, v.2.* Alfred Deller (c-tnr).   Bach Guild BG 639;
                                    BGS 5051 and Amadeo AVRS 6292
[ARCADELT. Il bianco e dolce cigno. COSTELEY. Allons, gay bergères;
Mignonne, allons voir si la rose. GESUALDO. Morro lasso al mio duolo.
JONES. Fair Oriana seeming to wink at folly. MARENZIO. Solo e
pensoso; Leggiadre Ninfe. MONTEVERDI. Lagrime d'amante; Zefiro
torna. PASSEREAU. Il est bel et bon. RORE. Ancor che c'ol partire.]
(sch 12/63)
N.B.: Volume 1 is in First Supplement, p.100; volume 3 in this list under
title, *Lamento d'Arianna.*

Madrigal Masterpieces, v.3. See *Lamento d'Arianna* (No.644).

663. *Madrigals Across the Centuries.* Riverside Chamber Singers.
Music Guild MG 107
[ARCADELT. S'infinita bellezza. BENNET. Weep, O mine eyes.
COSTELEY. Mignonne, allons voir. DEERING. Quem vidistis pastores.
FARMER. Fair Phyllis. A. GABRIELI. Ecco l'aurora. GASTOLDI. Amor
vittorioso. JANEQUIN. Petite nymphe folastre. LASSUS. Bonjour mon
coeur. LE JEUNE. Revecy venir du printans. LUZZASCHI. Quivi sospiri.
MONTEVERDI. Ecco mormorar l'onde. MORLEY. Fire, fire; Though
Philomela. PILKINGTON. Rest sweet nymphs. VICTORIA. O vos omnes.
WEELKES. Hosanna to the Son of David. Also Schütz and Debussy.]

664. *Madrigals and Instrumental Music.* Telemann Society; T. Schulze, cond.
Counterpoint/Esoteric 618; 5618
[FARNABY. Blind love was shooting; Curtain drawn. MORLEY.
Clorinda false; Now is the gentle season; On a fair morning; Since my
tears and lamenting. PILKINGTON. All in a cave; Rest sweet nymphs.
ANON. (Cosyn Virginal Book): Bullfinch; Filliday floutes me;
Brunswick's toy. ANON. No man's jig; Rapper sword dance; Shepherd's
hey. Also late English dances.]   (sch 7/65)

Madrigals and Songs. See *English, French and Italian Madrigals and Songs*
(No.542).

Madrigals Concerto. See *Recital de Madrigale, v.2* (No.819).

665. *Madrigals of Italy, Germany, England, France.* Wiener Sängerknaben;
Furthmoser, cond.   Philips PHM 500011; PHS 900011
[CERTON. Niemals war ich so voll Freude. GASTOLDI. An einem guten
Orte; An hellen Tagen; Mein Gedanken. LEJEUNE. Die schöne Schwalbe.
MORLEY. Der Lenz all Äst bekleiden tut; Warum nicht lustig?
WIDMANN. Kommt her Studenten frei; Wer Lust und Lieb zur Musik
hat; Wohlauf Soldatenblut. Also eight German folk songs and Frescobaldi.]
(Myers 6/63)

666. *Madrigals, Villancicos and Part Songs, 16th and 17th Centuries.* The
Riverside Singers.   Project 3 PR 7002 SD
Side 1
[BATESON. Have I found her? BENNET. All creatures now. BYRD.
This sweet and merry month. GIBBONS. The silver swan. WEELKES.
The nightingale. WILBYE. Draw on sweet night; Lady, when I behold.
Side 2
ESCOBAR. Secaróme los pesares. GONCALES. Navego en Hondo Mar.
MORATA. Ninpha gentil; Ojos claros serenos; Ojos que ya no véis.
VASQUEZ. Naome firays, madre. ANON. Ay, luna que reluzes; Pobre
Joan.]

Madrigals, Villanelles und Chansons. See *Ihr Musici, frisch auf* (No.618).

667. *Maîtres anciens de la Polyphonie.* Choeur Académique "Moravian";
Veselka, cond.   10" Supraphon SUP 20327
[CAMPANUS VODNANSKY. Favete linguis singuli. HANDL. Ascendit
Deus; Ecce quomodo moritur justus. HASSLER. Cantate Domino.
LASSUS. Eccho. PALESTRINA. Pueri Hebraeorum; Popule meus.
VICTORIA. Duo Seraphim; O vos omnes.]   (dia 64)

668. *Maîtres de luth au XVIIe siècle.* Castet (lute).   Boite à Musique C 106
[BALLARD. Trois branles de village. BELLEVILLE. Courante.
DUFAUT. Gavotte, sarabande et son double, gigue. DOWLAND.
Lachrymae; My Lord Willobie's welcome home. GAULTIER. Courante;
Son adieu et la redouble. MELII. Capriccio cromatico. PERICHON.
Prélude et courante. WITHEFELDE. The English hunt's up. ANON.
Bransle; Courante; En me revenant; Quatre ballets; Wilson's wilde.]
(dia 70)

669. *Masque Music.* Concentus Musicus of Denmark; Aksel Mathiesen, dir.
                                         Nonesuch H 1153; 71153
[CAMPION. Now hath Flora. COPERARIO. Come ashore; Cuperaree
or Grayes Inne; Squiers masque; While dancing rests. CUTTING. Alman,
Galliard; The squirrels toy - a jig. JOHNSON. The fairy masque; The
gypsies metamorphosed; The satyres masque. ANON. The divell's
dance; The goates masque; The king's mistress; The mountebanks dance
at Grayes Inne; The second witches dance; Waters his love; Williams his
love; Wilsons love. Also Lawes.]   (Myers 3/69)

670. *Masterpieces of the Early French and Italian Renaissance.* Société de
Musique d'Autrefois (singers and instrumentalists).
                                         Nonesuch H 1010; 71010
[BINCHOIS. Deul angoisseux, rage desmesurée; Triste plaisir et
douloureuse joie. BUSNOIS. Pucelotte. CARA. Occhi miei. COMPERE.
Che fa la ramacina; Ne doibt-en prendre. DELAHAYE. Mort, j'appelle de
ta rigeur. DUFAY. Donnes l'assault a la forteresse; Les doleurs dont me
sens. DUNSTABLE. O rosa bella. GHISELIN. La Alfonsina. ISAAC. La
morra; Morte che fai? TROMBONCINO. Non peccando altri che'l core;
Ostinato vo seguire. VAROTER. Voi che passate. ANON. Coda di volpe;
Dit le bourguignon; Epitaphe de l'amant vert; Perla mya; Tuba gallicalis.]

Masters of Early English Keyboard Music, v.5: John Bull. See under
BULL in Part II. (Volumes 1-4 are in original edition, Nos.236-39.)

671. *Masterwork Chorus.* David Randolph, cond.   Westminster 9622
[LASSUS. Ola! O che ben eccho. MONTEVERDI. Lagrime d'amante
(complete). Also Allegri, Lotti, Schütz.]

Masterworks for Organ, v.7. See *Anthologie de la musique d'orgue,
no.4* (No.455).

Medieval and Renaissance Andalusian Songs. See *Music from the Middle
Ages ...* (No.718).

672. *Medieval and Renaissance Music for the Irish and Medieval Harps, Vièle, Recorders and Tambourin.* Polonska, Durand and Cotte, soloists.
                                            Turnabout TV 4019; STV 34019
[ATTAINGNANT. Magnificat primi toni; Te deum laudamus (excerpts). BRIHUEGA. Villancico. BRUMEL. Vray dieu d'amours. V. GALILEI. Saltarello. GASTOLDI. Bicinium. GERVAISE. Dances. GHIZEGHEM. Gentil Gallans. ISAAC. Carmen saecularis. LANDINO. Angelica beltà. J. LEGRANT. Entre vous nouveaux mariés. MONACHUS. Gymel. OBRECHT. Ricercare. SERMISY. Du bien qu'oeil absent ne peut choisir; Puisqu'en amour. WALTHER VON DER VOGELWEIDE. Palestinalied; Wie sol ich den gemynen. ANON. Clausolae (Domino); Danse royale; Ductia; Estampie royale. In saeculum artifex; In saeculum viellatoris; Lamento di Tristano; La Manfredina; La Rotta; Saltarello; Trotto; Veri Floris sub Figura; La volonté.]

673. *Medieval Carols and Dances.* Renaissance Chamber Players; Paul Ehrlich, cond.   Baroque 9006

674. *Medieval English Carols and Italian Dances.* New York Pro Musica; Noah Greenberg, cond.   Decca DL 9418; 79148 and Brunswick AXA 4517;
                                                              SAXA 4517
[ANON. Nowel synge we bothe al and som; Lullay, lullow, lully, lullay; Ave Maria gracia dei plena; Saltarello; Istampita "Palamento"; Ther is no rose of swych vertu; Ave, rex angelorum; Nova, nova; Make we joye nowe in this fest; Hayl, Mary, ful of grace; Mervele noght, Josep, on Mary mylde; Saltarellos (2); Nowell, nowell, nowell; Salve, sancta parens; Deo gracias anglia (Agincourt carol).]

675. *Medieval English Lyrics.* John Whitworth (c-tnr); Grayston Burgess, and others.   Argo ZRG 5443
[HENRY VIII. Green growith th'holy. PHILIPS. This day day daws. ST. GODRIC. Sainte Marie virgine. ANON. Deo gracias anglia; Edi be thu; Gabriel fram heven king; Go hert, hurt with adversitee; Foweles in the frith; Miri it is; Now wold y fain; Nowel, nowel; Perspice Christicola; Pray for us; Sumer is icumen in; Stabat juxta Christi crucem; Stond wel, moder.]   (gram 12/70)

Medieval Motets and Carols for the Nativity. See *Carols and Motets for the Nativity of Medieval and Tudor England* (No.483), and cf. *Christmas Carols and Motets of Medieval Europe* (No.500).

676. *Medieval Music and Songs of the Troubadours.* Vocal soloists and Instrumental Ensemble; Musica Reservata; J. Beckett, cond.
                                                          Everest 3270
[ADAM DE LA HALLE. Amours et ma dame aussi; Li dous regars; Robin m'aime; Tan con je vivrai. GACE BRULÉ. De bone amor. RAIMBAUT DE VAQUIERAS. Kalenda maya. ANON. Amor potest / Ad amorem / Tenor; Au cuer ai un mal / Je ne m'en repentirai / Jolietement; Danse

676. *Medieval Music and Songs of the Troubadours.* (Continued)
royale; Ductia; Flor de lis / Je nepu is / Douce dame; In seculum
viellatoris; J'ai un cuer / Docebit; Jolietement; Mout me fu grief / Robin
m'aime / Portare; On parole / A Paris / Frese nouvele; Prisoner's song;
Pucelete / Je langui / Domino; La quarte estampie real; La quinte estampie
real; La seconde estampie real; La sexte estampie real.]

Medieval Music for Ancient Instruments (Musica Antiqua Polonica).
See *U Zrodel Muzyki Polskiej* (No.890).

677. *Medieval Songs of Praise (Ms.91, Cortona, Biblioteca comunale).* Choir
of the Papel Chapel of St. Francis of Assisi; Alfonso Del Farraro, dir.
                                                   Heliodor HS 25076
[Puer natus in Bethlehem; O virgo pulcherrima; O spes mea cara;
Concordia laetitia; Cristo riusati in tutti i cuori; Altà Trinitá beata; Laude
novella sia cantata; Omne omo ad alta voce; Venite a laudare; Laudar
vollio; Troppo perde'l tempo; De la crudel morte di Cristo; Martir
glorioso aulente flore.]   (hi fi 8/68)

678. *The Medieval Sound.* Early woodwind instruments played by David
Munrow, with Gillian Reid (psaltery and perc) and Christopher Hogwood
(regal and harpsi).   (gram 7/71)   Oryx EXP46

Meister der Laute (W. Gerwig). See *Lautenmusik aus Frankreich und
England* (No.648).

Meisterwerke der Madrigalkunst. See *Madrigal Masterpieces* (Nos.365,662,644).

679. *Messe et polyphonies.* Choeurs français; J. Chailley, dir.
                                                   Studio S.M. SM 3354
[MAUDUIT. Versets du Requiem pour Pierre de Ronsard. PRAETORIUS.
C'est l'agneau de Dieu. ANON. Le Dieu d'amour est mon verger. Also
Kedroff and Chailley.]   (dia 68)

680. *Metaphysical Tobacco; Songs and Dances by Dowland, East and
Holborne.* Musica Reservata; M. Morrow, dir; Purcell Consort of Voices;
G. Burgess, dir.   Argo ZRG 572
[DOWLAND. Away with these self-loving lads; Can she excuse; In this
trembling shadow; Lasso vita mia; Mr. Thomas Collier his galiard; Pavan
no.5 à 4; Pipers galliard (arr. Bull); Sorrow stay; Welcome black night;
What if I never speed. EAST. O metaphysical tobacco; Poor is the life;
Weep not dear love; Your shining eyes. HOLBORNE. The fairie round;
Heigh ho holiday; The honie suckle; Pavan Ploravit.]

681. *Minnesang und Spruchdichtung um 1200-1300.* Studio der frühen
Musik.   Telefunken SAWT 9487-A
[FRAUENLOB. Ez waent ein narrenweise. NEIDHARDT VON
REUENTHAL. Blozen wir den anger ligen sahen; Fürste Friderich; Meie
din; Meienzit. REINMAR. Wol mich des tages. WALTHER VON DER
VOGELWEIDE. Mir hat her Gerhart Atze; Nu alerst / Palästinalied;

Under der Linden. "DER UNVÜRZAGHETE." Der kuninc Rodolp.
WIZLAW III. Ich warne dich; Loibere risen. ANON. Chançonetta
Tedescha I; Chançonetta Tedescha II.]   (sch 1/67)

Minnesong and Prosody, ca.1200-1300. See *Minnesang und Spruchdich-tung um 1200-1300* (No.681).

682. *Missa cantantibus organis, Caecilia.* Prague Madrigal Singers.
                              Supraphon SUAST 50776
[DRAGONI. Kyrie; Qui tollis. GIOVANELLI. Et in spiritum. HANDL.
Missa super Elisabethae impletum est tempus. PALESTRINA. Et in
terra pax. STABILE. Kyrie; Patrem Omnipotentem - Crucifixus.
SURIANO. Christe; Et ascendit. Also Mancini and Santini.]   (gr 8/69)

683. *Missa L'Homme armé;* a composite, with the Proper for the Common of
Doctors of the Church, and instrumental interludes. The Columbia
University Collegium Musicum; R. Taruskin, dir.
                              Collegium Stereo JE 109/110
[L'homme armé - DEPRES. Asperges me - BINCHOIS. Introit,
Sacerdotes ejus induant - ISAAC. L'homme armé - ANON (set by
MORTON). Kyrie - BERTRAND VAQUERAS. Gloria - FAUGUES.
Gradual, Os justi - DUFAY (attr.). Alleluia, Inveni David - ISAAC.
Sequence, Ad laudes salvatoris - ISAAC. Il est de bone heure ne /
L'homme armé - JAPART (instr). Credo - DUFAY. Offertory, Veritas
mea - DUFAY (attr.). D'ung altre amer / L'homme armé - BASIRON.
Sanctus - DE ORTO. Agnus Dei - BASIRON. Communion, Domine
quinque talenta - ISAAC. Ite missa est - ANON. (Trent 88).]   (adv)

684. *Missa Salve.* Ambrosian Singers; D. Stevens, cond.   Dover HCR 5263
[An anonymous 13th-century English mass from the edition of L.
Dittmer of the Worcester Fragments, 1957. Verso is Missa De Sancta
Maria, an anonymous 13th-century mass from El Codex de las Huelgas,
1931. Pieces from each Ms. have been selected by Denis Stevens to form
the masses.]

685. *Missa Tournai - Motets, ca.1320.* Capella Antiqua of Munich; Konrad
Ruhland, cond.   Telefunken SAWT 9517 A
[Missa Tournai (Kyrie, Gloria, Credo, Sanctus-Benedictus, Agnus Dei,
Ite missa est). Motets: Ad solitum / tenor: Regnat (from Wolfenbüttel,
W2); Ad solitum / Ad solitum / tenor: Regnat (from W2); Ave Regina /
Alma redemptoris / tenor: Alma (Montpellier); Condicio nature / O
nacio / tenor: Mane prima sabbati (from Roman de Fauvel); Depositum /
Ad solitum / tenor: Regnat (from Bamberg Codex). Also works by
PHILIPPE de VITRY, q.v., in Part II.]

686. *El Misterio de Elche.* Capilla del Misterio de Elche; Dolores Perez (sop);
Gines Roman, cond.   Musical Heritage Society MHS 729/730
Act I
[ANON. (in order of performance): Germanes míes; !Ay, trista vida
corporal! Gran desig me a vengut al cór; Deu vos salve Verge imperial;
Saluts, honor e salvament; O Apostols e germans meus; Verge humil, flor
de honor; O poder del alt imperi (Ternario); Salve Regina princessa; O
cós sanct glorificat; Espons e Mare de Deu.
Act II
Par nos germans devem anar; A vosaltres venim pregar; Preneu vos Joan
la palma pretiosa; Flor de virginal bellessa; Aquesta gran novetat; O deu
Adonay; Promens Jueus si tots creeu; Nosaltres tots creem; In éxitu
Israel d'Egipto; Ans d'entrar en sepultura; O besfort desaventura; Vos
siau ben arribada; Gloria Patri et Filio.]

687. *Mittelalterliche Musik.* Capella Antiqua, München; K. Ruhland, cond.
Nonesuch H 71171 (Voices of the Middle Ages)
and Christophorus SCGLP 75891
[ADAM DE ANTIQUIS VENETUS. Senza te. DUFAY. Alma redemptoris; Hymnus in adventu Domini; Magnificat 8. toni; Spiritus Domini
replevit; Veni Creator Spiritus. RESINARIUS. Komm, Gott Schöpfer.
ANON. Alleluja; Ave virgo virginum; Brumans est mors; Dies est
laetitiae; Fulgent nunc; Gaudens in Domino; Komm, Heiliger Geist; O
Maria, maris Stella; O miranda dei karitas; Sei willekommen; Herre
Christ; Der Tag, der ist so freudenreich; Veni, Sancte Spiritus; Veni
virgo beatissima.]   (biel 2/67)

Mittelalterliche vokale Musik (Muza SXL 0294). See *U Zrodel Muzyki
Polskiej* (No.890).

688. *Monteverdi and His Contemporaries.* Ambrosian Consort; D. Stevens,
dir.   Guide International du Disque SMS 2580
[GASTOLDI. Vezzosette ninfe. GESUALDO. Luci serene e chiare.
MONTEVERDI. Ch'io t'ami; Io ardo; Luci serene e chiare; Ohimè, il
bel viso; O primavera; Sfogava con le stelle; Zefiro torna. STRIGGIO.
Il gioco di primiera. WERT. Vezzosi augelli.]

689. *Monumentos Históricos de la Música Española, v.1: La Música en la
Corte de Los Reyes Catolicos.* Ars Musicae, Barcelona; Enrique Gispert
cond.   Discoteca Educative Nacional, Madrid, 1001
(a series by subscription only)
[ENCINA. Es la causa bien amar; Más vale trocar; Pues que jamás
olvidaros; Quédate, Carrillo; Revelóse mi cuidado; Romerico, tu que
vienes; Qué es de tí, desconsolado? Todos los bienes del mundo.
ESCOBAR. Las mis penas, madre. LOPE DE BAENA. Todo cuanto y
serví. GABRIEL. Sola me dexaste. MILAN. Temeroso de sufrir.
MILARTE. Todos van de Amor Heridos. PENALOSA. El triste que

nunca os vío; Per las sierras de Madrid. PONCE. Allá se me ponga el sol.
ANON. Dentro en el vergel; Dindirindín.]

690. *Morley Canzonets and Music from the Fitzwilliam Virginal Book.*
V. Aveling (hpsi); Ambrosian Consort; D. Stevens, cond.

Penn State PSMS 101; 101S

[BULL. Piper's galliard. BYRD. Galiarda; Queen's alman; La volta.
FARNABY. Tell me, Daphne; Tower Hill. MORLEY. Adieu, you kind
and cruel; Ay me, the fatal arrow; Cruel, wilt thou persevere; False love
did me inveigle; Love took his bow and arrow; My nymph the deer; Lo,
where with flowery head; O grief; Our bonny-boots. PEERSON. Fall
of the leaf; The primerose. PHILIPS. Galiarda dolorosa.]   (sch 7/66)

691. *Motets.* King's College Chapel Choir; D. Willcocks, cond.

H.M.V. ALP 2111

[BYRD. Hodie beata virgo. DERING. Quem vidistes pastores.
GIBBONS. Hosanna to the Son of David; Gloria in excelsis Deo.
PALESTRINA. Hodie Christus natus est. SWELINCK. Hodie Christus
natus est. VICTORIA. O magnum mysterium. Also Händel and others.]
(gram 2/69)

692. *Motets from the 16th and 17th Centuries.* Harvard Glee Club; E. Forbes,
cond.   Carillon 124

[DEPRES. Missa Mater Patris et Filia. (motets): BRUMEL. Mater Patris
et Filia. CLEMENT. Adoramus te. HASSLER. Domine Deus; Laetentur
coeli. PALESTRINA. Supplicationes. Also Allegri.]

693. *Motets, Madrigals, Chansons.* Riverside Chamber Singers.

Music Guild M 20; S 20

[ARCADELT. S'infinita bellezza. BENNET. Weep, o mine eyes.
COSTELEY. Mignonne, allon voir si la rose. DERING. Quem vidistis
pastores? FARMER. Fair Phyllis I saw. A. GABRIELI. Ecco l'aurora
con l'aurata fronte. GASTOLDI. Tutti venite armati. JANEQUIN.
Petite nymphe folastre. LASSUS. Bon jour mon coeur. LEJEUNE.
Revecy venir du printans. LUZZASCHI. Quivi sospiri pianti. MONTE-
VERDI. Ecco mormorar l'onde. MORLEY. Fire, fire, my heart; Though
Philomela lost her love. PILKINGTON. Rest, sweet nymphs.
VICTORIA. O vos omnes. WEELKES. Hosanna to the Son of David.
Also Schütz and Debussy.]   (Myers 6/63)

694. *Motetten alter Meister.* Dresdner Kreuzchor; R. Mauersberger, dir.

Eurodisc 80274

[ANERIO. Christus resurgens. ECCARD. Zu dieser österlichen Zeit.
G. GABRIELI. Jubilate Deo. HANDL. Ecce quomodo moritur justus;
Pater Noster; Duo Seraphim. HASSLER. Cantate Domino canticum
novum. SWELINCK. Hodie Christus natus est; Venite exultemus
Domino. Also Schein, Durante, Homilius, and others.]   (biel 2/70)

695. *Motetten alter Meister.* Der Tölzer Knabenchor; Instrumental ensemble;
Gerhard Schmidt, dir.   Harmonia Mundi HM 30154 L; HMS 30803
[BODENSCHATZ. Joseph, lieber Joseph mein. ECCARD. Ich steh an
deiner Krippe hier. HANDL. Omnes de Saba venient. LASSUS. Angelus
ad pastores ait; Resonet in laudibus. Also arranged Christmas carols.
And Scheidt.]   (biel 2/70)

696. *Il Mottetto.* Coro Vallicelliano; Padre Sartori, cond.
                                          Italian Victor ML 20207
[AICHINGER. Regina Coeli. ANERIO. O salutaris hostia. DEPRES.
Ave verum. INGEGNERI. Ecce quomodo moritur. PALESTRINA.
Hodie Christus; Laudate Dominum; Popule meus; Super flumina
Babylonis. VICTORIA. Animam meam; Caligaverunt; Gloria, Sanctus,
Benedictus. Also A. Scarlatti.]

Music at Hampton Court. See *Music of the Court Homes and Cities of
England, v.2* (No.728).

697. *Music at Notre Dame in Paris.* Deller Consort.
                  Harmonia Mundi HMS 30823 and Angelicum LPA 5951
[PEROTINUS. Sederunt principes; Viderunt omnes - Alleluia nativitas.
ANON. Alleluja Christus resurgens (with clausula 'Mors'); Dic Christi
veritas; Pater noster commiserans (conductus).]
N.B.: Combined issue on 12" of material on HM 25143 and HM 25147,
both 10" records. Both were in original list (No.370) with different
issue numbers, q.v.

 # 407 ?

698. *Music at Notre Dame in Paris.* Deller Consort.
                                          Harmonia Mundi HM 30898
[MACHAUT. Missa de Notre Dame. PEROTINUS. Sederunt principes.
ANON. Dic Christi veritas; Pater noster commiserans.]   (biel 2/70)

699. *Music at the Burgundian Court.* Pro Musica Antiqua, Brussels; S. Cape,
dir.   Bach Guild BG 634 and Amadeo AVRS 5028
[BINCHOIS. Adieu, adieu, mon joieulx souvenir; Agnus Dei; Amoreux
suy; Amours merchi; De plus en plus; Filles à marier; Beata nobis gaudia;
Je loe amours; Triste plaisir. DUFAY. He! Compaignons; J'atendray
tant qu'il vous playra; Veni sancte Spiritus; Missa Se la face ay pale
(Hosanna). LANTINS. Puisque je voy, belle. MORTON. N'arraige
jamais mieulx. OBRECHT. Tsat een meskin. OCKEGHEM. D'un autre
amer cueur s'abesseroit? ANON. Dit le Bourguynon.]   (sch 12/62)

Music at the Court of King Henry VIII. See *Music of the Renaissance
and Baroque* (No.739).

Music at the Royal Castle in Warsaw. See *Muzyka na zamku Warszawskim*
(No.781).

700. *Music Dedicated to the Virgin Mary.* The Columbia University Collegium
Musicum; R. Taruskin, dir.   Collegium Stereo JE 102/103
[BRUMEL. Missa de Beata Virgine (Gloria). COMPERE. Omnium bonorum;

Virgo mites (Missa Galeazescha). DEPRES. Missa de Beata Virgine (Credo);
Missa Gaudeamus (Kyrie); Virgo prudentissima. DUFAY. Ave Maris Stella.
ISAAC. Alleluia, Assumpta est Maria; Gaudeamus omnes; O decus ecclesiae
virgo. LA RUE. Deo Gratias; Ite missa est; Missa Ave Sanctissima Maria
(Agnus Dei). OBRECHT. Missa Salve Diva Parens (Sanctus). OCKEGHEM.
Intemerata dei mater. SENFL. Ave Maria (after Depres). ANON.
Communio, Dilexisti justitiam; Magnificat quinti toni (Trent 89).] (adv)

701. *Music for Brass Quintet.* American Brass Quintet.   Folkways FM 3651
[DEPRES. Vive le roi. EAST. Desperavi. G. GABRIELI. Canzona "La
spiritata." HOLBORNE. The Fairie round; The Honie-suckle; My Linda;
The night watch; Pavana ploravit; Wanton. Also Bach, Kay, Whittenberg.]

702. *Music for Guitar from the Spanish Renaissance and Rococo.* Brigitte
Zaczek (guit).   Musical Heritage Society MHS 991
[MILAN. Fantasia de Consonicias y redobles; 5 Pavannes; Fantasia
MUDARRA. Diferencias sobre il conde claros; Fantasia; Gallarda.
NARVAEZ. Baxa de Contra Ponto; Conciòn del Emperador; Diferencias
sobre Guardáme las vacas. Also Sanz and D. Scarlatti.]

Music for Henry VIII and His Court. See *To Entertain a King* (No.877).

703. *Music for Holy Week.* Ambrosian Singers; J. McCarthy, cond.
                              Everest 3256 and Delysé ECB 3200; DS 3200
[ANERIO. Christus factus est. BYRD. Haec dies; Lamentationes.
DEERING. O vos omnes. GESUALDO. In Monte Oliveti; Jesum
tradidit. HANDL. Ecce quomodo. JOHN (JOÃO) IV. Crux fidelis.
PALESTRINA. Improperia; Pueri Hebraeorum portantes. VICTORIA.
Caligaverunt oculi mei; Pueri Hebraeorum vestimenta; Tenebrae factae
sunt. ANON. (chant): Hosanna filio David.]

Music for Maximilian. See *Musik in alten Städten und Residenzen:
Innsbruck* (No.765).

704. *Music for Passiontide.* Guildford Cathedral Choir; Gavin Williams (org);
Barry Rose, cond.   Guild GRM 7001; GRS 7001
[BYRD. Lord, hear my prayer; Miserere mei. GIBBONS. Drop, drop
slow tears. MORLEY. Out of the deep. Also Bach and Allegri.] (gr 4/69)

705. *Music for the Common of Apostles.* Renaissance Singers; Michael
Howard, cond.   Argo R 186; ZRG 5186
[Hymnus Aeterna Christi Munera; Vos qui reliquistis omnia (antiphon);
Benedictus (with organ verses by Titelouze). Verso: PALESTRINA,
q.v. in Part II.]

706. *Music for the Kings and Queens of England.* Choir of the Chapel Royal of
St. Peter ad Vincula within the Tower of London; A. Davis (org and hpsi);
M. Goosens (harp); Philip Jones Brass Ensemble; members of the Hurwitz
Chamber Ensemble; J. Williams, cond.   RCA International INTS 1115
[BYRD. O Lord, make thy servant Elizabeth the Queen. GIBBONS.
Hosanna to the Son of David. HENRY VIII. Pastime with good company.

706. *Music for the Kings and Queens of England.* (Continued)
TALLIS. O Sacrum Convivium. WEELKES. O Lord, grant the king a
long life. ANON. Greensleeves. Also Blow, Locke, S. S. Wesley, Prince
Albert, Purcell and Langford.]   (gram 1/71)

707. *Music for the Lute; The Art of Suzanne Bloch.*   Vox 1240; 501240
[ADAM DE LA HALLE. Dieux soit. ALFONSO EL SABIO. 5 Cantigas
de Santa Maria. BIANCHINI. Tant que vivray. BULL. The Spanish pavan.
DALZA. Calata Spagnola. FUENLLANA. Duo de Josquin. GIBBONS.
The woods so wilde. LA HAYE. Orchésographie; Hexachord (Byrd).
MILAN. Fantasia. MOULINIE. Air à boire. MUNDY. Fantasia.
PEROTINUS. Beata viscera. ROBINSON. Spanish pavan. SACHS.
Klingende Ton. SERMISY. Tant que vivray. SPINACCINO. Ricercare.
ANON. Alle, psalite, alleluya (Montpellier); Branle (Thesaurus
Harmonicus); Bryng us in goode ale; Now wolde y fair; Nowell, nowell;
Why aske you.]   (sch 11/65)

708. *Music for the Virginals.* S. Robb (virg).   Folkways FM 3321
[AMMERBACH. Passamezzo; Passamezzo d'Angleterre. ASTON. Horne-
pype. ATTAINGNANT. Basse danse; Galliarde. BULL. Courante: Jewel;
Pavana; St. Thomas wake. GIBBONS. The Lord of Salisbury His pavin.
MILAN. 2 pavanas. ANON. Bassa imperiale; Prelude; Saltarello. Also
Bach, Bendusi, Frescobaldi, and others.]   (Myers 9/64)

709. *Music for Twelfth Night.* Renaissance Quartet.   Project 3 (S) 7000
[CORNYSH. A robyn, gentil robyn. CUTTING. A jig. DUFAY. Bon
jour, bon mois; Craindre vous vueil; Festun nunc celebre; Vergine bella.
GUERRERO. Que buen año. HOLBORNE. The night watch. JONES.
Farewell, dear love. MORLEY. Though Philomela lost her love; O
mistress mine. PRAETORIUS. Es ist ein' Ros'. PYGOTT. Quid petis o
fili. RAVENSCROFT. Remember, O thou man. WALTHER. Nun freut
euch. WEELKES. The nightingale. ANON. E la don don; Hayl, Mary,
full of grace; Verbum caro factum est; Clangat tuba; Witches dance.]   (sch)

710. *Music for Vihuela and Guitar.* Renata Tarragó.
                                                      DGA Archive SAPM 198457
[DEPRES. Cancion I, del Emperador; Mille regretz. FUENLLANA.
Fantasia. MILAN. Pavana no.3; Pavana no.5. MUDARRA. Pavana
primera; Gallarda. NARVAEZ. Siete diferencias sobre el tema
Guardáme las vacas. VALDERRÁBANO. Fantasia 28. Also Sor, Sanz,
and others.]   (gr)

711. *Music for Voices and Viols in the Time of Shakespeare.* Elizabethan
Consort of Viols; Pugh (hpsi); Leeb (lute); Golden Age Singers; Field-
Hyde, cond.   Westminster 19076; 17076
[BYRD. The Earl of Salisbury (pavan and galliard). CORNYSH. A
robyn, gentle robyn. DEERING. The cryes of London. DOWLAND.
My Lady Hunsdon's puffe. EDWARDS. Where gryping grief. FERRA-
BOSCO. I saw my lady weeping & Vias tuas. JOHNSON. Carman's

whistle. JONES. Farewell, dear love. MORLEY. About the maypole;
It was a lover and his lass; My bonnie lass she smileth; Now is the month
of Maying. MUNDY. My Robbin. WEELKES. As Vesta was from
Latmos Hill. WILBYE. I love alas yet am not loved; The Lady Oriana.
ANON. Greensleeves; Hold thy peace (canon); Sick tune.] (Myers 3/69)

712. *Music from the Chapel of Charles V.* Roger Blanchard Vocal Ensemble;
Pierre Froidebise (org).   Nonesuch H 1051; 71051
[CRECQUILLON. Caesaris auspiciis magni; Erravi sicut ovis; Salve crux
sancta. GOMBERT. Mass Je suis desheritée. SCHLICK. Hommage à
l'empereur Charles-quint; Maria zart.]

713. *Music from the Chapel of Philip II of Spain.* Roger Blanchard Vocal
Ensemble; Pierre Froidebise (org).   Nonesuch H 1016; 71016
[CABEZÓN. D'où vient cela; Pavane; Variations sur le Chant du
Chevalier. MORALES. Ave Maria; Lamentabatur Jacob; Magnificat
septimi toni; Missus est Gabriel. MUDARRA. Israel; Psalmo II por el
primo tono; Triste estaba el Rey David. VICTORIA. Laetatus sum
(Ps.121).] (Myers 6/66)

714. *Music from the Court and Chapel of Henry VIII.* Société de la Chorale
Bach de Montréal; G. Little, dir.   Vox DL 950; STDL 500950
[BLITHEMAN. Eterno rerum conditor (org, Mulliner Book).
CORNYSHE. Pleasure it is; Trolly lolly lo. FAYRFAX. O Lux Beata
Trinitas (motet). HENRY VIII. Green grow'th the holly; Pastime with
good company. REDFORD. Jam lucis orto sidere; Salvatore (with a
meane); Sermone blando angelus (org, Mulliner Book); Rejoice in the
Lord alway (anthem). SMERT. In Die Nativitatis; Nowelle - Who ys
there that syngith so. TALLIS. Magnificat; Nunc Dimittis; O Nata Lux
de Lumine; This is my commandment. TAVERNER. Christe Jesu, Pastor
bone; In nomine. TYE. I will exalt Thee, O Lord; O God, be merciful;
Praise ye the Lord, ye children. R. WHITE. In nomine. ANON. Boar's
head carol; My Lady Carey's dompe (instr); O Lord, the Maker of all
things.]

715. *Music from the Court of Burgundy.* Roger Blanchard Vocal and
Instrumental Ensemble; R. Blanchard, cond; Pierre Poulteau Recorder
Trio.   Nonesuch H 1058; 71058
[BINCHOIS. Files à marier; Je loe amours; Magnificat primi toni.
BUSNOIS. Bel Acueil; In hydraulis. DUFAY. Lamentatio sanctae
matris Ecclesiae Constantinopolitanae; Vergine bella. FONTAINE.
Pastourelle en un vergier. GHIZEGHEM. Allez regretz. GRENON. La
plus belle et doulce figure. MORTON. La Perontina. MUREAU. Grace
attendant. ANON. J'ay prins amour a ma devise.]

Music from the Court of Mantua. See under WERT in Part II (Vanguard
VCS 10083).

716. *Music from the Courts of Spain.* Celedonio Romero (guit).
　　　　　　　　　　　　　　　　　　　　　　Mercury 50296; 90296
[DOWLAND. King of Denmark's galliard. GALILEI. Suite of 6 dances.
MILAN. 3 pavanas. NARVAEZ. Diferencias sobre Guárdame las Vacas.
Also Visée, Bach, Rameau, Sanz.] (sch 10/63)

717. *Music from the 100 Years War.* Musica Reservata; Beckett, dir.
　　　　　　　　　　　　　　　Philips 839753 and SAL 3722 (Eng.)
[ACOURT. Je demande ma bienvenue. ALANUS. Sub arcturo plebs.
COOKE. Alma prolez. DUFAY. Donnés l'assault; Franc cuer gentil;
Magnes me gentes; Se la face ay pale. FONTAINE. J'ayme bien celui.
MACHAUT. Plange, regni respublica. SOLAGE. S'aincy estoit.
VAILLANT. Par maintes foys. ANON. Anglia tibi turbidas; Blance
flour; Deo gracias, Anglia; Deus tuorum militum; Estampie; L'homme
armé; Mutato modo geniture; Patrie pacis; Tappster, fyll another ale;
Tuba gallicalis.] (gr 12/69)

718. *Music from the Middle Ages and Renaissance; Mediaeval and Renaissance
Andalusian Songs.* Victoria de los Angeles; Barcelona Ars Musicae;
Enrique Gispert, dir.　　　　Angel S 36468 and H.M.V. SAN 194
[ALFONSO EL SABIO. Rosa das rosas; Maravillosos e piadosos.
GUERRERO. Dexó la venda. MORALES. Si no's huviera mirado.
MORATA. Aquí me declaró. MUDARRA. Díme a do tienes. NARVAEZ.
Paseábase el rey moro. ORTEGA. Pues que me tienes Miguel. TORRE.
Damos gracias a ti. ANON. Sobre Baça estaba el rey; Ay! que non hay!
Tres moriscas; Puse mis amores. TRADITIONAL SEPHARDIC. Ah, el
novio no quiere dinero; Como la rosa; Estava la mora; Aquel rey de
Francia.]

719. *Music from the Time of Boccaccio's Decameron.* Musica Reservata; John
Beckett, cond.　　　　　Philips 802904 and SAL 3781 (Eng.)
[GHIRARDELLO DA FIRENZE. Tosto che l'alba. GIOVANNI DA
FIRENZE. O tu chara scientia; Per larghi prati. LANDINO. Chosi
pensoso; Gram piant'agli occhi; Musicha son; Non avrà ma' pietà;
Questa fanciull', amor; Se la rimica mie. ANON. Ghaetta; In pro;
Lamento di Tristano; Non avrà ma' pietà; Questa fanciull', amor;
Saltarello; Tre fontane.] (gr 4/70)

720. *Music from the Time of Christopher Columbus.* Musica Reservata; John
Beckett, cond.　　　　　Philips SAL 3697; 839714 LY
[CABEZÓN. Diferencias sobre Las Vacas; Pavana (La Gamba) con su
glosa; Sobre el canto llano de La Alta. CAVALLOS. Amargas oras.
ENCINA. Cucú, cucú, cucucú; Triste España sin ventura. GARCIA
MUNOS. Una montaña pasando. JUAN FERNANDEZ DE MADRID.
Pues que Dios. MILAN. Durandarte. MUDARRA. Triste estaba el rey
David. TORRE. Danza alta. ANON. Calabaca, no sé, buen amor; Dale, si
le das; Dizen a mi; Está la reyna del cielo; La gamba; Pasa el agoa, ma
Julieta.]

Music in Catalonia until the 14th Century. See *Anthologie de la musique médiévale espagnole, v.3* (No.457).

Music in Honor of Queen Elizabeth. See *The Cries of London* (No.512).

721. *Music in Medieval and Renaissance Life.* Collegium Musicum of the University of Missouri; Andrew Minor, cond.
University of Missouri Press UMPR 1001
[BARTLET. Of all the birds that I do know; A prety ducke there was. CARA. Non e tempo (frottola). DUFAY. Conditor alme siderum (hymn). GERVAISE. Pavane d'Angleterre avec sa Gaillarde. HANDL. Hodie Christus natus est (motet). ISAAC. Hora e di Maggio. MOUTON. In illo tempore Maria Magdalene (motet); La rouse du moys de may. MUSET. Quand je voi yver retorner. PADOVANO. Aria della Battaglia per sonar d'istrumenti da fiato a 8. PIERS. He, Trola, there boys are. SENFL. Das Gläut zu Speyer. WEELKES. The ape, the money, and baboon. ANON. La Ballete de la Reine d'Avril; Estampie; Gaite de la tor; Nota; Prima chiamata di Guerra; Seconda chiamata, che va sonata avanti la Battaglia; The strake to the fields; Tappster, Dryngker, fylle another ale; The uncoupling of the coverte side.]

Music in Old Cities and Residences. See *Musik in alten Städten und Residenzen* (Nos.764-768).

722. *Music in Shakespeare's England.* Krainis Consort.
Mercury MG 50397; SR 90397
[BYRD. 2 Fantasias à 3. CAMPIAN. Never weather-beaten sail. GIBBONS. 2 Fantasias. HUME. Life, touch me lightly. JOHNSON. La Vecheo gallyerde. LUPO. Fantasia à 3. MORLEY. Il doloroso; La Girandola; It was a lover and his lass; Mine own sweet jewel. ANON. Daphne; Fortune, my foe; Heartsease; The King's morisco; Miserere, my maker; My Lady Carey's dompe; My Robbin; Tickle my toe; A toy; La Volta; Willow, willow.]

Music in the Aachen Cathedral. See *Musik im Dom zu Aachen* (No.762).

Music in the Basilica of St. Marks in Venice. See *Musique en la Basilique Saint-Marc de Venise* (No.774).

Music in the Castle Blois. See *Concerts pour deux princes au château de Blois* (No.509).

723. *Music of Eastern Europe.* The Columbia University Collegium Musicum; R. Taruskin, dir.
Collegium Stereo JE 106/107
[CARON. Ave sidus clarissimum. HANDL. St. John Passion. HAUSMANN. 3 Polish dances. MIKOLAJ Z RADOMIA. Gloria. PICCHI. Ballo Ongaro. SCHIAVETTO. Pater noster. STOLTZER. Erzürne dich nicht über die Bösen. ZIELINSKI. Ave Maria. ANON. (from the Glogauer Liederbuch): Bonum vinum; Carmen (instr); Christ ist erstanden; Entrepis (instr); Iteitas; Jaegerhorn (instr); Natter schwancz

723. *Music of Eastern Europe.* (Continued)
(instr); Sempiterna; Swatheo Martina (instr). ANON. (from the Chapel
of Peter the Great): Blazhenna pervovo glasa; Budyi imya gospodnye;
Gospodu Iisusu; Mnogoletstvovaniye. ANON. Cracowia civitas; Heyduck;
Heyduczky (Jan of Lublin Tablature); Kosakenballett; New song of
victory at Byczyna.] (adv)

724. *Music of Medieval France (1200-1400).* Deller Consort; A. Deller, cond;
Concentus Musicus, Vienna; Ensemble of ancient instruments; N.
Harnoncourt, cond.   Bach Guild BG 656; BGS 70656
[GRIMACE. Alarme, alarme. MACHAUT. Comment qu'ay moy; S'il
estoit. PEROTINUS. Alleluja Nativitas. PERUSIO. Andray soulet; Ne
me chant. SOLAGE. Helas je voy; Pluseurs gens voy. VAILLANT. Par
maintes foy. ANON. Alleluja Christus resurgens; Amor potest conqueri;
Dic Christi veritas; Hoquetus "in seculum"; In seculum d'Amiens longum;
La Manfredina; El mois de mai; Or sus vous dormez trop; Pater noster
commiserans.]

725. *Music of Shakespeare's Time.* Dolmetsch Consort; Schola Cantorum
Basiliensis Viols; Eileen Poulter (sop); Wilfred Brown (tnr).
            2-Nonesuch 3010; 73010 and H.M.V. CLP 1633/4; CSD 1487/8
[BARTLETT. Whither runneth my sweetheart? BRADE. Almain;
Coranto. BYRD. O mistress mine; Sellenger's rounde; La volta.
CAMPION. Never weather-beaten sail. CORKINE. Sweet, let me go.
CORNYSHE. Ah Robin, gentle Robin. DOWLAND. Captain Digorie
Piper's galliard; Come heavy sleep; Lachrimae antiquae; Mr. George
Whitehead's almand. FERRABOSCO. O eyes; O mortal stars.
HOLBORNE. Galliard (the Sighs); Pavan Paradiso; Pavan the Marigold.
HUME. Fain would I change that note. J. JOHNSON. Lavecheo, pavan
and galliard. R. JOHNSON. Full fathom five; Where the bee sucks.
JONES. Sweet Kate. LASSUS. Mouncier Mingo. MORLEY. Frog
galliard; O grief even on the bud. ROBINSON. A toy. TOMKINS.
Fusca, in thy starry eyes. WEELKES. Hark all ye lovely saints.
WHYTHORNE. Buy new broom. WILBYE. Weep, weep mine eyes.
ANON. Coranto; Daphne; Fortune my foe; Greensleeves; Holly berry;
Lord Zouche's masque; Master Newman's pavan; My true love hath my
heart; Nobody's jig; Sweet was the song the Virgin sang; A toy; Willow
song.] (sch 12/66)

726. *Music of the Ars Nova.* The Columbia University Collegium Musicum; R.
Taruskin, dir.   Collegium Stereo JE 101
Side 1
[MATHEUS DE PERUSIO. Andray soulet; Pres du soloil. ISAAC. Es
wolt eyn Maydleyn grasen gan; Der Hundt; J'ay pris amours; La Morra;
La my la sol.
Side II
A composite 14th-century mass: Kyrie - GUYMONT (Apt Ms.); Gloria -
ANON. (Torino Ms.); Credo - ANON. (Torino Ms.); Sanctus - ANON.

(Ivrea); Agnus Dei - ANON. (Barcelona C); Ite missa est - MACHAUT.]
(adv)

727. *Music of the Court Homes and Cities of England.*
v.1: Composers of the Chapel Royal. Various groups and soloists; R.
Leppard, cond; Martindale Sidwell, cond.   H.M.V. HQS 1140
[BULL. St. Thomas wake. FAYRFAX. Somewhat musing. GIBBONS.
This is the record of John; The silver swan. MORLEY. Out of the deep.
PARSONS. Pandolpho. TALLIS. Gloria tibi trinitatis (antiphon); Like
as the doleful dove. Also Purcell, Locke and Humfrey.]

728. *v.2: Music at Hampton Court.* Musica Reservata; Ely Consort; Jaye
Consort. Conductors: Michael Morrow; R. Leppard; Francis Baines;
Ian Harwood, and others.   H.M.V. HQS 1141
[ALBARTE. Pavan and galliard. BAXTER. Sacred galliard. BYRD. Ye
sacred muses. CORNYSHE. Fa la sol. DOWLAND. Love stood amazed.
HAYLES. O eyes leave off your weeping. HENRY VIII. Consort II.
MERBECKE. A virgin and mother. MORLEY. Sacred end pavan.
ANON. Bransle. Also Purcell.]

729. *v.3: Composers of Whitehall Palace and Wilton House.* Various artists.
                                                      H.M.V. HQS 1146
[CONVERSI-MORLEY. Sola soletta. DEERING. Gaudent in coelis.
DOWLAND. The Right Honourable Lady Rich, her galliard. FERRA-
BOSCO. Fair cruel nymph. HOLBORNE. Countess of Pembroke's
paradise. MORLEY. Do you not know; Who is it that this dark night?
TESSIER. In a grove. TOMKINS. A sad pavan for these distracted
times. ANON. Sir Philip Sydney's lamentation. Also Lawes and
Laniere.]   (gr 6/68)

730. *v.4: Composers of Greenwich House and Ingatestone House.* April
Cantelo (sop); Helen Watts (cont); Sybil Michelow (cont); Gerald
English (tnr); Christopher Keyte (bass); R. Leppard, cond; Jaye Consort
of Viols; C. Bishop, cond; E. Müller-Domboise (lute), and others.
                                                      H.M.V. HQS 1147
[BYRD. Browning; Hey ho to the greenwood; Lullaby, my sweet little
baby; The nightingale so pleasant is; Pavana Bray; Susanna fair; This day
Christ was born; Victimae Paschalis. CAMPION. Shall I come sweet love.
COPERARIO. Suite. FARNABY. Almande. FERRABOSCO II. Four
note pavan. GIBBONS. The silver swan. JOHNSON. As I walked forth;
Allemayne; Witty wanton.]   (gr 6/68)

731. *v.5: Composers of Hatfield House and Hengrave.* April Cantelo, Eileen
Poulter (sop); Helen Watts (cont); Gerald English (tnr); Christopher
Keyte (bass); R. Leppard, cond; Jaye Consort; C. Bishop, cond; E.
Müller-Domboise (lute), and others.   H.M.V. HQS 1151
[BYRD. Queens alman. EDWARDS. Where griping grief. FERRABOSCO
I. Lady if you so spite me; Pavin. HENRY VIII. Pastime with good

731. *Music of the Court Homes and Cities of England.* (Continued)
v.5: Composers of Hatfield House and Hengrave. (Continued)
company. JOHNSON. Allmaine. MORLEY. Now is the month of
Maying; Sing we and chant it. TALLIS. Psalm tune no.3. WILBYE.
Draw on sweet night; Fantasia; Ne reminiscaris; Oft have I vowed; O
God the Rock; Sweet honeysucking bees; Unkind stay thy flying.
ANON. Fortune my foe.]   (gr 7/68)

732. *v.6: Composers of Chichester and Worcester.* Various artists.
H.M.V. HQS 1158
[TOMKINS. In nomine for 3 viols; Love cease lamenting; My beloved
spake; Oyez! has any found a lad; Pavan for five viols; When David
heard; Worcester brawls. WEELKES. All people clap; Alleluia; Cease
sorrows now; Lady, the birds right fairly; Lord to Thee I make my
moan; O how amiable; Pavan no.3; Thule, the period of cosmography.]
(gr 8/68)

Music of the Early Middle Ages (Stevens). See *History of European
Music, Part I* (No.615).

733. *Music of the Early Renaissance; John Dunstable and His Contemporaries.*
The Purcell Consort of Voices; Grayston Burgess, cond; Musica
Reservata (instr ensemble).   Turnabout TV 4058; 34058
[ADNEMAR. Salve Regina, Mater Misericordiae (plainsong). DUFAY.
Ave Regina coelorum (motet); Franc cuer gentil. DUNSTABLE. Ave
maris stella (hymn); O rosa bella; Quam pulchra es (motet); Veni sancte
spiritus / Veni creator (isor. motet). FRYE. Ave regina coelorum (motet).
HERMANNUS CONTRACTUS. Alma redemptoris mater (plainsong).
LANTINS. In tua memoria (motet). ANON. Deo gratias Anglia (Agincourt carol); Filles à marier; Reges Tharsis (plainsong); Sing we to this
merry company; La Spagna (basse dance); La Spagna (another basse
dance).]

734. *Music of the High Renaissance in England.* The Purcell Consort of
Voices; Jaye Consort of Viols; Grayston Burgess, cond.
Turnabout TV 4017; 34017 and Vox STV 34017 (Ger.)
[BULL. In nomine; Prelude. BYRD. The Earle of Salisbury pavan; In
nomine à 5; O Lord, how vain; Elegy on the death of Thomas Tallis:
Ye sacred muses. FERRABOSCO. Pavan. GIBBONS. Great Lord of
Lords; Lord Salisbury's pavan; O God, the king of glory. MORLEY.
Hard by a crystal fountain. TOMKINS. The Lady Folliott's galliard;
WEELKES. As Vesta was descending.]

Music of the Hundred Years War. See *Music from the 100 Years War*
(No.717).

Music of the Medieval Age. See *Medieval and Renaissance Music for the
Irish and Medieval Harps, Vièle, Recorders and Tambourin* (No.672).

735. *Music of the Middle Ages, v. 7: The French Ars Antiqua (13th Century)*.
Oberlin (c-tnr); Bressler (tnr); Myers (bar); Price (tnr); Blackman (viol).
Experiences Anonymes 35
[PEROTINUS. Salvatoris hodie (conductus). ANON. (from the
Montpellier Ms.): Deus in Adiutorium (1); Dame qui j'aim et desir /
Amors vaint tot / Au tans d'esté que cil oisel / Et gaudebit (23); Li doz
maus m'ocit que j'ai / Trop ai lonc tens en folie / Ma loiautés m'a nuisi /
In seculum (28); Cest quadruble sans reison n'ai pas fet / Voz n'i
dormirés jamais / Biaus cuers renvoisiés / Fiat (30); Mors a primi patris
uicio / Mors, que stimulo nos urges / Mors morsu nata uenenato / Mors
(35); Povre secors ai encore recovré / Gaude, chorus omnium / Angelus
(39); Quant voi l'erbe reverdir et le tans / Salue, virgo virginum Dei
plena / C[umque evigilasset Iacob] (43); O natio que uitiis / Hodie
perlustravit (47); Desconfortés ai esté longuement / Amors, qui tant m'a
grevé / Et super (124); J'ai si bien mon cuer assiz / Aucun m'ont par
leur envie / Angelus (128); Ja n'amerai autre que cele que j'ai / Sire Dieus,
li doz maus m'ocit que j'ai / In seculum (137); Flor de lis, rose espanie /
Je ne puis, amie / Douce dame que j'aim tant (164); Blanchete comme
fleur de lis / Quant je pens a ma douce amie / Valare (168); Ne m'a pas
oublié / In seculum (207); J'ai mis toute ma pensée lonc tans / Je n'en
puis mais se je ne chant / Puerorum (255); Qui amours veut maintenir /
Li dous pensers / Cis a cui je sui amie (280); Salue, uirgo nobilis, Maria /
Verbum caro factum est / Verbum (284); Deus in adiutorium Intende
laborantium (303); On parole de batre et de vanner / A Paris soir et
matin / Frese nouvelle (319).]   (Myers 12/61)
N.B.: Volumes 1-6 of this series were included in original edition.

736. *Music of the Middle Ages and Renaissance.* Syntagma Musicum Ensemble;
Kees Otten, dir.   2-H.M.V. HQS 1195/6
N.B.: This disc contains almost the same repertoire as the Seraphim
Guide to Renaissance Music (SIC 6052, 3 discs), q.v., but includes Dalza's
Tastar de corde, which does not appear in the Guide. It lacks works by
Legrant, Paumann and several anonymous compositions which are in the
Guide. This set is also similar to the disc Cinq siècles de joyeuse musique
(VSM SME 191761/2), q.v.

737. *Music of the Pre-Baroque, from Josquin Des Pres to the End of the 16th
Century.* No performers indicated.   Lyrichord LL 109
[ATTAINGNANT. A court dance. BYRD. O magnum mysterium;
Fantasia à 6. BULL. Galiardo. DEPRES. Ave verum. FARNABY. Giles
Farnaby's dreame. GIBBONS. Hosanna to the Son of David; Earl of
Salisbury's pavan. LASSUS. In hora ultima. PALESTRINA. Super
flumina. SWELINCK. Hodie Christus natus est. TALLIS. O ye tender
babes. VICTORIA. O magnum mysterium. Also Lotti and Monteverdi.]

738. *Music of the Renaissance.* Vocal Arts Ensemble; Richard Levitt, cond.   Counterpoint 601; SD 5601
[BANCHIERI. Contrapunti bestiale; Nobili spettatori. BENNET. Weep, o mine eyes. CORNYSHE. A robyn. DEPRES. Ave Maria. LASSUS. Gallans qui par terre et mer; Je l'ayme ben; Mon coeur se recommande a vous. LEJEUNE. Revecy venir du printans. MONTEVERDI. Se nel partir da voi. MORLEY. I go before my darling; Miraculous love's wounding. OCKEGHEM. Missa Fors seulement; Fors seulement. VAUTOR. Mother I will have a husband. WEELKES. Hark all ye lovely saints above.]

Music of the Renaissance (Walther von der Vogelweide Chamber Choir).
See *Gesellschaftsmusik der Renaissance* (No.592).

739. *Music of the Renaissance and Baroque.* Trio Flauto Dolce; R. White (tnr).   Flauto Dolce TFD1
[CAMPION. Never weather-beaten saile. CORNYSHE. Adieu, mes amours; Blow thine horn, hunter. DOWLAND. Sorrow, stay. FEVIN. Fors seulement. GIBBONS. Fantasia (D major). HENRY VIII. Consort "no.5." MORLEY. O mistress mine. ANON. Have you seen but a whyte lillie grow?; Si fortune m'a si bien pourchassé. Also Boismortier, Campra, Lupo, Schütz.] (Myers 9/66)

740. *Music of the Renaissance and Baroque for Brass Quintet.* The American Brass Quintet.   Folkways FM 3652; 33652
[DOWLAND. 3 dances from Lachrimae antiquae. FINCK. Greiner Zanner. G. GABRIELI. Canzona prima a cinque. ISAAC. Der Hund; La mi la sol. SUSATO. Galliard mille Ducas; Pavane Si par soufrir; Ronde; Saltarelle Pour quoy. ANON. Die Bänkelsängerlieder sonata. Also Scheidt and Pezel.]

741. *Music of the Royal Courts of Europe, 1150-1600.* London Early Music Consort; D. Munrow, cond.   World Record Club ST 1108
[ADAM DE LA HALLE. Fines amouretes ai; Tan con je vivrai. ALONSO. La tricotea Samartin. CABEZON. Diferencias sobre La dama le demanda. CARA. Non e tempo (frottola). DUFAY. Vergine bella. ENCINA. Ay triste que vengo. ISAAC. Innsbruck, ich muss dich lassen. LEGRANT. Entre vous noviaux mariés. MUSET. Quant je voi yver retorner. ORTIZ. Recercadas primera y segunda. SENFL. Nun wölt ihr hören. WECK. Spanyöler Tanz und Hopper Dancz. ANON. Ductia; Estampie: Souvent souspire mon cuer; Pase el agua; Rodrigo Martinez; La sexta estampie real; La Spagna (basse danse); 3 carnival songs; 6 dances.] (gram 6/71)

742. *The Music of the Royal Courts of Their Most Illustrious Majesties Queen Elizabeth I, James I of England (and Scotland) and Charles I.* S. Armstrong (sop); English Consort of Viols.   PAN 6208; SPAN 6208
[BULL. Queen Elizabeth's pavan. BYRD. Susanna fair. COPERARIO. Fantasy Chi può mirarvi. DEERING. Pavan and almaine in C major.

FARRANT. Abradad. JENKINS. Fantasy in D major; Pavan in A minor. MICO. Pavan in F major. TOMKINS. Fantasy in G minor. ANON. Ah! Silly poor Joas; Sweet was the song the Virgin sang; This merry, pleasant spring. Also Lawes and Simpson.] (gram 8/67)

743. *Music of the Spanish Renaissance.* Société de la Chorale Bach de Montréal; George Little, cond.

Vox DL 890; STDL 500890 and Turnabout TV 34264S [ALONSO. Gritos davan en aquella sierra (Cancionero de Palacio). ANCHIETA. Missa quarti toni (Kyrie). CABEZON. Dic nobis, Maria; Verso de primo tono; Verso de quarto tono; Verso de quinto tono. ENCINA. Mi libertad en sosiego (Cancionero). PEDRO DE ESCOBAR. Las mis penas, madre (Cancionero). FUENLLANA. Four tientos. MILAN. Ved, comadres (Cancionero). ORTIZ. Recercada segunda sobre el mesmo madrigal. PONCE. Todo mi bien é perdido (Cancionero). SANTA MARIA. Clausulas de primo tono. VALENTE. La Romanesca con cinque mutanze. VICTORIA. Ne timeas, Maria; O magnum mysterium. ANON. Dadme albricias, híjos d'Eva!; Ríu, ríu, chíu. (Following are all from Cancionero de Palacio): Dale si le das; Deh fosse la qui mecho; Dolce amoroso focho; Rodrigo Martínes.]

744. *Music of the Spanish Theater of the Golden Age.* New York Pro Musica; J. White, dir.   Decca DL 79436 [CORREA DE ARAUXO. Bailete: Con las mozas de Vallecas. FLECHA. Ensalada: El fuego. GUERRERO. Villanesca; Todo quanto pudo dar; Virgen sancta. HIDALGO. Quedito, pasito. MARIN. Passacalle: Desengañemonos ya; Passacalle: No piense Minguilla; Passacalle: Qué bien canta un ruisenor. MUDARRA. Fantasia que contrahaze la harpa. PATINO. Cuatro: Pastorcillo triste; Cuatro: Cantar las gracias de Flora. VALENCIANO. Tonada: Ay del amor. ANON. El villano; Matachín; Marizápalos; Jácara; No hay que decirle el primor.]

745. *Music of the Waits.* Various artists; Don Smithers, dir.   Argo ZRG 646 [ADSON. Courtly masquing ayres à 6; Courtly masquing ayres à 5. BASSANO. Oyme dolente. BRADE. Canzon. FARNABY. A maske. PARSONS. Trumpetts. VECCHI. Saltavan ninfe. ANON. Almande Est-ce-Mars.] (gr 12/70)

Music Played on the Virginal. See *Music for the Virginals* (No.708).

746. Musica Antiqua, Vienna. R. Clemencic, cond; Prague Madrigal Singers; M. Venhoda, cond.   Supraphon SUA 10558; SUAST 50558; Crossroads 22 16 0043; 22 16 0044 [A. GABRIELI. Ricercare IX del XII tono à 4. G. GABRIELI. Audi Domine hymnum; Deus in nomine tuo. MONTEVERDI. Missa a cappella.] (biel 2/65)

Musica Antiqua Polonica. See separate recordings under titles: *Muzyka na Zamku Warszawskim* (No.781); *Muzyka na Zamku Wawelskim* (No. 782); *Polska Muzyka Organowa* (No.813); *U Zrodel Muzyki Polskiej* (No.890), and recordings under these composers in Part II: JARSZEBSKI, MIELCZEWSKI, GOMOLKA, LEOPOLITA, and PEKIEL.

747. *Musica Britannica, 1560-1730.* L. Ströbel; Collegium Musicum St. Martini, Bremen.   Psallite PSC 47/180667
[BYRD. Fantasia. DOWLAND. From silent night; Pavane. GIBBONS. The Lord of Salisbury pavan. HOLBORNE. A third set of quintets. MORLEY. Fire, fire, my heart. MUNDY. Fantasia. WEELKES. Come sirrah Jack; Hark all. Also Humphries, Lawes, D. Purcell.]   (biel 2/70)

748. *Musica en la Corte de Carlos V.* Agrupación Instrumental de Música Antiqua de Madrid; Alejandro Mass, dir.   Odeon ASDL 951
[BLONDEAU. Gallardas 1 y 11; Pavana - Gallarda - La Magdalena. CABEZON. Diferencias sobre el canto del Caballero; O lux beata trinitas; Tiento V del primer tono; Tiento IX del primer tono; Tres sobre el cantollano de la Alta. SUSATO. Sans Roch - Final y vuelta de danza. ANON. A su albedrio; Caballero, si a Francia ideas; Miralo como llora (villancico); Pastorella; Pavana; Pavana sobre La re do si la.] (Peters Intl. catalog)

749. *Musica Hungarica.* Various performers.
                                           Qualiton/Hungaroton SLPX 1214
[BAKFARK. Fantasia for the lute. PICCHI. Ballo ongaro. ANON. Eger vár (The Siege of Eger); Emlékezzél, mi történék (Remember, I Lord, what has come upon us); Imhol vayok (Here I am, Sweet Lord); Siralmas énékem (It is sorrow to be parting from you); Sok király oknak (After the death of many kings); Sokféle részögösrol (You many drunkards); Ungarescha (instr). Also folk songs from "The Period of Migration and Conquest."]

750. *Musica Iberica, v.1: Hasta 1500.* Estudio de la Música Antiqua, Munich.
                                                    Odeon J 063 20114
[CORNAGO (villancicos). Gentil dame; Pues que Dios; Señora, qual soy venido. URREDA (villancicos). De vos is de mi; Muy triste será mi vida; Nunca fue pena mayor. ANON. Quant ay lo mon consirat; Nénbressete Madre (cantiga); A Madre (cantiga); Benedicamus - Catholicorum concio (trope); Ex illustri nata prosapia; Salve Virgo / Ave Gloriosa.]   (Peters Intl. catalog)

751. *Musica Italica, 1540-1650.* Collegium Musicum St. Martini, Bremen; L. Ströbel, dir.   10" Psallite PSA 24/180965
[BIVI. Responsorium mit Vers zu 4 Stimmen (2). BONELLI. Artemisia (Canzona à 4). GRANDI. Motette. GUSSAGO. La Leona. MASSAINO. Canzon à 8. PACELLI. Madrigal zu 4 Stimmen. ROSSI. Sinfonia und Galliarde.]   (biel 2/67)

752. *Musica Maximiliana.* Les Menestrels; Franz Haselböck (org).
Tudor 0531
[FINCK. Chiara luce; Ich stand an einem Morgen; O du armer Judas; Ich werde erlöst (org). HOFHAIMER. Herzliebstes Bild; Meiner Traurigkeit; Ohne Freunde; Salve Regina (org); Tröstlicher Liebe. ISAAC. Carmen; Fanfare; Intrada; Lasso, quel altri fugge; O Venus; Le serviteur; Je mehr ich trinke; Un di lieto. SENFL. Ach Elslein; Deinen Namen; Die Brünnlein; Fortuna; Nun grüss' dich Gott; O Herr, rufe ich an.] (Tudor catalog)

753. *Musica Polonica, 1530-1730.* Collegium Musicum St. Martini, Bremen; L. Ströbel, dir. 10" Psallite 33210566 PSB
[DEMANTIUS. Polnischer Tanz. DLUGORAJ. Fantasia (lute). JARSZEBSKI. Canzon I; Concert 4. KRHKOW. Madrigal zu 4 Stimmen; PODBIELSKI. Praeludium. POLAK. Courante (lute). SZADEK. Dies est laetitia (Kyrie, Sanctus, Benedictus). SZARZYNSKI. Concerto à 3. ANON. Taniec.] (biel)

Musica religiosa del 1400. See *Geistliche Musik um 1400* (No.589).

754. *Musica Reservata.* J. Beckett, cond. Delyse ECB 3201
[ADAM DE LA HALLE. Tan con je vivrai. GACE BRULÉ. De bone amours. RAIMBAUT DE VAQUEIRAS. Kalenda Maya. ANON. In seculum viellatoris; La quinte estampie real; Prisoner's song; La quarte estampie real; Mout me fou grief - Robin m'aime - Portare; Amore potest - Ad amorem - Tenor; Pucelete - Je langui - Domino; Danse royale. Jolietement; Au cuer si un mal? Je ne m'en repentirai - Jolietement; J'ai un cuer - Docebit; La seconde estampie real; Ductia; On parole - A Paris? Frese nouvele.] (gram 12/70)

Musical Renaissance. See *Sixteenth-Century Vocal Works* (No.852).

Musical Riches of Henry VIII and Elizabeth I. See *Les riches heures musicales* ... (No.832).

Musiche del medioevo e del rinascimento per arpa ... See *Medieval and Renaissance Music for the Irish and Medieval Harps, Vièle, Recorders and Tambourin* (No.672).

Musiche del primo Rinascimento. See *Music of the Early Renaissance; John Dunstable and His Contemporaries* (No.733).

Musiche fiorentine del XIV sec. See *Florentine Music of the 14th Century* (No.570).

Musiche inglesi per virginale. See *Englische Virginalmusik* (No.539).

755. *Musiche profane nel basso medio evo: Ars Nova.* Bozza Lucca (sop); Nobile (ten); Rapp, Poli, Smith, con viole, liuti, flauti, spinettino e strumenti a percussione. Carosello BCA 7011
(sant 5-6/71 - no contents)

756. *Musiche Rinascimentali.* Bozza Lucca (sop); Rapp, Poli, Smith, Ferraresi
con liuti, viole, flauti, spinetta.   Carosello BCA 7014
(sant 5-6/71 - no contents)

Musik am burgundischen Hof. See *Music at the Burgundian Court*
(No.699).

Musik am elisabethanischen Hofe. See *An Evening of Elizabethan Music*
(No.559).

757. *Musik am englischen Königshofe.* Camerata Lutetiensis.
                                Schwann VMS 2009 and Charlin CL 5
[ALL selections are instrumental. BATESON. If flood of tears. BYRD.
Elisabethan suite; Fantasia a sei; Pavana. FARNABY. Dream; A toy.
GIBBONS. Fantasia a tre. MORLEY. Sing we and chant it. NICHOL-
SON. Der Kuckuck. WILBYE. Fantasia a sei [unnamed madrigal].
ANON. Pavane des Königs Henry VIII. Also Purcell and Lawes.]
(biel 2/67; gr 4/67)

Musik auf Schloss Wawel zu Krakau. See *Muzyka na Zamku Wawelskim*
(No.782).

Musik aus dem königlichen Schloss zu Warschau. See *Muzyka na Zamku
Warszawskim* (No.781).

758. *Musik aus dem Trecento.* Silvia and Walter Frei.
                                Fono. Ges. Luzern S 30-4703
[BARTOLINO DA PADUA. Quel sole. [JACOPO DA?] BOLOGNA.
Con gran furor; Non al suo amante. GIOVANNI DA CASCIA. Nel
mezzo a sei paon. CICONIA. Dolce fortuna. GIOVANNI DA FIRENZE.
Morrà la invida. LANDINO. L'antica flamma; Per allagreca; El mie
dolce sospir; Cara mie donna; Deh'sospir. MASINI. Sanctus. MATHEUS
DA PERUSIO. Non so, che di me fia. PIERO. Cavalcando. REYNALDUS.
L'adorno viso. ANON. Cum altre uccele; Trotto; Lamento di Tristano;
Saltarello.]   (biel 2/70)

759. *Musik aus Italien 1300-1650.* Kees Otten; Syntagma Musicum, Amsterdam.
                Voce del Padrone SME 191761/2 and Electrola 1 c 063-24182
[BANCHIERI. Fantasia. BENDUSI. Desiderata; Galante. CIMA. Bicinium.
GANASSI. Ricercar. JACOPO DA BOLOGNA. Fenice fu. LANDINO.
Amor c'al tuo suggetto; Fatto m'a serr' amore; La dolce vista; Sy dolce non
sono. MONTEVERDI. Non cosi tosto; Salve, O Regina. VIADANA. Salve
Regina. ANON. Saltarello.]   (biel 2/70)

760. *Musik der Renaissance.* Capella Antiqua, Munich.
                                Christophorus SCGLX 75941
[ATTAINGNANT. Mille regretz; Pavane-Gaillarde-Bransle; Pavane -
Gaillarde; Propter bonos geschwenkos. BRUMEL. Vrai dieu d'amours.
CLEMENT. Ich sag ade. DUFAY. Vostre bruit. HASSLER. Mein Gmüt
ist mir verwirret. ISAAC. O liebes Herz. REGNART. All mein gedanken;

Wann ich gedenk. SCANDELLUS. Schein uns, du liebe Sonne.
STOCKEM. Brunete. VOIT. Für all ich kröh. ANON. Adieu madame;
Lieblich hat sich gesellet; Chanson.]   (biel 2/70)

761. *Musik des Mittelalters und der Renaissance.* Various performers.
                                                            DGG 136306
[ADAM DE LA HALLE. Fines amourettes; Le jeu de Robin et Marion.
BYRD. Allemand; La Volta. GESUALDO. Ecco mirirò dunque.
GIBBONS. Fantasia I. HASSLER. Nun fanget an. JANEQUIN. Au joli
jeux. LASSUS. Echo song; Miserere mei. LECHNER. Gott b'hüte dich.
LEONINUS. Judea et Jerusalem (organum duplum. Part 1). MACHAUT.
Notre-Dame mass (Agnus Dei). NEUSIEDLER. Elsleijn, liebstes Elslein.
PALESTRINA. Missa Papae Marcelli (Benedictus, Hosanna). SENFL.
Entlaubet ist der Walde. VAQUEIRAS. Estampida. VENTADOUR.
Lancan vei la folha. ANON. Alleluia (chant for Easter Sunday mass);
Chanconnète / A la cheminée / tenor: Veritatem (motet); Elzeleyn,
lipstis, Elzeleyn (Glogauer); Christe Redemptor Omnium (chant for first
Christmas vespers); Chanson de toile; La Rotta; Stantipes; Trotte;
Victimae paschali laudes (chant for Easter Sunday mass).]

762. *Musik im Dom zu Aachen.* Aachener Domsingknaben; R. Pohl, cond.
                                        10" Harmonia Mundi HM 25153
[CLEMENT. O Maria, vernans rosa (motet). HERMANNUS
CONTRACTUS. Salve Regina. LASSUS. Audi dulcis amica mea (motet).
MANGON. Ave Maria; Assumpta est Maria; Magnificat.]   (biel 2/65)

763. *Musik im Dom zu Münster.* Domchor Münster; Leiwering, cond;
Stockhorst (org).   10" Harmonia Mundi HM 25144
[ANERIO. O pretiosum. GIACOBBI. Caro mea vere est cibus.
PALESTRINA. Fratres ego enim accepi. ANON. Chant. Also Cifra,
Gratiani and Lucca.]   (biel 2/65)

764. *Musik in alten Städten und Residenzen: Augsburg. Im Hause der Fugger.*
Various soloists; Windsbacher Knabenchor; W. Thamm, cond; RIAS
Kammerchor; G. Arndt, cond; J. Brenneke (org).
            Odeon C 91109; STC 91109 and Electrola 91109; S 91109
[AICHINGER. Beati omnes, qui timent Dominum (motet). BESARD.
Galliarda. ERBACH. Ricercar VII. toni (org). FERRABOSCO. Io mi
son giovinett'e volontieri. G. GABRIELI. Canzon duodecimo toni à
8; In nobil sangue. GUMPELZHAIMER. Ach wie elend; Die finster
Nächte. HASSLER. Canzon (Amoenitatum musicalium hortulus);
Chiara e lucente stella; Herzlich lieb hab ich dich; Ich scheid von dir;
Mein Lieb will mit mir kriegen; Mi sento ohimè morire; O tu che mi
dai pene. MONTE. Sottile e dolce ladra. NEUSIEDLER. Fuggerin Tanz.
ANON. La fantina; Saltarello de megio.]

765. *Musik in alten Städten und Residenzen: Innsbruck.* RIAS Kammerchor;
G. Arndt, cond; J. Brenneke (org); E. Müller-Dombois (lute).
Odeon C 91107; STC 91107 and H.M.V. HQM 1045; HQS 1045
			and Angel 36379 under title Music for Maximilian
[DEPRES. Adieu mes amours; J'ai bien cause; Plus nulz regretz. FINCK.
O schönes Weib. GREFINGER. Wohl kömmt der Mai. HOFHAIMER.
Nach Willen dein (org); Nach Willen dein (chor); In Gottes Namen
fahren wir; Meins Traurens ist Ursach; Zucht, Ehr und Lob. ISAAC.
All mein Mut; Illumina oculos meos (motet); Innsbruck ich muss dich
lassen; Mein Freud allein; Questo mostrarsi adirata di fore; Sempre giro
piangendo; Süsser Vater, Herre Gott. JUDENKÜNIG. Ain niederlandisch
runden Dantz; Rossina ain welscher Dantz; Zuch, Ehr und Lob. KLEBER.
Praeambulum in Sol b-moll (org). KOTTER. Provenium in re. SENFL.
Mag ich, Herzlieb, erwerben dich; Mag ich Unglück nit widerstahn; Mein
Fleiss und Müh; Pacientiam muss ich han.]

766. *Musik in alten Stadten und Residenzen: Kassel. Am Hofe des Landgrafen
Moritz von Hessen.* Soloists; RIAS Kammerchor; G. Arndt, cond.
						Odeon SMC 91116
[DEMANTIUS. Diese Nacht hatt' ich ein' Traum; Galliarde; Herr nun
lässt du; Zart schönes Bild. DOWLAND. Can she excuse; Say, love, if
ever; Semper Dowlands. MORITZ, LANDGRAF VON HESSEN.
Aventurose più d'altro terreno; Fuga à 4; Gagliarda Brunsvicese; Pavana
del Francisco Segario; Pavana del pover soldato - Gagliarda del
sopradetto; Pavana del Tomaso di Canora. PRAETORIUS. Christ unser
Herr. Also Schütz.]

767. *Musik in alten Städten und Residenzen: München. Die Hofkapelle
unter Orlando di Lasso.* RIAS Kammerchor; G. Arndt, cond.
						Odeon C 91108; STC 91108
[FALLAMERO. Canzonetta al Napolitana "Vorria, Madonna, fareti a
sapere." FERRABOSCO. Canzonetta "Che giovarebbe haver
bellezza"; "Se si spezzasse sta dura catene." A. GABRIELI. O sacrum
convivium. G. GABRIELI. Sacro tempio d'honor. LASSUS. Princeps
Marte potens, Guilielmus; Si le long temps; Un aduocat dit à sa femme;
Wie lang, O Gott, in meiner Not; Motette in hora; Al gran Guilielmo
nostro. PHALESE. Pavane and Galliarde ferrarese. REGNART.
Venus, du und dein Kind; Nach meiner Lieb viel hundert Knaben
trachten. RORE. O sonno o della queta humida ombrosa. STRIGGIO.
Il gioco di primiera; Caccia. SUSATO. Allemainge and Pavane; Ronde
and saltarello; Pavan and galliarde. VENTO. Ich bin elend, wo ich
umfahr; Ich weiss ein Maidlein hübsch und fein; Vor etlich wenig Tagen.
ANON. Aufzug; Der gestreifft Danntz; Der Gassenhauer darauff; Der
Maruscat Danntz; Der Auff und Auff.]

768. *Musik in alten Städten und Residenzen: Venedig. Festliche Kirchen-musik.* Soloists; RIAS Kammerchor; G. Arndt, cond; R. Ewerhart (org).
Odeon SMC 91117; STC 91117
[CAVAZZONI. Ave maris stella; Christe Redemptor omnium. FANTINI. L'Imperiale. A. GABRIELI. Ricercare II toni. G. GABRIELI. Canzon à 10 (Sacrae Symphoniae); Intonazione d'organo; Magnificat I toni; Quis est iste; Sonata pian' e forte. GUAMMI. Canzon. MONTE-VERDI. Ave maris stella.]

769. *Musik in der Klosterkirche Einsiedeln.* Choralschola; P. Bannwart, cond; Stiftschor; P. Meier, cond; P. Winnig (org).
10" Harmonia Mundi HM 25-126 and FONO FGL 25-4302
[AICHINGER. Regina coeli. VICTORIA. Missa O quam gloriosam (Kyrie, and ? Sanctus and ? Benedictus). ANON. Alma redemptoris (chant); Ego sum. Also Clérambault.]   (biel 1/64)

770. *Musique ancienne tchèque.* Soliste et choeurs de la Philharmonie tchèque; M. Veselka, dir; Ensemble des Madrigalistes de Prague; M. Venhoda, dir.
Supraphon SUA 19453
[Hospodine pomiluo ny; Svaty Vaclave; Buoh Vsemohuci; Jezu Kriste, scedry kneze; Jizt mne vse radost ostava; Drevo se listem odie va; Andeliku Rozkochany; Pravdo mila tiezit tebe; Slyste, rytieri bozi; O slovanie Konstantske; Pustan, povstan, velike mesto Prazske; Dietky, v hrodmadu se sendeme; Ktoz Jsu bozi bojovnici; Astra solum qui regis (Tropaire de Saint-Vith); O quantum sollicitor (chant); Planctus Mariae.] (dia 64)

771. *Musique au temps de la Renaissance.* The London Ambrosian Singers and Consort; Franz Tenta Consort, Salzburg; Ensemble Les Ménestrels, Vienna.   Belvédère ELY 0501
[ATTAINGNANT. Pavenne. BOESSET. Objet dont les char. CABEZON. Duo pour positif. DALZA. Vexilla Regis prodeunt. DEPRES. Cueurs desolez; Mille regretz. GUÉDRON. Si jamais mon âme blessée. ISAAC. Optime Pastor. JANEQUIN. Quand je bois du vin claret. NARVAEZ. Variations sur Guardame las vacas. ORTIZ. O felici occhi. M. PRAETORIUS. Bransle de la Grenée; Reprinse; Bransle de village; La Mouline. VASQUEZ. Ojos morenos. WILLAERT. Madonna io non lo so. ANON. Imperitante Octaviano, Virtute vuius (Trent Codex). Also G. Martini.]

772. *Musique de l'époque gothique et de la renaissance.* Palestrina Kantorei; Stadlmaier, dir; Choeur Collège Saint-Lievain d'Anvers; Hellinckx, dir; Petits Chanteurs "Les Pinsons de Saint-Martin"; Kaufbeuren dir; Ensemble instruments anciens.   Orphée ORP 51070
[AICHINGER. Regina coeli. BERCHEM. Laet ons nu al verblyden; O Jesu Christe. HOFHAIMER. Erst weiss ich, was die Liebe ist. JANE-QUIN. Ce moys de may. LASSUS. Matona mia cara; Surrexit pastor bonus.

772. *Musique de l'epoque gothique et de la renaissance.* (Continued)
AICHINGER. Schöns Maedlein, murr nur nit. MARENZIO. Estote
fortes. NEIDHARDT VON REUENTHAL. Mailied. PALESTRINA. O
crux ave; Peccatem me quotide. SACHS. Silberweis. SENFL. Entlaubet
ist der Wald. SWELINCK. Hodie Christus natus est. VICTORIA. Ave
Maria. WALTHER VON DER VOGELWEIDE. Kreuzfahrerlied.
WOLKENSTEIN. Wach auf, mein Hort. ANON. Kunig Rudolf; In
saeculum viellatoris.]   (dia 67)

La musique d'orgue aux Pays Bas du 16e au 18e siècle. See *De Orgelkunst
in de Nederlanden ...* (No.795).

773. *Musique du siècle d'or Espagnol.* Ochoa (bar); Bon (   ); A. Ponce (guit).
                              Chant du Monde LDXA 48321; LDXA 8321
[DAZA. Fantasia. FUENLLANA. De Antequera sale el moro; La
Girigonza. MILAN. Pavan no.1; Pavan no.5; Todo mi vida os amé.
MUDARRA. Conde claros; Dime a do tienes las mientes; Gallarda;
Gentil Cavallero; Romanesca; Si viesse e me levasse; Triste estaba el Rey
David. NARVAEZ. Arded corazon, arded; Baixa de contrapunto;
Cancion de Emperador; Diferencias sobre Guardame las vacas; Paseabase
el Rey Moro; Ya se asienta el Rey Ramiro. PISADOR. Villancico;
Villancico Si te vas a banar, Juanica; Pavana; Villancico En la fuente
del rosel. VALDERRABANO. Pavanas. ANON. Dindirindin.]   (dia 67)

774. *Musique en la Basilique Saint-Marc de Venise.* Soloists; instrumentalists;
Orchestra of the Teatro Comunale, Bologna; Tito Gotti, dir.
                  Erato STU 70724 and Musical Heritage Society MHS 860
[G. GABRIELI. Canzon à 12; Canzon IX à 12; Canzon VIII à 8; Canzon
VII et VIII toni à 12. GRILLO. Canzon in echo a 8; Canzon II à 8.
TROFEO. Canzon XIX à 8. Also Caldara, Cavalli, Vivaldi.]   (arg 5/69)

775. *Musique espagnole XVIe, XVIIe et XVIIIe siècles.* Mancha (org).
                                            Ducretet DUC 320 C 156/7
[ALVARADO. Fantaisie Pange lingua espagnole. CABEZON. Fantaisie
sur le Ier ton; Deux gloses sur l'Ave Maris Stella; Magnificat (6 versets sur
le IVe ton); Variations sur El canto del caballero. CASTILLO. Fantaisie
sur le IIe ton. CORREA DE ARAUXO. Fantaisies sur le registre haut du
Ier ton, ie registre plein du Xe ton, le registre bas du Xe ton, en forme
de chansons sur le IVe ton. HEREDIA. Oeuvre sur le Ier ton; Fantaisie
sur le IVe ton; Salve de leno. TOMAS DE SANTA MARIA. Quatre
fantaisies brèves. Also Cabanilles, Oxinagas, Elias and Soler.]   (dia 64)

776. *La musique flamand dans la société des XV. et XVI. siècles.* Various
performers (selections from the Archiv-Produktion catalog plus some
new performances, to accompany book of the same title by Wangermée).
                                            DGG Archiv 629517/8
[BINCHOIS. Files à marier. CLEMENT. Souterliedekens. DEPRES.
Basiez moy; Bergerette Savoyene; Missa Pange Lingua (Gloria); N'esse
pas un grand deplaisir; Parfons regretz. DUFAY. Flos florum; Missa

l'homme armé (Agnus Dei II); Vexilla regis. GOMBERT. Angelus
Domini (motet). ISAAC. Fortuna in mi; Innsbruck, ich muss dich
lassen; La Mora; Proprium missae in Dominica Laetare (Introit).
JAPART. Il est de bonne heure. LA RUE. Autant en emporte le vent;
Porquoy non? LASSUS. Baur, was traegst im Sacke; Io ti vorria contar;
O la, o che bon echo; Or sus, filles, que l'on me donne; Domine, ne in
furore tuo (Ps.6); Scais-tu dire l'ave? Super flumina Babylonis (motet);
Un doux nenny; Un dubbio verno. OCKEGHEM. L'autre d'antan;
Missa L'Homme armé (Kyrie); Ma maistresse. RORE. Crudele acerba
inexorabili morte. SUSATO. Danserye. WILLAERT. Allons, allons gay;
O dolce vita mia; Quidnam ebrietas. ANON. Entree suis en pemsee; God
is myn licht (Ps.26); Hoort myn ghebet, o Heere (Ps.101).]

777. *Musique flamande: Renaissance et baroque.* Ensemble Alarius; Quatuor
vocale de Bruxelles.　　　　　　　　　　　　　　　Alpha DB 129
[ARCADELT. Voi ve n'andat'al cielo. Van BERGHEM. Que feu
craintif. BRUMEL. Ach, gheldeloos. ESPISCOPIUS. Laet varen alle
fantasie. FAIGNENT. De Seghenings. HELLINCK. Compt alle vaart by
twee dry. LA RUE. Myn hert alyt heeft verlangen. TURNHOUT. Ghy
meyskans. WEERBECK. Panis Angelicus. WILLAERT. O dolce vita
mia. Also Hacquart, Kempis, Richard, Wichel.] (dia 2/68)

Musique instrumentale à la cour de la reine Elisabeth Ière. See
Instrumental Music from the Courts of Queen Elizabeth and King James
(No.623).

778. *Musique Portugaise polyphonique.* Choeurs de la Fondation Gulbenkian;
Olga Violante, Pierre Salzmann, conds.　　　　　Philips 835 771 LY
[CARDOSO. Missa Miserere mihi Domine. LOPES MORAGO. Gaudete
cum laetitia; Jesu Redemptor II; Laudate pueri II; Quem vidistis pastores;
Oculi mei. PEDRO DE CRISTO. O magnum mysterium; Quaeramus
cum pastoribus.] (dia)

Musique pour cuivres au temps de Jacques I. See *The Royal Brass Music
of James I* (No.834).

779. *Musique profane à la cour papale de Rome.* Camerata Lutetiensis.
　　　　　　　　　　　　　　　　　　　　　　　　Charlin CL 6
[G. GABRIELI. Canzona La spiritata. MONTEVERDI. 3 madrigals.
PALESTRINA. 8 ricercare. VECCHI. Fantasia à 4. Also Frescobaldi,
Legrenzi.] (dia)

Musique sacrée de la Renaissance à Salzbourg. See *Kirchenmusik der
Salzburger Renaissance* (No.640).

780. *Musiques héraldiques.* Vocal ensemble; Groupe instrumental anciens,
Paris; Cotte, cond.　　　　　　　　　　　　　　Pathé CPTC 2035
[DA CACCIA (i.e., GIOVANNI DA CASCIA). Nel mezzo a sei paon.
CICONIA. Una panthera. GRIMACHE. Alarme. LE JEUNE. L'un

780. *Musiques héraldiques.* (Continued)
émera le violet. ANON. Marche pour les chevaliers faits par Henri III;
Non mudera ma constance et firmesse; Un lion say. Also Verdier and
Lully.]   (dia 2/68)

781. *Muzyka na Zamku Warszawskim (Music of the Royal Castle in Warsaw).*
Musicae Antiquae Collegium Varsoviense; S. Sutkowski, dir.
                        Muza XL 0295; SXL 0295 and Orpheus OR 342
[CATO. Chorea Polonica (lute). DLUGORAJ. 3 lute dances.
JARSZEBSKI. Susanna Videns. MIELCZEWSKI. Deus, in Nomine Tuo.
PEKIEL. Dulcis amor. ROZYCKI. Magnificat. SCACCHI. Vivat et
floreat rex. ANON. Preludium i fuga (hpsi); 3 Polish folk songs.]   (adv)

782. *Muzyka na Zamku Wawelskim.* Zespoe Madrygalistrow; Capella Bydgostiensis pro Musica Antiqua.
                Muza XL 0296 and Orpheus 355 (Musica antiqua polonica)
[CATO. Fantazja. KLABON. Hetmanowi Koronnemu; Jesle Greccy
Hektorowie; Slawne Potomstwo Lechowe; Sluchajcie mnie wszystkie
kraje; Szerokie sarmackie wlòsci; Tryumfuj wierny poddany.
LEOPOLITA. Cibavit eos. MIKOLAJ Z CHRZANOWA. Protexisti me
Deus. MIKOLAJ Z KRAKOWA. Date siceram maerentibus; Wesel sie
polska korona. MIKOLAJ Z RADOMIA. Hystorigraphi acie; Utwor
bez tytulu. WACLAW Z SZAMOTUL. Nunc scio vere. ANON. Napis
nad grobem zacnej krolowej barbary radziwillowny; Piesn o posiedzeniu
i o zniewoleniu zalosnym ziemi wegierskiej; Piesn o smierci krola
zygmunta pierwszego; Piesn o weselu krola zygmunta wtorego. ANON.
(Dances from the Jan of Lublin tablature): Ad novem saltus; Conradus;
Rex; Rocal fuza; Taniec.]

783. *Nativity to Candlemas.* King's College Choir, Cambridge; Willcocks, cond.
                        Angel S36275 and H.M.V. ALP 2111; ASD 653 and
                                    Voix son Maître ASOF 882; FALP 882
[BYRD. Hodie beata virgo; Senex puerum portabat. DEERING. Quem
vidistis, pastores? ECCARD. When to the temple Mary went. GIBBONS.
Hosanna to the son of David. HANDL. Ecce concipies; Omnes de Saba.
PALESTRINA. Hodie Christus natus est. SWELINCK. Hodie Christus
natus est. VICTORIA. O magnum mysterium; Senex puerum portabat.
WEELKES. Hosanna to the son of David; Gloria in excelsis Deo.]
(dia 67)

784. *Neuf noëls anciens.* Chanteurs Saint-Eustache; Ensemble instrumental;
Martin, cond.   10" Lumen 2516
[COSTELEY. Allons, gai gai bergère. DU CAURROY. Un enfant du ciel
nous est venu. MOUTON. Allons ouïr sur nos têtes. ANON. Les anges
dans nos campagnes; Douce nuit; Il est né le divin enfant; Jacobin;
Quaeramus cum pastoribus; Saint Joseph a fait un nid.]   (dia 64)

785. *Niederländische und deutsche Motetten des 16. und 17. Jahrhunderts.*
Windsbacher Knabenchor; Thamm, cond; Utrechts Motetgezelschap;
Mudde, cond; Heinrich-Schütz-Chor, Heilbronn; Werner, cond; West-
fälische Kantorei; Ehmann, cond.   Cantate 640215
[ECCARD. Herr Christe, tu mir gehen; O Freude über Freud; Übers
Gebirg Maria geht. HAMMERSCHMIDT. O Vater aller Frommen.
LASSUS. Die Klagen des Hiob (part 7). LECHNER. Christ, der du bist
der helle Tag; Deutsche Sprüche von Leben und Tod. Also Kuhnau and
Schein.] (biel 2/65)

*Noah Greenberg Conducting the New York Pro Musica: An Anthology
of His Greatest Works.* See MORLEY, BANCHIERI (Festino), *English
Medieval Christmas Carols* (No.548), and *Children's Songs of
Shakespeare's Time* (No.853).

De Noël à la Chandeleur. See *Nativity to Candlemas* (No.783).

786. *Notre Dame de Paris in the 13th Century.* Vocal and Instrumental
Ensemble; T. Dart, dir.   Fontana Special SFI 14133
[PEROTINUS. Alleluia nativitas. ANON. A combrais; A vos, douce
debonaire; Hyer main chevauchole; In saeculum; Benedicamus Domino;
En bon Diu; Mariae Assumptio; On parole; Post partum; Portare;
Pucelete; Salve Virgo; Studentes conuigo.] (gr 2/70)

787. *Now Make We Merthe.* Boys Choir of All Saints Church; Purcell Consort
of Voices; London Brass Ensemble; instrumentalists; S. Preston (org);
G. Burgess, cond.   Argo ZRG 526
N.B.: Issued in Germany, lacking seven pieces, as *Weihnachtsmusik aus
Mittelalter und Renaissance* (No.898), q.v.
[MOUTON. Noe, noe, psallite. SMERT. Nowell: Dieus vous garde.
WALTHER. Joseph lieber, Joseph mein. ANON. The Bory's hede;
Conditor fut le non-pareil; Fines amouretes; Fulget hodie de l'espine;
Gabriell off hye degre; I saw a sweete; In this valey; El lobo rabioso;
Lullay, lullow; Lux hodie; Nova, nova; Now God Almighty; Now make
we merthe; Orientis partibus; Pray for us; Resonet in laudibus; Riu, riu,
chiu; Verbum caro: Dies est laetitiae; Verbum caro; In hoc anni
circulo; Verbum patris hodie; Verbum patris humanatur.] (adv)

788. *Nun bitten wir den Heiligen Geist; Pfingstgesänge aus dem 13. bis 16.
Jahrhundert.* Capella Antiqua, Munich; K. Ruhland, cond.
                    10" Christophorus CLP 73314
[DUFAY. Veni, Creator Spiritus / Spiritus Domini. FINCK. Veni,
Creator spiritus / Accipite spiritum sanctum. RESINARIUS. Komm,
Gott Schöpfer, Heiliger Geist. ANON. Alleluja / Veni, Sancte Spiritus
(Glogauer); Komm Heiliger Geist, Herre Gott; Nun bitten wir den
heiligen Geist (Glogauer).] (biel 2/70)

789. *O Great Mystery: Unaccompanied Choral Music of the 16th and 17th Centuries.* The Canby Singers; E. T. Canby, cond.
Nonesuch H 1026; 71026 and Chant du Monde LDX-A 48354
[BYRD. O magnum mysterium. FRANCK. Ihr Lieben. GUERRERO. Canite tuba in Sion. HANDL. O admirabile commercium; Mirabile mysterium. LASSUS. Resonet in laudibus. MONTEVERDI. Sfogava con le stelle. MORALES. O magnum mysterium. VICTORIA. O magnum mysterium. WAELRANT. Musiciens qui chantez à plaisir. Also Schein, Schütz and Canby (arr.).]

790. *O Ravising Delight.* A. Deller (c-tnr); D. Dupré (lute); D. Munrow and R. Lee (rcdrs); R. Elliot (cemb).
Harmonia Mundi 30708 M and Victor VICS 1492
[BARTLET. Of all the birds. CAMPION. The cypress curtain; I care not for these ladies. DOWLAND. Come heavy sleep; I saw my lady weep; Shall I sue; Wilt thou unkind. PILKINGTON. Rest, sweet nymphs. ROSSETER. What then is love. ANON. Miserere, my maker. Also Blow, Clarke, Croft, Eccles, Purcell.]   (Myers 12/70)

791. *Oberrheinische und süddeutsche Orgelmeister.* K. P. Schuba (org).
10" Christophorus CLP 75416
[BUCHNER. Kyrie eleison. ISAAC. Herrgott, lass dich erbarmen. LUSCINUS. In patienta Vestra (a 3). VON SALEM. Resonet in laudibus. Also Fischer, Kerll and Murschhauser.]   (biel 2/65)

Of Castles and Cathedrals. See *Concert Renaissance au château de Chenonceaux* (No.507).

792. *Old English Vocal Music.* Prague Madrigal Singers.
Crossroads 22-16-0144
[BROWNE. O Mater Venerabilis. BYRD. Have mercy upon me, O Lord. COOPER. I have been a foster. DOWLAND. What if I never speed. DUNSTABLE. Ave Regina coelorum. GIBBONS. I feign not friendship where I hate. MORLEY. My bonny lass. TALLIS. Audivi vocem. ANON. Alleluia psallat; Ductia; Ecce quod natura; Rex Virginum; St. Magnus hymn; Sumer is icumen in.]

Oldest Czech Monody (13th Century). See *Musique ancienne tchèque* (No.770).

793. *Oldest Czech Polyphony, Pt. I.* Prague Madrigal Singers; M. Venhoda, cond.   10" Supraphon SUF 29094 and Supraphon MAB 22
[Ave generosa; Ave Maria ancilla Trinitatis; Beati qui esuriunt; Christum ducem; Flos florum; Nas mily asvaty Vaclave; Primo tempore; Procendentum sponsum; O Regina; Omnis mundus jucundetur.]   (dia 64)

794. *Oldest Czech Polyphony, Pt. II.* Musica Antiqua, Vienna; Clemencic, cond; Prague Madrigal Singers; M. Venhoda, cond; Czech Philharmonic Chorus, J. Veselka, cond. (Side 2)   Supraphon SUA 19564; ST 59564

Side 1
[8 ANON. Excerpts from Hymnbook from Benešov.
Side 2
KAROLIDES. Ps.XCVI. RYCHNOVSKÝ. Decantabat populus.
VODŇANSKÝ. Favete linguis singuli; Oda XLVI. ANON. Alleluja,
panna syna porodila; Officium Dunaj voda hluboká; Otče náš; Vzhůru,
Vzhůru Čechové.]

The Organ and Its Music. See *De Orgelkunst in de Nederlanden van de
16de tot de 18de Eeuw* (No.795).

Organ Music of the Polish Renaissance. See *Polska Muzyka Organowa*
(No.813).

795. *De Orgelkunst in de Nederlanden van de 16de tot de 18de Eeuw.* Flor
Peeters, (org).   Musique Royal DP 19201/2
Record 1
[BULL. Fantasia on Een kindekeyn is ons geboren. CORNET. Fantasia
in Mode VIII. ISAAC. Herr Gott lass dich erbarmen. MACQUE.
Canzona a la Francese. PHILIPS. Trio du premier mode. SWELINCK.
Variations on Est-ce mars; Wo Gott der Herr nicht bei uns hält. Also
Kerckhoven, Fiocco and Gheyn.
Record 2
BULL. Fantasia on Laet ons mit hertzen reyne. CORNET. Salve Regina.
PHILIPS. Fantasia in A minor. SWELINCK. Echo fantasia in A minor;
O lux beata trinitas; Toccata in A minor. WILLAERT. Ricercare. Also
Kerckhoven.]
N.B.: To accompany Peeters book, The Organ and Its Music.

796. *Orgelwerke des 16. Jahrhunderts.* Julio-M. Garcia Llovera and Montserrat
Serra (org).   DG Archive 198455
[ALBERTO. Salmo II (Qui habitat). BAEZA. Tiento de VII tono.
BERMUDO. Exemplo del modo primero por Elami. CABEZON.
Diferencias sobre Guardame las vacas; Diferencias sobre el Canto del
Cavallero; Tientos del I & VI toni; Tres sobre el canto llano de la alte.
LACERNA. Tiento del VI tono. MORALES. Verso de V tono.
PALERO. Glosado del Verso de Morales; Tiento sobre Cum sancto
Spiritu. PERAZA. Tiento de medio registro alto de I tono. TOMAS DE
SANTA MARIA. Fantasia no.3 and no.9. SOTO. Tiento de VI tono.]
(gram 12/70)

797. *Orgues Danoises (Frederiksborg).* Chapelet (org).
                                    Harmonia Mundi HM 30579 and Oryx 502
[SWELINCK. Ricercare brevis; Toccata; Variations on Est-ce Mars;
Variations on Mein junges Leben hat ein End. ANON. La shy muse; My
Lady Careys dompe; La doune cella. Also Scheidt, Cabezon and
Pasquini.]   (dia 69)

798. *Orgues Espagnols: Covarrubias.* Chapelet (org).
                                  Harmonia Mundi HM SO 30540 and Oryx 506
[CABEZON. Diferencias sobre la Galliarda Milanesa; Magnificat de IV
tono; Tiento de I tono; Tiento Ut queant laxis. CORREA DE ARAUXO.
Canto llano de la Immaculada Concepcion; Tiento de II tono; Tiento de
IV tono; Tiento de VII tono; Tiento de X tono. Tiento pequeno y facil
de VII tono. LOPEZ. Quarto versos de I tono; Dos versos de VII tono;
Dos versos de IV tono. PERAZA. Tiento de I tono. ANON. Three
Fauxbourdons.] (biel 2/67)

799. *Orgues Espagnols: Salamanque.* Chapelet (org).
                                      Harmonia Mundi HM SO 530541
[CABEZON. Tiento. CORREA DE ARAUXO. Tiento de VII tono;
Tiento de X tono. MODENA. Tiento de IV tono. XIMENEZ. Batalla.
ANON. Four 16th-century Fauxbourdons. Also Alvarado, Cabanilles,
Casanoves, Lopez.] (biel 2/67)

800. *Orgues espagnols: Trujillo. Musique à la cour de Charles-Quint et*
[Side 2] *Musiques a la cour de Philippe II.* F. Chapelet (org).
                                          Harmonia Mundi HMO 30705
Side 1
[ALBERTO. Trois pièces. CORREA DE ARAUXO. Tiento de 4ᵉtono;
Tiento de baxon sexo tono. CRECQUILLON. Cancion Pour ung plaisir.
DEPRES. Kyrie. GOMBERT. Fabordono llano y Fabordon glosado.
JANEQUIN. Réveillez-vous. SOTO DE LANGA. 2 tientos. ANON. Je
vous; Sacris solemnis; Te matrem Dei laudamus; Jesucristo hombre y
dios.
Side 2
All works by Cabezon. See Index, Part II, under his name.]

801. Oxford Schola Cantorum (Schola Cantorum Oxoniensis). J. Byrt, dir.
                                              Audiovision APR 266
[BYRD. Laetentur coeli. DOWLAND. What if I never speed. G.
GABRIELI. Timor et tremor. MUNDY. O Lord, the Maker. PILKING-
TON. Rest, sweet nymphs. Also Poulenc, Byrt, Holst, Vaughan Williams.]
(gr 7/66)

802. *Parthenia, or the Maydenhead.* Colin Tilney (hpsi).
                                      Golden Guinea/Pye GSGC 14129
[BULL. Galiardo; Pavana - St. Thomas wake; Galiardo - St. Thomas
wake; Parthenia. BYRD. Parthenia; Earl of Salisbury pavan and gailiard.
GIBBONS. Earl of Salisbury pavan; Galiardo; Preludium; Fantasia of
four parts; Queenes command.] (gram 12/69)

Peasant Dances and Popular Street Music. See *Bauern-, Tanz- und
Strassenlieder in Deutschland um 1500* (No.470).

803. *Petrucci: First Printer of Music.* New York Pro Musica; J. White, dir.
Decca DL 79435
[BOSSINENSIS. Recercar and Lauda Processionale: Se mai per
maraveglia. BRUHIER. Latura tu. COMPERE. Loudault, lourdault.
DALZA. Pavana alla veneziana; Saltarello; Piva. DEPRES. De tous bien
playne; El grillo; Missa Ave Maris Stella. GHISELIN. La Alfonsina.
GHIZEGHEM. De tous biens playne. MANTUANUS. Un sonar da piva
in fachinesco (Lirium bililirum). NINOT LE PETIT. Ela la la.]

804. *Plainsong to Polyphony.*
v.1: Carmelite Priory Choir; McCarthy, cond.
Odeon CSD 1617 and Everest 3174/3 and H.M.V. CLP 1895; CSD 1617
[BYRD. Christe, qui lux es et dies. LASSUS. De Profundis (from
Penitential Psalms). MONTEVERDI. Ave Maris Stella. PALESTRINA.
Missa Assumpta est Maria (part 1); Missa Ecce Sacerdos magnus (Kyrie);
Missa Aeterna Christi munera (Kyrie). SHEPHERD. Deus tuorum
militum (Sarum Hymnary). TALLIS. Salvator mundi; Te lucis ante
terminum; Veni creator spiritus. VICTORIA. Ave Maria.]

805. *v.2:* Carmelite Priory Choir; McCarthy, cond.
Odeon CSD 3519 and Everest 3174/3 and H.M.V. CLP 3519; CSD 3519
[BYRD. Pange lingua. DEPRES. La Déploration de Johannes Ockeghem.
KERLE. Missa Regina coeli (Kyrie). MARENZIO. Hodie Christus natus
est. MORALES. Magnificat VIII tone. PALESTRINA. Salve Regina;
Missa Lauda Sion (Benedictus); Magnificat. SHEPHERD. Haec dies.
TALLIS. Jerusalem (Lamentations of Jeremiah). VICTORIA. Estoto
Fortes in bello.]

806. *v.3:* Carmelite Priory Choir; McCarthy, cond.
Odeon CSD 3606 and Everest 3174/3 and H.M.V. CLP 3606; CSD 3606
[ANERIO. Alma redemptoris. DUFAY. Vexilla Regis. MORALES.
Jubilate Deo omnis terra. PENALOSA. Missa Beata Virgine (Kyrie).
VICTORIA. Libera me, Domine. Also Wright and S. Wesley.]

807. *The Pleasures of Cervantes.* Polyphonic Ensemble of Barcelona; M. Q.
Gavalda, dir.   Nonesuch H 1116; 71116 and Eurodisc 70939 MK
[ARANES. Un sarao de la chacona. MILAN. Con pavor recordó il moro;
Durandarte. MENA. De la dulce mi enemiga. NARVAEZ. Paseábase el
rey moro. RIBERA. Por unos puertos arriba. ROMERO. Romerico
florido. VALDERRABANO. Pavane (guit). ANON. Caballeros, si a
Francia ides; Canario (hpsi, two versions); Chaconne (hpsi); Folia (hpsi);
La perra mora; Rompase la sepultura; Tres morillas. Also some 17th
century works.]

La plus ancienne polyphonie tchèque. See *Oldest Czech Polyphony*
(Nos. 793-94).

808. *Polifonia de Navidad.* Coros de Radio Nacional de España, Madrid; A.
Blancafort.   Pax P 355
[CABEZON. De la Virgen que alumbró. CASTRO. Angelus ad pastores.
ESQUIVEL. Gloria in excelsis Deo. GUERRERO. A un Niño llorando
al hielo; Los reyes siguen la estrella; Pastores loquebantur; Vamos al
portal. MORALES. Pastores dicite, quidnam vidistis? VICTORIA. Jesu
redemptor omnium; O magnum mysterium. ANON. Christus natus est
nobis; Riu, riu, chiu; Un Niño nos es nacido. Also anonymi from the
17th century.]   (adv)

809. *Polifonia de Semana Santa.* Coros de Radio Nacional de España, Madrid;
A. Blancafort, cond.   Pax P 367
[CEBALLOS. Possuerunt super caput ejus. ESQUIVEL. O vos omnes.
MORALES. O Crux, ave spes unica; Per tuam Crucem. ORTIZ.
Canticum Zachariae "Benedictus Dominus." SÁNCHEZ. Christus
factus est. VICTORIA. Popule meus; Vere languores. VIVANCO.
De Lamentatione Jeremiae prophetae (Lectio I). ZORITA. Pueri
Hebraeorum. Also Guerau.]   (adv)

810. *Polifonia Eucaristica.* Coros de Radio Nacional de España, Madrid; A.
Blancafort, cond.   Pax P 377
[BERNAL. Ave, sanctissimum Corpus. COMES. Alabado sea el
Santisimo Sacramento; Hombres, qué más bien quéreis; No tenéis de
qué tener cuidado; Venid, mortales, venid. GUERRERO. Alma, si
sabes de amor; Antes que comáis a Dios; Caro nea; Qué te daré, Señor?
Oh venturoso dia! LOBO. O quam suavis est. TAFALLA. Oh memorable
Sacramento! TORRE. Adorámoste, Señor. TORRES. Oh admirable
Sacramento! VICTORIA. Domine, non sum dignus; O sacrum convivium;
Pange lingua. ANON. Vuelve tus ojos claros.]   (adv)

811. *Polifonia Mariana del Siglo de Oro Español.* Coros de Radio Nacional
de España, Madrid; A. Blancafort, cond.   Pax P 353
[COMES. Que el alba se rie. ENCINA. A quién debo yo llamar; Pues que
tú, Reina del Cielo; Ya no quiero tener fe. ESCOBAR. Virgen bendita
sin par. FERNANDO DE LAS INFANTAS. Virgo prudentissima. F.
GUERRERO. Benedictu; Esclarecida Madre; Oh, Virgen; Rogad vos,
Virgen; Santisima Maria. P. GUERRERO. O Beata Maria. MORALES.
Ecce Virgo concipiet. ROBLEDO. Magnificat (Modus III). VICTORIA.
Sancta Maria. VILLALAR. Regina coeli laetare. VIVANCO. Stabat
Mater. ANON. Alta Reina; Gózate, Virgen sagrada.]   (adv)

Polish Medieval Music. See *U Zrodel Muzyki Polskiej* (No.890).

812. *Polish Renaissance.* Sebestyen (hpsi and org).   Candide 31019
[BAKFARK. 2 Fantasias. CATO. Fantasia & fugue. DLUGORAJ.
Chorea Polonica; Fantasia; Villanella Polonica; 4 villanelles. LOEFFEL-
HOLTZ. Good Polish dance. LOHET. 3 fugues (from Woltz Organ
Tablature). MIKOLAJ OF CRACOW. Hayducky. POLAK. Galliard
(from Besard's "Novus partus"). WAISSELIUS. 2 Polish dances. ANON.

Aliud praeambulum (Lublin Organ Tablature); Bransle de St. Nicholas (Fuhrmann's Lute Tablature); Colenda; Dance Poznanie; Dziwny Sposob; Ortus (Monastery of the Holy Spirit, Krakow, Tablature); 5 Polish dances (Gdabak Tablature); Wesel.] (sch 3/70)

Polish Renaissance Organ Music. See *Polska Muzyka Organowa* (No.813).

813. *Polska Muzyka Organowa (Organ Music of the Polish Renaissance).*
Joachim Grubich (org). Muza XL 0235 and Orpheus OR 339
[From the Jan of Lublin tablature: MIKOLAJ Z KRAKOWA. Ave Jerarchia (Chorale prelude); Haiduk dance; Praeambulum in F. ANON. Colende (chorale prelude); Accede Nuntia (chorale prelude); Alia Poznanie; Praeambulum in D; Praeambulum in G.
From Holy Ghost Monastery Tablature, Krakow: ANON. "By thy Holy Resurrection"; Per merita Sancti Adalberti; Praeambulum.
From the Pelplin Tablature: ANON. Canzona on Ps.XLIII.
From Warsaw Music Society Tablature: SOWA. Salve Regina. PODBIELSKI. Praeludium.
Plus: CATO. Fantasia - motet - fuga. LEOPOLITA. Resurgente Christo Domino; Ricercare. ROHACZEWSKI. Canzona a 4. ZELECHOWSKI. Fantasia.]

814. *Polyphonies belges, anciennes et modernes: Chants polyphoniques de la Renaissance.* La Groupe Vocal Fritz Hoyois. 10"? Alpha 3013
[BERCHEM. O Salutaris Hostia. LA RUE. Autant en emporte le vent. LASSUS. Las! Voulez-vous qu'une personne chante; Madonna ma pieta; Petite folle, estes-vous pas contente; Que dis-tu, que fais-tu; Timor et tremor. MONTE. La premier jour du mois de may. WILLAERT. O Bene Mio; O dolce vita.] (adv)

815. *Popular Medieval Music.* Jaye Consort of Viols; G. Burgess, cond.
Pye/Golden Guinea GGC 4092; GSGC 14092
[ADAM DE LA HALLE. Li mans d'Amer. RAIMBAUT DE VAQUEIRAS. Kalenda maya. RICHARD I. Ja nun mons pris. ANON. Alta; C'est la fin; Ductia; English dance; Estampie; Estampie royale; In saeculum artifex; Lamento di Tristano; Moulin de Paris; Novus miles sequitur; Pour mon coeur; Rege mentem; Saltarello; Sol evitur; Song of the ass; Die suss Nachtigall; Trotto; Vierhundert Jahr uff diser Erde; Worlde's bliss.]
(gram 12/70)

Portugaliae Musica, v.8. See *Cancioneiro musical e poetico* (No.476) and CARDOSO. Missa Tui sunt coeli in Part II.

816. *Portugal's Golden Age, v.3.* Gulbenkian Foundation Chorus; Salzmann, cond. Mercury SR 4-9122 (Record 3 of 4)
[CARDOSO. Mass for 6 voices. LOPEZ DE MORAGO (motets). Gaudete cum laetitia; Jesus Redemptor II; Laudate Pueri II; Oculi mei; Quam vidistis pastores. PEDRO DE CRISTO (motets). O magnum mysterium; Quaeramus cum pastoribus.] (sch 10/67)

Praetorius et son temps. See *Ten Christmas Songs from the Time of Praetorius* (No.874).

817. *Pueri cantores.* Petits Chanteurs à la Croix de Bois; ensembles and soloists; Maillet, dir.   Pathé STX 155
[BERCHEM. O Jesu Christe. HANDL. Radix Jesse. HASSLER. Es kam ein Engel. MAUDUIT. En son temple sacré. ANON. Venite! Exultemus. Also Perosi, Gruber, Haug, Cottau, Trexler, Metayer, Rameau, Bach, and traditional folk songs.]   (dia 67)

818. *Recital de Madrigale.*
[v.1]: Corul "Madrigal" al Conservatorului "Ciprian Porumbescu."
M. Constantin, dir.   Electrecord St-ECE 0264
[ARCADELT. Il bianco e dolce cigno. BONNET. Mon père et ma mère. DONATO. Chi la gagliarda. HASSLER. Ach Lieb hier is das Herze. LASSUS. Ich weiss mir ein Meidlein. PALESTRINA. I vaghi fiori. PASSEREAU. Il est bel et bon. PLANCON. Où estes-vous. SCANDELLO. Bongiorno madonna. SERMISY. Languir me fais.]   (Peters Intl. catalog)

819. [v.2]: Corul "Madrigal" al Conservatorului "Ciprian Porumbescu."
M. Constantin, dir.   Electrecord ST-ECE 0265; ECD 1076
[BENNET. Weep o mine eyes. BONNET. Francion vint l'outre jour. GASTOLDI. Speme amorosa. GOUDIMEL. Par le désert de mes peines. HANDL. Ecce, quomodo moritur. JANEQUIN. Au joli jeu. LASSUS. Matona mia cara. MONTEVERDI. Lasciatemi morire. MORLEY. Fire, fire. WIDMANN. Wohlauf ihr Gäste.]   (Peters Intl. catalog)

820. *The Renaissance Band.* New York Pro Musica; N. Greenberg, dir.
                                                      Decca DL 9424; 79424
[ISAAC. A la bataglia. LASSUS. Chi chilichi; Echo-valle profonda; Hor che la nuova; Passan vostri triomphi. M. PRAETORIUS. Courant de la Royne; Galliarde; Galliarde de la guerre; Galliarde de Monsieur Wustrow; La bouree. Passameze; Passameze pour les cornetz; Reprinse. With demonstrations of early instruments.]

821. *The Renaissance Band.* Stanford University Collegium Musicum; Nordstrom, cond.   Orion 6905
[HASSLER. Ihr musici, frisch auf. HOFHAIMER. Meins traurens ist. ISAAC. La la hö hö. LAPICIDUS. Tander naken. LASSUS. Ich weiss ein Mädlein hübsch und fein. PRAETORIUS. Volte: Bransle de la Royne. SCHMIDT. Io mi son giovanetta. SENFL. Ach Elselein; Es taget vor dem Walde; Es wollt' ein Mädlein Wasser hol'n; Wann ich des Morgens früh aufsteh'.]   (sch 12/69)

822. *Renaissance Choral Music for Christmas.* N.C.R.V. Vocaal Ensemble, Hilversum; M. Voorberg, cond. Kaufbeurer Martinsfinken; L. Hahn, cond. Niedersächsischer Singkreis, Hannover; W. Träder, cond.
                                                    Nonesuch H 1095; 71095
[DEPRES. Praeter rerum seriem. A. GABRIELI. Quem vidistis pastores.

G. GABRIELI. Hodie Christus natus est; O Jesu mi dulcissime. HANDL.
Egredietur virga / Radix Jesse. GESIUS. Ein Kind geborn zu Bethlehem
(verse 2 by M. PRAETORIUS; verse 3 by M. VULPIUS). M. PRAETO-
RIUS. Es ist ein Ros entsprungen. WALTHER. Joseph, lieber Joseph
mein. Also Scheidt, Schütz.]

823. *Renaissance Chorus.* Brown, cond.   Baroque 9003
[OBRECHT. Missa Je ne demande (Gloria and Credo). OCKEGHEM.
Credo sine nomine. Also Johannes Martini.]   (hi-fi 8/62)

Renaissance Dances from the 14th through the 16th Centuries. See
Estampies, Basses Dances, Pavanes (No.557).

824. *La Renaissance espagnole.* Choeur Madrigal, Barcelona; M. Cabero, dir.
                                          10" Harmonia Mundi HM 25305
[BRUDIEU. Ma voluntat amb la rao s'envolpa. CARCERES. Toca, Juan
tu rabelejo. ENCINA. Ay, triste que vengo. ESCOBAR. La mis penas
madre. GUERRERO. Prado verde y florido. PALOMARES. En el
campo florido. VICTORIA. Ave Maria; Caligaverunt. ANON. Dadme
albricios.]   (dia 64)

825. *Renaissance Festival Music: Flemish Dances and Venetian Music.* New
York Pro Musica; N. Greenberg, cond.
                Decca DL 9419; 79419 and Brunswick AXA 4511; SXA 4511
[A. GABRIELI. Ricercar del XII tono. G. GABRIELI. Canzon terza;
Canzon quarta; Canzon VII toni. GRILLO. Canzon. MASCHERA.
Canzon "La Fontana." SUSATO. Allemaingne and Recoupe; Basse
danse and Reprise; Basse danse "La mourisque"; Branle and "Fagot";
Pavane Mille regretz; Pavana La Bataille; 2 Rondes. VIADANA. Canzon
La Padovana.]

826. *La Renaissance Flamande.* Chorale et Ensemble d'instruments Anciens
de la "Halewyn Stichting d'Anvers"; W. Weyler, cond.
                                          10" Harmonia Mundi HMO 25306
[BASTON. Verheugt u nu, bedruckte geesten. BELLE. Laat ons nu al
Verblyden. LASSUS. Gallans qui par terre. LATTRE. Al Hadden wy en
veerting Bedden. RORE. Anchor che col partire; Hélas comment; Musica
dulci sono; En vos adieux. SUSATO. Allemande du "Muziekboeksken"
de Tieleman; Ronde du "Muziekboeksken" de Tieleman. SWELINCK.
Pavana Philippi; Von der Fortuna werd' ich getrieben. WALHOUT.
Musiciens qui chantez à plaisir. ANON. Ik zeg adieu.]   (Harmonia
Mundi catalog)

827. *Renaissance Lieder and Chansons.* Dowland Consort; B. Boydell, dir.
                                                     Alpha AVM 021
[CERTON. La, la, la, je ne l'ose dire. COSTELEY. Arreste un peu, mon
coeur; Quand le berger. ISAAC. Innsbruck, ich muss dich lassen.
LASSUS. Ich weiss mir ein Maidlein; Mon coeur se recommande; La nuict
froide et sombre; Un jour vis un foulon qui fouloit. LECHNER. Deutsche

827. *Renaissance Lieder and Chansons.* (Continued)
Sprüche von Leben und Tod. LEJEUNE. La belle aronde. MAUDUIT.
Voyci le verd et beau May. PASSEREAU. Il est bel et bon. REGNARD.
Petite nymfe folâtre.] (gr 7/65)

828. *Renaissance Music.* Hanover Singkreis; Bremen Camerata Vocale;
N.C.R.V. Vocaal Ensemble, Hilversum; Kaufbeurer Martinsfinken.
                    Nonesuch H 1097; 71097 and World Record Club H 71097
[ARCADELT. O felici occhi miei; Sapet' amanti; Voi ve n'andate.
BENNET. All creatures now. COSTE. Pour faire plustost mal.
DOWLAND. Say love; Shall I sue. EUSTORG. Voici le bon temps.
FESTA. Se'l pensier. JEEP. Musica, die ganz lieblich Kunst. LAYOLLE.
La fille qui n'a point d'amye. MORLEY. Sing we and chant it.
MORNABLE. L'Heur d'amitie. PEUERL. O Musica, du edle Kunst;
Frischauf und lass uns singen. PILKINGTON. Rest, sweet nymphs.
RORE. De la belle contrade. SANDRIN. Qui vouldra scavoir. SERMISY.
Pourtant si je suis brunett. SWELINCK. Tes beaux yeux; Tu as tout seul.
WEELKES. Hark all ye lovely saints.] (gr 12/69)
(N.B.: Compare English and Italian contents with *Chansons und
Madrigale der Renaissance* (No.492).)

Renaissance Music. (Capella Antiqua, Munich). See *Staatsmusik der
Renaissance* (No.862).

829. *Renaissance Music for Brass.* Brass ensemble; G. Masson, cond.
                    Nonesuch H 1111; 71111
[ADSON. 3 Courtly masquing ayres (Nos.9, 1, 2). ATTAINGNANT. 2
Galliardes. BANCHIERI. 4 Fantasie overo canzoni alla francese. M.
FRANCK. Intrada II. A. GABRIELI. Ricercare IX del XII tono. G.
GABRIELI. Canzon I, La Spiritata. STOLTZER. 4 Pieces from Octo
tonorum melodiae (No.1, dorian; No.2, hypodorian; No.3, phrygian;
No.7, mixolydian). Also Scheidemann, Schütz and Frescobaldi.]

830. *Renaissance Music from Advent to Christmas.* Ambrosian Singers; J.
McCarthy, cond.   Delysé ECB 3204; DS 3204
[AICHINGER. Jubilate Deo (Ps.99). ASOLA. Quem vidistis pastores.
BERNARDI. Benedixisti Domine. BYRD. Beata viscera; Tollite portas.
ESQUIVEL. Veni Domine. G. GABRIELI. Deus, Deus meus (Ps.62);
Hodie Christus. GUERRERO. Canite tuba in Sion. MONTEVERDI.
Angelus ad pastores. PALESTRINA. Ad te levavi; Ave Maria. VAET.
Ecce apparebit. VICTORIA. Ne timeas Maria; O magnum mysterium.
ANON. (Plainsong). Christus natus est nobis; O radix Jesse. Also
Schein.] (gr 12/68)

831. *Requiem und Totenklagen um 1500-1550.* Capella Antiqua, Munich; K.
Ruhland, cond.   Telefunken SAWT 9471
[APPENZELLER. Musae Jovis ter Maximi. BRUMEL. O Domine Jesu
Christe. LA RUE. Missa pro defunctis (Requiem). SENFL. Non moriar
sed vivam; Quis dabit oculis nostris. VAET. Continuo lacrimas. VINDERS.

O mors inevitabilis.]   (biel 2/67)

832. *Les riches heures musicales d'Henry VIII et d'Elisabeth I.* Ensemble
polyphonique de Paris; Charles Ravier, cond.
Erato STU 70363 and Musical Heritage Society MHS 905
[BENNET. Weep, o mine eyes. CORNYSHE. Ah Robin, gentle Robin.
DOWLAND. M. Bucton's galliard; Lord Chamberlaine's galliard; M.
Thomas Collier, his galliard. GIBBONS. Galliard. HENRY VIII. Consort
XXIV; It is to me; The time of youth; Though some saith; Hélas Madame.
MORLEY. Clorinda false; Canzonet; Fire, fire; O grief e'en on the bud.
WEELKES. Hark all ye lovely saints above. ANON. Bonny sweet Robin;
Cloris sighed; Drewries accord; Madame d'amours; O death rock me to
sleep; Where be ye, my love.]

833. *Royal Brass Music.* The London Gabrieli Brass Ensemble.
Pye/Golden Guinea GGC 4072; GSGC 14072 and
Nonesuch H 1118; 71118
[Suite from the Royal Brass Music of King James I: BASSANO. Fantasia.
BUSSANE. Pavan. FARNABY. Almande. GUY. Almande. HARDING.
Almande. ANON. Almande.
Plus: G. GABRIELI. Sonata pian e forte. HOLBORNE. As it fell on a
holy eve; The choice; The fairy round; The fruit of love; Gaillard.
LASSUS. Adoramus te Christe. TROMBONCINO. Sarà forsi ripres' il
pensier mio. Also Schein and Locke.]

834. *The Royal Brass Music of James I.* Brass ensemble; T. Dart, dir.
L'oiseau-lyre OL 50189; SOL 60019 and
London AWO 9943; SAWO 9943
[A. BASSANO. Pavane no.16. J. BASSANO. Fantasia. COPERARIO.
Fantasia no.76. DERING. Fantasia. FARNABY. Almande. FERRA-
BOSCO II. Almande no.5; Pavane; Almande. GUY. Almande no.13.
HARDING. Almande. HOLBORNE. As it fell on a holy eve; The choice;
The fairy round; The fruit of love; Galliard. JOHNSON. Almande no.7.
LEETHERLAND. Pavane. LUPO. Almande. SIMPSON. Intrada.]
(Myers 12/61)

Royal Court Music. See *The Music of the Royal Courts of Their Most
Illustrious Majesties ...* (No.742).

Sacred and Secular Music of the Gothic Period. See *Music of Medieval
France* (No.724).

Sacred Music Around 1400. See *Geistliche Musik um 1400* (No.589).

835. *Sacred Polyphony of the 16th Century.* St. Mary of the Angels Choir,
Wellington; M. Fernie, dir.   Kiwi SLD 10
[JOHN (JOÃO) IV. Crux fidelis. PALESTRINA. Ad te levavi; Sicut
cervus; Super flumina. PHILIPS. Gaudent in coelis; Tibi laus, tibi gloria.
VICTORIA. Jesum tradidit impius; Recessit Pastor Noster; Seniores
populi consilium fecerunt.] (gr 4/68)

836. *Sacred Songs and Instrumental Music of Luther's Time.* Studio der
frühen Musik, Munich.   Telefunken S 9532
[ALDER. Da Jakob nu das Kleid ansach. BRUCK. Aus tiefer Not.
HELLINCK. Capitan Herrgot. HOFHAIMER. Carmen. ISAAC. Carmen
in fa; Carmen in G; Suesser Vatter. KOTTER. Aus tiefer Not. KUNGS-
BERGER. Urbs beata. SCHLICK. Maria zart (org). SENFL. Christ ist
erstanden; Da Jesus an dem Kreuze hing; O du armer Judas. ANON.
Gelassen had eyn sustergen; Mit got so wöln wirs heben; O Jesu Christ;
Pro eomium; Urbs beata / In dedicatione.]

837. *San Carlo di Brescia.* René Saorgin (org).   Harmonia Mundi HMO 30728
[A. GABRIELI. Ricercare Arioso; Ricercare du 7e ton. G. GABRIELI.
Canzon La Spiritata. GUAMI. Toccata du 2e ton. MALVEZZI. Canzon
du 2e ton. MERULO. Canzon La Marca; Toccata du 2e ton. SODERINI.
Canzon La Scaramuccia.]

838. *Schweizer Musik aus Mittelalter und Renaissance.* Walter and Silvia Frei
(various ancient instruments).   Fono-Gesellschaft Luzern FGL 24-4315
[APIARIUS. Es taget vor dem Walde. BALBULUS. Sancti spiritus assit
(hymn). CYEAT. Nabi sid in te cathe. GLAREANUS. Donec gratus
eram tibi. FENIS. Nun ist niht mêre. HEINRICH VON LOUFENBERG.
Ich wöllt das ich doheime wer. MEYER. Fuga. SENFL. Ich armes
Käuzlein kleine. TUOTILO. Hodie cantandus. WANNEMACHER. Aus
tiefer Not; Min Gmüet und Blüet. WÜRZBURG. Des soltu clein
geniessen. ANON. Ave Virgo virginum (sequence); Constans esto, fili
mi; Appenzeller Kuhreien; Ad regnum epulentum; Gaudens in Domino
(motet); Ich scheid mit Leid.]

Scottish Keyboard Music and Dances. See *Early Scottish Keyboard
Music ...* (No.530).

Secular Music Around 1300. See *Weltliche Musik um 1300* (No.899).

839. *Secular Music of the Renaissance.* Capella Monacensis; K. Weinhöppel,
dir.   Musical Heritage Society MHS 713 and Amadeo AVRS 5030
[ARCADELT. O felici occhi miei. DEPRES. Il grillo. ENCINA.
Gasajémonos de husla. HASSLER. Tanzen und springen. ISAAC.
Innsbruck, ich muss dich lassen. LAURENTIUS (THE ELDER).
Waer is hij nu. NEUSIEDLER. Ein guter Gassenhauer (instr).
OBRECHT. Laet u ghenoughen, liever Johan (instr). ORTIZ. Recercada;
Diferencias sobre O felici occhi miei. SENFL. Ein Maidlein zu dem
Brunnen ging. SUSATO. Ronde and Saltarello. TORRE. Alta.
WAELRANT. Als ick u vinde. ANON. Dale, si le das; Es gingen drei
Baurn; In carnevale; Kehraus (instr); Mij heeft een Piperken; Pase el
agoa; Rodrigo Martines (villancico); Venid a sospirar (instr); Das
Yegerhorn.]

840. *Secular Spanish Music of the Sixteenth Century.* The Ambrosian
Consort; D. Stevens, cond; R. Jesson (hpsi).
Penn State Music Series PSMS 102-S and Oryx 717 and
Da Camera Magna SM 94025
[CABEZON. Diferencias sobre el canto llano del Caballero; Duviensela;
Pavan; Pavana Italiana. FLECHA. Que farem del pobre Joan?; Teresica
hermana. SCOTTO (?). No so yo. ANON. Ay luna que reluzes;
Falalalera, de la guarda riera; Hartaos ojos de llorar; Riu, riu, chiu;
Si amores me han de matar; Si de vos mi bien me aparto; Si la nocha
haze escura.]

841. *Secular Vocal Music of the Renaissance.* Ambrosian Singers and Players;
D. Stevens, cond.   Dover HCR 5262
Side 1
[Spanish Music (from the *Cancionero musical de Palacio)*: ALDOMAR.
Ha, Pelayo. ALONSO. La tricotea Samartin. BADAJOZ. O desdichado
de mi. ENCINA. Cucú, cucú; Oy comamos; Tan buen ganadico; Una
sañosa porfia. VILCHES. Ya cantan los gallos.
Side 2
LUZZASCHI. O dolcezze amarissime d'amore; O primavera. RORE.
Ancor che col partire; En vos adieux. STRIGGIO. Il gioco di primiera.
WERT. Non è si denso velo; Un jour je m'en allai; Vezzosi augelli.]

842. *Sei willekommen, Herre Christ.* Capella Antiqua, Munich; K. Ruhland,
cond.   10" Christophorus CLP 75482
[DUFAY. Hymnus in adventu Domini. PRAETORIUS. Ein Kind geborn
zu Bethlehem; Wachet auf. SENFL. Puer natus est nobis. ANON. Dies
est laetitae (Glogauer); Fulgent nunc (Glogauer); Gaudens in domino; O
miranda dei karita (Bamberg); Sei willekommen, Herre Christ (Erfurt Ms);
Der Tag, der ist so freudenreich.]   (biel 1/64)

843. *Sept motets pour le temps de la passion avec méditations bibliques.*
Quatuor Vocal Caillat.   10" Jericho 401
[GAGLIANO. Tristus est anima mea. LASSUS. Adoramus te.
PALESTRINA. O Domine Jesu Christe. VICTORIA. Tenebrae factae
sunt. Also Martini, Genet, Lotti.]   (dia 64)

844. *Seraphim Guide to Renaissance Music.* Syntagma Musicum, Amsterdam;
Kees Otten, dir.   3-12" Seraphim SIC 6052
[ADAM DE LA HALLE. Dieus soit en cheste maison; Robin m'aime.
ALFONSO EL SABIO. Rosa das rosas. CORNYSHE. Trolly, lolly.
DEPRES. Missa de Nostra Domina (Agnus Dei); Basiez moy; La
Bernardina. DUFAY. Flos florum; Resvelons nous, resvelons amoureux.
DUNSTABLE. Sancta Maria. ENCINA. O reyes magos benditos.
FACOLI. Aria della Marchetta Saporita; Aria della Signora Moretta.
GANASSI. Ricercar. GASTOLDI. Musica a due voci. GHERARDELLO
DA FIRENZE. Agnus Dei. GULIELMUS. La bassa castiglia. HENRY
VIII. O my hart. ISAAC. Ecce Virgo; Innsbruck ich muss dich lassen.

844. *Seraphim Guide to Renaissance Music.* (Continued)
JACOPO DA BOLOGNA. Non al suo amante. JAN Z LUBLINA.
Doulce memoire. LA RUE. Mijn hert altijt heeft verlanghen. LANDINO.
Echo la primavera. LEGRANT. Or avant, gentiltz fillettes; Wilhelmus
Legrant. LORENZO DA FIRENZE. Sanctus. MACHAUT. Trop plus /
Biauté / Je ne suis. OBRECHT. Fuga. OCKEGHEM. Missa Quinti toni
(Kyrie). ORTIZ. Recercade segonda sobre La misma cancion. OTHMAYR.
Vom Himmel hoch. PAUMANN. [untitled piece from *Fundamentum
Organisandi*]. PEROTIN. Alleluja. PERRIN D'AGINCOURT. Ballade.
PESENTI. Gagliarda. RESINARIUS. Nun komm der heiden Heiland.
RICHARD I. Ballade. SACHS. Salve ich grüsz dich schöne. SANDRIN.
Doulce memoire. SUSATO. De Post. SWELINCK. Marchans qui
traversez; Toccata. TASSIN. Chose Tassin I, II. TURNHOUT. Compt al
wt (uyt) zuyden. VALDERRABANO. Pavana. WALTHER. Ein feste
Burg. ANON. Agnus Dei (Worcester 68); Alle psallite cum luya
(Montpellier); Ave Maria (Paris Lat.15139); Benedicamus Domino
(Paris It.568); Bruder Konrad (Glogauer); Chanson (Paris B.N. Ms.);
Ciz chans veult boire (Roman de Fauvel); Contre le temps (Reina);
Czenner Greyner (Glogauer); Danse Real (Paris Fr.844); Deus in
adjutorium (Turin Ms); Di molen van Paris; Ductia; Es suld eyn Man
(Glogauer); Het dunct mi wesen verre (Prague Ms); Ich sachz eyns Mols
(Glogauer); Das Jägerhorn (Glogauer); Kyrie (instr. Faenza); Lamento
di Tristano (British Museum Add 29987); Lasse! que deviendrai je
(Paris H.12483); Missa Tournai (Kyrie and Sanctus); Motet, Je gart le
bois (Montpellier); Robin m'aime (Montpellier); Trotto (British Museum
Add 29987).]
N.B.: Contents of this set similar to those issued under title: *Cinq
siècles de joyeuse musique,* Voix son maître SME 191.761/2 (No.503),
and *Music of the Middle Ages and Renaissance,* H.M.V. HQS 1195-6
(No.735).

845. *Shakespearean Songs and Consort Music.* Deller Consort; D. Dupré
(lute); A. Deller (c-tnr).
Victrola VIC 1266; VICS 1266 and Oryx 726;
1526 and Harmonia Mundi DR 202
[BYRD. Non nobis Domine. CUTTING. Walsingham variations (instr).
JOHNSON. Full fathom five; Where the bee sucks. MORLEY. It was a
lover and his lass; O mistress mine. WEELKES. Strike it up, Tabor.
WILSON. Take, O take those lips away. ANON. Bonny sweet Robin;
Caleno custure me; Greensleeves; He that will an alehouse keep; How
should I your true love know; Kemp's jig; Then they for sudden joy did
weep; We be soldiers three; When griping griefs; When that I was; Willow
song.]
N.B.: Oryx 1526 has title *Shakespearian Songs and Lute Solos.*

846. *Siècle de la réforme.* Maîtrise Oratoire Louvre; Hornung, cond; Chanteurs Traditionnels, Paris; M. Honegger, cond.   Studio S.M. 33-64
[BOURGEOIS. Oraison de Notre-Seigneur. CHAMPION. Ps.34. CAULERY. Ps.13. GOUDIMEL. Ps.25; Ps.47; Ps.133. JANEQUIN. Ps.5. L'ESTOCART. Ps.32; Ps.91. LUPI. Ps.149.] (dia 67)

847. *The Silver Swan: Madrigals of Gibbons, Byrd, Ward and Pilkington.* Deller Consort.   Bach Guild BG 624
[BYRD. This sweet and merry month; Though Amaryllis dance. GIBBONS. Ah! dear heart; Dainty fine bird; The silver swan; What is our life. PILKINGTON. Amyntas with his Phyllis fair; Diaphena like the daffdown-dilly; Have I found her; O softly singing lute; Rest sweet nymphs. WARD. Out from the vale; Retire my troubled soul; Upon a bank with roses.]

848. *Sing Joyfully.* St. Michael's College Choir, Tenbury; L. Nethsingha, cond.
                               Argo RG 423; ZRG 5423
[BYRD. Sacerdotes Domini; Sing joyfully. GIBBONS. Nunc dimittis. MORLEY. Agnus Dei; Magnificat. REDFORD. Rejoice in the Lord. TALLIS. If you love me. TYE. O come, ye servants of the Lord. Also Britten, Murrill, Stanford, Vaughan Williams and Ouseley.] (gr 1/65)

Sing We at Pleasure. See *English Madrigals* (No.544).

849. Sistine Chapel Choir. L. Perosi, dir.   10" Voce del Padrone QBLP 5048
[ANERIO. Requiem aeternum. ARCADELT. Ave Maria. PALESTRINA. Improperia; Sicut cervus; Super flumina Babylonis. VICTORIA. Factae sunt.] (sant 5-6/71)

850. *Sistine Chapel Choir at the Vatican.* D. Bartolucci, cond.   Everest 3193
[DEPRES. Ave Maria. MARENZIO. Innocentes pro Christo. MORALES. Pastores dicite; Natum vidimus. PALESTRINA. Benedictus qui venit; Hodie Christus natus est; Surge illuminare Jerusalem. ANON. Dio s'ei fatto fanciullo; Sopra il fieno colcato. Also Bartolucci and Perosi.]

851. *Sixteenth-Century Love Songs.* Rome Polyphonic Chorus; Q. Petrocchi.
                               Victor VIC 1231; VICS 1231
[AZZAIOLO. L'amanza mia si chiama Saporita; Ti parti cor mio caro. DEPRES. El grillo. DONATO. Chi la gagliarda. GASTOLDI. Amor vittorioso. LASSUS. Matona mia cara; O occhi manza mia. PALESTRINA. Da cosi' dotta man; Vaghi pensier. VECCHI. Con voce dai sospiri interrotta; Cruda mia tiranniella; Leva la man di qui; Quando mirai la bella faccia d'oro; So ben mi ch'a' bon tempo.] (gr 10/67)

Sixteenth-Century Spain. See *Anthologie der mehrstimmigen Volksmusik des 16. Jahrhunderts* (No.460).

Sixteenth-Century Spanish Music. See *Secular Spanish Music of the Sixteenth Century* (No.840).

Sixteenth-Century Spanish Vocal Polyphony. See *Anthologie der mehrstimmigen Volksmusik des 16. Jahrhunderts* (No.460).

852. *Sixteenth-Century Vocal Works.* Les Petits Chanteurs du Mont-Royal.
                                                                Oryx EXP 36
[ARCADELT. Margot, laboures les vignes. COSTELEY. La, je n'yray.
HASSLER. Cantate Domino. JANEQUIN. Le chant des oyseaux; La
guerre. LASSUS. L'echo; Matona mia cara; La nuit. LEJEUNE. Tu
ne l'enten pas. PALESTRINA. Missa Lauda Sion (Sanctus); Precatus est.
PASSEREAU. Il est bel et bon. VICTORIA. Victimae Paschali Laudes.]
(gr 6/70)

Songs and Dances by Dowland, East and Holborne. See *Metaphysical Tobacco* (No.680).

Songs for Tenor and Guitar. See *Songs with Guitar* (No.856).

853. *Songs from Shakespeare's Plays and Popular Songs of Shakespeare's Time.* T. Kines (tnr with lute); J. Steele (rcdr); J. Sands (vlc); E.
McCuaig (hpsi).   Folkways 8767
[HENRY VIII. Pastime with good company. MORLEY. It was a lover
and his lass. ANON. Agincourt song; Ah, the sighs that come fro' the
heart; All in a garden green; Caleno custore; Cobbler's jig; Greensleeves;
Heart's ease; Heigh-ho for a husband; High Barbaree; Light o'love; O
mistress mine; Peg o'Ramsey; The Spanish lady; The three ravens; When
that I was a little tiny boy; Willow song.]   (arg 7/64)

Songs of Andalusia in Middle Ages and Renaissance. See *Music from the Middle Ages and Renaissance* (No.718).

854. *Songs of Birds, Battles and Love, and the Flowering of the French Chanson.* A. Deller (c-tnr); Deller Consort.   Vanguard SRV 298-SD
[COSTELEY. Allons gay bergères; Mignonne allons voir si la rose.
DEPRES. La déploration de Jean Okeghem; Parfons regretz. GRIMACE.
Alarme, alarme. JANEQUIN. Au joly boys; La Bataille de Marignan; Le
chant de l'alouette; Le chant des oiseaux; Ce moys de May. LASSUS. La
nuit froide et sombre; Mon coeur se recommande à vous. MACHAUT.
Comment qu'a moy. PASSEREAU. Il est bel et bon. ANON. Or sus
dormez trop.]   (Myers 12/70)

855. *Songs of Shakespeare; Authentic Musical Versions from 14 Plays, with Lute Accompaniment.* C. Casson.   Spoken Word 159
[MORLEY. It was a lover and his lass; O mistress mine. ANON. How
should I my true love know; When that I was a little tiny boy. Other
works, 18th century or later.]   (sch 10/60)

856. *Songs with Guitar.* W. Brown (tnr); J. Williams (guit).
                                Odyssey 32160398 and CBS Classics 61126
[BARTLETT. Of all the birds that I do know. CAMPION. I care not for
these ladies. DOWLAND. Fantasie; Melancholy galliard; My Lady

Hunsden's puffe. JONES. Go to bed, sweet Muse. PILKINGTON.
Diaphena. ROSSETER. When Laura smiles. ANON. The willow song.
Also Britten, Dodgson.]   (gr 4/70)

Spanische Chormusik des 16. Jahrhunderts. See *Secular Spanish Music
of the Sixteenth Century* (No.840).

857. *Spanish Guitar Music of Five Centuries, v.1.* N. Yepes (guit).
                                                               DGG 139365
[MILAN. 6 pavanas. MUDARRA. Fantasia que contrabaze la harpa en la
manera de Ludovico. NARVAEZ. Cancion del Emperador; Differencias
sobre Guardame las vacas. PISADOR. Pavana muy llana para taner;
Villanesca. Also Sanz and Soler.]   (Myers 9/69)

858. *Spanish Harp Music of the 16th and 17th Centuries.* N. Zabaleta (harp).
                                                           DGG Archive 198458
[CABEZON. Diferencias sobre el Canto del caballero; Diferencias sobre
la Gallarda milanesa; Pavana con su glosa; Pavana italiana. MUDARRA.
Tiento para harpa. And works by PALERO, ALBERTO, RIBAYAS,
HUETE, RODRIQUEZ, and ANON.]   (gr 4/70)

859. *Spanish Keyboard Music of the 16th and 17th Centuries.* P. Wolfe (hpsi).
                Expériences Anonymes EA 0026; Music Heritage Society MHS 681
[CABEZON. Diferencias sobre La Gallarda Milanesa; Diferencias sobre
La Pavana Italiana; Diferencias sobre el Canto del Cavallero; Diferencias
sobre La dama le demande; Romance para quien crie yo cabellos; Tiento
del primero tono. ALBERTO. Tiento de falsas. SOTO. Tiento del sesto
tono. ANON. Pues no me quereis hablar; Fantasia sobre fa mi ut re; Al
revuelo de una garza. Also Cabanilles.]

860. *Spanish Medieval Music.* New York Pro Musica; N. Greenberg, cond.
                Decca DL 9416; 79416 and Brunswick AXA 4513; SXA 4513
[ALFONSO EL SABIO. (from Cantigas de Santa Maria): Porque trobar
(1); Santa Maria (7); Por nos de dulta livrar (18); Pagar ben pod' o que
dever' (25); Nas mentes senpre tẽer (29); O que a Santa Maria (35);
Tanto son da Groriosa (48); Ben com' aos que van per mar (49); Da que
Deus (77); Maravillosos (139); Como poden per sas culpas (166). ANON.
(from Codex Calixtinus): Annua Gaudia (conductus); Alleluia / Vocavit
Jesus Jacobum; Benedicamus Domino / Congaudeant catholici. ANON.
(from Las Huelgas, Mass in Honor of the Blessed Virgin Mary): Agnus
Dei / Regula moris; Kyrie / Rex virginum; Sanctus / Cleri cetus; Maria
virgo virginum (sequence).]

Spanish Music of Five Centuries. See *Spanish Guitar Music of Five
Centuries* (No.857).

Spanish Organ Works of the 16th Century. See *Orgelwerke des 16.
Jahrhunderts* (No.796).

861. *Spanish Songs of the Renaissance.* V. De Los Angeles (sop); Ars Musica
Ensemble; Lamaña, cond.
Angel 35888 and Voix de son Maître ASDF 729; FALP 729
[CORNAGO. Gentil dama non se gana. DAZA. Dame acogida en tu hato;
Enfermo estaba Antioco. ENCINA. Ay triste que vengo. ENRIQUE. Mi
querer tanto vos quiere. FUENLLANA. De Antequera salió el moro; De
los alamos vengo, madre; Duélete de mi Señora. GABRIEL. No soy yo
quién la descubre. MILAN. A quel caballero, madre. VASQUEZ.
Morenica, dame un beso. VALDERRABANO. De dondé venis, amore?;
Señora, si te olvidare. ANON. Una hija tiene el rey; Una matica de ruda;
Pase el agua; Julieta; Pastorcico non te aduermas; Si la noche se hace
oscura.]

Spanish Vocal and Instrumental Music of the 15th-17th Centuries. See
The Pleasures of Cervantes (No.807).

862. *Staatsmusik der Renaissance.* Capella Antiqua, Munich; K. Ruhland,
cond.   Telefunken SAWT 9561/2
[APPENZELLER. Plangite Pierides. BARBION. Gallis hostibus in fugam
coactis. BRUBIER. Vivite felices. CLEMENT. O quam moesta dies.
COMPERE. Da pacem; Quis numerare queat. CORTECCIA. Ingredere
felicissimis. COURTOIS. Venite populi. DEPRES. Absolve, quaesumus,
Domine; Carmen gallicum; Cueurs desolez. GASCOGNE. Bone Jesu
dulcissime. ISAAC. Imperii proceres; Sancti spiritus assit nobis.
JACHET DE MANTOVA. O Angele Dei. LASSUS. Heroum soboles.
MODERNE. La bataille. MOUTON. Exultet coniubilando; Quis dabit
oculis nostris. FILIPPO DI LURANO. Quercus iuncta columna est.
SERMISY. Quosque non reverteris pax. WILLAERT. Victor io salve ...
Quis curare neget. ZWINGLI. Herr, nun heb' den wagen selb. ANON.
Julia dic experta meas vires; Proch dolor ... Pie Jesu.]   (biel 2/70)

863. *Storico organo construito da Antegnati nel 1581.* Zanaboni (org).
Vedette VPC 1505; VST 6005
[ANTEGNATI. Ricercare del X tono. CAVAZZONI. Christe Redemptor
Omnium; Ave Maris Stella. A. GABRIELI. Canzone ariosa; Intonazione
del VII tono. G. GABRIELI. Fuga del IX tono; La Spiritata. Also
Frescobaldi.]   (sant 5-6/71)

Streichmusik und Blasmusik der Renaissance. See *Cuivres et violes de la
Renaissance* (No.513).

864. Syntagma Musicum Ensemble, Amsterdam.   Odeon CO63 24011
[DUFAY. 6 hymns [unspecified]. A. de LANTINS. Missa Verbum
incarnatum. H. de LANTINS. Cesla sublimatur.]   (Peters Intl. catalog)

865. *Tablatures de Sicher (1490-1546).* Ensemble d'orgues W. von Karajan.
Charlin AM 67
[Resonet in laudibus; Ave Maris Stella; In dulci jubilo; Canzone à tte.
[sic]   (dia 2/70)

866. *Tänze und Chansons - Instrumental Musik un 1500.* Capella Antiqua, Munich; K. Ruhland, cond. 10" Christophorus CLP 75514; SCLP 75515 [Attaingnant, Susato, Dufay, Caron, Brumel, Stockhem and Anon.] (biel 2/69)

867. Talsma, Willem R. Organ Recital.   DGG Archive 198445 [ATTAINGNANT. Tant que vivray. CLEMENT. Ick segh adieu; Ps.65. ISAAC. Herr Gott lass dich erbarmen. MACQUE. Durezze et ligatura, Seconda strauaganze. SERMISY. Tant que vivray. SWELINCK. Echo-Fantasia in d minor; Fantasia; Malle Sijmen; Toccata in G major; Variations on Von der fortuna werd' ich getrieben. SUSATO. Mon désir (basse dance); Wo bistu; Rondo / Saltarello. WILLAERT. Ricercare. ANON. Allemande; Branle Champagne; 2 untitled works. Also Abraham von der Kerckhoven and Steenwick.]

868. *Tanzmusik aus vier Jahrhunderten.* Pro Arte Antiqua, Prague.
                                                Supraphon SUA 10412; SUA 50037 [BINCHOIS. Rondeau. DEMANTIUS. Intrada. DEPRES. Fantasia. ISAAC. Tmeiskin was jonck. LASSUS. 2 madrigals. OCKEGHEM. Ut heremita solus (motet). SCHMELZER VON EHRENRUFF. Die Fachterschule: Allegro, Moderato, Sarabande, Courante, l'Ecole d'escrime, Aria. TOLAR. Balletto: Sonata, Intrada, Courante, Sarabande, Gigue, Retirada. WILLAERT. Fantasia. ANON. [PRAGENSIS XVI]. 2 gotische Tänze.] (biel 1/64)

869. *Tanzmusik der Gotik und Renaissance.* Les Menestrels; Wiener Ensemble für alte Musik; E. Kölz, dir.
                                    Amadeo AVRS 5052 and [Fr.] 66003 and
                                          Musical Heritage Society MHS 761 [GERVAISE. Allemande; Pavane-Passamezzo; Galliarde; Bransles de Bourgogne; Bransles de Champagne. JEAN LE GRAND. Entre vous. SUSATO. Pavan, The Battle; Allemande. TORRE. Alta danza. ANON. Trotto; Nota; Lamento di Tristan; Saltarello; Istampita ghaetta; Molendium de Paris; Stantipes; Allemande (lute); Pavane (lute); Galliarde (lute).]

870. *Tanzmusik der Renaissance.* Various performers.
                                    Victrola VICS 1328 and Harmonia Mundi HM 30610
                                                          and Discaphon 4231 [ATTAINGNANT. Galliarde; Pavane; Tourdion. DEMANTIUS. Galliarde; Polnischer Tanz. FRANCK. Galliarda; Pavana. GERVAISE. Bransle simple. HASSLER. (Lustgarten). Prima intrada; Quinta intrada; Septima intrada. MODERNE. Branle gay nouveau; 3 bransles de Bourgogne. PHALESE. L'arboscello ballo Furlano. SUSATO. Hoboecken dans; Pavane Mille regretz; Pavane Si pas souffrir; Ronde; Ronde Il estoit une fillette; Ronde and Saltarello.]

871. *Tanzmusik und Tischsitten der Renaissance.* Collegium Aureum.
Harmonia Mundi 30157
[DEMANTIUS. 2 galliarda. FRANCK. Galliarde; Pavane. GERVAISE.
Branle. MODERNE. 2 Bransles de Bourgogne. PHALESE. L'arboscello
ballo Furlano. PRAETORIUS. 2 Tänze. SUSATO. Hexentanz;
Hoboeckentanz; Hupfauf; 2 rondos.]   (biel 2/70)

872. *Tanzsätze der Renaissance aus der Orgeltabulatur des Jan de Lublin.*
Lautenensemble Pöhlert.   Da Camera Song SM 93-603
[Bona cat; 2 Conradi; 2 Coreae; Corea ad novem saltus; Corea ad unum
saltum Poznanie; Corea Ferdinandi - proportio Ferdinandi ulterius; Corea
Hispaniarum; 2 Coreae italicae; Corea Simonis; 2 Coreae super duos
saltus; Czayner thancz; Hayduczky; Jeszcze marczynye; Paur thancz;
Poznania; Poznanie; Rex; Rocal fuza; Schephczyk ydzye po ulyczy
szydelko noszacz; 9 Tänze (without titles); Tanz (without title) -
sequuntur Corea N.C. 1541; Zaklolam szya tharnem ad unum saltum.]

873. *Ten Centuries of Music.* Various performers.
10 DGG Archive KL 52/61; SKL 152/161
N.B.: A 10-record set which includes music from most periods and offers
the following medieval and renaissance works:
Chant: Tertia missa in Nativitate Domini Nostri Jesu Christi.
[Previously issued as DGG Archive 3143; 73143 and included in original
edition of this present work as No.324.]
PALESTRINA. Missa Papae Marcelli and (motets): Ascendit Deus; Ego
sum panis vivus; Illumina oculos meos; Incipit oratio; Jubilate Deo;
Laudate Dominum; Pueri Hebraeorum; Terra tremuit.
[Performed by Regensburger Domspatzen and Domchor; T. Schrems,
cond, and issued separately as DGG Archive 3182; 73182.]

874. *Ten Christmas Songs from the Time of Praetorius.* Soloists; Eppendorf
Boys' Choir; Hamburg Town Choir; Archive Ancient Instrument
Ensemble; A. Detel, cond.
DGG Archive 3216; 73216 and 14316; 198316
[BODENSCHATZ. Gelobet seist du Jesu Christ. CRAPPIUS. Nun ist es
Zeit zu singen hell. ECCARD. O Freude über Freud; Vom Himmel hoch,
da komm ich her. FREUNDT. Wie schoen singt uns der Engelschar.
GUMPELZHAIMER. Gelobet seist du Jesu Christ. OSIANDER. Gelobet
seist du Jesu Christ. OTHMAYR. Gelobet seist du Jesu Christ; Vom
Himmel hoch da komm ich her. J. PRAETORIUS. Vom Himmel hoch
da komm ich her. M. PRAETORIUS. Cum pastores laudavere; In dulci
jubilo; Wie schoen leuchtet der Morgenstern. SCHAERER. Gelobet
seist du Jesu Christ. WALTHER. Gelobet seist du Jesu Christ. Also
Schein and Scheidt.]

875. Thomanerchor, Leipzig. G. Ramin, cond.   Cantate 640217
[G. GABRIELI. Timor et tremor. HANDL. Alta trinita; Pater noster.
Also Kodaly and Weismann.]   (biel 2/65)

876. Thomas, Michael. (org, hpsi and clavichord)
                                        Pan PAN 6002; SPAN 6002
[BULL. Doctor Bull's juell; Doctor Bull's myselfe; Duchesse of
Brunswick's toye; Duke of Brunswick's alman; Gigge. BYRD. Callino
casturame; Lord Willoby's welcome home; O mistress mine. FARNABY.
Maske. GIBBONS. Galliard. MUNDY. Mundy's joye. OSTERMAYR.
Galiarde. ANON. Almans.] (gr 11/66)

877. *To Entertain a King: Music for Henry VIII and His Court.* Musica
Reservata; Purcell Consort of Voices; G. Burgess, cond.
                                        Argo RG 566; ZRG 566
[BARBIREAU. En frolyk weson. BUSNOIS. Fortune esperée.
CORNYSH. Adieu, mes amours; Blow thy horn, hunter. DAGGERE.
Downderry down. HENRY VIII. Pastime with good company; Taunder
naken. ISAAC. La my. RICHEFORT. De mon triste desplaisir. ANON.
Allemande prince; The antyck; He trolly lolly lo; Il buratto; Henry VIII's
pavan; I am a jolly foster; Il me suffit; La morisque; My Lady Carey's
dumpe; Passo e mezzo; Rocha el fuso; La traditor; Vegnando da
Bologna; Where be ye, my love?] (Myers 3/70)

878. *Tournai Mass (13th-14th Century).* Vocal soloists and instrumentalists;
M. Honegger, cond.   10" Christophorus CLP 75486 and Lumen 2128A
(biel 2/65)

879. Tower of London Chapel Choir.   RCA International INTS 1115
[BYRD. O Lord, make thy servant Elizabeth. HENRY VIII. Pastime
with good company. GIBBONS. Hosanna to the son of David.
WEELKES. O Lord, grant the king a good life. TALLIS. O sacrum
convivium. Also Wesley, Purcell, Langford, Blow.] (gr 12/70)

880. *Transeamus usque Bethlehem (Breslauer Originalfassung).* Rheinischer
Kammerchor; H. Schröder, dir; Rheinisches Konzertorchester; F.
Schmitz, dir.   Harmonia Mundi HMS 17077
[SCHRÖTER. Freut euch ihr lieben Christen; Lobt Gott ihr Christen
allzugleich.]

881. *Treasury of Early Music* (to accompany book of same title by Carl
Parrish). Various performers.
                                 4-12" Haydn Society HSE 9100/3; St-HSE 9100/3
Record 1
[ALFONSO EL SABIO. Gran dereit'. BERNARD DE VENTADOUR.
Be m'an perdut. LEONINUS. Viderunt omnes. ANON. Ave gloriosa
mater / Ave virgo / Domino; Gaudete populi; In seculum longum (motet);
Infantem vidimus; Je n'amerai autre (motet); Ogne homo; Populo meus;
Redde mihi; Veni creator spiritus.
Record 2
ANTHONELLO DE CASERTA. Notes pour moi. CAPIROLA. O mia
cieca e dura sorte. CARA. O mia cieca e dura sorte. DUNSTABLE.

881. *Treasury of Early Music.* (Continued)
Veni sancte spiritus. ENCINA. Soy contento y yos servido.
FRONCIACO. Kyrie Jhesu dulcissime. GIOVANNI DA FIRENZE.
Con brachi assai. GOUDIMEL. Mon Dieu me paist. HASSLER.
Laudate Dominum. MORALES. Magnificat octavi toni. SACHS.
Gesangweise. TALLIS. Heare the voyce and prayer of thy servants.
TOURNAI MASS. (Agnus Dei). WALTHER. Komm, Gott Schöpfer,
heiliger Geist.
Record 3
BULL. Pavana. DOWLAND. My thoughts are wing'd with hope.
GESUALDO. Moro lasso. GIBBONS. In nomine (viols). MERULO.
Toccata for organ. SENFL. Oho, so geb' der Mann ein'n Pfenning.
ANON. Fricassée; Passamezzo d'Italie. Also Cavalieri, Schein, Gaultier,
Poglietti and Buxtehude.
Record 4
Baroque.]

882. *The Treasury of English Church Music, v.1, 1100-1545.* The Ambrosian
Singers; D. Stevens, cond.   E.M.I. and Odeon CSD 3504
[CORNYSH. Ave Maria, mater Dei. DAMETT. Beata Dei genetrix.
DUNSTABLE. Veni sancte spiritus. EXCETRE. Sanctus and Benedictus.
FRYE. Salve virgo mater. QUELDRYK. Gloria in excelsis (Old Hall Ms.).
ANON. Alleluia psallat; Ave miles caelestis curiae; Conditor alme siderum;
Perspice, Christicola; Salve sancta parens; Sancte Dei pretiose; Sanctus and
Benedictus.]

883. *The Treasury of English Church Music, v.2, 1545-1650.* Choir of West-
minster Abbey, D. Guest, cond.   E.M.I. CLP 3536; CSD 3536
[BYRD. Ave verum corpus; Sing joyfully. CHILD. O God, wherefore
art Thou absent from us? DEERING. Factum est silentium. FARRANT.
Hide not thou thy face. GIBBONS. Nunc dimittis. MERBECKE. Nunc
dimittis. MORLEY. Nolo mortem peccatoris; Out of the deep. MUNDY.
Ah, helpless wretch. PARSONS. Nunc dimittis. PHILIPS. Ascendit
Deus. TALLIS. Wherewithal shall a young man cleanse his way?
TOMKINS. Nunc dimittis. WEELKES. Gloria in excelsis Deo.]

Triomphe de Maximilien Ier. See *Triumph of Maximilian I* (No.884).

Triumph der Renaissance: Maximiliana. See *Triumph of Maximilian I*
(No.884).

884. *Triumph of Maximilian I.* Ambrosian Singers; Vienna Renaissance
Players; J. McCarthy, cond.
              Nonesuch 2-12" 73016 and ELY 0520/21 and (?) Tudor 0531
[FESTA (arr. SENFL). Quis dabit oculis. HOFHAIMER. Carmen
magistri Pauli; Hertzliebstes bild, beweiss; Meins traurens ist; On frewd
verzer ich; Salve regina; Tröstlicher Lieb. ISAAC. Carmen; Carmen in
fa; Et ie boi d'autant; Innsbruck, ich muss dich lassen; J'ay pris amours;
La la hö hö; Lasso, quel ch'altri fugge; O Venus bant; Le serviteur; Un

di lieto giamai; Tricinium; Virgo prudentissima. SENFL. Ach Elslein;
Die Brünnlein; Das gläut zu Speyer; Es taget vor dem Walde; Ich stünd an
einem Morgen; Maecenas atavis; Magnificat primi toni; Nun grüss dich
Gott; O Herr, ich ruf' dein'n Namen an. ANON. Tocceda.]

885. *The Triumphs of Oriana.* Purcell Consort of Voices; London Sackbut
Ensemble; Elizabethan Consort of Viols; G. Burgess, dir.
                                          Argo ARG 643; ZRG 643
[BENNET. All creatures now. EAST. Hence stars. FARMER. Fair
nymphs. HOLMES. Thus bonny-boots. HUNT. Hark! Did ye ever hear.
MARSON. The nymphs and shepherds. MORLEY. Arise, awake; Hard
by a crystal fountain. MUNDY. Lightly she whipped. PEELE. Descend
ye sacred daughters; Long may she come. TOMKINS. The fauns and
satyrs. WEELKES. As Vesta was from Latmos hill. WILBYE. The Lady
Oriana. ANON. Daphne; Strawberry leaves; A toye; La volta.] (gr 4/70)

Troubadour Songs of the 13th Century. See *Chansons der Troubadours*
(No.489).

886. *Trouvères et troubadours; Minnesänger et Meistersinger.* Ensemble
Gaston Soublette.   Bôite à Musique C 103
[ADAM DE LA HALLE. Dieu comment pourrait; Or est Bayard en la
pasture; Tant que vivray. FREIDRICH VON HAUSEN. Ich denke
under wilen. GAUTIER DE COINCY. Ma vièle. GRENON (NICOLE).
La plus belle et doulce figure. GUY DE COUCY. Li nouviau tenz.
JAUFRÉ RUDEL. Lanquan li jorn. L'ESCUREL. Plainte de celle.
MARCABRU. Pastourelle. MEISTER ALEXANDER. Hie vor dô wir
Kynder wâren. MEISTER RUMELAND. Untruwe. MONIOT D'ARRAS.
Ce fut en mai. RICHARD DE SEMILLI. Dame qui a mal mari. SACHS.
David und Jonathan. THIBAUT IV DE CHAMPAGNE. Pour mal temps
ni pour gelée. WALTHER VON DER VOGELWEIDE. Palästina Lied.
WIZLAW III. Loybere Risen; We Ich han gedacht. WOLKENSTEIN. In
Suria. ANON. A la charté (Montpellier); A la fontenelle; La belle au
rossignol; J'ai vu la beauté.] (dia 67)

887. *Tudor Church Music.* London Ambrosian Singers; J. McCarthy, dir.
                                          2-12" Belvédère 0540/1
[BYRD. Anthem; Agnus Dei; Kyrie; Magnificat; Nunc dimittis; Ps.114;
Répons. GIBBONS. Ps.57; Ps.118; Te Deum. MUNDY. Introitus.
SMITH. Response. STONE. Lord's Prayer. TALLIS. If you love me;
Gloria. TAVERNER. Sanctus. TOMKINS. Credo. WEELKES. Gloria.
WHITE. O praise God.] (dia 67)

Tudor Church Music. See also under TALLIS and WEELKES in Index,
Part II.

888. *Turmmusiken und festliche Intraden.* Süddeutsches Bläservereinigung;
W. Kloor, cond.   Saba SB 15039
[BARBIREAU. Der Pfobenswancz. DEPRES. Königsfanfaren. ISAAC.
Innsbruck, ich muss dich lassen. SENFL. Quodlibet. SUSATO. Rondo
e saltarello. WALTHER. Christ lag in Todesbanden. ANON. Christ ist
erstanden; Das Yeger Horn. Also Fischer, Hindemith, Rosenmüller,
Schilling.]   (biel 2/65)

Twenty-One French Chansons of the Renaissance. See under JANEQUIN
and BERTRAND (Erato STU 70519) in Part II.

889. *Two Centuries of English Organ Music.* T. Dart (on various English
instruments).   Odeon CLP 1212
[BULL. Fantasia; Salvator mundi Deus. BYRD. A fancie; A voluntarie.
GIBBONS. Fantasia; In nomine. TOMKINS. Fancy. Also Blow, Boyce,
Greene, Händel, Locke, Nares, Purcell, Stanley.]   (Myers 9/64)

Two Medieval Masses. See under *Missa Salve* (No.684).

890. *U Zrodel Muzyki Polskiej.* (Musica Antiqua Polonica). Chor Chlopiecy i
Meski Filharmonii Pomorskiej; Capella Bydgostiensis Pro Musica
Antiqua; various soloists; S. Galonski, cond.
                            Muza XL 0294; SXL 0294 and Orpheus OR 341
[GALKA. Piesn o wiklefie. LADYSLAW Z GIELNIOWA. Zoltarz
Jezousow. MIKOLAJ Z RADOMIA. Et in terra Pax; Magnificat; Patrem
omnipotentem. ANON. Angelus ad Virginem; Ave in coelum; Badz
wiesiola; Bogurodzica; Chwala tobie Gospodzinie; Cracovia civitas;
Cristicolis secunditas; O najdrozsy kwiatku; Pastor gregis egregius; Salve
sancta parens.]

891. *Ungarische Lieder aus 5 Jahrhunderten.* Soloists and Orchestra József
Pécsi.   Qualiton/Hungaroton SLPX 1292
[Balassi-Lieder; Historische Lieder; Kuruzenlieder; Volkslieder;
Blumenlieder; Csokonai-Lieder; Volksartige Kunstlieder.]

Venetian Polychoral Music. See *Venezianische Mehrchörigkeit um 1600*
(No.892).

892. *Venezianische Mehrchörigkeit um 1600.* Capella Antiqua, Munich; K.
Ruhland, cond.   Telefunken AWT 9456-A; SAWT 9456-A
[G. GABRIELI. Canzon VI a 7; Jubilate Deo; Magnificat I toni; Nunc
dimittis; O domine, Jesu Christe; Sonata XV a 12. GIOVANELLI. Salve
Regina. GRILLO. Canzona II à 8. GUSSAGO. Sonata La Leona.
ROGNONI TAEGGIO. Sonata La Porta.]

893. Verschraegen, Gabriel. (org).   Supraphon SUA 10548
[BRUMEL. Bicinium. LUYTON. Fuga suavissima. OBRECHT. Ein
frohlich Wesen. SCKRONX. Echo. Also Cornet, Fiocco, Kerckhoven,
Loeillet.]   (gram 12/70)

894. *Victimae Paschalis: A Sequence of Music for Lent, Passiontide and Easter.* Choir of Ely Cathedral; A. Wills, dir.   Alpha AVM 015
[BARCROFTE. O Lord we beseech Thee. BYRD. Ave verum corpus; Terra tremuit. CORNYSHE. Woefully arrayed. DUFAY. Vexilla regis prodeunt. KYRBIE. O Jesu, look. MORLEY. Agnus Dei. PHILIPS. Surgens Jesus. SWELINCK. Durch Adams Fall ist ganz verderbt. WEELKES. Hosanna to the Son of David. ANON. Haec Dies (Sarum plainchant). Also Bach, Blow, Dandrieu.]

895. *Vielles orgues en Flandre, no.2.* G. Verschraegen (org).   Alpha CL 3017
[ISAAC. Zwischen Berg und tiefem Tal. OBRECHT. Hélas mon bien. SCKRONX. Courante avec variations; Fantaisie sur le huitième ton. Also Gheyn, Fiocco, Loeillet, Kerckhoven, Raick.]   (gr 12/70)

896. *Vocal and Instrumental Works of 16th Century Venice.* Lausanne Vocal and Instrumental Ensemble; M. Corboz, cond.   Erato STU 70638/9
[ANNIBALE PADOVANO. Amor è gratiosa e dolce voglia; Padre del ciel; Pasce la pecorella. BELL'HAVER. Sparve e ogni stella in cielo; Non rumor di tamburi. DONATO. Tratto fuora del Mar. A. GABRIELI. A le Guancie di Rose; Battaglia; Echo Vinegia bella; Hor che nel suo bel seno; Io mi sento morire; Ricercare per sonar; Risonanza di Echo. G. GABRIELI. Canzon Fa Sol La Ré; Canzon seconda; Canzone prima La Spiritata; Canzone quarta. GUAMI. Canzona a quattro; Gravi pene in amor. MERULO. Canzon per sonar; Lieti fiori e felici; L'Olica. PARABOSCO. Niuna sconsolata; Non dispregiate i merelli amanti. VECCHI. Boscareccia pastorale. VEGGIO. Canone à l'unisono. ZARLINO. Canzona a cinque. ANON. Poi ch'il mio largo pianto.]   (gram 7/71)

Vocal and Instrumental Works of the 13th Century. See *Ars Antiqua* (No.462).

Voices of the Middle Ages. See *Mittelalterliche Musik* (No.687).

Weihnachtsgesänge des 13. bis 15. Jahrhundert. See *Sei Willekomen, Herre Christ* (No.842).

897. *Weihnachtsmusik alter Meister.* Madrigalchor der Staatlichen Hochschule für Musik, Cologne; H. Schroeder, cond. Die Salzburger Turmbläser; J. Dorfner, cond. M. G. Förstemann (org); A. Heiller (org).
                                        Philips S 08497 L; 850020 SG
[ECCARD. In dulci jubilo. G. GABRIELI. Canzona quarta; Canzona terza. GUMPELZHAIMER. Vom Himmel hoch. PRAETORIUS. Es ist ein Ros'. ROGNONI. La mazza. SCANDELLO. Gelobet seist du, Jesu Christ. WALTHER. Nun komm der Heiden Heiland. Also Speer, Bach, Liebhold, Schein, Niedt.]

898. *Weihnachtsmusik aus Mittelalter und Renaissance.* Purcell Consort of
Voices; G. Burgess, cond.   Decca SAWD 9977-B
[ANON. The borys hede; Conditor fut le non-pareil; Dies est laetitiae;
Dieus vous garde; Fines amouretes; Fulget hodie l'espine; Gabriell off
hye degre; I saw a sweete; In hoc anni circulo; In this valley; Joseph
lieber, Joseph mein; El lobo rabioso; Noe, noe, noe, psallite; Now let
God Almighty; Orientis partibus; Resonet in laudibus.]   (biel 2/70)
N.B.: With the addition of several other works issued in England as
Now we Make Merthe, q.v. (No.787).

899. *Weltliche Musik um 1300.* Studio der frühen Musik, Munich.
                                        Telefunken SAWT 9504 A
[ADAM DE LA HALLE. Le jeu de Robin et Marion. MEISTER
ALEXANDER. Hie vor dô wir kinder wâren. MONIOT D'ARRAS. Ce
fut en mai. PIEREKINS DE LA COUPELE. Chançon faz non pas
vilainne. PSEUDO-NEIDHARDT. Winter diner künfte. ANON. L'autre
jour / Au tens pascour / In seculum; Bryd one brere; La chasse, Se je
chant; He, Marotele / En la praerei / Aptatur; El mois d'avril / O quam
sancta / Et gaudibit; Mout me fu grief / Robins m'aime / Portare; O
natio / Hodie perlustravit; Souvent souspire; Trotto. ANON. (from the
Llibre Vermell Ms.): Ad mortem festinamus; Cuncti simus; Imperayritz
de la ciutat; Laudemus verginem; Los set gotex; Mariam, matrem; O
virgo splendens; Polorum regina; Splendens ceptrigera; Stella splendens.]

900. *William Byrd and Masters of His Time.* King:s College Choir; D. Willcocks,
dir.   Electrola SME 91469 and Voix de son Maître ASDF 875;
                        FALP 875 and H.M.V. ASD 641; ALP 2094
[BYRD. Ave verum corpus; Haec Dies; Justorum animae; Miserere mei;
O quam gloriosum; Tu es Petrus. G. GABRIELI. Miserere mei. LASSUS.
Justorum animae. PALESTRINA. Haec Dies; Tu es Petrus. PHILIPS.
Ave verum corpus. VICTORIA. O quam gloriosum.]   (biel 2/67)

Worcester Fragments. See under *Missa Salve* (No.684).

901. Zanaboni (org).   Vedette VPC1505; VST 6005
[ANTEGNATI. Ricercare del X tono. CAVAZZONI. Christe Redemptor
Omnium; Ave Maris Stella. A. GABRIELI. Canzone ariosa; Intonazione
del VII tono. G. GABRIELI. Fuga del IX tono; La Spiritata. Also
Frescobaldi. (sant 5-6/71)

Zehn festliche Sätze der Praetorius-Zeit. See *Ten Christmas Songs from
the Time of Praetorius* (No.874).

PART II

Index to Anthologies and Individual Discographies by Composer

Discs devoted mainly to the works of one or two composers are listed here, immediately following the composer's name, rather than with the anthologies in Part I. In most cases, contents for the individual discographies are indicated only by underlined numbers, which correspond to the list of works which follows. Within the list of works, numbers not underlined following each title refer to the anthologies in Part I.

Example:

1   ARCADELT, JACOB (ca.1514-ca.1562)
2   *Capella Cordina (Planchart).*   Lyrichord 7199
3   1,2,5,6,7,8,9,10,13,16

4   1. Amour ne sçauriez. 2. At trepida. 3. Ave Maria:849. 4. Il bianco e
5   dolce cigno:510,660,662,818. 5. Helas amy. 6. L'hiver sera. 7. Hor
6   tregua. 8. Io mi rivolgo. 9. Margot, labourez les vignes:656,852.
7   10. Missa Noe noe. 11. Nous voyons que les hommes:656. 12. O
8   felici occhi miei:492,629,828,839. 13. Gli prieghi miei. 14. Sapet'-
9   amanti:492,828. 15. S'infinita bellezza:663,693. 16. Voi ve n'andat'al
10   cielo:492,612,777,828. Also 499.

Line   1. Composer.
Line 2-3. A whole disc devoted to Arcadelt.
Line   2. Performer (in this case, performing group), followed by Conductor in parentheses. Disc number at far right.
Line   3. These numbers refer to item numbers in the list of works (Lines 4-10), e.g., this Lyrichord disc contains: 1. Amour ne sçauriez. 2. At trepida. 5. Helas amy, etc.
Line   4. No.2, "At trepida," is on this Lyrichord disc but not in an anthology.
Line   4. No.4, "Il bianco e dolce cigno," is NOT included on the Lyrichord disc, but is included in anthology numbers following title. See Part I.
Line   9. No.16, "Voi ve n'andat'al cielo," is on the Lyrichord disc and also included in anthology numbers following title. See Part I.
Line 10. "Also 499." Anthology 499 includes a composition by Arcadelt whose title could not be identified.

Index to Anthologies and Individual Discographies by Composer

Composer entries are arranged alphabetically by title. Some are also indexed under the names of collections, such as, *Glogauer Liederbuch,* or in some cases, names of manuscripts, such as, *Bamberg Codex.* These entries, integrated with those for composers, are listed in italics and followed by numbers of anthologies in Part I containing pieces from the cited works. Entries under the names of collections and manuscripts are by no means complete, since many anonymous works could not be so identified with any degree of certainty from the information available. Anonymous compositions are listed at the end of the Index (p.223) following the composer entries.

The titles which appear in this index have been shortened to minimal length; a fuller and more detailed entry (including in some cases medium of performance) will often be found by referring to the corresponding anthology.

In spite of attempts to avoid this, some compositions may have been listed under two or more different titles or variant spellings. Since secondary sources often had to be relied upon, it was not possible to establish the exact identity of every composition.

Composer Index

ACOURT (15th century)
Je demande ma bienvenue:717.
ADAM DE ANTIQUIS VENETUS
Senza te, sacre Regina:467,687.
ADAM DE LA HALLE (ca.1235-ca.1288)
A Dieu comant:576. Amours et ma dame aussi:676. Bonnes amouretes:
576. Dieu comment pourrait:886. Dieus soit en cheste maison:615,707,
844. Fi, maris:576. Li dous regars:676. Fines amourettes:576,741,761.
Je muir, je muir:576. Li mans d'amer:615,636,815. Le jeu de Robin et
Marion:761,899. Robin m'aime:676,844. Tanzlied (Robin et Marion):
575. Tant con je vivrai:615,676,741,754,886. Or est Baiars:576,886.
ADAM DE SAINT-VICTOR (d.1192)
Jubilemus salvatori:615.
ADAM VON FULDA (d.1505)
Ach hülf mir leid:594.
ADSON, JOHN (d.1640?)
Courtly masquing ayres:469,745,829.
AGAZZARI, AGOSTINO (1578-1640)
Dimmi donna gentile:630.
Agincourt, Perrin d'. See PERRIN d'AGINCOURT
AGRICOLA, ALEXANDER (1446-1506)
Her, her, ich verkünd euch neue Mär:448.
AGUILERA DE HEREDIA, SEBASTIAN (b. ca.1570)
Oeuvre sur le Ier ton:775. Fantaisie sur le IVe ton:775. Salve de leno:
775. Salve Regina:593. Tiento de falsas du VIe ton:593.
AICHINGER, GREGOR (1564-1628)
Beati omnes:764. Confirma hoc:638. Factus est repente:638. Jubilate
Deo:830. Regina coeli:654,696,769,772. Schöns Maedlein, murr nur
nit:772. Ubi est Abel:484.
ALANUS, MAGISTER (15th century)
Sub arcturo plebs:717.
ALBARTE
Pavan and galliard:728.
ALBERT, HEINRICH (1604-1651)
Du mein einzig Licht:520.

ALBERTO, LUIS (16th century)
   Salmo II:796. Tiento de falsas:859. Trois pièces:800.
ALDER, COSMAS (ca.1497-1550)
   Da Jakob nu das Kleid ansach:836.
ALDOMAR (15th-16th centuries)
   Ha, Pelayo:841.
ALEXANDER, MEISTER (13th century)
   Hie vor dô wir kinder wâren:886,899.
ALFONSO EL SABIO (1252-1284)
   (N.B.: Underlined numbers correspond to the Cantigas numbers.)
   Capilla Musical y Escolania de Santa Cruz del Valle de los Caidos (Lozano);
   Atrium Musicum (Paniagua). Musical Heritage OR 302; Erato STU 70694
      Prologo. 1,20,25,29,40,58,79,100,118,159,166,179,216,222,279,
      302,320,353,380,384,401, Apéndice I:11; Apéndice II:2.
   Ochoa, Rondeleux (vocalists); Lepauw (vièle); Depannemaker (tambourin).
                                             10" Harmonia Mundi OPUS 9
      Prologo. 11,118,139,226,244,320,340,383. (cf. No.478)

   Prologo. Porque trobar:860. 1. Des oge. 7. Santa Maria amar:860.
   10. Rosa das rosas:718,844. 11. Macar ome per folia:478. 18. Por nos
   de dulta livrar:860. 20. Virga de Jesse. 25. Pagar ben:860. 29. Nas
   mentes:860. 35. O que a Santa Maria:860. 40. Deus te salve. 48. Tanto
   son da Groriosa:860. 49. Ben com' aos:860. 58. De muitas guisas.
   77. Da que Deus:860. 79. Ay, Santa Maria. 100. Santa Maria, strela.
   118. Fazer pode:478. 139. Marovillosos:478,718,860. 159. Non sofre
   Santa Maria. 166. Como poden:860. 179. Ben sab. 216. O que en
   Santa Maria. 222. Quen ouver. 226. Assi pod'a Virgen:478. 244. Gran
   dereit:478,881. 279. Santa Maria, valed. 302. A madre de Jhesucristo.
   320. Santa Maria leva:478. 340. Virgen, madre groriosa:478. 353. Quen
   a omagen. 380. Sen calar. 383. O ffondo do mar:478. 384. A que por
   muy. 401. Macar poucos cantares (Peticon). Apéndice I:11. Nenbre
   ssete. Apéndice II:2. Pos que dos reys. 5 cantigas:707.
ALISON (ALLISON, ALOYSON), RICHARD (16th-17th centuries)
   Bachelors delight:559. De la tromba pavin:559. Shall I abide:546.
ALONSO
   Gritos davan en aquella sierra:743. La tricotea Samartin:741,841.
ALVARADO, DIEGO d' (d.1643)
   Fantaisie Pange lingua espagnole:775.
AMMERBACH, ELIAS NIKOLAUS (ca.1530-1597)
   Gagliarda:515. Herzog-Moritz-Tanz mit proportio:556. Passamezzo:
   515,557,708. Passamezzo antico:613. Passamezzo d'Angleterre:708.
   La riprese:515.
AMNER, JOHN (d.1641)
   O ye little flock:172.
ANCHIETA, JUAN DE (ca.1450-1523)
   Missa quarti toni:743 (Kyrie). O bone Jesu:460.

Andrea da Firenze. See ANDREAS DE FLORENTIA
ANDREA DI GIOVANNI (d.1415)
    Sotto candido vel:463.
ANDREAS DE FLORENTIA (14th-15th centuries)
    Non più doglie ebbe Dido:569.
ANERIO, FELICE (ca.1560-1614)
    Carmelite Priory Choir, London (Malcolm).
      [Missa pro defunctis.]   L'Oiseau-Lyre OL 50211; SOL 60042
    Chor der Kirchenmusikalische Schule Münster; Santini Kammerorchester
    (Ewerhart).   Turnabout STV 34172
      [La conversione di S. Paolo; Vivean felici (Historia von Adam und Eva).]

    Alma redemptoris:806. Christus factus est:703. Christus resurgens:694.
    O pretiosam:763. O salutaris hostia:696. Requiem aeternum:849.
ANNIBALE PADOVANO (1527-1575)
    Ensemble Cuivres Gabriel Masson (Delmotte).   Belvedere ELY 0531
      [Aria della battaglia.] (verso: Janequin)

    Amor è gratiosa:896. Aria della battaglia:721. Padre del ciel:896. Pasce
    la pecorella:896.
ANTEGNATI, COSTANZO (1549-1624)
    Ricercare del X tono:863.
ANTHONELLO DE CASERTA (14th century)
    Notes pour moi:881.
ANTIPHONAIRE MOZARABE DE LEON: 458
ANTIPHONAIRE MOZARABE DE SILOS: 458
Antiquis Venetus, Adam de. See ADAM DE ANTIQUIS VENETUS
APIARIUS, MATHIAS (ca.1500-1554)
    Es taget vor dem Walde:622,838.
APPENZELLER, BENEDICTUS (16th century)
    Musae Jovis ter Maximi:831. Plangite Pierides:862.
APT MS.: 589,726
ARANIES (ARANES), JUAN (16th-17th centuries)
    Un sarao de la chacona:807.
Arauxo, Francisco Correa de. See CORREA DE ARAUXO, FRANCISCO
Arbeau, Thoinot. See TABOUROT, JEHAN
ARCADELT, JACOB (ca.1514-ca.1562)
    Capella Cordina (Planchart).   Lyrichord 7199
    1,2,5,6,7,8,9,10,13,16

    1. Amour ne sçauriez. 2. At trepida. 3. Ave Maria:849. 4. Il bianco e
    dolce cigno:510,660,662,818. 5. Helas amy. 6. L'hiver sera. 7. Hor
    tregua. 8. Io mi rivolgo. 9. Margot, labourez les vignes:656,852.
    10. Missa Noe noe. 11. Nous voyons que les hommes:656. 12. O
    felici occhi miei:492,629,828,839. 13. Gli prieghi miei. 14. Sapet'-
    amanti:492,828. 15. S'infinita bellezza:663,693. 16. Voi ve n'andat'al
    cielo:492,612,777,828. Also 499.

ARCHILEI, ANTONIO (16th century)
Dalle più alte sfere:464.
Arnold de Lantins. See LANTINS, ARNOLD DE
ARNOLD VON BRUCK (d.1554)
Aus tiefer Not:527,588,611,836. O du armer Judas:518. So trinken wir alle:524,591.
Arras, Monio d'. See MONIO D'ARRAS
ASOLA, GIOVANNI MATTEO (d.1609)
Quem vidistis pastores:830.
ASTON, HUGH (d.1522)
Hornpipe:525,556,557,708.
ATTAINGNANT, PIERRE, ed.
Darasse (org). Turnabout TV 4126; (Ger.) Vox STV 34126
[L'espoir que j'ay; Basse danse; 2 gaillardes; Tant que vivray; Branle.] (verso: Titelouze)

Also 509,515,556,557,573,574,575,577,619,648,672,708,737,760,771, 829,866,867,870.
ATTEY, JOHN (d. ca.1640)
Vain hope, adieu:461.
AZZAIOLO (AZZAIUOLO), FILIPPO (16th century)
Petit Ensemble Vocal, Montreal (Little). Vox DL 900; 500900
[Al di, dolce ben mio; Chi passa per 'sta strada; Come t'aggio lasciat'o vita mia; Dall'orto sè ne vien; Gentil madonna del mio cor; L'amanza mia si chiama Saporita; O spazzacamini; Occhio non fu giammai che lagrimasse; Quando la sera; Sentomi la formicula; Tanto sai fare; Ti parti, cor mio.] (verso: Gesualdo)

L'amanza mia si chiama Saporita:851. Ti parti cor mio:851.

BADAJOZ (15th-16th centuries)
O desdichado de mi:841.
BAENA, LOPE DE (15th-16th centuries)
Todo cuanto y servi:689.
BAEZA, GARCIA DE (d.1560)
Tiento del VII tono:796.
BAKFARK, VALENTIN (1507-1576)
Fantasias for lute:659,749,812.
BALLARD, ROBERT
Arias:446. Branles:649,668. Entrées:649.
BAMBERG CODEX: 462,576,685,842
BANCHIERI, ADRIANO (d.1634)
Il Nuovo Madrigaletto Italiano (Grani). Turnabout TV 4067; 34067
[Festino.] (verso: Vecchi)

Primavera Singers (New York Pro Musica). (Greenberg)
[Festino.] Esoteric 516; Everest LPBR 6145/7

Sestetto Italiano Luca Marenzio.   Heliodor 25060; HS 25060;
          DGA 14132 APM; 198021 SAPM; ARC 3136; (Ger.) MR 199035
          [La pazzia senile.] (verso: Monteverdi)

Contrappunto bestiale:454,498,738. Fantasia:759. Fantasia in eco:513,
635. Fantasia vigesima:635. Fantasie overo canzoni alla francese:829.
Festino:630. Nobili spettatori:738. Omnes gentes:628.

Barahona, Juan Esquivel de. See ESQUIVEL DE BARAHONA, JUAN

BARBION, EUSTACHIUS (d.1556)
     Gallis hostibus in fugam coactis:862.

BARBIREAU, JACOB (d.1491)
     En frolyk weson:877. Der Pfobenswancz:888.

BARCROFTE, GEORGE (16th-17th centuries)
     O Lord we beseech thee:894.

BARTLET, JOHN (16th-17th centuries)
     Of all the birds that I do know:721,790,856. A pretty duck there was:
     721. Whither runneth my sweetheart:627,725.

BARTOLINO DA PADUA (14th-15th centuries)
     Quel sole:758. Also 561.

BASIRON, PHILIPPE (15th-16th centuries)
     Agnus Dei:683. D'ung altre amer / L'homme armé:683.

BASSANO, ANTHONY (16th-17th centuries)
     Pavane no.16:834.

BASSANO, GIROLAMO (JEROME) (16th-17th centuries)
     Fantasia:833,834.

BASSANO (?)
     Galliard:515. Oyme dolente:745.

Bassiron, Philippe. See BASIRON, PHILIPPE

BASTON, JOSQUIN (16th century)
     Verheugt u nu, bedruckte geesten:826.

BATAILLE, GABRIEL (b. ca.1575)
     Beautés qui residés:446. Ma bergère non légère:490. Qui veut chasseur:
     446. Un satyre:446.

BATCHELAR, DANIEL (16th century)
     Monsieurs almaine:549.

BATESON, THOMAS (ca.1570-1630)
     Camilla fair tripped o'er the plain:547. Come follow me:547,655.
     Come, sorrow:547. Cupid in a bed of roses:547. Cytherea smiling said:
     547. Down from above:544. Have I found her:666. I heard a noise:
     547. If flood of tears:757. She with a cruel frown:547. Sister, awake:
     546. When to the gloomy woods:547.

BATTEN, ADRIAN (ca.1585-1637)
     Peterborough Cathedral Choir; Latham (org). (Vann)
                    Argo RG 318; ZRG 5318; (Ger.) Decca SAWD 9980-B
          [Fourth evening service; Hear my prayer; O clap your hands; O Lord,
          thou has searched me out; O sing joyfully; Out of the deep.]
          (verso: Deering)

Baude Cordier. See CORDIER, BAUDE

BAXTER, JOHN
  Sacred galliard:728.

Baziron, Philippe. See BASIRON, PHILIPPE

BEATRITZ DE DIA (COMTESSA DE DIA)
  A chanter m'er de so qu'eu no volria:489.

BEAULIEU, EUSTORG DE (d.1552)
  Voici le bon temps:828.

BELLE, JAN VAN (16th century)
  Laat ons nu al verblyden:826. O amoureusich mondeken root:492.

BELLEVILLE, JACQUES DE (d. ca.1650)
  Courante:668.

BELL'HAVER, VINCENZO (d.1587)
  Non rumor di tamburi:896. Sparve e ogni stella in cielo:896.

BENDUSI, FRANCESCO (16th century)
  Desiderata:759. Cortesana padoano:557. Galante:759.

BENEDICTUS
  Mijn liebkens bruin oghen:492.

BENEŠOV HYMNBOOK: 794

BENNET, JOHN (16th-17th centuries)
  All creatures now:492,512,546,666,828,885. Eliza, her name gives
  honour:512. The hunt is up:533,655. O sleep, fond fancy:544. Weep,
  o mine eyes:474,498,521,663,693,738,819,832.

BERCHEM, JACHET (16th century)
  Jehan de Lagny:656. Laet ons nu al verblyden:772. O Jesu Christe:
  772,817. O salutaris hostia:814. Que feu craintif:777.

BERENGUIER DE PALAZOL (BERENGUER DE PALOU) (12th century)
  Dona, la ienser:456. De la iensor:456.

BERMUDO, JUAN (b. ca.1510)
  Exemplo del modo primero por Elami:796.

BERNAL, JOSE (16th century)
  Ave, sanctissimum corpus:810.

BERNAL GONZALEZ, FRANCISCO (16th century)
  Navego en hondo mar:666.

BERNARD DE VENTADOUR (d.1195)
  Be m'an perdut:615,881. Can vei la lauzata mover:489. Lancan vei la
  folha:761. Quan vei la laudets mover:478.

BERNARDI, STEFFANO (16th-17th centuries)
  Benedixisti Domine:830.

BERTRAND, ANTOINE DE (16th century)
  Caillard Ensemble Vocal.   Erato STU 70519; MHS 1158
  [Beauté dont la douceur; Ces deux yeux bruns; Dans le serain de sa
  jumelle flamme; Hâtez-vous, petite folie; Je vis ma nymphe; Las! pour
  vous trop aimer; Marie, qui voudrait; O doux plaisir; Vivons, mignarde.]
  (verso: Janequin)

Ensemble Polyphonique de Paris (Ravier). Valois MB 473; MB 773; MB 973
[Les amours de Ronsard (Beauté qui sans pareille; Ce ris plus doux;
Certes mon oeil; Ces deux yeux bruns; Le coeur loyal; Je ne suis seulement amoureux; Je suis tellement amoureux; Je vy ma nymphe; Las!
pour vous trop aymer; Mon Dieu! que ma maitresse est belle; Nature
ornant la dame; O doux plaisir; Oeil qui mes pleurs; Prenez mon coeur).]

Certes mon oeil:507. Je ne suis seulement:507.

Bertrand Vaqueras. See VACQUERAS, BELTRAME

BESARD, JEAN-BAPTISTE (ca.1567-ca.1625)
Air de cour:659. Bransles:574,648,659. Bransle gay:574,577,596,648.
Bransle volte:648. Courante:574,648. Les cloches de Paris:577.
Galliardes:574,648,764. Préludes:574,648. Villanella:574,648. Volte:
574.

BEVIN, ELWAY (16th-17th centuries)
Browning:551,625,643.

BIANCHINI (prob. FRANCESCO) (16th century)
Tant que vivray:707.

BINCHOIS, GILLES (ca.1400-1460)
Adieu, adieu, mon joieulx souvenir:578,699. Adieu mes très belles
amours:488. Agnus Dei:699. Amoreux suy:699. Amour et souvenir de
celle:488. Amours merchi:699. Asperges me:683. Beata nobis gaudia:
699. De plus en plus:586,609,699. Deul angoisseux:670. Filles à
marier:586,609,699,715,776. Je loe amours:488,699,715. Magnificat
primi toni:715. Mon seul et souverain desire:578. Plaine de plours:575.
Rondeau:868. Seule esgarée:488,535. Toutes mes joyes:488. Triste
plaisir:670,699.

BIVI, PAOLO (1508-1584)
Responsorium mit Vers:751.

BLITHEMAN, WILLIAM (d.1591)
Eterne rerum alias IV:661. Eterne rerum conditor:714. In pace:537.

BLONDEAU
Gallardas 1 & 11:748. Pavana & gallarda La Magdalena:748.

BODENSCHATZ, ERHARD (1576-1636)
Gelobet seist du Jesu Christ:874. Joseph lieber, Joseph mein:448,620,
695. Also 599.

BOESSET, ANTOINE (ca.1585-1643)
Blanchard Vocal Ensemble.   Epic LC 3515
[Magnificat.] (with later composers)

N'espérez plus, mes yeux:509. Objet dont les char:771.

Bologna, Jacopo da. See JACOPO DA BOLOGNA

BOLTON, EDMUND (16th-17th centuries)
A cánzon pastoral:655.

BONELLI (AURELIO?)
Artemisia:751.

BONNET, PIERRE (1538-1608)
    Francion vint l'autre jour:487,491,492,819. Mon père et ma mère:818.
    La vertu d'un personnage:446. Voulez-vous donc toujours Madame:490.
BORLET (14th century)
    Ma très dol rosignol:535,586,619.
Bornelh, Guiraut de. See GUIRAUT DE BORNELH
BOSSINENSIS, FRANCISCUS (15th-16th centuries)
    Recercar and lauda: Se mai per maraviglia:803.
BOURGEOIS, LOUIS (16th century)
    Oraison de notre Seigneur:846. Qui au conseil:612.
Bourgogne, Marie de. See MARIE DE BOURGOGNE
BRADE, WILLIAM (1560-1630)
    Alman:466,515,725. Canzon:745. Coranto:515,725. Galliard:515.
BRANDT, JOBST VOM (1517-1570)
    Es wurb ein's Königs Sohn:524. Frisch auf, in Gottes Namen:524.
BRASART, JOHANNES (15th century)
    O flos flagrans:589.
BRETON, NICHOLAS (16th century)
    Shepherd and shepherdess:655.
BRIHUEGA
    Villancico:672.
BRITISH MUSEUM, ADD. 27630: 462
BRITISH MUSEUM, ADD. 29987: 844
BRITISH MUSEUM, ARUNDEL 248: 462
BROCCHUS, JOANNES (15th century)
    Alma svegliate ormai:510.
Broda, Paulus de. See PAULUS DE BRODA
BROWNE, JOHN (ca.1426-1498)
    O Mater venerabilis:792. Stabat Mater:558.
Brubier, Antoine. See BRUGIER, ANTOINE
Bruck, Arnold von. See ARNOLD VON BRUCK
BRUDIEU, JOAN (d.1591)
    Ma voluntat amb la rao:824.
BRUGIER (BRUBIER, BRUHIER), ANTOINE (16th century)
    Latura tu:803. Vivite felices:862.
Brulé, Gace. See GACE BRULE
BRUMEL, ANTOINE (ca.1480-ca.1520)
    Ach, gheldeloos:777. Bicinium:624,893. Ecce panis angelorum:508.
    Fors seulement:624. Mater Patris et Filia:508,511,692. Missa de
    Beata Virgine:700 (Gloria). Noe noe:465. O Domine Jesu Christe:831.
    Tandernac:465. Vray dieu d'amours:624,672,760. Also 866.
BUCHNER, HANS (1483-1538)
    Ach hülf mich Leid:557. Kyrie eleison:791.

BULL, JOHN (d.1628)

   Dart (hpsi).   L'Oiseau-Lyre OL 255; SOL 255; OLS 118

    [Bonny sweet Robin; Bull's goodnight; Coranto Kingston; Dallying alman; Duchess of Brunswick's toye; Duke of Brunswick's almain; Dutch dance; English toy; Galliard; My grief; My jewel; My self; Pavan and galliard; Pavan and Galliard Symphony; Pavan in the second tone; Queen Elizabeth's galliard; Welsh dance, Why ask you?] (Masters of English Keyboard Music, v.5)

   Johannes Koch Gamba Consort; Jeans (virg); Cameron (org).

                                           DGG Archive 198472

    [(Chamber): Fantasia à 3, G minor; Dorick à 4, A major; In nomine à 5, G minor. (Keyboard): My self; My choice, My jewel; Dallying alman; Alman; Regina galliard; Galliard; My grief; What care you. (Organ): In nomine XII; Dorick music, 4 parts; Fantasia; Te lucis ante terminum; Pavan Symphony; Galliard Symphony; Germans almaine; Dutch dance; Galyard italiano; English toy; French almaine; Carol: Den lustelijcken meij; Bull's goodnight.]

   Les buffons: 596. Doctor Bull's my selfe: 876. Duchess of Brunswick's toye: 186,539,566,876. Duke of Brunswick's alman: 186,566,876. English toy: 538. Fantasia: 565,889. Fantasia in D minor: 538. Galiarda: 737,802. Gigge: 876. Hexachord fantasia: 539. In nomines: 514,541,550, 564,565,566,581,734. Jewel: 550,708,876. The king's hunt: 538,550, 554,596. Een kindekeyn is ons geboren: 795. Laet ons met herten reijne: 455,795. Parthenia: 802. Pavana: 708,881. Piper's galliard: 690. Prelude: 734. Prince's galliard: 543. Queen Elizabeth's pavin: 543,742. Spanish pavin: 564,707. St. Thomas wake: 582,708,727,802. Salvator mundi Deus: 889. Walsingham: 550.

BURGK, JOACHIM A. (d.1610)

   Der Herr mit seinen Jüngern: 518.

BURNETT

   Pavan: 530.

BUSNOIS, ANTOINE (d.1492)

   Nonesuch Consort (Rifkin).   Nonesuch 71247

    [A une dame; A que ville; Acordes moy; Amours nous traicte; Bel acueil; Je m'en vois; Maintes femmes; Seule apart moy; Terrible dame.]

   Bel acueil: 715. Fortune esperée: 877. In hydraulis: 715. Pucelotte: 670.

BUSSANE, ANTHONY

   Pavan: 833.

BUXHEIMER ORGELBUCH: 610

BYRD, WILLIAM (1642 or 3-1623)

   Cantores in Ecclesia (Howard).   L'Oiseau-Lyre SOL 311/3

      SOL 311: 6,8,28,44,71

      SOL 312: 42,53,65,78

      SOL 313: 22,23,25,30,44,56,81,87 (verso: Tallis)

BYRD, WILLIAM (1642 or 3-1623) (Continued)
Choir of New College, Oxford (Lumsden).   Abbey S 629
 36,40,43,60,62,79 (verso: Victoria)
Deller Consort.   Harmonia Mundi HM DR 2.110/11
 50,51,52
Deller Consort.   Harmonia Mundi HM DR 211
 9,18,20,50,66,68,74,77
Deller Consort.   Harmonia Mundi HM DR 212
 3,11,38,43,51,60,68,78
Deller Consort.   Harmonia Mundi HM DR 213
 4,9,18,20,40,52,56,57
Deller Consort.   Harmonia Mundi HMS 30827
 [Mass (not spec.); Puer natus est; Viderunt omnes; Dies sanctificatus;
 Tui sunt coeli.]
Elizabethan Singers (Halsey).   Pan PAN 6204; SPAN 6204
 12,13,14,29,52,76,90
King's College Choir (Willcocks).
 50,51   London 5795; 25795; Argo RG 362; ZRG 5362
Maynard (hpsi and org).   Decca DL 10040; 711040
 96,101,105,106,107,108,113,115,116,122,123,124,125,128,134,136
Saltire Singers; Jesson (org).   Lyrichord LL 156; LLST 7156
 7,11,15,16,20,26,32,35,37,46,58,93,111,115,127,129
Société Chorale Bach, Montréal (Little). Vox DL 880; STDL 500880
 51,52
Westminster Abbey Choristers (McKie).
 51,97,101,114,122 ARC 3201; 73201; (Ger.) DG 14301; 198301

(vocal): 1. Agnus Dei:887. 2. Ah silly soul:466. 3. Alleluia ascendit
Deus. 4. Alleluia cognoverunt discipuli. 5. Anthem:887. 6. Aspice
Domine. 7. Assumpta est Maria. 8. Attollite portas. 9. Ave Maria.
10. Ave Regina coelorum. 11. Ave verum corpus:474,498,583,654,
883,894,900. 12. Beata es, virgo Maria. 13. Beata viscera:830.
14. Benedicta et venerabilis. 15. Boy, pity me. 16. Cast off all doubtful
care. 17. Christ rising:613. 18. Christe qui lux:804. 19. Cibavit eos.
20. Civitas sancti tui. 21. Come to me grief:541. 22. Da mihi auxilium.
23. Diliges Dominum. 24. Domine, praestolamur:496. 25. Domine,
secundum actum meum. 26. An earthly tree. 27. Ego sum panis vivus:
454,498. 28. Emendemus in melius. 29. Felix es, sacra Virgo.
30. Gloria Patri. 31. Haec dies:537,583,703,900. 32. Have mercy upon
me, O Lord:792. 33. Hey, ho, to the greenwood:582,730. 34. Hodie
beata Virgo Maria:552,691,783. 35. I thought that love. 36. In
resurrectione tua. 37. Is love a boy. 38. Justorum animae:537,900.
39. Kyrie:887. 40. Laetentur coeli:801. 41. Lamentationes:582,703.
42. Laudate pueri. 43. Laudibus in sanctis:537. 44. Libera me, Domine.
45. Like as the lark:614. 46. Lord, hear my prayer:704. 47. Lullaby,

my sweet little baby:546,567,730. 48. Magnificat:887. 49. Make ye joy to God:472. 50. Mass for 3 voices. 51. Mass for 4 voices. 52. Mass for 5 voices. 53. Memento homo. 54. Miserere mei:537,704,900. 55. Miserer Gloria tibi trinitatis:536. 56. Miserere mihi, Domine. 57. Ne irascaris Domine. 58. The nightingale:730. 59. Non nobis Domine:845. 60. Non vos relinquam:587,613. 61. Nunc dimittis:887. 62. O God, whom our offences. 63. O Lord, how vain:734. 64. O Lord, make thy servant Elizabeth:706,879. 65. O lux beata trinitas. 66. O magnum mysterium:737,789. 67. O mistress mine:533,643,725,876. 68. O quam gloriosam:583,900. 69. O sacrum convivium. 70. Pange lingua:805. 71. Peccantem me quotidie. 72. Psalm 81. 73. Psalm 114:887. 74. Répons:887. 75. Sacerdotes Domini:598,848. 76. Salve, sancta parens. 77. Senex puerum portabat:783. 78. Siderum rector. 79. Sing joyfully:848,883. 80. Susanna fair:627,730,742. 81. Te deprecor. 82. Terra tremuit:894. 83. This day Christ was born:730. 84. This sweet and merry month:512,544,546,583,666,847. 85. Though Amaryllis dance:546,661,847. 86. Tollite portas:830. 87. Tribue, Domine. 88. Tu es Petrus:900. 89. Victimae paschali:730. 90. Virgo Dei genetrix. 91. While the bright sun:495. 92. Who made thee hob forsake:466. 93. Wounded am I. 94. Ye sacred muses (Elegy on the death of Thomas Tallis):461,728,734.

(instrumental): 95. Alman:540,556,566,761. 96. The bagpipe and the drone. 97. The battell:540,554. 98. The bells:529,540,554. 99. Browning:536,541,551,562,627,730. 100. Callino casturame:529, 876. 101. The carmans whistle:453,554,566. 102. Coranto:540,556, 564,565. 103. The Earle of Oxford's marche:529. 104. Elizabethan suite:757. 105. A fancie:889. 106. Fantasias:536,566,584,643,722, 737,747,757. 107. The flute and the droome:186. 108. French coranto no.2. 109. Galliardas passamezzo:550. 110. Galliarde for the victorie:186. 111. A gigg: F. Tregian:543,556,566,637. 112. In nomines:551,734. 113. John come kiss me now. 114. Lord Willobies welcome home:453,614,623,639,876. 115. Miserere:566. 116. Mr. Bird's upon a plainesong. 117. Monsieurs alman:559,564,566. 118. My Lord of Oxenford's maske:559. 119. My Lord of Oxenford's march:643. 120. (deleted) 121. Parthenia:802. 122. Pavan Earl of Salisbury:543, 711,734,802. 123. Pavan and galliard no.10. 124. Pavan and galliard of Mr. Birde. 125. Pavan and galliard of Mr. Peter:538. 126. Pavana Bray:639,730. 127. Pavans and galliards (misc.):515,536,539,540, 543,559,564,565,566,639,690,757. 128. Pipers galliard. 129. Praeludium. 130. The Queen's alman:512,543,614,690,731. 131. Sellengers round:533,725. 132. Tedesca dita l'Austria:556. 133. Tedesca dita la Proficia:556. 134. Ut, re, mi, fa, sol, la. 135. La volta:186,556,566,596, 690,725,761. 136. A voluntarie:889. 137. Wolsey's wilde:186,543,566.
BYTTERING (or GYTTERING) (15th century)
Nesciens Mater:500.

CABEZON, ANTONIO DE (1510-1566)
    Chapelet (org).   10" Harmonia Mundi OPUS 15
    [Dic nobis Maria; Magnificat du Ier ton; Magnificat du IVe ton;
    Magnificat du VII ton; O lux beata trinitas; Quatre versets sur Ave
    maris stella; Tiento du Ier ton; Tiento Malheur me bat; Quatre versets
    du Ier ton sur Saeculorum amen.]

    Chapelet (org).   12" Harmonia Mundi HMO 30075
    Side 1
    [Magnificat du Ier ton; Dic nobis Maria; O lux beata trinitas; Quatre
    versets du Ier ton sur Saeculorum amen; Tiento du Ier ton; Tiento du
    IIe ton; Tiento Malheur me bat; Tres diferencias sobre Ave maris stella.]
    Side 2 (See No.800)

    Ave maris stella:593,775. De la Virgen que alumbró:808. Dic nobis,
    Maria:743. Diferencias sobre El canto del caballero:593,612,713,748,
    775,796,840,858,859. Diferencias sobre Guardame las vacas:720,796.
    Diferencias sobre La dama le demande:741,859. Diferencias sobre La
    galliarda milanesa:798,858,859. Diferencias sobre La pavana italiana:859.
    D'où vient cela (Duviensela):713,840. Duo pour positif:771. Fantasia
    del primer tono:775. Magnificat del cuarto tono:775,798. O lux beata
    trinitas:748. Pavane:713,720,840,858. Pavana italiana:840,858.
    Romance para quien crie yo cabellos:859. Tiento del primer tono:450,
    748,796,798,859. Tiento del segundo tono:593. Tiento del cuarto
    tono:593. Tiento del sexto tono:796. Tiento (unspec.):799. Tiento
    Ut queant laxis:798. Diferencias sobre El canto llano de la alta:720,748,
    796. Verso del primer tono:743. Verso del cuarto tono:743. Verso del
    quinto tono:743. Versos del sexto tono:612.
CADEAC, PIERRE (16th century)
    Je suis déshéritée:487,491,656.
CADENAL, PEIRE (13th century)
    Un sirventés:456.
CALIXTINUS CODEX: 458,860
CAMPANUS, JOANNES VODNIANUS (VODNANSKY) (d. ca.1618)
    Favete linguis singuli:667,794. Oda XLVI:794.
CAMPION, THOMAS (1567-1620)
    Miskell (tnr); Leeb (lute).   HMV HQM 1035
    [Fair, if you expect admiring; Follow the sun; It fell on a summer's
    day; Thus the curtain of night is spread; Turn back you wanton
    flyer.] (verso: Dowland)

    Come, you pretty false-eyed wanton:571. The cypress curtain:790. I
    care not for these ladies:790,856. It fell on a summer's day:461,559.
    Jack and Joan:655. Never weather-beaten sail:722,725,739. Now hath
    Flora:669. Oft have I sighed:583. Shall I come sweet love:582,730.
    Turn back you wanton flyer:541.
CANCIONERO DE PALACIO: 743,841

CAVENDISH, MICHAEL (ca.1565-1628)
Down in a valley:655. Sly thief:545.
CEBALLOS (CEVALLOS) (FRANCISCO?)
Possuerunt super caput ejus:809. Quam bienaventurado:460.
CEBRIAN, ANTONIO (16th century)
Lagrimas de mi consuelo:460.
CERTON, PIERRE (ca.1510-1572)
Mid-America Chorale (Dexter).   Greg. Inst. of Amer. EL 35
[Magnificat; Missa pro defunctis; Cantantibus organis; Domine, si tu
es; Laus et perennis; Pater noster; Ave Maria.]

I cannot conceal it:498. J'ai le rebours:507. Je ne fus jamais si aisé:
656,665. La, la, la, je ne l'ose dire:474,487,491,827. Que n'est-elle
auprès de moi?:507. Also 651.
CERVEAU, PIERRE (16th-17th centuries)
Comme nous voyons la rose:446.
CESARIS, JOHANNES (15th century)
A virtutis ignitio / Ergo beata nascio / Benedicta:563.
Cevallos. See CEBALLOS
CHAMPION (prob. THOMAS) (d. ca.1580)
Psalm 34:846.
CHANSONNIER MOAILLES: 576
CHARITE, PIERRE DE LA (d.1451)
Jusqu'à tant:621.
CHILD (WILLIAM?)
O God, wherefore art Thou absent from us?:883.
Chrzanowa, Mikolaj z. See MIKOLAJ Z CHRZANOWA
CICONIA, JOANNES (15th century)
I cani sono fuora:463. Doctorum principem:589,631. Dolce fortuna:758.
Et in terra pax:500,608. Gloria in excelsis:589. Ingens alumnus Padue:
589. Melodia suavissima:589,631. O Padua sidus praeclarum:485. O
virum, o lux, o beata Nicolae:589. Una panthera:780. Ut te per omnes:
589. Venetia mundi splendor:485.
CIMA, GIAN PAOLO (b. ca.1570)
Bicinium:759.
CIMELLO, THOMAS (16th century)
Gli occhi tuoi:221.
CLEMENT, JACQUES (called Clemens non Papa) (d. ca.1556)
Collegium Musicum Antwerpen (Weyler).   10" Cantate 64220
[Aanhort mijn volk (Ps.78); Als ich riep met verlangen (Ps.130); Here
lieve Here (Ps.4); Hoort mijn gebed, O Here (Ps.102); O God, aanhort
mijn klagen (Ps.64); Wilt danken loven Gods naam (Ps.34).]

Adoramus te:474,498,692. Une fillette bien gorriere:490. Ich sag ade:
650,760,867. De lustelijcke mey:492. O Maria, vernans rosa:762. O
quam moesta dies:862. Pastores, quidnam vidistis?:473. Ps.65:867.
Souterliedekens:776. Vox in rama:612.
Codex Calixtinus. See *CALIXTINUS CODEX*

CORREA DE ARAUXO, FRANCISCO (before 1575-ca.1663)
Bailete: Con las mozas de Vallecas:744. Canto llano de la Immaculada Concepcion:798. Fantasias:775. Tiento de II tono:798. Tiento de IV tono:798,800. Tiento a modo de cancion du IV ton:593. Tiento de baxon VI tono:800. Tiento de VII tono:798,799. Tiento pequeno y facil de VII tono:798. Tiento de X tono:798,799.

CORTECCIA, FRANCESCO (d.1571)
Ingredere felicissimis:862.

CORTONO. LAUDARIO: 535,646,647,677

COSTANTINI, ALESSANDRO (17th century)
Pastores loquebantur:448.

COSTE, GASPARD (16th century)
Pour faire plustost mal:828.

COSTELEY, GUILLAUME (1531-1606)
Allons au vert bocage:491. Allons gai, bergères:507,517,613,662,784, 854. Arreste un peu, mon coeur:827. Je vois des glissantes eaux:492, 507. La, je n'yray:852. Mignonne allons voir si la rose:490,495,507, 567,662,663,693,854. Quand le berger:492,827. Que de passions et douleurs:492,507,555,626. Que vaut catin:517. Also 499.

Coucy, Guy de. See GUY DE COUCY

COURTOIS, JEAN (16th century)
Venite populi:862.

CRAPPIUS, ANDREAS (ca.1542-1623)
Nun ist es Zeit zu singen hell:874.

CRASSOT, RICHARD (b. ca.1530)
Psalm 51:281.

CRAUS (prob. STEPHAN) (16th century)
Pavan Fuchs beiss mich nicht:522.

CRECQUILLON, THOMAS (d. ca.1557)
Caesaris auspiciis magni:712. Cancion pour ung plaisir:800. Erravi sicut ovis:712. Salve crux sancta:712.

CREMA, GIOVANNI MARIA DA (16th century)
Bertoncina:653. Bolognese:653. Louetta:653. 2 ricercari:653.

Cristo, Pedro de. See PEDRO DE CRISTO

CROCE, GIOVANNI (ca.1557-1609)
Dies sanctificatus:473. O sacrum convivium:484. Veni Domine:444.

Cruce, Petrus de. See PETRUS DE CRUCE

CUTTING (FRANCIS or THOMAS) (16th-17th centuries)
Alman:669. Galliards:549,669. Greensleeves:549. A jig:709. The squirrels toy:669. Walsingham variations:538,845.

CYEAT, RENWARD (1545-1614)
Nabi sid in te cathe:838.

DAGGERRE, WILLIAM (16th century)
Downderry down:877.

DALZA, JEAN-AMBROSIO (15th-16th centuries)
Calata spagnola:707. Pavana alla ferrarese:515. Pavana alla veneziana:
607,803. Piva:507,803. Saltarello:803. Tastar de corde con il ricercar
dietro:610,736. Vexilla Regis prodeunt:771.
DAMETT, THOMAS (d.1473)
Beata Dei genetrix:609,882.
Da Nola, Gian Domenico. See NOLA, GIOVANNI DOMENICO DA
DANYEL (DANIEL), JOHN (d.1630)
Stay, cruel, stay:657.
DARMSTADT 3317: 462
Dascanio, Josquin. See DEPRES, JOSQUIN
DASER, LUDWIG (ca.1525-1589)
Fratres, sobrii estote:471.
DAVY, RICHARD (15th-16th centuries)
All Saints Chorus; Purcell Consort of Voices (Burgess).　　Argo ZRG 558
[Passion according to St. Matthew.]
DAZA, ESTEBAN (16th century)
Dame acogida en tu hato:600,861. Enfermo estaba Antioco:861.
Fantasia:773. Tiento:600.
DEERING, RICHARD (d.1630)
Peterborough Cathedral Choir; Latham (org). (Vann)
1,2,5,6,8,10　　Argo RG 318; ZRG 5318; (Ger.) Decca SAWD 9980-B

1. Ave verum corpus. 2. Contristatus est Rex David. 3. Country cries:
532,553. 4. Cries of London:512,711. 5. Duo seraphim. 6. Factum est
silentium:883. 7. Fantasia:834. 8. Gaudent in coelis:528,537,729.
9. Jesu, dulcis memoria:552. 10. O bone Jesu:528,537. 11. O vos
omnes:703. 12. Pavan and almaine:742. 13. Quem vidistis pastores:537,
663,691,693,783.

De Haspre, Johannes Simon. See HASPRE, JOHANNES SIMON DE
de la Halle, Adam. See ADAM DE LA HALLE
DELAHAYE, JEAN (15th century)
Mort, j'appele de ta rigeur:670.
de La Rue, Pierre. See LA RUE, PIERRE DE
de la Torre, Francisco. See TORRE, FRANCISCO DE LA
DELATRE, CLAUDE PETIT JEAN (16th century)
Al hadden wy en veerting bedden:826.
Del Giovane, Giovanni Domenico. See NOLA, GIOVANNI DOMENICO DA
Del Melle, Renatus. See MEL, RENATUS DEL
DEMANTIUS, CHRISTOPH (1567-1643)
Concentus Musicus of Denmark (Mathiesen).　　Nonesuch 1064; 71064
[5 Polish and German dances.] (verso: Widmann)

Junge Kantorei Mannheim (Schweizer).　　Da Camera CH 94005
[Ach bleib bei uns; Deutsche Passion ... St. Johannes; Ich bin die
Auferstehung; Ich bin ein guter Hirte; Leidenweissagung des Jesaia.]

DEMANTIUS, CHRISTOPH (1567-1643) (Continued)
NCVR Vocaal Ensemble Hilversum (Voorberg).
Camerata CMS 30014 LPM; Nonesuch 1138; 71138
[Deutsche Passion ... St. Johannes; Leidenweissagung des Jesaia.]
NCVR Vocaal Ensemble Hilversum (Voorberg).
Camerata CMS 30015 LPM
[Das ist mir lieb (Ps.116); Denn wer sich selbst erhöhet; Es ward ein
Stille; Steh auf und nimm das Kindlein; Und wie Moses.]

Spandauer Kantorei (Behrmann). Turnabout TV 34175
[Weissagung des Leidens und Sterbens Jesu Christi.] (verso: Lechner)

Spandauer Kantorei (Behrmann). Odyssey 32160360
[Das ist mir lieb (Ps.116).] (verso: Schein and Schütz)

Deutsche Passion nach dem Ev. St. Johannes: 518. Dies Nacht hatt'ich
ein' Traum: 766. Du sollst Gott, deinen Herren lieben: 605. Es ward
eine Stille: 605. Galliards: 766, 870, 871. Herr nun lässt du: 766.
Hertzlich thut mich erfrewen: 590. Ich bin ein guter Hirte: 605. Intrada:
868. Polnischer Tanz: 753, 870. Zart schönes Bild: 766.
De Melle, Renatus. See MEL, RENATUS DEL
de Monte, Philippe. See MONTE, PHILIPPE DE
De Orto, Marbriano de. See ORTO, MARBRIANUS DE
DEPRES, JOSQUIN (d.1521)
Blanchard Vocal Ensemble. Disc. DF 730063; 740015
35

Caillard Choir and Instrumentalists. Musical Heritage MHS 1000
18,41

Capella Antiqua, Munich (Ruhland). Telefunken AWT 9480; SAWT 9480
3,4,5,6,8,10,24,27

Capella Cordina (Planchart). Lyrichord LLST 7214
9,17,42,45,51,63

Chanteurs St.-Eustache (Martin). Boîte à Musique 022
18 (verso: Manchicourt)

Chanteurs St.-Eustache (Martin). Boîte à Musique 040
50 (verso: Lassus)

Chanteurs St.-Eustache (Martin). Lumen AMS 4
11,31,38

Collegium Musicum; UCLA Madrigal Singers (Weiss). Everest 3210
12,13,14,21 (verso: Schütz)

Kaufbeurer Martinsfinken (Hahn). Nonesuch H 1084; 71084
4 (verso: Isaac, Lassus)

NCVR Vocaal Ensemble Hilversum (Voorberg). Cantate CMS 30031
23,25 (verso: Isaac)

Prague Madrigal Singers; Vienna Musica Antiqua (Venhoda).
5,25,30,39,50,57   Crossroads 22 16 0093; 22 16 0094

Prague Madrigal Singers (Venhoda).   Valois MB 794
3,6,22,23,41

Purcell Consort (Burgess).   Argo ZRG 681
5,45,50,52,53,61,64,69

Spandauer Kantorei (Behrmann).   Turnabout 34431
41 (verso: La Rue)

University of Illinois Chamber Chorus (Hunter).   Nonesuch 71216
1,20,26,29,33

Vocal and Instrumental Ensemble; Cochereau (org). (Birbaum)
5,7,27   Philips 835785

Wiener Kammerchor & Musica Antiqua (Gillesberger).
11,15,31,34,38   Bach BG 620; BGS 5042; Amadeo AVRS 5008

(motets): 1. Absolon fili mi. 2. Absolve, quaesumus, Domine:862.
3. Alma redemptoris Mater. 4. Ave Christe immolate. 5. Ave Maria:738,
850. 6. Ave Regina caelorum. 7. Ave vera virginitas:454,498. 8. Ave
verum:484,598,696,737. 9. Benedicite omnia opera. 10. Benedicta es,
coelorum Regina. 11. De profundis. 12. Dulces exuviae. 13. Fama
malum. 14. Huc me sydereo. 15. In principio erat verbum. 16. In te
Domine:610. 17. Laudate pueri. 18. Miserere. 19. Misericordias
Domini. 20. Mittit ad virginem. 21. O Domine Jesu Christe. 22. O Jesu
filii David. 23. O Virgo virginum. 24. Planxit autem David. 25. Praeter
rerum seriem:822. 26. Salve Regina. 27. Stabat Mater. 28. Tu pauperum
refugium:610,622. 29. Tu solus, qui facis mirabilia. 30. Tulerunt
Dominum meum:486. 31. Veni sancte Spiritus. 32. Virgo prudentissima:
700.

(masses): 33. Ave maris stella:803. 34. Da pacem. 35. De beata Virgine:
700 (Credo). 36. De nostra Domina:844 (Agnus). 37. Gaudeamus:700
(Kyrie). 38. Hercules Dux Ferrariae. 39. L'homme armé. 40. Mater
Patris et Filia:692. 41. Pange lingua:497,776 (Gloria). 42. Sine nomine.
From unspecified masses: Kyrie:800. Agnus Dei:610.

(chansons): 43. Adieu mes amours:511,624,656,765. 44. Allégez-moy:
511,656. 45. Basiez-moy:624,776,844. 46. Bergerette Savoyene:776.
47. Carmen gallicum:862. 48. Coment peult:465. 49. De tous biens:
624,803. 50. La deploration de Jehan Okeghem (Cueurs desoles):578,
644,771,805,854,862. 51. Faulte d'argent:610. 52. Fortuna desperata.
53. El grillo:660,803,839,851. 54. L'homme armé:621,683. 55. In
meine Sinn:591. 56. J'ai bien cause:765. 57. Milles regrets:487,517,
555,578,597,626,656,710,771. 58. Une mousse de Biscaye:656.
59. N'esse pas un grand deplaisir:776. 60. Parfons regretz:644,776,854.
61. Petite camusette:621. 62. Plus nulz regretz:765. 63. Plusieurs
regretz.

DEPRES, JOSQUIN (d.1521) (Continued)
  (instrumental): 64. La bernardina:844. 65. Cancion I, del Emperador:
  710. 66. Fantasia:868. 67. Royal fanfares for the consecration of
  Louis XII:560,888. 68. Petrus et Johann currunt in puncto:624.
  69. Vive le roy:469,504,511,624,701.
Dering, Richard. See DEERING, RICHARD
de Rore, Cipriano. See RORE, CYPRIAN DE
Dia, Beatriz (Comtessa) de. See BEATRITZ DE DIA
DIESSEN. Clm.5511: 462
Diomedes, Cato. See CATO, DIOMEDES
DLUGORAJ, WOJCIECH (16th-17th centuries)
  Chorea polonica:812. Dances:781. Fantasias:659,753,812. Finales:659.
  Villanellas:659,812.
DONATO (DONATI), BALDASSARE (1548-1603)
  Chi la gagliarda:818,851. Tratto fuora del mar:896. Wenn wir
  hinausziehn:521.
Donato da Cascia. See DONATUS DE FLORENTIA
Donato da Firenze. See DONATUS DE FLORENTIA
DONATUS DE FLORENTIA (14th century)
  L'aspido sordo:463. Come da lupo:586. I'fuggià usignol:569.
DOWLAND, JOHN (1563-1626)
  Bream (lute).   RCA LM 2987; LSC 2987; (Br.) RB 6751; SB 6751
    62,63,64,66,71,75,78,79,82,88,89,94,95,96,98
  Deller Consort. ,   Bach BG 673; BGS 70673;
                      (Ger.) Amadeo AVRS 6396; (Fr.) AVRS 66009
    1,3,5,13,14,15,19,24,25,26,33,41,42,58,93
  Elizabethan Consort of Viols.   Music Guild S872
    70
  Golden Age Singers (Field-Hyde).   Argo RG 290; ZRG 5290
    1,2,5,6,9,10,15,23,27,39,41,44,49,53,58,59
  Golden Age Singers (Field-Hyde).
                      Westminster W9619 (reissue of XWN 18762)
    4,11,18,21,25,30,34,36,44,45,47,51,55,57
  Miskell (tnr); Leeb (lute).   HMV HQM 1035
    5,14,22,26,35,40 (verso: Campian)
  Saltire Singers; Dupré (lute).
                      Lyrichord 153; 7153; Musical Heritage MHS 870 S
    2,13,24,27,33,36,39,44,45,46,54,56,57
  Studio der frühen Musik, Munich (Binkley).
                      DGA ARC 3245; 73245; APM 14345; SAPM 198345
    3,8,19,22,26,33,40,42,45,47,72,75
  Schola Cantorum Basiliensis (Müller-Dombois).
                      RCA VIC(S) 1338; Harmonia Mundi 30623
    60,64,69,80,81,83,84,85,86,87,94,97,99,100

Vocal and Instrumental Ensemble (Leppard).

Nonesuch 1167; 71167; Odeon CLB 1894

12,13,18,20,25,28,31,37,38,39,40,42,45,50,51,52,53,57

(Ayres): 1. Awake sweet love. 2. Away with these self-loving lads:680. 3. Can she excuse:453,531,657,680,766. 4. Clear or cloudy. 5. Come again:521,583,657. 6. Come, heavy sleep:531,725,790. 7. Come when I call:461. 8. Come ye heavy states of night:453. 9. Dear, if you change:531. 10. Disdain me still. 11. Faction that ever dwells. 12. Farewell, unkind. 13. Fine knacks for ladies:587. 14. Flow my tears:584. 15. Flow not so fast, ye fountains:461. 16. Fortune my foe:657. 17. From silent night:747. 18. Go, cristall tears. 19. Go nightly cares. 20. An heart that's broken and contrite. 21. I must complain. 22. I saw my lady weep:453,531,790. 23. If flood of tears. 24. If my complaints. 25. If that a sinner's sighs. 26. In darkness let me dwell:639. 27. In this trembling shadow:680. 28. Lady, if you so spight me. 29. Lasso vita mia:680. 30. Love stood amazed:728. 31. Love, those beams that breed. 32. The lowest trees have tops:639. 33. Me, me and none but me:453. 34. My thoughts are wing'd with hope:881. 35. Now cease my wandering eyes. 36. Now, oh now I needs must part:466. 37. Psalm 51. 38. Psalm 100. 39. Say, love:492, 583,639,661,766,828. 40. Shall I sue:453,492,531,790,828. 41. Sleep, wayward thoughts. 42. Sorrow, stay:453,627,639,680,739. 43. Stay, time:531. 44. Sweet, stay awhile:531. 45. Tell me, true love. 46. Think's thou then by this feigning. 47. Thou mighty God. 48. Time's esdest son:639. 49. To ask for all thy love. 50. Up, merry mates. 51. Weep you no more:531. 52. Welcome black night:680. 53. Were every thought an eye. 54. What if I never speed:466,657,680, 792,801. 55. What poor astronomers. 56. When Phoebus first did Daphne love. 57. Where sin sore wounding. 58. Wilt thou, unkind:639, 790. 59. Woeful heart.

(instrumental): 60. Captain Digori Piper's galliard:549,639,680,725. 61. Dowlands adew:559. 62. Dowland's first galliard. 63. The Earl of Derby his galliard. 64. Earl of Essex Galliard:642. 65. Fantasias:559, 659,856. 66. Frog galliard:643. 67. Galliard:549. 68. Galliard: Can she excuse:559. 69. King of Denmark's galliard:507,549,716. 70. Lachrymae:668. 71. Lachrimae antiquae:549,642,725,740. 72. Lachrimae antiquae novae. 73. Lachrimae pavin:559. 74. Lachrymae triste:643. 75. Lachrimae veraè. 76. Lady Clifton's spirit:639. 77. Lord Chamberlaine's galliard:832. 78. Lord d'Lisle's galliard. 79. Melancholie galliard:549,550,856. 80. M. Bucton's galliard:832. 81. Mrs. Nichols' allemande. 82. Mrs. Vaux's gigge. 83. Mr. George Whitehead's almand:642,725. 84. Mr. Giles Hoby's galliard. 85. Mr. Henry Noel his galliard. 86. Mr. Nicholas Gryffith his galliard:627. 87. Mr. Thomas Collier his galliard:680,832. 88. My Lady Hunsdon's puffe:550,711,856. 89. My Lady Rich's galliard:534,582,729.

DOWLAND, JOHN (1563-1626) (Continued)
    90. My Lord Willobye's welcome home:534,668. 91. Orlando sleepeth:
    507. 92. Pavane:680,747. 93. Queen Elizabeth's galliard:549,627,639,
    659. 94. Semper Dowland:583,766. 95. The shoemaker's wife:550.
    96. Sir Henry Gifford's almaine. 97. Sir Henry Umpton's funeral.
    98. Sir John Smith's almaine. 99. Sir John Gouch his galliard:532.
    100. Sir John Langton's pavan:639. 101. Tarleton's resurrection:559,
    639.
DRAGONI, GIOVANNI ANDREA (ca.1540-1598)
    Kyrie:682. Qui tollis:682.
DUBLIN VIRGINAL MS.: 530
DU CAURROY, FRANÇOIS EUSTACHE (1549-1609)
    Deliette, mignonette:491. Un enfant du ciel:784. 5 fantasias on Une
    jeune fillette:625. 2ème fantaisie:523. 5ème fantaisie:513. Te Deum:
    508.
DUFAY, GUILLAUME (d.1474)
    Ambrosian Singers and Players (Stevens).   Dover HCR 5261
    24,31,35,48,49,51,57,58,63,64,69

    Berkeley Chamber Singers (Gilchrist).
    40   Lyrichord LL 150; LLST 7150; Oryx 722

    Caillard Vocal Ensemble.   Erato LDE 3023
    42

    Capella Antiqua, Munich (Ruhland). Telefunken AWT 9439; SAWT 9439
    3,5,6,19,29,43,44,45,46

    Capella Cordina (Planchart).   Lyrichord LL 190; LLST 7190
    2,12,23,39

    Capella Cordina (Planchart).   Lyrichord 7233
    6,38,61,68,72

    Capella Cordina (Planchart).   Lyrichord 7234
    42 (verso: ANON. Missa Fuit homo.)

    Capella Cordina (Planchart).   Lyrichord 7237
    7 (verso: Ockeghem)

    Frauenchor der Fachschule für Musik Györ (Szabó).   Qualiton S 11441
    39 (verso: Lassus)

    Musica Reservata (Beckett).   Philips 6500085
    35,47,49,50,52,65,66,67,70,72 (verso: Morton)

    Petit Ensemble Vocal de Montreal (Little).   Vox DL 990; STDL 500990
    1,4,6,13,15,16,18,21,22,26,27,28,32,41 (Kyrie & Sanctus), 48,50,
    53,55,60,63,69

    Tölzer Knabenchor.   Harmonia Mundi HM 30683; 530683
    8,9,41

Vienna Chamber Choir (Gillesberger). Bach BG 653; 70653;
__41__ (Br.) BG 653; BGS 5065; (Ger.) Amadeo AVRS 5026

(sacred): 1. Alma redemptoris mater:467,575,579,609,687. 2. Apostolo
glorioso. 3. Audi benigne. 4. Aures ad nostras. 5. Ave maris stella:700.
6. Ave Regina coelorum:733. 7. Benedicamus Domino. 8. Christe
redemptor omnium. 9. Conditor alme siderum:721. 10. Festun nunc
celebre:709. 11. Flos florum:776,844. 12. Fulgens iubar. 13. Hi sunt
quos ritenens. 14. Hymnus in Adventu Domini:687,842. 15. Hymnus in
Festis Plurimorum Martyrum. 16. Hymnus in Festo Pentecostes.
17. Hymns (misc.):864. 18. Jesu, corona virginum. 19. Magnificat VI
tone. 20. Magnificat VIII tone:467,687. 21. Nobis datus. 22. Nova
veniens a caelo. 23. Nuper rosarum flores:485. 24. O beate Sebastiane.
25. Os justi:683. 26. Pange lingua. 27. Qui paraclitus. 28. Respice
clemens. 29. Salve Regina. 30. Spiritus Domini replevit:687,788.
31. Supremum est mortalibus:485. 32. Urbs beata Jerusalem. 33. Veni
creator Spiritus:146,687,788. 34. Veni sancte Spiritus:699. 35. Vergine
bella:709,715,741. 36. Veritas mea:683. 37. Vexilla regis:146,776,806,
894.

(masses): 38. Ave Regina caelorum. 39. Caput. 40. L'homme armé:609
(Kyrie & Agnus),683 (Credo),776 (Agnus II). 41. Se la face ay pale:699
(Hosanna). 42. Sine nomine. 43. Gloria:587. 44. Kyrie (Ms. Cambrai).
45. Kyrie paschali. 46. Sanctus papale.

(secular): 47. Adieu ces bons vins. 48. Adieu m'amour:468,578,609,619.
49. La belle se siet. 50. Bon jour bon mois:578,709. 51. Ce jour de
l'an. 52. Colinetto. 53. Craindre vous vueil:709. 54. Les doleurs dont
me sens:670. 55. Donna, i ardente. 56. Donnes l'assault:670,717.
57. Franc cuer gentil:468,578,717,733. 58. He! compaignons:699.
59. J'attendray tant qu'il vous plaira:621,699. 60. Je ne vis oncques.
61. Lamentatio sanctae matris Ecclesiae Constantinopolitanae:621,715.
62. Magnes me gentes:717. 63. Malheureux cueur. 64. Mon chier amy:
609. 65. Mon coeur me fait:621. 66. Par droit je puis bien complaindre.
67. Pour l'amour de ma doulce amye:619. 68. Puisque vous estez
campieur. 69. Quel fronte signorille. 70. Resvelliés vous et faites chiere.
71. Resvelons nous resvelons amoureux:844. 72. Se la face ay pale:468,
717. 73. Vostre bruit:760. Also 866.

DULICHIUS, PHILIPPUS (1562-1631)
Ich hebe meine Augen auf:526.

DUNSTABLE, JOHN (ca.1370-1453)
Purcell Consort of Voices (Burgess). Argo ZRG 681
[Ave maris stella; Alma redemptoris mater; O rosa bella; Sancta
Maria; Veni sancte Spiritus.] (verso: Depres)

Ave maris stella:733. Ave Regina coelorum:792. Kyrie:483. O rosa
bella:609,670,733. Quam pulchra est:483,589,622,733. Sancta Maria:
500,609,844. Veni sancte Spiritus:733,881,882.

EAST, THOMAS (ca.1540-ca.1608)
 Desperavi:701. Farewell, sweet woods:655. Hence stars:885. O
 metaphysical tobacco:680. Poor is the life:680. Sweet muses:655.
 Thyrsis, sleepest thou:655. Weep not dear love:680. When Israel
 came out of Egypt:627. Your shining eyes:680.
Ebreo. See GUGLIELMO EBREO
ECCARD, JOHANNES (1553-1611)
 Ein feste Burg:527. Herr Christe, tu mir gehen:785. Ich lag in tiefer
 Todesnacht:444,616. Ich steh an deiner Krippe hier:447,599,695. In
 dulci jubilo:897. Nun schürz dich:520,524. O Freude über Freud:
 785,874. Resonet in laudibus:580. Übers Gebirg Maria geht:444,785.
 Vom Himmel hoch:448,617,874. When to the temple Mary went:783.
 Zeit tut Rosen bringen:591. Zu dieser österlichen Zeit:523,694.
EDWARDS, RICHARD (ca.1523-1566)
 Where griping grief:582,661,711,731.
ELVAS. BIBL. PUBLIA HORTENSIA. MS.: 476
ENCINA (ENZINA), JUAN DEL (1469-1534)
 A quién debo yo llamar:811. Ay triste que vengo:741,824,861.
 Congoxa mas que cruel:610. Cucú, cucú:720,841. Es la causa bien
 amor:689. Fata la parte:581,585. Gasajémonos de husla:495,839.
 Guarda no lo seas tu:477. Hoy comamos:581,841. Mas vale trocar:
 610,689. Mi libertad en sosiego:460,743. O reyes magos benditos:844.
 Pues que jamás olvidaros:454,477,498,610,689. Pues que tú:811. Qué
 es de tí, desconsolado:689. Quédate, Carrillo:689. Revelóse mi
 cuidado:689. Romerico, tú que vienes:689. Una sañosa porfia:477,841.
 Soy contento y vos servido:881. Tan buen ganadico:841. Te do los:477.
 Todos los búenes del mundo:460,689. Triste España:477,485,581,720.
 Villancicos:505. Vuestros amores:477. Ya no quiero tener fe:811.
ENRIQUE (16th century)
 Mi querer tanto vos quiere:861.
EPISCOPIUS, LUDOVICUS (ca.1520-1595)
 Laet varen alle fantasie:777.
ERBACH, CHRISTIAN (ca.1570-1635)
 Canzon del VI tono:580. Intonatio II toni:580. Ricercar VII toni:764.
ERFURT MS.: 842
ESCOBAR, PEDRO (early 16th century)
 In nativitate Domini:500. Las mis penas:477,689,743,824. Pásame
 por Dios:460. Secaróme los pesares:666. Virgen bendita:811.
ESCORIAL MS.: 457
Escurel, Jehannot de l'. See L'ESCUREL, JEHANNOT DE
ESQUIVEL DE BARAHONA, JUAN (16th-17th centuries)
 Gloria in excelsis:808. O vos omnes:809. Veni Domine:830.
Este, Thomas. See EAST, THOMAS
Estocart, Pascal de l'. See L'ESTOCART, PASCAL DE
ETON CHOIRBOOK: 558
Eustorg de Beaulieu. See BEAULIEU, EUSTORG DE

EXCETRE, JOHN (14th century)
Sanctus and Benedictus:882.

FABRICIUS (prob. PETRUS) (1587-1651)
Es ist ein Bauer in Brunnen:522. Gut Gsell:522. Polnischer Tanz:522.
Studentenlob:522. Studententanz:522.
FACOLI, MARCO (16th century)
Aria della Marcheta Saporita:844. Aria della Signora Lucilla:556. Aria
della Signora Moretta:844.
FAENZA CODEX: 535,844
Faidit, Gaucelm. See FAYDIT, GAUCELM
FAIGNIENT, NOE (16th century)
De Segheninge:777.
FALLAMERO, GABRIELE (16th century)
Vorria, Madonna:767.
FANTINI, GIROLAMO (17th century)
178,513,768
FARMER, JOHN (16th-17th centuries)
Fair nymphs:546,885. Fair Phyllis:567,663,693. A little pretty bonny
lass:544,545. O stay, sweet love:655.
FARNABY, GILES (ca.1564-ca.1600)
Almande:730,833,834. Ay me, poor heart:544. Blind love was shooting:
664. Bonny sweet robin:566. Construe my meaning:546,587. Curtain
drawn:664. Fantasia:539,543,566. Farnabye's conceit:566. Giles
Farnaby's dream:566,737,757. His rest:566. Loath to depart:543,565,
566. Maske:538,745,876. The new sa-hoo:186. Pearce did dance with
Petronella:655. Pearce did love fair Petronella:655. Rosasolis:529,643.
Spagnioletta:602. Tell me, Daphne:637,690. Tower hill:543,566,690.
A toye:186,565,566,757. Wooddy-cock:529,564.
FARNABY, RICHARD
Fayne would I wed:566. Nobodye's gigge:550.
FARRANT, RICHARD (ca.1530-1580)
Abradad:742. Call to remembrance:474,498. Hide not thou thy face:883.
FAUGUES, GUILLERMUS (VINCENT) (15th century)
Gloria:683.
FAWKYNER (15th century)
Gaude rosa:558.
FAYDIT, GAUCELM (b. ca.1150)
Fort chausa aujatz:478.
FAYRFAX, ROBERT (d.1521)
Ambrosian Singers (Stevens).   Lumen AMS 38; Musica 38
[Missa Tecum principium; Aeterne laudis lilium (motet).]

O lux beata Trinitas:714. Somewhat musing:727.
Fenis, Rudolph von. See RUDOLPH VON FENIS-NEUENBURG

FERAGUT, BELTRAME (15th century)
Excelsa civitas Vincentia:485.
Fernandez de Madrid, Juan. See MADRID, JUAN FERNANDEZ
Fernando de las Infantas. See LAS INFANTAS, FERNANDO DE
FERRABOSCO, ALFONSO II (ca.1575-1628)
Almandes:541,834. Che giovarebbe haver bellezza:767. Fair cruel
nymph:729. Fantasy in G:541. Fantasia on the hexachord:466.
Four-note pavan:475,730. I saw my lady weeping:711. Io mi son
giovinett'e volontieri:764. Lady, if you so spite me:731. O eyes:725.
O mortal stars:725. Pavans:659,731,734,834. Pavan Dovehouse:515,
541. Se si spezzasse:767. Vias tuas:711.
FESTA, CONSTANZO (d.1545)
Deus, venerunt gentes:569. Quando ritrova:568,612. Quis dabit
oculis nostris:465,884. Se'l pensier:492,828.
FEVIN, ANTOINE DE (d.1515)
Faulte d'argent:586. Fors seulement:739. Gaude Francorum regia
corona:511. Missa mente tota:611 (Agnus).
Filippo di Lurano. See LURANO, FILIPPO DE
FINCK, HEINRICH (1445-1527)
Renaissance Chorus (Brown).   Baroque 9005
[Missa de Beata Virgine.]

Ach herzigs Herz:652. Chiara luce:752. Greiner Zanner:469,624,740.
Habs nun getan:590. Ich stund an einem Morgen:752. Ich werde
erlöst:752. In Gottes Namen:524. O du armer Judas:752. O schönes
Weib:765. Sauff aus und machs nit lang:652. Der Tag der ist so
freudenreich:580. Tanz:652. Veni Creator Spiritus:609,788. Veni
redemptor gentium:640. Veni Sancte Spiritus:609. Wach auf:520.
Firenze, Andrea di. See ANDREAS DE FLORENTIA
Firenze, Donato da. See DONATUS DE FLORENTIA
Firenze, Lorenzo da. See LAURENTIUS DE FLORENTIA
FITZWILLIAM VIRGINAL BOOK: 564,565,566
FLECHA, MATEO (1481?-1553?)
El fuego:744. Que farem del pobre Joan:840. Teresica hermana:840.
FLORENCE. PLUTEUS 29.1: 462,576,615
Florentia, Andreas de. See ANDREAS DE FLORENTIA
Florentia, Donatus de. See DONATUS DE FLORENTIA
Florentia, Ghirardellus de. See GHIRARDELLUS DE FLORENTIA
Florentia, Johannes de. See GIOVANNI DA CASCIA
Florentia, Laurentius de. See LAURENTIUS DE FLORENTIA
FOGLIANO, GIACOMO (1468-1548)
L'amor donna:586. Ave Maria:500,610.
FOGLIANO, LUDOVICO (d. ca.1538)
Quodlibet:632.
FOLQUET DE MARSEILLE (ca.1155-1231)
En cantan m'aven a membrar:478.

FONTAINE, PIERRE (d. ca.1450)
Fontaine à vous dire:488. J'ayme bien celui:717. Mon coeur pleure:621.
Pastourelle:535,621,715. Sans faire de vous départie:557.

FORD, THOMAS (ca.1580-1648)
Almighty God who hast me brought:454,498. Come, Phyllis:531. Fair
sweet cruel:531. Since first I saw your face:495.

FOREST (d.1446)
Qualis est dilectus tuus:589.

FORSTER (GEORG?)
I say adieu:454,498.

Francesco de Layolle. See LAYOLLE, FRANCESCO DE

Franciscus Bossinensis. See BOSSINENSIS, FRANCISCUS

FRANCISCUS REYNALDUS (14th century)
L'adorno viso:758.

FRANCISQUE, ANTOINE (ca.1565-1605)
Branle de Montirandé:596.

FRANCK, MELCHIOR (d.1639)
Camerata Vocale.   Musica Rara MUS 1; Da Camera 94017
[Hosianna dem Sohne Davids; Fürchtet euch nicht; Das alte Jahr
vergangen ist; O du Bethlehem; Die Menschen alle bewunderten sich;
Kommt her zu mir; Hüt dich weg; Fürwahr er trug unser Krankheit;
Entsetzet euch nicht; Ich bin ein guter Hirte; Wahrlich ich sage euch;
Gehst hin in alle Welt. Also hat Gott die Welt geliebt; Gleich wie
Moses; Gelobet sei der Herr; Es werden nicht alle; Machet euch
Freunde nicht; Wer sich selbst erhöhet; Und ich hörte eine grosse Stimm';
Warum denket ihr; Gleich wie der Blitz; Kommt her, ihr Gesegneten.]

New York Pro Musica (Greenberg).   Decca 9412; 79412
[Du bist aller Dinge schön; Meine Schwester, liebe Braut; Ich sucht
des Nachts in meinem Bette.] (verso: Schütz)

Das Bergwerk wolln wir preisen:519. Galliarda:523,870,871. Ihr Lieben:
789. Intrada II:829. Intrada VII:560. Kommt, ihr G'spielen:520. Lobet
den Herren alle Heiden:605. Pavana:870,871.

François de Lille. See FRANCUS DE INSULA

FRANCUS DE INSULA (INSULIS) (15th century)
Je ne vis pas:468.

FRAUENLOB (HEINRICH VON MEISSEN) (d.1318)
Ez waent ein narrenweise:681.

FRESNEAU, HENRI (16th century)
J'ay la promese de m'amye:578.

FREUNDT, CORNELIUS (ca.1535-1591)
Wie schön singt uns der Engel Schar:620,874.

FRIDERICI, DANIEL (1584-1638)
Drei schöne Dinge:519. Wir lieben sehr im Herzen:520.

FRIEDRICH VON HAUSEN (ca.1155-1190)
Ich denke under wilen:886.

FRONCIACO (14th century)
Kyrie Jhesu dulcissime:881.
FRYE, WALTER (15th century)
Ave Regina:733. Salve virgo mater:882.
FUENLLANA MIGUEL DE (16th century)
De Antequera salió el moro:773,861. De los alamos vengo:861. Duo
de Josquin:707. Duélete de mi:505,861. Fantasia:710. La girigonza:
773. Morenica dáme un beso:600. Ojos claros serenos:600. Paseábase
el rey moro:612. Four tientos:743.
FUHRMANN'S LUTE TABLATURE: 812
Fulda, Adam von. See ADAM VON FULDA

GABRIEL (or MENA) (15th-16th centuries)
De la dulce mi enemiga:477,807. No soy yo quién la descubre:861.
Sola me dexaste:689.
GABRIELI, ANDREA (ca.1510-1586)
Ambrosian Consort; Ensemble Cuivres Gabriel Masson (Delmotte).
Belvedere (Centrocord) ELY 0530
[Aria della battaglia.] (verso: Janequin)

Ambrosian Singers; Brass Ensemble (Stevens).
Angel S 36443; HMV HQS 1093
[Benedictus Dominus; Gloria; O crux splendor; Ricercare.]
(verso: G. Gabrieli)

Dalla Libera (org). Vedette VPC 1508; VST 6008
[Canzon ariosa; Cappriccio sopra il Pass'e mezzo antico; Praeambulum
quarti toni; Ricercar arioso 1, 3; Toccata del X tono.]
(verso: G. Gabrieli)

Eastman Wind Ensemble (Fennell). Mercury MG 50245; SR 90245;
(Br.) Mercury MMA 11169; AMS 16119
[Aria della battaglia.] (verso: G. Gabrieli)

Paris Instrumental Ensemble (Hollard). Vox 540; 500540
[Ricercare del VI tono; Ricercare del XII tono; Ricercare del II tono.]
(verso: G. Gabrieli)

A le guancie di rose:896. Aria della battaglia:896. Benedictus Dominus:
582. Benedixisti:444. Canzonas:506. Canzone ariose:450,863. Dimmi
cieco:629. Ecco l'aurora:629,663,693. Echo Vinegia bella:896. Gloria:
583. Hor che nel suo bel seno:896. Imploration pour un temps de
détresse:506. Intonazione del VII tono:612,863. Io mi sento morire:
896. Magnificat:501. Missa brevis:628. O crux splendidior:582. O
sacrum convivium:767. Quem vidistis pastores:822. Ricercare del II
tono:768. Ricercare del VI tono:635. Ricercare del VII tono:450,837.
Ricercare del VIII tono:450. Ricercare del XII tono:612,746,825,829.
Ricercare arioso:837. Ricercare (unspec.):583,896. Risonanza di
echo:896.

GABRIELI, GIOVANNI (1557-1612)
Ambrosian Singers; Brass Ensemble (Stevens).
Angel S 36443; HMV HQS 1093
[Canzona VII toni; Buccinate in neomenia; In ecclesiis; Timor et tremor.] (verso: A. Gabrieli)

Capella Antiqua, Munich (Ruhland). Telefunken AWT 9456; SAWT 9456

Collegium Musicum of Radio Vienna; Urbancic (org). (Kneihs)
Musical Heritage MHS 998
[Canzon a 7; Fuga IX toni; Sonata no.13 for double orchestra; Canzon for brass; Canzon for recorders; Canzon for double orchestra; Toccata XI toni; Canzon for reeds; Fantasia IV toni; Canzon La spiritata.]

Dalla Libera (org). Vedette VPC 1508; VST 6008
[Fantasia VI toni; Fuga IX toni; Ricercar 5; Canzon 2; Ricercar X toni; Toccata.] (verso: A. Gabrieli)

Eastman Wind Ensemble (Fennell).
Mercury MG 50245; SR 90245; (Br.) MMA 11169; AMS 16119
[Sonata VIII toni; Canzon XII toni; Canzon IX toni; Canzon VII toni; Canzon IV toni; Sonata pian'e forte.] (verso: A. Gabrieli)

Edward Tarr Brass Ensemble; Gabrieli Consort La Fenice; E. Power Biggs (org). (Negri) Columbia MS 7142
[(canzonas): IX toni a 8; VII toni a 8; IX toni a 12; VII toni a 12; VIII toni a 12; XII toni a 10; I toni a 10; XII toni a 6. Sonata IX toni a 8; Sonata for three violins and organ; Ricercare for organ.]

Gregg Smith Singers; Texas Boys Choir; Edward Tarr Brass Ensemble; E. Power Biggs (org). (Negri)
Columbia ML 6471; MS 7071; (Br.) CBS 72663
[Intonations for organ; Plaudite, psalite; In ecclesiis; O magnum mysterium; Hodie Christus natus est; Deus qui beatum Marcum; Kyrie; Gloria; Sanctus.]

Gregg Smith Singers; Texas Boys Choir. Columbia MS 7334
[Deus, in nomine tuo; Beata es, Virgo Maria; Jubilemus singuli; Deus, Deus meus; O quam suavis est; Cantate Domino; Domine exaudi; Hodie completi sunt; A cappella Mass.]

Paris Instrumental Ensemble (Hollard). Vox 540; 500540
[(canzonas): I toni; VII toni; XII toni; IX toni; IV toni.]
(verso: A. Gabrieli)

Philadelphia Brass Ensemble; Cleveland Brass Ensemble; Chicago Brass Ensemble. Columbia MS 7209; CBS 72729
[Canzon VII toni 2; Canzon XII toni: Canzon a 12 in echo; Sonata VIII toni; Canzon per sonar 27; Canzon IV toni; Canzon a 12; Canzon per sonar 28; Sonata pian'e forte; Canzon I toni; Canzon VII toni 1; Canzon IX toni; Canzon per sonar 2.]

St. Hedwig's Cathedral Choir (Forster).   Da Capo SMVP 8075
[Jubilate Deo.] (verso: Palestrina)

Stuttgart Chamber Orchestra (Münchinger).   Decca SXL 6441
[Sonata XIII; Canzon VII; Canzon a 7; Canzon per sonar I toni; Canzon 10; Canzon 2; Sonata pian'e forte; Sonata con tre violini.]

Vienna State Opera Orchestra (Scherchen).   Westminster 19013; 17013
[Canzon I toni.] (verso: Beethoven, Orff)

Ahi, senza te:496. Alma cortes'e bella:496. Audi Domine hymnum: 746. Beata est virgo Maria:501. Buccinate in neomenia:583. Canzon La spiritata:701,779,829,837,863,896. Canzon prima a cinque:740. Canzon per sonar no.2:469. Canzon seconda:896. Canzon terza:825, 897. Canzon quarta:825,896,897. Canzon VI a 7:892. Canzon VIII a 8:774. Canzon VII toni a 12:774. Canzon VIII toni a 12:774. Canzon IX a 12:774. Canzon per sonar, I toni:513. Canzon VII toni:825. Canzon XII toni a 8:764. Canzon a 4:625. Canzon a 8, Fa sol la re: 625,896. Canzon a 10:768. Canzon a 12:774. Canzona:583. Deus, Deus meus:830. Deus in nomine tuo:746. Dolce care parole:496. Dormiva dolcemente:496. Fuga del IX tono:863. Hodie Christus natus est:595,616,822,830. In ecclesiis:583,613. In nobil sangue:764. Intonazione d'organo:768. Jubilate Deo:501,654,694,892. Magnificat: 582. Magnificat I toni:768,892. Miserere mei:900. Nunc dimittis:892. O che felice giorno:496. O Domine Jesu Christe:892. O Jesu mi dulcissime:473,822. Quis est iste:768. Sacro tempio d'honor:767. S'al discoprir:496. Se cantano gl'augelli:496. Sonata pian'e forte:560,768, 833. Sonata XV a 12:892. Timor et tremor:582,801,875. Vagh'-amorosi:496.

GACE BRULE (d. ca.1220)
Au renouviau de la doucor d'este:535. De bone amor:535,676,754. Les oisellons de mon pais:535.

GAFFURIO (GAFORI), FRANCHINO (1451-1522)
Polifonica Ambrosiana (Biella).   Musica Sacra S pab 303
Missa de carneval. (verso: Palestrina)

GAGLIANO, MARCO DA (d.1642)
Tristus est anima mea:843.

GALILEI, MICHELANGELO (16th century)
Correnta:633.

GALILEI, VINCENZO (d.1591)
Io mi son giovinetta:633. Ricercare:633. Saltarello:672. Il vostro gran valore:633. Dances:716.

GALKA, JEDRZEJ
Piesn o wiklefie:890.

GALLO, R. (15th century)
Je ne vis pas:468.

Gallus, Jacobus. See HANDL, JACOB

GANASSI, SYLVESTRO DI (16th century)
Ricercar:586,611,759.
GARSI, SANTINO, DA PARMA (d.1604)
Aria de Gran Duca:633. Ballo del Serenissimo Duca di Parma:633,634.
Correnta:633,634.
GASCOGNE, MATIEU (16th century)
Bone Jesu dulcissime:862. Christus vincit:494. Missa Pourquoy non:494.
GASTOLDI, GIOVANNI GIACOMO (16th-17th centuries)
Amor vittorioso:663,851. An einem guten Orte:665. An hellen Tagen:
521,665. Bicinium:672,844. Mein Gedanken:665. Speme amorosa:819.
Tutti venite armati:618,693. Vezzosette ninfe:688. Also 499,651.
GAULTIER (DENIS?)
668
GAUTIER DE COINCY (ca.1177-1236)
Ma vièle:886.
GDABAK TABLATURE: 812
GENTIAN (16th century)
Je suis Robert:542.
GERONA. COLLEGIALE DE SAN FELIU. MS.: 457
GERVAISE, CLAUDE (16th century)
Allemandes:178,515,577,642,869. Basse danse:515. Bransles:515,871.
Bransle de Bourgogne:178,449,577,642,869. Bransle de Champagne:
178,449,577,642,869. Pransle de Poitou:178,449,577. Bransle gay:
178,577. Bransle simple:178,870. Galliarde:869. Gaillarde variée:509.
M'amy est tout honneste:178. Passamezzo:642. Pavane:178. Pavane
and gaillarde:515,642. Pavane d'Angleterre:178,515,577,721. Pavane-
passamezzo:178,869. Tourdion:515. Dances:491,560,612,672.
GESIUS, BARTHOLOMAUS (ca.1555-1613)
Christum wir sollen loben schon:447. Freut euch, ihr lieben Christen:
599. Ein Kind geboren zu Bethlehem:447,822. Verleih uns Frieden:527.
GESUALDO, CARLO, PRINCIPE DE VENOSA (ca.1560-1613)
Accademia Monteverdiana (Stevens). Dover HCR 7287; HCR 5287
19,20,25,27,30,42,52,58 (verso: Schütz)

Accademia Monteverdiana (Stevens). Pye Virtuoso TPLS 13012
3,5,8,10,13,14,32,36,45,51,59,61,63,64

Deller Consort. RCA Victrola VIC(S) 1364; (Ger.) HMS 203
3,4,6,9,10,17,26,36,37,43,44,53

Hamburg Cappella Vocale (Behrmann). Candide 31036
1,3,6,10,19,30,33,34,38,50,53,54,55,58,60,66,73,76,78

Monteverdi Choir (Gardiner). Argo ZRG 645
3,6,10,36,37,53 (verso: Monteverdi)

NCRV Vocaal Ensemble Hilversum (Voorberg). Philips 839789
2,7,12,14,17,36,37,43,44,47,53

GESUALDO, CARLO, PRINCIPE DE VENOSA (ca.1560-1613) (Continued)

Niedersachsischer Singkreis (Träder).   Camerata CMS 30034
17,37,43,44,47,53

Petit Ensemble Vocal, Montreal (Little).   Vox DL 900; 500900
17,35,36,37,43,44,45,47,62

Prague Madrigal Singers (Venhoda).   Valois MB 785
[Responsoria et alia ad Officium Sabbati Sancti.]

Quintetto Vocale Italiano (Ephrikian).   Arcophon ARCO 300/306
[Madrigals, complete.]

Quintetto Vocale Italiano (Ephrikian).   10" Harmonia Mundi OPUS 8
16,22,44,45,65,71,75

Schlean; Foti; Mazzoni; Farolfi; Sarti; Nabokov (vocal quintet).
18,23,24,31,39,41,48,49,56,57,69,70,72,74,77   Amadeo AVRS 5013

Various performers (Craft).
Columbia KL 5718; KS 6318; (Br.) CBS BRG 72276; SBRG 72276
1,11,20,21,28,29,36,40,59,67,68,79

Venosa Singers (Craft).   Columbia MS 7441
[Madrigals: Book 6, complete.]

(sacred): 1. Aestimatus sum. 2. Animam meam dilectam. 3. Ave
dulcissima Maria. 4. Ave Regina coelorum. 5. Caligaverunt oculi mei.
6. Hei mihi, Domine. 7. In Monte Oliveti:582,703. 8. Jesus tradidit:
582,703. 9. O crux benedicta. 10. O vos omnes:628. 11. Recessit
pastor. 12. Tenebrae factae sunt. 13. Tradiderunt me. 14. Tribulationem et dolorem. 15. Tristis est anima mea.

(secular): 16. Ahi, dispietata e cruda. 17. Ahi, già mi discoloro:521.
18. Amore, pace non chero. 19. Ancide sol la morte. 20. Ardita
Zanzaretta. 21. Ardo per te. 22. Asciugate i begli occhi. 23. Baci
soavi e cari. 24. Bell'angioletta. 25. Beltà poi che t'assenti:644.
26. Bene o miei sospiri. 27. Candido e verde fiore. 28. Canzon
francese del Principe. 29. Che fai meco. 30. Chiaro resplender sole.
31. Com'esser può. 32. Correte, amanti. 33. Deh, come invan sospiro.
34. Dolce spirto d'amore. 35. Dolci parole e care. 36. Dolcissima mia
vita:592. 37. Ecco, morirò dunque:521,761. 38. Ed ardo e vivo.
39. Felice primavera. 40. Gagliarda:515. 41. Gelo ha madonna.
42. Già piansi nel dolore. 43. Invan dunque. 44. Io tacerò. 45. Itene,
o miei sospiri. 46. Languisce al fin:583. 47. Luci serene e chiare:688.
48. Madonna, io ben vorrai. 49. Mentre madonna. 50. Meraviglia
d'amore. 51. Merce grido piangendo. 52. Mille volte il dì moro.
53. Moro lasso:662,881. 54. Non mai. 55. Non mi toglia. 56. Non
mirar. 57. O dolce mio martire. 58. O dolce mio tesoro. 59. O
dolorosa gioia. 60. O mal nati messagi. 61. O miei sospiri. 62. O
miracol d'amore. 63. O tenebroso giorno. 64. O voi, troppo felici.
65. Or, che in gioia. 66. Per uscir di dolore. 67. Quando ridente.

Composer Index

Gielniowa, Ladyslaw. See LADYSLAW Z GIELNIOWA
Gines de Morata. See MORATA, GINES DE
GINTZLER, SIMON (b. ca.1490)
    Recercar quarto:522.
Giovane, Giovanni Domenico del. See NOLA, GIOVANNI DOMENICO DA
GIOVANELLI, RUGGIERO (ca.1560-1625)
    Et in spiritum:682. Salve regina:892.
Giovanni, Andrea di. See ANDREA DI GIOVANNI
GIOVANNI DA CASCIA (GIOVANNI DA FIRENZE, JOHANNES DE
FLORENTIA) (14th century)
    Con brachi assai:570,881. Da, da a chi avareggia:570. Morrà la
    invida:758. Nel mezzo a sei paon:758,780. O tu chara scientia:719.
    Per larghi prati:463,719. Tosto che l'alba:608. Madrigal:601.
Giulio da Modena. See SEGNI, GIULIO
GLAREANUS, HENRICUS (1488-1563)
    Donec gratus eram tibi:838.
GLOGAUER LIEDERBUCH: 610,650,723,761,788,842,844
GODARD (prob. ROBERT) (16th century)
    Hault le boys:517. M'amye Margot:517.
GODRIC, SAINT (d.1170)
    Crist and Sainte Marie:500. Sainte Marie virgine:615,675.
GÖTZ, JOHANN
    Vil lieber zit:557.
GOMBERT, NICOLAS (16th century)
    Angelus Domini:776. Fabordono llano y fabordon glosado:800. Hors
    envieux:454,498. Missa Je suis désheritée:712. Ricercar:611. Super
    flumina:611.
Gonzáles (Gonçales), Bernal. See BERNAL GONZALES, FRANCISCO
GORZANIS, GIACOMO (b. ca.1525)
    La dura partita:653. Passamezzo e padoana:633,634.
GOUDIMEL, CLAUDE (d.1572)
    Deba contre mes debateurs:612. Mon Dieu me paist:881. Par le désert
    de mes peines:819. Psalm 25:846. Psalm 47:846. Psalm 56:281. Psalm
    133:846.
GRANDI, ALESSANDRO (d.1630)
    Motette:751.
GREAVES, THOMAS (16th-17th centuries)
    Come away sweet love:546.
GREFINGER, WOLFGANG (15th century)
    Wohl kömmt der Mai:765.
GREITER, MATTHIAS (d.1550)
    Es hüdri hüt:590.
GRENON, NICOLAS (14th-15th centuries)
    Ave virtus virtutum / Prophetarum / Infelix:563. Nova vobis gaudia:
    589. La plus belle et doulce figure:715,886. La plus joilie et la plus
    belle:488.

GRILLO, GIOVANNI BATTISTA (d.1622)
Canzon:825. Canzon II a 8:774,892. Canzon in echo a 8:774. Canzon quintadecima:635.

GRIMACE (14th century)
Alarme, alarme:724,780,854.

GUAMI, GIUSEPPE (d. ca.1611)
Canzone:625,768,896. Gravi pene in amor:896. Toccata:837.

GUEDRON, PIERRE (d. ca.1621)
C'est une demoiselle:491. Si jamais mon âme blessée:771.

GUERRERO, FRANCISCO (1527-1599)
A un niño:808. Alma, si sabes de amor:810. Antes que comáis a Dios: 810. Benedictu:811. Canite tuba:789,830. Caro nea:810. Dexó la venda:718. Esclarecida madre:811. Hermosa Catalina:460. Hoy, José:454,498. Huyd, huyd o ciegos amadores:460. Oh venturoso dia: 810. Oh virgen:811. Oyd, oyd una cosa:448. Pastores loquebantur:808. Que buen ano:709. Qué te daré, Señor:810. Prado verde y florido:824. Los reyes siguen la estrella:808. Rogad vos, virgen:811. Salve Regina: 612. Santisima Maria:811. Todo quanto pudo dar:744. Vamos al portal:808. Villanesca:744. Virgen sancta:744.

GUERRERO, PEDRO (16th century)
O beata Maria:811.

GUETFREUND, PETER (ca.1570-1625)
Jubilate Deo:640. Tu es Deus:640.

GUGLIELMO EBREO (15th century)
Falla con misuras:468.

GUILIELMUS MONACHUS (15th century)
Faubourdon and gymel:483. Gymel:672. La bassa castiglia:844.

Guillaume de Machaut.   See MACHAUT, GUILLAUME DE
Guillaume Le Heurteur.   See LE HEURTEUR, GUILLAUME

GUILLAUME LE VINIER (d.1245)
Espris d'ire:615.

Guillaume l'Hébreu.   See GUGLIELMO EBREO

GUILLEMETTE
Volte:659.

GUIRAUT DE BORNELH (12th century)
Leu chansonet'e vil:489. Reis glorios:456,615.

GUIRAUT RIQUIER (d.1292)
Canco a la Maire de Deus:456. Fis e verays:456. Jhesu Christ, filh de Diu viu:478.

Gulielmus Monachus.   See GUILIELMUS MONACHUS

GUMPELZHAIMER, ADAM (1559-1625)
Ach wie elend:764. Deutsches Magnificat:444. Die finster Nächte:764. Gelobet seist du, Jesus Christ:599,626,874. Maria durch ein'n Dornwald ging:444. Vom Himmel hoch:447,897. Wir danken dir:605.

GUSSAGO, CESARIO (16th-17th centuries)
La fontana:635. La leona:751,892.

GUY, NICHOLAS (16th-17th centuries)
Almande: 833,834.
GUY DE COUCY (d.1203)
Li nouviau tenz: 886.
GUYARD (15th century)
M'y levay par ung matin: 586.
GUYMONT
Kyrie (Apt Ms.): 726.
Gyttering. See BYTTERING

HAGIUS, KONRAD (ca.1550-ca.1615)
Herzlich tut mich erfreuen: 521.
Halle, Adam de la. See ADAM DE LA HALLE
HANDL, JACOB (JACOBUS GALLUS) (1550-1591)
Prague Madrigal Singers (Venhoda); Musica Antiqua, Vienna (Clemencic).
Bach BG 655; BGS 70655; (Br.) BG 655; BGS 5007;
(Ger.) Amadeo AVRS 5037
[Ecce quomodo; Erravi sicut ovis; Jerusalem gaude; O salutaris hostia;
Omnes de Saba; Peccantem me quotidie.] (verso: Monte)

Alta Trinita: 875. Ascendit Deus: 667. Canite tuba: 595. Duo Seraphim:
694. Ecce concipies: 783. Ecce quomodo: 269,613,667,694,703,819.
Egredietur virga: 822. Hodie Christus natus est: 721. Jerusalem gaude:
473,486,555,626. Mirabile mysterium: 789. Missa super Elisabethae
impletum est tempus: 682. O admirabile commercium: 789. Omnes de
Saba: 473,695,783. Orietur stella: 454,498. Pater noster: 526,694,875.
Radix Jesse: 817,822. Resonet in laudibus: 474,498,595. St. John
Passion: 723.
HARANT (HARANTZ), CHRISTOF, FREIHERR VON POLZIC (1564-1621)
Tschechischer Sängerchor (Veselka). 10" Supraphon SUF 29118
[Missa quinta vocibus.]
HARDING, JAMES (ca.1560-1626)
Almande: 833,834.
HARLEIAN 978: 462
HASPRE, JOHANNES SIMON DE (15th century)
Ma doulce amour: 468.
HASSLER, HANS LEO (1564-1612)
Regensburger Domspatzen (Schrems).
10" Christophorus CLP 75404; SCLP 75405
[Angelus ad pastores ait; Cantate Domino; VIII. Messe à 8; Verbum
caro factus est.]

Ach Lieb hier ist das Herze: 818. Angelus ad pastores ait: 473,616.
Cantate Domino: 667,694,852. Canzon (Amoenitatum musicalium
hortulus): 764. Canzon duodecimi toni: 635. Canzon noni toni: 635.
Chiara e lucente stella: 764. Domine Deus: 692. Es kam ein Engel: 817.
Feinslieb, du hast mich gfangen: 519,591. Das Herz tut mir aufspringen:

454,498,519,520. Herzlich lieb hab ich:526,764. Ich scheid von dir:764. Ihr musici, frisch auf:520,618,821. Im kühlen Maien:618. Jungfrau, dein schön Gestalt:519,521,618. Laudate Dominum:881. Laetentur coeli:692. Mein g'müt ist mir verwirret:520,650,760. Mein Lieb will mit mir kriegen:618,764. Mi sento ohime morire:764. Nun fanget an: 520,591,761. O tu che mi dai pene:764. Prima intrada (Lustgarten):870. Quinta intrada (Lustgarten):870. Septima intrada (Lustgarten):870. Tanzen und Springen:474,498,839. Verbum caro factum est:616. Vom Himmel hoch:617. Also 499.

HAUCOUR, JOHANNES (14th century)
Je demande ma bien venue:621.

Hausen, Friedrich von. See FRIEDRICH VON HAUSEN

HAUSSMANN, VALENTIN (d. ca.1611)
German dances:515,523. Polish dances:723. Tanz mir nicht mit meiner Jungfer Käthen:524.

HAYLES, ROBERT (d.1616)
O eyes leave off your weeping:728.

HAYNE VAN GHIZEGHEM (15th century)
Allez regretz:715. De quatre nuys:488. De tous biens playne:803. Gentil gallans:672. Pour ce que j'ai joui:488.

Hébreu, Guillaume l'. See GUGLIELMO EBREO

Heinrich von Laufenberg. See LAUFENBERG, HEINRICH

HELLINCK, LUPUS (ca.1495-1541)
Capitan Herrgot:588,836. Compt alle vaart by twee dry:777. Pro oemium:588.

HENRY VIII, KING OF ENGLAND (1491-1547)
Consort II:582,728. Consort V:739. Consort XXIV:832. Green growith th'holy:675,714,832. If love now reynyd:562. It is to me:832. O my hart:844. Pastime with good company:533,582,706,714,731,853, 877,879. Sanctus:483. Tandernaken:643,877. Though some saith:832. The time of youth:832.

Herédia, Sebastián Aguiléra de. See AGUILERA DE HEREDIA, SEBASTIAN

HERMAN (NIKOLAUS?)
Lobt Gott, ihr Christen:616. Also 599.

HERMANNUS CONTRACTUS (1013-1054)
Alma redemptoris Mater:733. Salve Regina:762.

Hessen, Moritz von. See MORITZ, LANDGRAF VON HESSEN

Heurteur, Guillaume Le. See LE HEURTEUR, GUILLAUME

HIDALGO, JUAN (17th century)
744

HILTON, JOHN (d.1608)
Fair Oriana:512. My mistress frowns:587.

HINGSTON, JOHN (d.1683)
Fantazia:571.

HOFHAIMER, PAUL (1459-1537)
Ach Lieb mit Leid:652. Ave maris stella:579. Carmen:588,836. Carmen magistri Pauli:884. Erst weiss ich:772. Greiner Zanner:525. Herzliebstes Bild:520,752,884. Ich klag und reu:594. In Gottes Namen fahren wir:765. Meiner Traurigkeit:752. Mein's traurens ist:610,622, 765,821,884. Nach willen du:464,765. O werder mund:594. Ohne Freunde:752. On frewd verzer ich:884. Recordare, virgo Mater:640. Salve Regina:640,752,884. Tendernaken:465. Tristitia vestra:640. Tröstlicher Lieb:752,884. Zucht, Ehr und Lob:652,765.
HOLBORNE, ANTHONY (1565-1602)
As it fell on a holy eve:833,834. The chaise:623,833,834. Countess of Pembroke's paradise:729. The fairy round:623,680,701,833,834. The fruit of love:833,834. Galliard:469,475,515,551,833,834. Galliard The sighs:551,725. Hey, ho, holiday:541,551,623,680. The honie-suckel:466,469,515,551,623,680,701. My Linda:469,701. Night watch:469,551,701,709. Pavan:469,515,551,623. Pavan The funerals:466,625. Pavan The marigold:725. Pavana ploravit:623,680, 701. Pavan paradiso:725. Prelude:541. The Queen's gifte:614. See what a maze of error:534. Sic semper:623. Suite:529. Tears of the muses:541. A third set of quintets:747. The wanton:515,623,701.
HOLMES, JOHN (16th-17th centuries)
Thus bonny-boots:885.
HOWETT (HUWETT), GREGORIO (16th-17th centuries)
Fantasia:659.
LAS HUELGAS: 459,462,684,860
HUME, TOBIAS (d.1645)
Death and life:627. Fain would I change:725. Life, touch me lightly: 722. Tobacco is like love:466,571.
HUNT, THOMAS (16th-17th centuries)
Hark! Did ye ever hear:885.

ILEBORGH TABLATURE: 610
Infantas, Fernando de las. See LAS INFANTAS, FERNANDO DE
INGEGNERI, MARCO ANTONIO (ca.1545-1592)
Lausanne Vocal Ensemble (Corboz, Bruchez).
Musical Heritage MHS 700; Erato STU 70238
[Tenebrae factae sunt; 3 Lamentations of Jeremiah; 3 responses for matins of Holy Saturday.] (verso: Monteverdi)

Kissinger Kantorei (Walter, Nachtmann).
10" Christophorus CLP 73328
[Jerusalem surge; Tristis est anima mea; Velum templi.] (verso: Monteverdi)

Ecce quomodo moritur:696.
Insula, Francus de. See FRANCUS DE INSULA
Insulis, Francus de. See FRANCUS DE INSULA

ISAAC, HEINRICH (ca.1450-1517)
Capella Antiqua, Munich (Ruhland).   Christophorus SCGLY 75936
[Missa carminum.] (verso: Senfl)

Capella Antiqua, Munich (Ruhland).   Telefunken SAWT 9544
[Missa super O praeclara; La mi la sol; Tota pulchra es; Illumina
oculos meos; Maria, Jungfrau hochgeborn; Carmen; Es het ein Baur ein
Töchterlein; Donna di dentro.]

Collegium Cantorum Bonn (Tenta); Ensemble alter Instrumente (Siemann).
[Mass Ein fröhlich Wesen.]   10" Lumen AMS 5008

Columbia University Collegium Musicum (Taruskin).
     Collegium Stereo JE 100
[Missa Quant j'ay au cuer; Propers for Feast of the Holy Trinity.]

NCVR Vocaal Ensemble Hilversum (Voorberg).   Camerata CMS 30026
[Ave sanctissima Maria; O Maria, mater Christi; Regina caeli laetare;
Tota pulchra es.] (verso: Senfl)

Niedersächsiger Singkreis, Hannover (Träder).   Nonesuch H 1084; 71084
[Missa carminum.] (verso: Depres, Lassus)

Niedersächsiger Singkreis, Hannover (Träder).   10" Camerata CM 25004
[Missa carminum.]

A la bataglia:465,820. Ad laudes salvatoris:683. All mein Mut:765.
Alleluia, assumpta est Maria:700. Alleluia, inveni David:683. An buos:
465. Carmen:752,884. Carmen in fa:465,588,836,884. Carmen in sol:
588,836. Carmen saecularis:672. Christ ist erstanden:588. Christe qui
lux:471. Un di lieto:752,884. Dich, Mutter Gottes:524. Domine
quinque talenta:683. Ecco virgo concipiet:471,844. Es hatt ein Baur ein
Töchterlein:524,652. Es wolt eyn Maydleyn grasen gan:726. Et ie boi
d'autant:624,884. Fanfare:752. Fortuna in mi:465,776. Gaudeamus
omnes:700. Gross Leid muss ich jetzt tragen:652. Helas:624. Herrgott,
lass dich erbarmen:791,795,867. Hora e di Maggio:721. Der Hund:624,
726,740. Ich schrei und rief:594. Ich stund an einem Morgen:520,622,
652. Illumina oculos meos:765. Imperii proceres:465,485,862. In festo
Nativitatis S. Joannis Baptistae:569. Innsbruck, ich muss dich lassen:
465,519,521,524,590,618,622,624,652,741,765,776,827,839,844,884,
888. Intrada:752. J'ay pris amours:465,624,726,884. Je mehr ich
trinke:752. La la hö hö:624,821,884. La mi la sol:624,726,740,877.
Laetare Jerusalem:776. Lasso, quel ch'altri fugge:752,884. Lombre:624.
Maudit soyt:624. Mein Freud allein:622,765. Mein Mütterlein:524.
Mein Trost ob allen Weiber:652. Missa Magnae Deus potentiae:590. La
morra:465,670,726,776. Morte che fai:670. O decus ecclesiae virgo:700.
O liebes Herz:650,760. O Venus:752,884. Optime pastor:640,771.
Palle, palle:624. Par ung chies de cure:624. Puer natus:500. Questo
mostrarsi adirata:765. Quis dabit capiti:485. Rorate coeli:471.
Sacerdotes ejus:683. Sancti Spiritus assit nobis gratia:465,862. Schöne
Maruschka:521. Sempre giro piangendo:765. Le serviteur:752,884.

ISAAC, HEINRICH (ca.1450-1517) (Continued)
Süsser Vater:588,617,765,836. Tartara:624. Tmeiskin was jonck:868.
Tricinium:884. Virgo prudentissima:884. Zwischen Berg und tiefem
Tal:525,610,895. Also 624.
IVREA CODEX: 726

JACHET DE MANTUA (ca.1495-1559)
O angele Dei:862.
JACOB DE SENLECHES (JACOPINUS SELESSES) (14th century)
En attendant:608. En ce gracieux temps:463.
JACOPO DA BOLOGNA (14th century)
Aquil'altera / Creatura gentil / Ucel di Dio:631. Con gran furor:758.
Fenice fu:570,759. Lux purpurata / Diligite institiam:463. Non al suo
amante:608,758,844. O cieco mondo:463.
JACOTIN (pseud. of Jacob Godebrie) (d.1529)
Je suis désheritée:656.
JAMBE DE FER, PHILIBERT (d.1572)
Psalm 36:281. Psalm 99:281.
JAN Z JENSTEJNA (14th century)
Decet huius cunctis horis:500.
JAN Z LUBLINA (JEAN DE LUBLIN) (16th century)
Lautenquartett Pöhlert.   Da Camera 93603
[Pieces for lute quartet.]

Conradus:556. Douce memoire:844. Hayduczky:556. Hispaniarum:
556. Italica:556. Poznanie:556.
JAN OF LUBLIN ORGAN TABLATURE: 782,812,813
JANEQUIN, CLEMENT (ca.1495-ca.1560)
*Ambrosian Consort, Dupré (lute); Trumpet Ensemble Gabriel Masson
(Delmotte).*   Belvedere (Centrocord) ELY 0530
15,16,17,25,29 (verso: A. Gabrieli)

Ambrosian Consort.   Belvedere (Centrocord) ELY 0531
14,18,20,35,48 (verso: Annibale Padovano)

Blanchard Vocal and Instrumental Ensemble.
3,9,15,17,24,25,34,37,39,42,47   HMV HQM 1044; HQS 1044
Caillard Vocal Ensemble.   Erato LDEV 473
15,25

Caillard Vocal Ensemble. Musical Heritage MHS 1158; Erato STU 70519
6,8,16,17,38,40,41,44,52,53,54,55 (verso: Bertrand)

Ensemble Polyphonique de Paris (Ravier).   Valois MB 428; 928
1,7,10,12,13,14,15,21,23,25,27,30,31,32,33,36,40,47,51,52

Pro Arte Antiqua; Kann (cemb); Witoszynskyj (vihuela).   Tudor 0570
2,3,15,16,17,20,26,29

Vocal and Instrumental Ensemble; Cochereau (org). *(Birbaum)*
<u>20</u>,<u>25</u>,<u>26</u> (verso: Depres)   Philips 835785

<u>1</u>. A ce joli mois de may. <u>2</u>. Aller my fault. <u>3</u>. Aria della battaglia. <u>4</u>. Au joly boys:854. <u>5</u>. Au joli jeux:507,761,819. <u>6</u>. Au vert bois. <u>7</u>. Aussi tost que je voy ma mye. <u>8</u>. Bel aubépin. <u>9</u>. Le caquet des femmes. <u>10</u>. Ce may nous dit. <u>11</u>. Ce mois de mai:507,772,854. <u>12</u>. Ce petit dieu. <u>13</u>. Cent baysers. <u>14</u>. Le chant de l'alouette:487,611,644,854. <u>15</u>. Le chant des oiseaux:487,644,852,854. <u>16</u>. Le chant du rossignol: <u>479</u>. <u>17</u>. Chantons, sonnons, trompettes:517. <u>18</u>. La chasse. <u>19</u>. Cocu: 486. <u>20</u>. Les cris de Paris. <u>21</u>. Dur acier. <u>22</u>. Elle mérite:621. <u>23</u>. Est-il possible. <u>24</u>. Fiez-vous-y:656. <u>25</u>. La guerre (La bataille de Marignan): 487,517,852,854. <u>26</u>. La guerre de Renty. <u>27</u>. Il ferait bon planter. <u>28</u>. Il s'en va tard:507. <u>29</u>. La jalouzie. <u>30</u>. Je liz au cueur. <u>31</u>. Je ne connais femme en cette contrée:507. <u>32</u>. Je veux que ma mye. <u>33</u>. Ma peine n'est pas grande:507. <u>34</u>. Martin. <u>35</u>. Messe La bataille. <u>36</u>. O cruauté. <u>37</u>. O doulx regard. <u>38</u>. On vous est allé rapporter. <u>39</u>. Or viens ça. <u>40</u>. Or vit mon coeur. <u>41</u>. Ouvrez-mois l'huis. <u>42</u>. Ung petit coup mamye. <u>43</u>. Petite nymphe folastre:490,663,693. <u>44</u>. Plus ne suis. <u>45</u>. Psalm 5:846. <u>46</u>. Quand je bois du vin claret:771. <u>47</u>. Quant contrement. <u>48</u>. Qu'est-ce d'amour. <u>49</u>. Reveillez-vous:800. <u>50</u>. Si Dieu voulait:597. <u>51</u>. Si le coqu. <u>52</u>. Sus approchez ces levres. <u>53</u>. Toutes les nuits. <u>54</u>. Tu as tout seul. <u>55</u>. Va rossignol. <u>56</u>. Ville de Bloys:509. <u>57</u>. Voici le bois:507.

JAPART, JOHANNES (15th-16th centuries)
Il est de bonne heure:683,776.

JARZEBSKI, ADAM (1590-1649)
Chamber Orchestra of Warsaw National Philharmonic (Teutsch).
                                           Orpheus OR 337

[Bentrovata; Chromatica; 5 canzoni; Novas casa; Sentinella; Tamburetta.] (verso: Mielczewski)

Canzon I:753. Concert IV:753. Susanna videns:781.

JAUFRE RUDEL (12th century)
Lanquan li jorn:478,886.

Jean de Lublin. See JAN Z LUBLINA

JEEP, JOHANN (1582-1644)
Musica, die ganz lieblich Kunst:828.

Jehannot de l'Escurel. See L'ESCUREL, JEHANNOT DE

JENKINS, JOHN (1592-1678)
541,742

Jenstein, Jan of. See JAN Z JENŠTEJNA

Joachim à Burgk. See BURGK, JOACHIM A

Joan de Latre. See DELATRE, CLAUDE PETIT JEAN

Johannes de Florentia. See GIOVANNI DA CASCIA

JOHN (JOÃO) IV, KING OF PORTUGAL (1604-1656)
Crux fidelis:484,703,835.

JOHANNES DE LIMBURGIA (14th-15th centuries)
    Salve virgo regina:589. Surge propera amica mea:589.
JOHNSON, EDWARD
    Eliza is the fairest queen:521.
JOHNSON, JOHN (d.1594)
    Allmaine:753. The flatt pavin:559.
JOHNSON, ROBERT (1569-1633)
    Almans:540,564,566,655,730,834. As I walked forth:730. Away
    delights:541. Care charming sleep:542,571. The fairy masque:669.
    Full fathom five:725,845. The gypsies metamorphosed:669. The
    satyres masque:669. Where the bee sucks:725,845. Witty wanton:730.
JOHNSON (JOHN or ROBERT)
    Carman's whistle:711. La vecheo gallyerde:722,725.
JOHNSTON
    Pavan (arr. Kinloch):530.
JONES, ROBERT (16th-17th centuries)
    Allemande Disdaine that so doth:584. Fair Orianna:662. Farewell,
    dear love:709,711. Fie what a coil is here:461. Go to bed, sweet muse:
    856. Sweet Kate:528,725. What if I seek:541.
Josquin des Pres. See DEPRES, JOSQUIN
JOYE, GILLES (15th century)
    Non pas que le veuille penser:488.
Juan Fernández de Madrid. See MADRID, JUAN FERNANDEZ
JÜDENKUNIG, HANS (d.1526)
    Ain niederlandisch runden Dantz:522,765. Rossina ain welscher Dantz:
    522,765. Von edler Art:652. Wo soll ich mich hinkehren:522. Zuch,
    Ehr und Lob:765.

KARGEL, SIXT (16th century)
    Fantasia:522.
KAROLIDES, DANIEL
    Psalm XCVI:794.
KERLE, JACOBUS DE (1531 or 2-1591)
    Stiftschor der Benediktiner-Abtei Einsiedeln (Meier).
                            Harmonia Mundi HM 25161; Lumen AMS 5013
        [Responsorium pro concilio; Responsorium pro unione.]

    Exurge, Domine:613. Missa Regina coeli:805 (Kyrie).
KINLOCH, WILLIAM
    Galliarde of the lang paven:530. Kinloche his fantasie:530.
KIRBYE, GEORGE (ca.1570-1634)
    O Jesu, look:894. Sorrow consumes me:546.
KLABON, KRZYSZTOF (16th century)
    Hetmanowi Koronnemu:782. Tryumfuj wierny paddany:782.
KLEBER, LEONHARD (ca.1495-1556)
    Praeambulum:765.

Composer Index

KOTTER TABLATURE: 610
KRAKOW, MONASTERY OF THE HOLY SPIRIT. TABLATURE: 812,813
Krakowa, Mikolaj z. See MIKOLAJ Z KRAKOWA
KRHKOW, MIKOAJ VON (Mikolaj z Krakowa?) (16th century)
    Madrigal:753.
KUGELMANN, HANS (d.1542)
    Wir loben:523.
KUNGSBERGER, URBANUS
    Urbs beata:588,836.

LACERNA, ESTACIO DE (16th century)
    Tiento del VI tono:796.
La Charité, Pierre de. See CHARITE, PIERRE DE LA
LADYSLAW Z GIELNIOWA (d.1505)
    Zoltarz Jezousow:890.
LA HAYE
    Hexachord:707. Orchésographie:707.
LAMBE, WALTER (ca.1452-ca.1500)
    Nasciens mater:558.
LANDINO (LANDINI), FRANCESCO (ca.1325-1397)
    Amor c'al tuo suggeto:608,759. Amore:570. Angelica beltà:672.
    L'antica flamma:758. La bionda treccia:570. Biance flour:570.
    Cara mie donna:570,758. Chosi pensoso:719. De dimmi tu:570.
    Deh' sospir:758. La dolce vista:759. Donna'l tuo partimento:570.
    Ecco la primavera:570,586,844. Fatto m'a serr'amore:759. Giovine
    vagha:463. Gram piant' agli occhi:468,586,719. Giunta vaga bilta:570.
    I' prieg amor:468. Musicha son:719. El mie dolce sospir:535,758.
    Nessun ponga speranca:631. Non avrà ma' pietà:719. Per allegrezza:
    468,758. Questa fanciulla:570,719. Sy dolce non sono:463,608,631,
    759. Se la rimica mie:719. Va pure, amore:468. Also 561.
Langa, Francisco Sotto de. See SOTO DE LANGA, FRANCISCO
LANTINS, ARNOLD DE (fl.1431)
    In tua memoria:733. Missa Verbum incarnatum:864. Puisque je voy:609,
    699. Tota pulchra es:589.
LANTINS, HUGO (15th century)
    Ce ieusse fait:609. Cesla sublimatur:864.
LAPICIDA (LAPICIDUS), ERASMUS (15th-16th centuries)
    Tandernaken:821.
LA RUE, PIERRE DE (d.1518)

    Cappella Antiqua, Munich (Ruhland).   Telefunken S 9471
    [Requiem; motets.]

    Ensemble Polyphonique de Paris (Ravier).   Philips 9021
    [Requiem; Dolores gloriose recolentes.]

    Spandauer Kantorei (Behrmann).   Turnabout 34431
    [Requiem.] (verso: Depres)

LA RUE, PIERRE DE (d.1518) (Continued)
Autant en emport le vent:578,776,814. Deo gratias:700. Fors
seulement:465. Ite missa est:700. Kyrie:610. Missa Ave sanctissima
Maria:700 (Agnus). Missa Pro defunctis:831. Myn hert alyt heeft
verlangen:585,777,844. Porquoy non:776.

LAS INFANTAS, FERNANDO DE (b.1534)
Hodie Maria virgo:460. Virgo prudentissima:811.

LASSUS, ORLAND DE (d.1594)

Caillard Vocal Ensemble.   Musical Heritage MHS 624;
                    Erato R65 2573; 2574; Christophorus CGLP 75799
17,22,23,25,27,29,31,32,33,34

Frauenchor der Fachschule für Musik Györ (Szabo).   Qualiton S 11441
[Magnum opus musicum (selections).] (verso: Dufay)

Hamburg Cappella Vocale (Behrmann).   Da Camera SM 94022
90

Kaufbeurer Martinsfinken (Hahn).   Nonesuch H 1084; 71084
5,12,24 (verso: Depres, Issac)

Passaquet Vocal Ensemble.   Harmonia Mundi HMO 34761/2
90

Prague Madrigal Singers (Venhoda). Crossroads 22 16 0023; 22 16 0024;
                    Supraphon SUA 10434; SUAST 50434
44,52,53,57,71,72,75,77,79,82 (verso: Monteverdi)

Prague Madrigal Singers (Venhoda).   Bach BG 651; BGS 70651;
35,37   (Br.) 6063; Amadeo AVRS 5036

Prague Madrigal Singers (Venhoda).   Nonesuch 1053; 71053
36,94

Prague Madrigal Singers (Venhoda).   Valois MB 871
90

Regensburg Domchor; Archive Instrumental Ensemble (Schrems).
7,14,16,20,21,33,35   DGG Archive 198476

St.-Eustache Singers (Martin).   Boite LD 040
26,31 (verso: Depres)

Spandauer Kantorei (Behrmann).   Camerata CMS 30036
31,88 (motets 1-7, 15-21) (verso: Lechner)

Welch Chorale.   Lyrichord 113
1,18,27,38,69,76,82,85

(motets): 1. Adoramus te Christe:269,654,833,843. 2. Angelus ad
pastores ait:695. 3. Audi dulcis amica mei:762. 4. Ave verum corpus:471.
5. Cum essem parvulus. 6. De profundis:471,582,804. 7. Domine
convertere. 8. Domine, labia mea aperies:471. 9. Domine, ne in furore:
776. 10. Exaudi Deus orationem meam:471. 11. Exspectans exspectavi:
473. 12. Factus est Dominus. 13. Gloria Patri:471,605. 14. In conver-

tendo. 15. In hora ultima:737. 16. In Monte Oliveti. 17. Jesu nostra redemptio. 18. Jubilate Deo:473,638. 19. Justorum animae:471,583, 900. 20. Lauda Sion salvatorem. 21. Miserere mei:761. 22. Missus est angelus. 23. Nos qui sumus. 24. Nunc cognosco. 25. Pelli meae. 26. Pulvis et umbra. 27. Resonet in laudibus:448,473,695,789. 28. Super flumina Babylonis:776. 29. Surgens Jesus. 30. Surrexit pastor:772. 31. Timor et tremor:814. 32. Tribulationem. 33. Tristis est anima mea. 34. Tui sunt coeli:471.

(masses): 35. Bell'Amfitrit altera. 36. Ecco nunc benedicite Dominum. 37. In die tribulationis. 38. Vinum bonum.

(French chansons): 39. Un advocat dit à sa femme:767. 40. Bonjour mon coeur:474,498,613,618,663,693. 41. Un doux neny:490,776. 42. Fleure de quinze ans:490. 43. Fuyons tous d'amour le jeu:517,583. 44. Gallans qui par terre:738,826. 45. Il était une religieuse:490. 46. Je l'ayme bien:738. 47. Un jeune moine:487. 48. Un jour vis un foulon: 827. 49. Las! Voulez-vous qu'une personne chante:814. 50. Mon coeur se recommande:487,491,555,626,738,827,854. 51. Mouncier Mingo: 725. 52. La nuit froide et sombre:644,827,852,854. 53. O faible esprit. 54. O vin en vigne:567. 55. Or sus, filles:776. 56. Petite folle:814. 57. Quand mon mari:583,618. 58. Que dis-tu, que fais-tu:814. 59. Le rossignol:487. 60. Scais-tu dire l'ave:776. 61. Si le long temps:767.

(German Lieder): 62. Annelein, du singst fein:591. 63. Audite nova: 519,521,592. 64. Baur, was trägst im Sacke:519,776. 65. Ein guter Wein:520. 66. Ich liebe dich:521. 67. Ich weiss mir ein Maidlein:592, 818,821,827. 68. Tritt auf den rigel:519. 69. Wein. 70. Wie lang, O Gott:767.

(Italian madrigals): 71. Amor che fed'ogni pensier. 72. Ardo si. 73. Un dubbio verno:776. 74. Chi chilichi:820. 75. Come la notte. 76. L'eccho: 592,667,671,761,776,820,852. 77. Il grave de l'eta. 78. Hor che la nuova:820. 79. Hor vi riconfortate. 80. Io ti vorria:618,776. 81. Madonna ma pieta:814. 82. Matona mia cara:487,592,618,660,772, 819,851,852. 83. O bella fusa:495. 84. O occhi manza mia:851. 85. Passan vostri triomphi:820. 86. S'io ti vedess'una sol:618.

(miscellaneous): 87. Al gran Guilielmo nostro:767. 88. Busstränen des heiligen Petrus. 89. Heroum soboles:862. 90. Lamentations of Job:785 (part 7). 91. Motette in hora:767. 92. Penitential Psalms:613 (no.3). 93. Princeps Marte potens, Guilielmus:767. 94. Prophetiae Sibyllarum. Also 499,868.
Latre, Joan de. See DELATRE, CLAUDE PETIT JEAN
Laudario di Cortona. See *CORTONA. LAUDARIO*
LAUDE
    500,535,646,647,677
LAUFENBERG, HEINRICH VON (d.1460)
    Ich wöllt das ich daheime wer:838.

LAURENTIUS DE FLORENTIA (14th century)
A poste messe:631. Sanctus:758,844. Also 561.
LAURENTIUS THE ELDER (15th-16th centuries)
Mij heeft een piperken:585. Waer is hij nu:839.
LAWES (HENRY or WILLIAM)
Cupid detected:587.
LAYOLLE, FRANCESCO DE (1492-ca.1540)
La fille qui n'a point d'amye:578,828. Lasciar il velo:464.
LECHNER, LEONHARD (d.1606)

Capella Lipsiensis (Knothe). 7,9	DGA 19436
Gächinger Kantorei (Rilling). 10	10" Bärenreiter BM 25 R 610
Gachinger Kantorei (Rilling). 7,9,12,14	Cantate 640228
Gächinger Kantorei (Rilling). 7,9,10	Cantate 657606
Spandauer Kantorei (Behrmann). 7 (verso: Lassus)	Camerata CMS 30036
Spandauer Kantorei (Behrmann) 10 (verso: Demantius)	Turnabout TV 34175

1. Ach Lieb, ich muss dich lassen:650. 2. Allein zu dir, Herr Jesus Christ:
518. 3. Che più d'un giorno è la vita mortale:592. 4. Come nave ch'in
mezzo all'onde:592. 5. Christ, der du bist der helle Tag:785. 6. Christ
ist erstanden:524. 7. Deutsche Spruche von Leben und Tod:479,785,
827. 8. Gott b'hute dich:591,592,761. 9. Das hohelied Salomonis:479.
10. Johannespassion. 11. Die Musik g'schrieben auf Papier:592. 12. Nun
schein, du Glanz:622. 13. O Lieb, wie suss und bitter:519,622. 14. O
Tod, du bist ein bittre Gallen. 15. Der Unfall reit mich ganz und gar:592.
Also 599.
LEETHERLAND, THOMAS (15th-16th centuries)
Pavane:834.
LEGRANT, GUILLAUME (14th-15th centuries)
Or avant, gentiltz fillettes:621,844. Wilhelmus Legrant:844.
LEGRANT, JOHANNES (14th-15th centuries)
Entre vous nouviaux mariés:741,672,869.
LEGRANT (GUILLAUME or JOHANNES)
A l'aventure:621. Credo:608. Si vous saviez:621.
LEJEUNE, CLAUDE (d.1600)

Caillat Vocal Ensemble.
    2,3,12,14,17,19,24 (verso: Janequin. Re-issue of 10" Decca 133723 -
    see 1964 edition, p.59.)

Grimbert Vocal Ensemble. 1,5,7,11,13,16,18,28,31,33	(Fr.) Decca 154.053; SSL 40.518

LOHET, SIMON (d.1611)
    Fugues:812.
LONGUEVAL, ANTOINE DE (15th-16th centuries)
    Passio Domini nostri Jesu Christi:511.
Lope de Baena. See BAENA, LOPE DE
LOPEZ MORAGO, ESTEVÃO (16th-17th centuries)
    Gaudete cum laetitia:778,816. Jesu redemptor:778,816. Laudate
    pueri:778,816. Oculi mei:778,816. Quem vidistis pastores:778,816.
    Versos de I tono:798. Versos de IV tono:798. Versos de VII tono:798.
Lorenzo da Firenze. See LAURENTIUS DE FLORENTIA
Loufenberg, Heinrich. See LAUFENBERG, HEINRICH
Lublin, Jean de. See JAN Z LUBLINA
LUKACIC, IVAN (1587-1648)
    Panis angelicum:626.
LUPI SECOND, DIDIER (16th century)
    Psalm 149:846.
LUPO, THOMAS (16th-17th centuries)
    Almande:834. Fantasia a 3:623,722. Fantasia a 6:623.
LURANO (LUPRANO), FILIPPO DE (15th-16th centuries)
    Quercus iuncta columna est:862. Se me grato:586.
LUSCINIUS (NACHTGALL), OTHMAR (ca.1480-1537)
    Ein fröhlich wesen:594. In patienta vestra:791.
LUTHER, MARTIN (1483-1546)
    Vom Himmel hoch:617.
LUYTHON, CAROLUS (d.1620)
    Fuga suavissima:455,893.
LUZZASCHI, LUZZASCO (d.1607)
    Canzon a 4:513. O dolcezze:586,841. O primavera:841. Quivi sospiri:
    629,663,693.
Lymburgia, Johannes de. See JOHANNES DE LIMBURGIA

MACHAUT, GUILLAUME DE (d.1377)
    Ambrosian Singers (McCarthy).   Belvedere (Centrocord) ELY 0430
    17

    Burgess; Partridge; Burrey; Rogers; Shaw (vocal quintet).
    1,10,12,17,19,25,31,33   L'Oiseau-Lyre SOL 310

    Capella Antiqua, Munich (Ruhland).   Telefunken SAWT 9566
    3,9,20,35

    Capella Vocale & Instrumentale (Behrmann).   Da Camera SM 94033
    17

    Deller Consort.   Bach BG 622; BGS 5045
    17,29,36

    Schola Cantorum Basiliensis (Wenzinger).   DG ARC 2533054
    17 (and miscellaneous works)

1. Amours me fait desirer:468. 2. Ballade:575. 3. Bone pastor.
4. Comment qu'a moy:608,724,854. 5. De fortune me doy pleindre:
445. 6. De petit po:445,468. 7. De tour sui:575. 8. De triste cuer /
Quant vrais amans / Certes, je di:445. 9. Double hoquet. 10. Douce
dame jolie:445. 11. Felix Virgo:504. 12. Foys porter. 13. Hoquetus,
David:576. 14. Ite missa est:726. 15. Je puis trop bien:608. 16. Je
sui aussi:445,468. 17. Missa de Notre Dame:698,761 (Agnus).
18. Nesque on porroit:445,468. 19. Nuls ne doit avoir merveille. 20. O
livoris feritas. 21. Pas de tor en thies pais:445. 22. Plange, regni
respublica:717. 23. Plus dure:575,608. 24. Quant je suis mis:445.
25. Quant ma dame. 26. Sanz cuer:445. 27. Se je souspir:445. 28. Se
quanque amours:463. 29. Sederunt principes. 30. S'il estoit nulz /
S'amours:463,608,724. 31. Tant doucement. 32. Tres bonne et belle:
468. 33. Tres douce dame. 34. Trop plus biauté / Je ne suis:844.
35. Veni creator Spiritus. 36. Viderunt omnes.

MACQUE, GIOVANNI DE (ca.1550-1614)

Canzona a la francese:795. Durezze et ligatura:867. Seconda strava-
ganze:867. Toccata a modo di trompette:513.

MADRID, JUAN FERNANDEZ (15th century)

Pues que Dios:720.

MAHU, STEPHAN (15th-16th centuries)

Es gieng ein wilgezogner Knecht:470.

MALVEZZI, CRISTOFORO (1547-1597)

Canzon:837. Dal vago e bel sereno:568. O fortunato giorno:568.
O qual risplende nube:568.

MANCHICOURT, PIERRE DE (16th century)

Chanteurs St.-Eustache (Martin).   Boîte 022
   [Mass.] (verso: Depres)

MANGON, JOHANN (d. ca.1578)

Assumpta est Maria:762. Ave Maria:762. Magnificat:762.

Mantova, Jachet de. See JACHET DE MANTUA

Mantova, Rossino di. See ROSSINUS MANTUANUS

Mantovano, Rossini. See ROSSINUS MANTUANUS

Mantua, Jachet de. See JACHET DE MANTUA

Mantuanus, Rossinus. See ROSSINUS MANTUANUS

Marbeck, John. See MERBECKE, JOHN

MARCABRU OF GASCONY (d. ca.1147)

L'autrier jost' una sebissa:478. Pastourelle:886. Pax in nomine:456,615.

MARENZIO, LUCA (d.1599)

Quatuor Double (Courville).   Pirouette 19004; S 19004
   [Ahi! dispietata morte; Solo e pensoso; Vezzosi augelli; Zeffiro torna.]
   (verso: Palestrina)

A Roma:630. Ahi! dispietata morte:630. Belle ne fe natura:568. Cedan
l'antiche tue chiare vittorie:644. Chi dal delfino:568. Estote fortes:660,
772. Hodie Christus natus est:805. Innocentes pro Christo:850.
Leggiadre ninfe:662. Madonna mia gentil:613. O figlie di Piero:568.

MARENZIO, LUCA (d.1599) (Continued)
O rex gloriae:454,498. Scendi dal paradiso:510,630. Schau ich dir in die Augen:592. Se nelle voci nostre:568. Secondo intermedio:568. Sinfonia:568. Solo e pensoso:662. Zefiro torna:592.

MARIE DE BOURGOGNE
Basse dances:575.

MARIN, JOSE (1619-1699)
744

MARINI, BIAGIO (1597-1665)
O luci belle:630.

MARQUES, JUAN (1582-1658)
O vos omnes:451.

Marseille, Folquet de. See FOLQUET DE MARSEILLE
Marselha, Folquet de. See FOLQUET DE MARSEILLE

MARSON, GEORGE (d. ca.1631)
The nymphs and shepherds:885.

MARTIN CODEX: 456

MASCHERA, FLORENTIO (16th century)
Canzon da sonare:513. Canzon La fontana:825. Canzon terza:635. La mazzuola:635.

Masini, Lorenzo. See LAURENTIUS DE FLORENTIA

MASSAINO, TIBURTIO (16th century)
Canzon a 8:625,751. Illumina oculos:640.

MATHEUS DE PERUSIO (15th century)
Andray soulet:724,726. Le greygnour bien:463. Ne me chant:724. Non so che di me fia:758. Pres du soleil:726.

MAUDUIT, JACQUES (1557-1627)
Eau vive:446. En son temple sacré (Psalm 150):484,817. Versets du requiem pour Pierre de Ronsard:679. Voicy le verd et beau may:446, 487,827. Vous me tuez:487,491.

Meister Alexander. See ALEXANDER, MEISTER
Meister Rumeland. See RUMELAND, MEISTER

MEL (MELLE), RENATUS (RINALDO) DEL (ca.1554-ca.1600)
O Jesu Christe:454,498.

Melle, Renatus del. See MEL, RENATUS DEL

MELLI (MELII) (prob. PIETRO PAOLO) (16th-17th centuries) See also REGGIO
Capriccio cromatico:668.

Mena. See GABRIEL

MERBECKE, JOHN (ca.1510-ca.1585)
Nunc dimittis:883. A virgin and mother:728.

MERTEL, ELIAS (ca.1561-1626)
Ballett:522. Praeludium:522. So wünsch ich:522.

MERULO, CLAUDIO (1533-1604)
Canzon La marca:837. Canzon per sonar:896. Lieti fiori e felici:896. L'Olica:896. Toccatas:613,837,881. La Zambeccara:464.

MEYER, GREGOR (ca.1510-1576)
Fuga:838.

MICO
    Pavan: 742.
MIELCZEWSKI, MARCIN (d.1651)
    Chamber Orchestra of Warsaw National Philharmonic (Teutsch).
    [Canzona a 3 with bassoon.] (verso: Jarzebski)   Orpheus 337

    Deus, in nomine tuo: 781.
MIKOLAJ Z CHRZANOWA
    Protexisti me Deus: 782.
MIKOLAJ Z KRAKOWA (NICHOLAS OF CRACOW)
    Ave Jerarchia: 813. Date siceram maerentibus: 782. Hayducky: 812,813.
    Praeambulum in F: 813. Wesel sie polska korona: 782.
MIKOLAJ Z RADOMIA
    Et in terra pax: 890. Hystorigraphi acie: 782. Gloria: 723. Magnificat:
    890. Patrem omnipotentem: 890. Utwor bez tytulu: 782.
MILAN, LUIS (16th century)
    A quel caballero: 861. Con pavor recordo el moro: 600,807. Durandarte:
    452,610,720,807. Fantasias: 600,623,702,707. Fantasia de consonicias
    y redobles: 702. Fantasia del IV tono: 649. Oh dulce: 610. Pavan no. 1:
    773. Pavan no.3: 710. Pavan no.5: 710,773. Pavans: 507,601,657,702,
    708,716,857. Ricercare: 633. Temeroso de sufrir: 689. Todo mi vida
    os amé: 773. Ved, comadres: 743.
MILARTE, JACOBUS (15th century)
    Todos van de amor: 689.
Modena, Julius de. See SEGNI, GIULIO
MODERNE, JACQUES (16th century)
    La bataille: 862. Branle gay nouveau: 870. Bransles de Bourgogne: 870,871.
MOLINARO, SIMONE (ca.1565-ca.1615)
    Il conte Orlando: 659. Fantasia: 659. Saltarellos: 659.
Monachus, Guilelmus. See GUILELMUS MONACHUS
MONGE DE MONTAUDON (MAUTAUDON) (12th-13th centuries)
    Fort m'enoia: 456. Mout m'enoja s'o auzes dire: 478.
MONIOT D'ARRAS (13th century)
    Ce fut en mai: 886,899.
Montaudon, Monge de. See MONGE DE MONTAUDON
MONTE, PHILIPPE DE (ca.1521-1603)
    Prague Madrigal Singers (Venhoda); Musica Antiqua, Vienna (Clemencic).
                    Bach BG 655; BGS 70655; (Br.) BG 655; BGS 5007;
                                        (Ger.) Amadeo AVRS 5037
    [Deh fate homai col suon; In qual parte del ciel; Non fuggi Febo; Que
    me servent mes vers; Reviens vers moy; Sola te cerco ogn'hor.]
    (verso: Handl)

    La premier jour du mois de may: 814. Missa super Cara la vita: 613.
    Sottile e dolce ladra: 764.

MONTEVERDI, CLAUDIO (1567-1643)[1]
Ah, dolente partita:587. Angelus ad pastores ait:528,830. Ave maris
stella:768,804. Baci soavi e cari:542. Il ballo delle ingrate:583.
Cantate Domino:606. Ch'io t'ami:688. Chiome d'oro:582. Il
combattimento:464. Currite populi:528. Dolci miei sospiri:618.
Ecco mormorar l'onde:587,660,663,693. Fugge, fugge, anima mea:528.
Fugge il verno:618. Gloria:583. Hor che'l ciel:583. L'Incoronazione
di Poppea:583 (excerpts). Io ardo:688. Lagrime d'amante al sepolcro:
645,662,671. Lamento d'Arianna:479,644. Lamento della ninfa:542.
Lasciatemi morire:474,498,660,819. Luci serene e chiare:688. 3
madrigals:779. Missa a cappella:746. Non cosi tosto:759. O primavera:
688. Ohimè il bel viso:644,688. Orfeo:582 (Acts 2 and 3). Psalms:606.
Quel augellin che canta:521. Raggi dove'l mio bene:587. Salve Regina:
528,759. S'andasse amor a caccia:630. Se nel partir da voi:521,738.
Sfogava con le stelle:688,789. Si ch'io vorrei:626. Toccata:568.
Vattene pur crudel:630. Zefiro torna:582,662,688.
MONTPELLIER CODEX: 462,535,576,615,685,707,735,844,886
Morago, Estevão Lopes. See LOPES MORAGO, ESTEVÃO
MORALES, CRISTOBAL (ca.1500-1553)

Montserrat Abbey Choirs (Segarra). 1,2,19,20,23	10" Harmonia Mundi 25160
Montserrat Abbey Choirs (Segarra). 6,12	10" Harmonia Mundi 30621
Prague Madrigal Singers (Venhoda). 1,3,11,18,19,21	Valois MB 834

1. Andreas Christi famulus:451. 2. Ave Maria:451,713. 3. Christus
resurgens. 4. Ecce Virgo concipiet:495,811. 5. Emendemus in melius:
612. 6. Exaltata est sancta Dei genitrix. 7. Jubilate Deo omnis terra:
806. 8. Lamentabatur Jacob:713. 9. Magnificat VII toni:713.
10. Magnificat VIII toni:805,881. 11. Missa Mille regretz. 12. Missa
Quaeramus cum pastoribus. 13. Missus est Gabriel angelus:496,713.
14. Natum vidimus:850. 15. O crux ave:809. 16. O magnum mysterium:
789. 17. Parce mihi, Domine:460. 18. Pastores, dicite:448,808,850.
19. Per crucem tuam:451,809. 20. Quanti mercenarii:451. 21. Salve
Regina. 22. Si no's huviera mirado:718. 23. Tu es Petrus:451.
24. Verso de V tono:796. Also 505.
MORATA, GINES DE (16th century)
Aqui me declaró:718. Ninpha gentil:666. Ojos claros serenos:666.
Ojos que ya no veis:460,666.
MORITZ, LANDGRAF VON HESSEN (1572-1632)
Aventurose più d'altro terreno:766. Fuga a 4:766. Gagliarda
Brunsvicese:766. Pavan:659. Pavana del Francisco Segario:766.
Pavana & gagliarda del pover soldato:766. Pavana del Tomaso di
Canora:766.

---

[1] Not a complete discography. As in the original edition, only works included in
the anthologies have been indexed.

MORLEY, THOMAS (1557-ca.1603)
Ambrosian Singers; Aveling (hpsi). (Stevens)
DGA ARC 3209; 73209; (Br.) APM 14309; SAPM 14309
5,26,27,30,32,33,37,60,62,64,66,72,73,83,84

Deller Consort. Vanguard SRV 157; 157 SD; (Br.) Philips VSL 11078
9,34,36,38,43,50,57,65,76,79 (verso: Wilbye)

Morley Consort; Early Music Consort of London (Murrow).
[Dances for broken consort.] (verso: Susato) HMV HQS 1249

New York Pro Musica (Greenberg). Everest LPBR 6145/7
15,16,27,28,30,32,38,47,50,51,57,59,65,74,81

Rogers (tnr); Harnoncourt (viola da gamba); Dombois (lute).
Telefunken SAWT 9568
2,13,17,21,40,45,54,58,71,78,82,86,87,90,91,92

1. About the maypole: 711. 2. Absence: 531. 3. Adieu, you kind and
cruel: 690. 4. Agnus Dei: 848,894. 5. Alman: 550. 6. April is in my
mistress face: 544. 7. Aria: 657. 8. Arise, awake: 885. 9. Arise, get up:
547. 10. Ay me, the fatal arrow: 690. 11. Blow, shepherds, blow: 512.
12. La caccia: 551. 13. Can I forget. 14. Canzonet: 832. 15. Cease
mine eyes. 16. Clorinda false: 664,832. 17. Come, sorrow, come.
18. Cruel, wilt thou persevere: 690. 19. Do you not know: 729. 20. Il
doloroso: 722. 21. Fair in a morn. 22. False love did me inveigle: 544,
690. 23. Fantasia: 539. 24. Fantasia Il grillo: 625. 25. Fantasia La
rondinella: 559. 26. Farewell, disdainful: 453. 27. The fields abroad:
453,454,498. 28. Fire, fire, my heart: 454,498,547,663,693,747,819,
832. 29. Frog galliard: 559,725. 30. Galiarda. 31. La girandola: 551,
722. 32. Go from my window. 33. Good love: 453. 34. Good morrow,
fair ladies. 35. Hard by a crystal fountain: 734,885. 36. Hark, alleluia
cheerly. 37. Hark jolly shepherds: 453,547. 38. I go before, my darling:
528,547,587,738. 39. I love, alas: 534. 40. I saw my lady weeping.
41. I should for grief and anguish: 461. 42. If I through grief: 547.
43. In dew of roses: 547. 44. In every place: 547. 45. It was a lover and
his lass: 461,531,533,627,657,711,722,845,853,855. 46. Joyne hands:
559. 47. Lady, those cherries plenty. 48. Il lamento: 551,623.
49. Leave now mine eyes lamenting: 461,547. 50. Leave this tormenting.
51. Lo she flies. 52. Lo, where with flowery head: 690. 53. Love took
his bow and arrow: 690. 54. Love winged my hopes. 55. Magnificat: 848.
56. Mine own sweet jewel: 722. 57. Miraculous love's wounding: 528,
738. 58. Mistresse mine: 584. 59. My bonny lass: 472,545,547,711,792.
60. My lovely wanton jewel: 453. 61. My nymph the deer: 690.
62. Nancie: 539,614. 63. Nolo mortem peccatoris: 883. 64. Now is the
gentle season: 453,664. 65. Now is the month of maying: 546,547,582,
661,711,731. 66. O grief even on the bud: 453,547,645,690,725,832.
67. O mistress mine: 559,709,739,845,855. 68. On a fair morning: 664.
69. Our bonny-boots: 690. 70. Out of the deep: 704,727,883. 71. A

MORLEY, THOMAS (1557-ca.1603) (Continued)
painted tale. 72. Pasmeasz pavan. 73. Pavan:614. 74. Phyllis, I fain
would die. 75. Sacred end pavan:728. 76. Say, gentle nymphs. 77. See
mine own sweet jewel:657. 78. She straight her light. 79. Shoot false
love. 80. Since my tears and lamenting:664. 81. Sing we and chant it:
492,587,731,757,828. 82. Sleep slumbering eyes. 83. Stay heart:453.
84. Sweet nymph:453,528. 85. Though Philomela:663,693,709.
86. Thyrsis and Milla. 87. What if my mistress. 88. What saith my
dainty darling:627. 89. Whither away so fast:546. 90. Who is that this
dark night:461,531,729. 91. Will you buy a fine dog:512. 92. With my
love.

Der Lenz all Äst bekleiden tut:665. Tanzlied im Maien:521. Warum
nicht lustig:665. Also 651.
MORNABLE, ANTOINE DE (b. ca.1510)
L'heur d'amitie:828.
MORTON, ROBERT (d.1475)
Musica Reservata (Becket).   Philips 6500085
[Le souvenir de vous.]   (verso: Dufay)

Chanson:535. Est temps:488. L'homme armé:621. Mon bien ma
joyeuls:621. N'araige jamais mieulx:488,699. La Perontina:715. Pour
un plaisir:621. Also 488.
MOSSBURG GRADUAL: 462
MOULU, PIERRE (16th century)
Amy souffrez:656.
MOUTON, JEAN (d.1522)
Capella Cordina (Planchart).   Lyrichord 7199
[Noe, noe.]   (verso: Arcadelt)

Allons ouir sur nos têtes:784. L'amant content:573. La dialogue des
graces:573. Exultet coniubilando:862. In illo tempore:721. La, la, la
l'oysillon du boys:509. La Mallasis:573. Noe, noe:787. Non nobis
Domine:485. Quis dabit oculis:511,862. La rouse du moys de may:721.
MUDARRA, ALONSO (16th century)
Claros y frescos rios:600. Diferencias sobre El conde claros:702,773.
Dime a do tienes:718,773. Fantasia:659,702. Fantasia que contrehaze
la harpa:649,744,857. Gallarda:702,710,773. Gentil cavallero:773.
Isabel, perdiste la tu faxa:452,600. Israel:713. Pavana primera:710.
Psalmo II por el primo tono:713. Romanesca:773. Si viesse e me
levasse:773. Tientos VII, VIII:600. Tiento para harpa:858. Triste
estaba el Rey David:713,720,773.
MUDD, THOMAS (16th century)
Let thy merciful ears:552.
MULLINER BOOK: 661,714
MUNDY, JOHN (d.1630)
Ah, helpless wretch:883. Bonny sweet robin:550. Fantasia:554,707,
747. Goe from my window:566. Introitus:887. Lightly she whipped:

885. Munday's joy: 564,566,876. My prime of youth: 544. My Robbin: 711. O Lord, the maker: 801. Robin: 583,637. Tres partes in una: 643. Were I a king: 544.

MUNICH. MOSSBURG 156: 462

MUNOZ, GARCIA
Una montaña pasando: 720. Pues bien para esta: 477.

MUREAU, GILLES (d.1512)
Grace attendant: 715.

Muset, Colin. See COLIN MUSET

Nachtgall, Ottomar. See LUSCINIUS, OTHMAR

NANINO (NANINI), GIOVANNI MARIA (ca.1545-1607)
Hic est beatissimus: 613.

NARVAEZ, LUIS DE (16th century)
Arded corazon: 773. Baixa de contrapunto: 702,773. Canción del Emperador: 702,773,857. Con que la lavaré: 452. Diferencias sobre Guárdame las vacas: 649,702,710,716,771,773,857. Diferencias sobre O glorioso Domina: 612. Paseábase el rey moro: 718,773,807. Variaciones sobre el tema Conde claros: 600. Ya se asienta el Rey Ramiro: 773.

NASHE
Spring, the sweetest spring: 655.

NEGRI, CESARE (b. ca.1546)
Alemana d'amore: 653. Ameni colli: 632. Bianco fiore: 633,634,653. Catena d'amore: 633,634,653. Fedeltà d'amore: 653. Spagnoletta: 633, 634.

NEIDHARDT VON REUENTHAL (12th-13th centuries)
Blozen wir den anger: 681. Fürste Friderich: 681. Mailied: 772. Der May hat meing hercze: 615. Meie din: 681. Meienzeit: 681. Nu gruonet aver diu heide: 482. Sinc ein guldin Huon: 562. Winter diner künfte: 899. Winder wie ist nu dein kraft: 615.

NESBETT
Magnificat: 558.

NEUSIEDLER, HANS (ca.1508-1563)
Gerwig (lute). 10" DGA 13031 AP
[Pieces for lute.] (verso: Garsi da Parma -- See original edition, p.55)

Ach Lieb mit Leid: 652. Bettlertanz: 522,652. Elslein: 649,761. Entlaubet ist der Walde: 652. Fuggerin Tanz: 764. Gassenhauer: 601, 652,839. Ein guter welscher Tanz: 522. Hie' folget ein welscher Tanz: 659. Hoftanz: 611. Ich klag den Tag: 652,659. Ich sag adieu: 522. Judentantz: 557,611,659. Mein Herz hat sich mit Lieb verpflicht: 659. Nach Willen dein: 649. Niederlendisch Tantzlein: 649. Preambel: 649. Wachsa mesa: 522,649. Zeuner Tantz: 557.

NEUSIEDLER, MELCHIOR (d. ca.1590)
Der Fuggerin Tanz: 522.

NEWMAN (16th century)
Pavane: 643.
Nicholas of Cracow. See MIKOLAJ Z KRAKOWA
NICHOLSON, RICHARD (d.1639)
Der Kuckuck: 757. O pray for the peace of Jerusalem: 552.
NINOT LE PETIT (fl.1480)
Ela la la: 803.
NÖRMIGER, AUGUST (ca.1560-1613)
Intrada: 556. Der Mohren Auftzugh: 556.
NOLA, GIOVANNI DOMENICO DA (16th century)
Chichilichi: 586. Madonna nui sapimo: 584. Tri ciechi siamo: 568,630.
NOORDT, ANTHONI VAN (d.1675)
455
NOTKER BALBULUS
Sancti spiritus assit: 838.
NOVELLA, GUILHEM AUGIER
Bella donna cara: 478.

OBRECHT, JACOB (ca.1430-1505)
Cappella Lipsiensis (Knothe).   ARC SAPM 198406
[Missa Sub tuum presidium.] (verso: Ockeghem)

Renaissance Chorus (Brown).   Baroque 9004
[Missa Salve diva parens (Kyrie).] (verso: Ockeghem)

Vienna Chamber Choir (Gillesberger).
Bach BG 653; 70653; (Br.) BGS 5065; Amadeo AM AVRS 5026
[Missa Sub tuum praesidium.] (verso: Dufay)

Fors seulement: 624. Ein frohlich Wesen: 893. Fuga: 844. Hélas mon
bien: 895. Ic draghe de mutze clutze: 585,619. Laet u ghenoughen: 839.
Missa Je ne demande: 823 (Gloria & Credo). Missa Salve diva parens:
700 (Sanctus). Missa Sine nomine: 609 (Kyrie I, Agnus II). O beate
Basilii: 609. Ricercare: 672. Tsat een meskin: 624,699. Vavilment: 465.
OCKEGHEM, JEAN DE (d.1496?)
Berkeley Chamber Singers (Zes).
6,16,19   Lyrichord LL 108; Musical Heritage MHS 1003
Caillard Vocal Ensemble.   Electrola SME 95075
13,20
Capella Cordina (Planchart).   Lyrichord 7213
1,3,11,12,14,26,27
Capella Cordina (Planchart).   Lyrichord 7237
15 (verso: Dufay, Anon.: Missa Sanctissimae Trinitatis.)

Cappella Lipsiensis (Knothe).   ARC SAPM 198406
19 (verso: Obrecht)

OCHSENKUHN, SEBASTIAN (1521-1574)
  Innsbruck, ich muss dich lassen:522.
ODHECATON: 509
OKEOVER, JOHN (d.1663)
  Fantasia:475.
OLD HALL MS.: 882
ORFEO CATALA. MS.1: 457
ORTEGA (16th century)
  Pues que me tienes Miguel:718.
ORTIZ, DIEGO (16th century)
  Cervera (viola da gamba); Jaccottet (hpsi).
                Servicio de Publicaciones, Secretaría General Tecnica,
                Ministerio de Educación y Ciencia MEC 1002
  [Variaciones sobre O felici occhi miei; Variaciones sobre la canción
  Doulce memoire; Ocho recercadas sobre canto llano; Quinta pars.]

  Benedictus Dominus:809. Diferencias sobre O felici occhi miei:771,
  839. Recercada:839. Recercadas primera y segunda:741. Recercada
  segunda (sobre Douce memoire):743,844. Recercada: O le bonheur:
  505.
ORTO, MARBRIANUS DE (d.1529)
  Sanctus:683.

OSIANDER, LUCAS (1534-1604)
Christum wir sollen loben schon:448,616. Gelobet seist du Jesu Christ: 874.
Oswald von Wolkenstein. See WOLKENSTEIN, OSWALD VON
OTHMAYR, KASPAR (1515-1553)
Ach Gott, wie weh tut Scheiden:524. Bauerntanz:590. Ein beurisch tantz:652. Dem Maidlein ich mein Treu versprich:652. Es ist ein Schnee gefallen:652. Es liegt ein Schloss in Oesterreich:524. Es steht ein Lind in jenem Tal:592. Gelobet seist du Jesu Christ:616,874. Mir ist ein feins brauns Maidelein:520,618. Quisquis requiem quaeris:590. Vom Himmel hoch:844,874. Wie schön blüht uns der Maie:520.
OYSTERMAYRE, JEHAN (16th century)
Galiarde:876.

PACELLI, ASPRILIO (ca.1570-1623)
Madrigal:751.
Padova, Bartolino da. See BARTOLINO DA PADUA
Padovano, Annibale. See ANNIBALE PADOVANO
Padua, Bartolino da. See BARTOLINO DA PADUA
PAIX, JAKOB (b.1556)
Schirazula Marazula:556. Ungarescha & saltarello:556.
Palazol, Berenguier de. See BERENGUIER DE PALAZOL
PALERO, FERNANDEZ (16th century)
Ave maris stella:600. Glosado del verso de Morales:796. Tiento sobre Cum sancto Spiritu:796.
PALESTRINA, GIOVANNI PIERLUIGI DA (ca.1525-1549)
Aachener Domsingknaben (Rehmann).　　10" DGA 13032 AP
108

Bucharest Madrigal Chamber Choir (Constantin). Electrecord EXE 0422
100,113,114,115,119,120,121,123,125

Carmelite Priory Choir, London (McCarthy).
103,109　　L'Oiseau-Lyre OL 269; SOL 269

Carmelite Priory Choir, London (McCarthy).
11,48,82,90 (verso: Victoria)　　L'Oiseau-Lyre OL 283; SOL 283

Dessoff Choirs (Boepple). Counterpoint 602; CPT 5602; Pan SPAN 6203
10,30,31,49,52,71,74,82,91

Instrumental Ensemble (Verardo).　　Vedette VPC 1507; VST 6007
129-136 (verso: Frescobaldi)

King's College Choir, Cambridge (Willcocks).
36,47,48,72,76　　Argo RG 398; ZRG 5398; (Ger.) Decca SAWD 9958

King's College Choir, Cambridge (Willcocks).　　HMV HQS 1237
100,108

Netherlands Chamber Choir (de Nobel).　　　　　Philips A 00272
　96,100,108

Polifonica Ambrosiana (Biella).　　　　　Musica Sacra S pab 303
　109　(verso: Gaffurio)

Prague Madrigal Singers (Venhoda); Czech Philharmonic Choir (Veselka).
　Supraphon SUA 10578; SUST 50578; Parliament SD 612; PLPS 612
　4,59,62,108

Prague Madrigal Singers (Venhoda).
　　　　　　　　　Bach BG 647; BGS 5059; Amadeo AVRS 5011
　2,18,22,23,26,27,32,42,54,60,67,73,75,80,81,85,86,91,93,94,95

Quatuor Double (Courville).　　　　　Pirouette 19004; S 19004
　100　(verso: Marenzio)

Regensburger Domchor (Schrems).
　99,110　　DGA ARC 3241; ARC 73241; APM 14341; SAPM 198341

Regensburger Domchor (Schrems).
　39,105　　　　　　　DGA ARC 3243; 43243; SAPM 198343

Regensburger Domchor (Schrems).
　8,25,37,69,87,102　　　　　DGA ARC 3283; 73283; SAPM 198383

Regensburger Domchor (Schrems); Musica Antiqua Ensemble (Clemencic).
　　　　　　　　　　　　DGA ARC SAPM 198434
　112,116,117,118,122,124,127,132,134,136

Renaissance Singers (Howard).　　　　Argo RG 186; ZRG 5186
　97　(verso: See No.705)

Roger Wagner Chorale.　　　　　　　Angel S 36022
　108　(verso: Victoria)

Sacred Heart Cathedral Men's Choir, Newark (Oates).　　Gregorian CA-1
　3,57　(verso: Nieland)

St. Eustache Singers (Martin).　　　　Odyssey 32 16 0121; 32 16 0122;
　13,81,98,106　　　　　　　(Fr.) Harmonia Mundi HMO 30510

St. Hedwig's Cathedral Choir (Forster).　　　Da Capo SMVP 8075
　108　(verso: G. Gabrieli)

St. John's College Choir, Cambridge (Guest).　　Argo RG 578; ZRG 578
　14,31,43,50,88,91,111

St. Mary of the Angels Choir, Wellington, N.Z. (Fernie).　　Kiwi LD 5
　21,61,92,97,100 (Benedictus, Agnus)　(verso: Victoria)

Sistine Chapel Choir (Bartolucci).　　　　　ID IM 1007
　1,6,12,15,17,19,24,30,46,53,65,84

Slovak Philharmonic Chorus (Dobrodinsky).　　Crossroads 22 16 0186
　[Cantico canticorum: nos.1-3,5-7,10-14,17-18,21-23,26-27,29]
　(N.B.: Above numbers refer to those in Palestrina's Motets, Book IV a 5)

PALESTRINA, GIOVANNI PIERLUIGI DA (ca.1525-1549) (Continued)
Spandauer Kantorei (Behrmann).   Turnabout 34309
45,58,87,101

Treviso Cathedral Chapel Choir (d'Alessi).   Period SPL 756; 2756
109 (verso: Victoria)

Women's Choir of Music High School Györ (Szabó).
3,5,9,11,16,34,35,66,70,77,83,109   Qualiton LPX, SLPX 11328

(motets, etc.): 1. Ad te levavi:830,835. 2. Adjuro vos filiae.
3. Adoramus te. 4. Alleluia / Tulerunt Dominum. 5. Alma redemptoris
Mater:473. 6. Angelus Domini. 7. Ascendit Deus:873. 8. Assumpta
est Maria. 9. Ave Maria:830. 10. Ave maris stella. 11. Ave Regina.
12. Bonum est confiteri. 13. Cantantibus organis. 14. Conditur alme
siderum. 15. Confitebur. 16. Confitemini Domino. 17. De profundis.
18. Descendi in hortum meam. 19. Dextera Domini. 20. Dies
sanctificatus:474,498. 21. Diffusa est gratia. 22. Dilectus meus descendit.
23. Dilectus meus mihi. 24. Domine Deus. 25. Dum complerentur:638.
26. Duo ubera tua. 27. Ecce tu pulcher es. 28. Ecce veniet dies illa:595.
29. Ego sum panis vivus:484,873. 30. Exaltabo te. 31. Exultate Deo.
32. Fasciculus myrrae. 33. Fratres ego enim accepi:763. 34. Gloriosi
principes terrae. 35. Haec dies:900. 36. Hodie beata virgo. 37. Hodie
Christus natus est:473,500,501,691,696,783,850. 38. Illumina oculos
meos:873. 39. Improperia:703,849. 40. Incipit lamentatio:638.
41. Incipit oratiò:873. 42. Introduxit me rex. 43. Jesu Rex admirabilis.
44. Jubilate Deo:873. 45. Lauda Sion salvatorem. 46. Laudate Dominum:
696,873. 47. Litanea de beata vergine Maria. 48. Magnificat I toni.
49. Magnificat IV toni. 50. Magnificat VI toni. 51. Magnificat (not
spec.):805. 52. Martibus suis dixerunt. 53. Meditabor. 54. Nigra sum.
55. O bone Jesu:598. 56. O crux ave:772. 57. O Domine Jesu Christe:
843. 58. O magnum mysterium. 59. Oratione Jeremiae. 60. Osculetur
me. 61. Pange lingua. 62. Paucitas dierum. 63. Peccatem me quotide:
772. 64. Popule meus:667,696. 65. Precatus est:852. 66. Pueri
Hebraeorum:667,703,873. 67. Quam pulchri sunt. 68. Recordata:654.
69. Regina coelorum. 70. Salve Regina:805. 71. Salvete flores martyrum.
72. Senex puerum portabat. 73. Si ignoras te. 74. Sicut cervus:613,835,
849. 75. Sicut lilium. 76. Stabat Mater:583. 77. Sub tuum praesidium.
78. Super flumina:696,737,835,849. 79. Supplicationes:692. 80. Surgam
et circuibo civitatem. 81. Surge, amica mea. 82. Surge illuminare:850.
83. Surrexit pastor bonus. 84. Terra tremuit:873. 85. Tota pulchra es.
86. Trahe me post te. 87. Tu es Petrus:900. 88. Tua Jesu dilectio.
89. Veni dilecte mi. 90. Veni sancte spiritus. 91. Veni sponsa Christe.
92. Verbum caro:454,498. 93. Vineam meam. 94. Vox dilecti mei.
95. Vulnerasti cor meum.

(masses): 96. Ad fugam. 97. Aeterna Christi munera:804 (Kyrie).
98. Ascendo ad patrem. 99. Assumpta est Maria:804. 100. Missa

brevis. 101. De beata virgine. 102. Dum complerentur. 103. Ecce ego Joannes. 104. Ecce sacerdos magnus: 804 (Kyrie). 105. Hodie Christus natus est. 106. In festis apostolorum. 107. Lauda Sion: 852 (Sanctus), 444 (Benedictus), 805 (Benedictus). 108. Papae Marcelli: 582,873,613 (Agnus I), 506 (Agnus I, II), 761 (Benedictus). 109. Sine nomine. 110. Tu es Petrus: 638. 111. Veni sponsa Christi. (From unspec. masses): Et in terra pax: 682. Benedictus: 850. Agnus Dei: 495.

(madrigals, etc.): 112. Ahi che quest'occhi miei. 113. Alla riva del Tebro: 613. 114. L'amour a pris mon âme. 115. La cruda mia nemica: 510. 116. Da cosi dotta man: 851. 117. Il dolce sonno. 118. Io son ferito. 119. Non son le vostri mani. 120. O che splendor. 121. Ogni beltà. 122. Se fra quest'erb'e fiore. 123. Soave fia il morir. 124. Il tempo vola. 125. I vaghi fiori: 818. 126. Vaghi pensier: 851. 127. Vestiva i colli.

(instrumental and misc.): 128. Exercices sur la gamme: 517. 129. Ricercar del I tono: 529,641,779. 130. Ricercar del II tono: 779. 131. Ricercar del III tono: 513,779. 132. Ri cercar del IV tono: 779. 133. Ricercar del V tono: 513,779. 134. Ricercar del VI tono: 779. 135. Ricercar del VII tono: 779. 136. Ricercar del VIII tono: 779. Macht hoch die Tür: 444.

PALOMARES, JUAN DE (16th-17th centuries)
En el campo florido: 824.

Palou, Berenguer de. See BERENGUIER DE PALAZOL

PAMINGER, LEONHARD (1495-1567)
Hüt's Feur: 524. In dulci jubilo: 448,580. Omnis mundus: 580. Resonet in laudibus: 580.

PARABOSCO, GIROLAMO (d.1557)
Niuna sconsolata: 896. Non dispregiate: 896.

PARIS. BIBLIOTHEQUE DE L'ARSENAL: 535

PARIS. BIBLIOTHEQUE NATIONALE: 457,844

PARSONS, ROBERT (d.1570)
Nunc dimittis: 883. Pandolpho: 464,727. Trumpetts: 745.

PASSEREAU (16th century)
Hé, gentil mareschal: 517. Il est bel et bon: 474,487,492,498,555,567, 626,662,818,827,852,854.

PASTRANA, PEDRO DE (16th century)
Domine, memento mei: 460.

PATINO, CARLOS (d. ca.1660)
744

PAULUS DE BRODA (15th-16th centuries)
Der Pfauenschwanz: 590.

PAUMANN, CONRAD (ca.1410-1473)
Des kalffers neyden: 572. Mit ganczen willen: 572,607. Also 844.

PEARCE (PIERS), EDWARD (16th-17th centuries)
He, trola, there boys are: 721.

PEDRO DE CRISTO (ca.1545-1618)
O magnum mysterium:778,816. Quaeramus cum pastoribus:778,816.
PEELE, GEORGE (16th century)
Descend ye sacred daughters:885. Long may she come:885.
PEERSON (PEERESON, PEARSON), MARTIN (ca.1580-1650)
Alman:515,565. Blow out the trumpet:627. Fall of the leafe:186,540,
550,554,566,596,690. Look up, fair lids:541. Piper's pavan:515. The
primerose:554,596,690. La primevère:584. Sing, love is blind:553.
PEKIEL, BARTLOMIEJ (d.1670)
781
PELPLIN TABLATURE: 813
PENALOSA, FRANCISCO (15th-16th centuries)
Missa beata Virgine:806 (Kyrie). Per las sierras de Madrid:689. El triste
que nunca os vió:689.
PERAZA, FRANCISCO DE (1564-1598)
Tiento de I tono:796,798.
PERICHON (prob. JEAN) (16th century)
Prélude et courante:668. Courante:446.
PEROTINUS (12th century)
Deller Consort.   Bach BG 622; BGS 5045
[Sederunt principes; Viderunt omnes.]   (verso: Machaut)

Alleluia:844. Alleluia, Nativitas:576,697,724,786. Beata viscera:615,
707. Hec dies:607. Salvatoris hodie:735. Sederunt principes:697,698.
Viderunt omnes:697. Virgo (organum):597.
Perusio, Matheus de. See MATHEUS DE PERUSIO
PERRIN d'AGINCOURT (13th century)
Quant voi en la fin d'estey:615. Ballade:844.
PESENTI, MARTINO (ca.1600-ca.1648)
515,844
PESENTI, MICHELE (15th-16th centuries)
L'acqua vale a mio gran foco:632. Dal lecto me levava:660. Questa
èmia:632.
PETER VON BLOIS
Dum inventus:482. Vite perdite:482.
Petit, Ninot le. See NINOT LE PETIT
PETRUS DE CRUCE (13th century)
Aucun ont trouvé:615. Aucun / Lonctans / Annuntiantes:576.
PEUERL, PAUL (ca.1575-ca.1625)
Frisch auf und lass uns singen:828. O Musika:591,592,828.
PHALESE, PIERRE (b. ca.1510)
L'arboscello ballo:870,871. Passamezzo:515. Pavane and galliarde
ferrarese:767.
PHILIPPE DE VITRY (1291-1361)
Capella Antiqua, Munich (Ruhland).   Telefunken SAWT 9517-A
[Colla iugo / Bona condit / Libera me; Firmissime / Adesto / Alleluia;
Tribum / Quoniam / Merito hec patimur; Tuba sacre fidei / In arboris

/ Virgo sum; Vos qui admiramini / Gratissima / Gaude gloriosa.]
(verso: Missa Tournai -- See No.685)

Douce plaisance / Garison selon nature:463. Tuba sacre fidei / In
arboris:463.
PHILIPS, PETER (ca.1560-ca.1633)
Allemande:513. Amarilli di Julio Romano:564. Ascendit Deus:883.
Ave verum corpus:900. Bon jour, mon coeur (after Lassus):613.
Cantantibus organis:537. Chromatic pavan:659. Fantasia in A minor:
795. Galliardo:564. Galiarda dolorosa:596,690. Galliard to the
chromatic pavan:659. Gaudent in coelis:835. Ne reminiscaris:537.
Pavana:566. Pavana dolorosa:566,596. Phillips pavin:559. Regina
coeli:454,498. Surgens Jesus:894. This day day daws:675. Tibi
laus:835. Trio:795.
PICCHI, GIOVANNI (16th-17th centuries)
Puyana (hpsi).   Mercury 50259; 90259
[Intavolatura di balli d'arpicordo.]   (verso: Frescobaldi)

Ballo ongaro:723,749. Variations:613.
PIEREKIN DE LA COUPELE (13th century)
Chancon faz non pas vilainne:899.
PIERO, MAESTRO (14th century)
Cavalcando:758. Con dolce brama:463,570.
PIERO DA FIRENZE (PETRUS DE FLORENTIA) (14th century)
561
Pierre de la Charité. See CHARITE, PIERRE DE LA
Pierre de la Croix. See PETRUS DE CRUCE
Pierre de la Rue. See LA RUE, PIERRE DE
Piers, Edward. See PEARCE, EDWARD
PILKINGTON, FRANCIS (d.1638)
All in a cave:664. Amyntas with his Phyllis fair:847. Diaphena like
the daffdown-dilly:847,856. Have I found her:847. O softly singing
lute:534,847. Rest, sweet nymphs:492,663,664,693,790,801,838,847.
Sweet Phillida:545. Why should I grieve:544.
PIPELARE, MATTHAEUS (15th-16th centuries)
Fors seulement:594.
PISADOR, DIEGO (fl.1552)
En la fuente del rosel:773. Pavana:600,773. Pavana muy llana para
taner:857. Porques es dama tanto quereros:600. Si te vás a banar:600,
773. Villanesca:857.
PLANÇON, JEHAN (ca.1559-ca.1612)
Chambrière:446,491. Nous étions trois jeunes filles:656. Où estes-
vous:818.
PODBIELSKI, JAN (17th century)
753,813
POLAK, JAKUB (d. ca.1605)
Courante:753,601. Galliard:812.

POLLING. Clm. 11764: 462
PONCE, JUAN (fl.1500)
    Alegria:477. Alla de me ponga el sol:477,689. Como esta sola:477.
    Todo mi bien e perdido:743.
PONS D'ORTAFAS (12th-13th centuries)
    Si ay perdut:456.
POSCH, ISAAC (16th-17th centuries)
    Couranta:625. Intrada:625.
POWER, LIONEL (d.1445)
    Anima me liquefacta est:589. Beata progenies:500. Sanctus and
    Benedictus:609.
PRAETORIUS, MICHAEL (1571-1621)
Collegium Terpsichore, Bielefeld.
    ARC 3153; 73153; DGA 14166 APM; 198166 SAPM
    [From *Terpsichore*, 1612: Entrée-courante; Gavotte; Spagnoletta;
    Bourrée; Ballet, Volte.] (verso: Schein, Widmann)

*Niedersächsicher Singkreis, Hannover; Ferdinand Conrad Instrumental
Ensemble.* Nonesuch H 1128; 71128; Camerata
    [Nun komm, der Heiden Heiland; Ein Kind geboren; Hosianna dem
    Sohne Davids; Psallite unigenito Christo; Vom Himmel hoch.]
    (verso: Schein)

Westfälische Kantorei (Ehmann). Nonesuch H 71242; Cantate 658218
    [Als der gütige Gott; Omnis mundus jocundetur; Puer natus in
    Bethlehem; Vom Himmel hoch.]

A solis ortus:447. Ach Herr, du allerhöchster Gott:524. Allein Gott in
der Höh:620. La bourée:820. Bransle de la Grenée:771. Bransle de
village:771. C'est l'agneau de Dieu:679. Christ unser Herr:766. Courant
de la Royne:820. Cum pastores laudavere:874. Dances:871. Enatus est
Emanuel:473. Es ist ein Ros entsprungen:447,448,524,620,709,822,897.
Galliarde:820. Galliarde de la guerre:820. Galliarde de Monsieur Wustrow:
820. Gelobet seist du, Jesus Christ:620. Hosianna dem Sohne Davids:620.
In dulci jubilo:447,580,599,617,620,874. In natali Domini:448. Ein
Kind geborn zu Bethlehem:447,842. Maria zart:447. Der Morgenstern
ist aufgedrungen:592,620. La mouline:771. Ein neues Lied wir haben an:
527. O vos omnes:518. Passameze pour les cornetz:820. Psallite:448,
454,498. Puer natus in Bethlehem:473. Quem pastores laudavere:524,
616. Reprinse:771,820. Volte: Bransle de la Royne:821. Vom Himmel
hoch:620,874. Wach auf, wach auf:520. Wachet auf:842. Wie schön
leuchtet der Morgenstern:874. Wir glauben all an einen Gott:527.
PRAGENSIS XVI: 868
PRAGUE. UNIV. BIBL. VI G III a: 462
PYGOTT, RICHARD (ca.1485-1552)
    Quid petis o fili:483,502,709.

QUELDRYK, JOHN (d.1387)
Gloria in excelsis:882.

Radomia, Mikolaj z. See MIKOLAJ Z RADOMIA
RAIMBAUT DE.VAQUEIRAS (d.1207)
Estampida:761. Kalenda maya:489,535,615,636,676,754,815.
RAIMON DE MIRAVAL (12th-13th centuries)
Selh que no vol auzir causas:478.
RANDALL (prob. WILLIAM) (16th century)
Lachrimae and galliard on Can she excuse:539.
RASELIUS, ANDREAS (ca.1563-1602)
Gelobet seist du, Jesu Christ:617. Wir glauben an den Heil'gen Geist:523.
RAVENSCROFT, THOMAS (ca.1590-ca.1633)
Maids to bed:512. Remember O thou man:709. Rustic lovers:553.
Sing after fellows:655. Tomorrow the fox will come to town:655.
Where are you, fair maids:512.
REDFORD, JOHN (fl.1535)
Christe qui lux:661. Eterne Rex altissime:661. Glorificamus:661.
Jam lucis orto sidere:661,714. O lux, with a meane:661. Rejoice in
the Lord alway:714,848. Salvator, with a meane:661,714. Sermone
blando angelus:714. Veni redemptor:611. Untitled piece:661.
REGGIO (possibly same as Melli, q.v.)
Cappriccio cromatico:633,634.
REGIS, JOHANNES (15th century)
O admirabile commercium:563.
REGNART, FRANÇOIS (16th century)
Petite nymfe folâtre:827.
REGNART, JACOB (1540-1599?)
All mein Gedanken:650,760. Nach meiner Lieb:767. Puer natus est:501.
Venus, du und dein Kind:767. Wann ich gedenk:650,760.
REINA CODEX: 844
REINMAR VON BRENNENBERG (13th century)
Wol mich des tages:681.
RESINARIUS, BALTHASAR (fl.1543)
Nun komm der Heiden Heiland:844. Komm, Gott Schöpfer:687,788.
Wir glauben auch an Jesus Christ:523.
Reuenthal, Neidhardt von. See NEIDHARDT VON REUENTHAL
Reynaldus, Franciscus. See FRANCISCUS REYNALDUS
RHAW, GEORG, ed. (1488-1548)
Ach Elslein:652. Entlaubet ist der Walde:652. Mir ist ein feins brauns
Maidelein:652.
Rhoda, Paulus de. See PAULUS DE BRODA
RIBERA, ANTONIO DE (early 16th century)
Por unos puertos arriba:460,807.

RICHAFORT, JEAN (d. ca.1548)
De mon triste desplaisir:877.
RICHARD I, KING OF ENGLAND (1157-1199)
Ja nun hons pris:615,636,815,844
RICHARD DE SEMILLI (13th century)
Dame qui a mal mari:886.
RICHARDSON, FERDINAND (ca.1558-1618)
Pavane:550.
Riquier, Guiraut. See GUIRAUT RIQUIER
RIPOLL. MS.116: 457
RIVAFLECHA, MARTIN DE (d.1528)
Salve Regina:567.
ROBERTSBRIDGE CODEX (organ pieces): 409
ROBINSON, THOMAS (ca.1588-1610)
Almaine:549. Galliard:549. Merry melancholie:549. Spanish pavan:707.
A toy:725.
ROBLEDO, MELCHOR (d.1587)
Magnificat:460,811.
ROGNONI TAEGGIO, GIOVANNI DOMENICO (16th-17th centuries)
La basgapera:635. La mazza:897. Sonata La porta:892.
ROHACZEWSKI, ANDRZEJ (17th century)
813
ROMAN DE FAUVEL: 463,685,844
ROMERO, MATEO (d.1647)
Romerico florido:807.
RORE, CYPRIEN DE (1516-1565)
Ancor che col partire:464,662,826,841. Crudele acerba inexorabili
morte:776. Da le belle contrade:492,612,828. En vos adieux:826,841.
Hélas comment:826. Musica dulci sono:826. Non è lasso:629. O sonno:
767.
ROSSETER, PHILIP (ca.1575-1623)
If she forsake me:531. What then is love:531,790. When Laura smiles:
531,856.
ROSSI, SALOMONE (16th-17th centuries)
Sinfonia and galliarde:751.
ROSSINUS MANTUANUS (15th-16th centuries)
Lirum bililirum:632. Da poi ch'el tuo bel viso:632. Un sonar da piva:803.
Rudel, Jaufré. See JAUFRE RUDEL
RUDOLF VON FENIS-NEUENBURG (ca.1150-1196)
Nun ist niht mêre:838.
RUMELAND, MEISTER (13th century)
Untruwe:886.
RYCHŇOVSKY, JIŘI (ca.1545-ca.1616)
Decantabat populus:794.

SACHS, HANS (1494-1576)
Als ich, Hans Sachs, alt ware:572. David und Jonathan:886. Gesang-
weise:881. Gloria patri: lob und er:572. Ich lob ein brünnlein küle:
572. Klingende Ton:707. Lob sei Gott Vater:615. Nachdem David
war redlich:585. Salve ich gruss dich schöne:844. Silberweis:772.
Ein tigertier:572. Zu Venedig ein kaufman sass:572.
ST. GALL. MS. 462: 469
ST.-QUENTIN. MS. 86: 658
St. Victor, Adam of. See ADAM DE SAINT-VICTOR
SALEM, BERNHARD VON
Resonet in laudibus:580,791.
SANCHEZ
Christus factus est:809.
SANDRIN, PIERRE REGNAULT (16th century)
Douce memoire:464,844. Qui voudra scavoir qui je suis:578,828.
Santa Maria, Tomás de. See TOMAS DE SANTA MARIA
SAVILE, JEREMY (17th century)
533
SCACCHI, MARCO (17th century)
781
SCANDELLO (SCANDELLI, SCANDELLUS), ANTONIO (1517-1580)
Bongiorno madonna:818. Gelobet seist du, Jesu Christ:897. Ein
Hennlein weiss:474,498,521. Schein uns, du liebe Sonne:650,760.
SCHAERER, MELCHIOR (16th-17th centuries)
Gelobet seist du Jesu Christ:874.
SCHEIN, JOHANN HERMANN (1586-1630)[1]
Collegium Terpsichore, Bielefeld.
ARC 3153; 73153; DGA 14166 APM; 198166 SAPM
[Banchetto musicale, 1617: Suites 3,4,5.] (verso: Praetorius,
Widmann)

Ferdinand Conrad Instrumental Ensemble. Nonesuch H 71128
[Banchetto musicale, 1617: Suites 1,2.] (verso: Praetorius)

Der kühle Maien:591.
SCHIAVETTO, GIULIO (16th century)
Pater noster:723.
SCHLICK, ARNOLT (fl.1512)
Hommage à l'empereur Charles-Quint:712. Maria zart:579,588,610,
712,836. Salve Regina:610.
SCHMELZER VON EHRENRUFF, JOHANN (17th century)
868
SCHMID, BERNHARD, der ältere (1528-1592)
Alemando novelle -- Ein guter neuer Dantz -- Proportz darauf:556. Le
corante de Roy:556. Der hupfauf:556. Io mi son giovanetta:821.
Ein schöner englisher Dantz:556. Wie schön blüht uns der Maie:557.

---

[1] Not a complete discography.

56. Oho, so geb' der Mann ein'n Pfenning:881. 57. Pacientiam muss ich han:765. 58. Puer natus est nobis:842. 59. Quis dabit oculis:622, 831. 60. Quodlibet:470,520,590,888. 61. Salutatio prima:611. 62. Von edler Art:652. 63. Wann ich des Morgens:524,821. 64. Zwischen Berg und tiefem Tal. Also 499.

Senleches, Jacob de. See JACOB DE SENLECHES

SERMISY, CLAUDE DE (ca.1490-1562)
Chorale de l'Université de Strasbourg (Eller).
    [9 chansons]   10" Harmonia Mundi HMO 25.308

Agnus Dei:494. Au joly bois:474,498,660. C'est une dure départie:507. Contentez-vous, ami:491. Du bien qu'oeil absent:672. Dulcis amica Dei:494. Elle s'en va:621. Hau, hau, hau le boys:517. Languir me fais:618,818. Pourtant si je suis brunett:828. Puisqu'en amour:672. Quosque non reverteris pax:862. Si bona suscepimus:494. Tant que vivrai:507,542,656,657,707,867. Vous perdez temps:507.

SERVIN, JEAN (16th century)
La piafe guerrière:517.

SHELBYE, WILLIAM (16th-17th centuries)
Miserere:661.

SHEPHERD (SHEPPARD), JOHN (16th century)
Deus tuorum militum:804. Haec dies:805. Reges Tharsis et insulae:552.

SICHER, FRIDOLIN (1490-1546)
Ave maris stella:640. In dulci jubilo:640. Resonet in laudibus:580,640. Tripellied:640.

SIES, JOHANN (fl.1519)
Mich hat gross Leid umgeben:591.

SIGEFRID, CORNELIUS (16th-17th centuries)
Kyrie:523.

SIGNAC (16th century)
Psalms 131,146,147:281.

Silos. Antiphonaire Mozarabe. See ANTIPHONAIRE MOZARABE DE SILOS

SIMMES, WILLIAM (16th-17th centuries)
Fantasie:475.

SIMPSON, THOMAS (16th-17th centuries)
Bonny sweet robin:551. Intrada:834.

SMERT, RICHARD (15th century)
In die nativitatis:483,714. Nowelle: Who ys there that singeth so:714. Nowell: Dieus vous garde:787.

SMITH (prob. WILLIAM) (16th-17th centuries)
Response:887.

SODERINI, AGOSTINO (16th-17th centuries)
Canzon La scaramuccia:837.

SOLAGE (14th century)
Fumeux fume:463. Helas je voy:724. Pluseurs gens voy:724. S'aincy estoit:717.

SOMMER, JOHANN (16th-17th centuries)
Pavan and galliard:625.
SOPHRONIOS, Saint, Patriarch of Jerusalem (ca.560-ca.638)
Pro tis genniseos:502.
SORIANO (SURIANO), FRANCESCO (1549-ca.1621)
Christe:682. Et ascendit:682.
SOTO DE LANGA, FRANCISCO (ca.1539-1619)
Tiento de VI tono:796,859. 2 tientos:800.
SOULIAERT, CAROLUS (16th century)
Een costerken op sijn clocken clanc:492.
SOWA, JAKOB (d.1593)
Salve regina:813.
SPERVOGEL (12th century)
Swa eyn vriund:615.
SPEUY, HENDERICK (16th-17th centuries)
Psalm 118: Dancket den Heer:455.
SPINACCINO, FRANCESCO (16th century)
La cara cosa:653. Fantasie:653. Gagliarda:653. Paduana:653.
Pescatore che va cantando:653. Ricercar:610,653,707. Saltarello:653.
SQUARCIALUPI CODEX: 535
STABILE, ANNIBALE (16th century)
Kyrie:682. Patrem omnipotentem:682. Crucifixus:682.
STADEN, JOHANN (1581-1634)
Aufzug:617. Beati omnes:526. Pavana:617.
STADLMAYR, JOHANN (ca.1560-1648)
Christe redemptor omnium:640.
STOCKEM (STOCKHEM), JOHANNES (15th century)
Brunete:760. Also 866.
STOLZER, THOMAS (early 16th century)
Christ ist erstanden:611. Entlaubet ist der Walde:470,520,525,590.
Erzürne dich nicht über die Bösen:723. Foeno iacere:500. Ich klag
den Tag:652. Ich stund an einem Morgen:525,652. Octo tonorum
melodiae (4 pieces):829.
STONE, ROBERT (1516-1613)
Lord's prayer:887.
STRIGGIO, ALESSANDRO (ca.1535-1587)
Caccia:767. Il gioco di primiera:688,767,841.
STROGERS, NICHOLAS (16th-17th centuries)
Fantasia:564.
Suriano, Francesco. See SORIANO, FRANCESCO
SUSATO, TIELMAN (d. ca.1561)
Allemandes:617,767,825,826,869. Basse danse:825. Basse danse Mon
désir:867. Basse danse La mourisque:562,825. Basse danse Sans Roch:
515,748. Bergerette:562. Bransle:562. Branle and fagot:825.
Danserye:776. Galliarde le tout:562. Galliard mille Ducas:740.
Hexentanz:871. Hoboeckentanz:870,871. Hupfauf:871. Pavan:469,

562. Pavane La bataille:515,825,869. Pavane Mille regretz:825,870. Pavane Si pas souffrir:740,870. Pavan and galliarde:767. De post:844. Rondes:469,740,825,826,870,871. Ronde Il estoit une fillete:870. Ronde et saltarelle:562,583,767,839,867,870,888. Saltarelle:469. Saltarelle Pour quoy:740. Wo bistu:867. Also 866.

SWELINCK, JAN PIETERSZ (1562-1621)

Leonhardt (organ and hpsi). Cambridge 508; CRS 1508
[Echo fantasia; Est-ce Mars; Fantasia; Ich ruf zu dir; More Palatino; Paduana lachrimae; Toccatas 20,23; Von der fortuna.]

NCRV Vocaal Ensemble, Hilversum (Voorberg).
Bärenreiter BM 30 L 1305
[Ab oriente; De profundis; O Domine Jesu Christe; Te Deum; Incontinent que j'eus oui (Ps.122); O Dieu des armées (Ps.84); O Dieu, mon honneur (Ps.109); Or soit loué l'Eternel (Ps.150); Or sus, serviteurs (Ps.134); Sus mon âme (Ps.146); Tu as été (Ps.90).]

Netherlands Chamber Choir; Van Wering (hpsi); Kee (org). (De Nobel)
Donemus DAVS 6201
[Ecce Virgo; Madonna con quest' occhi; Psalm 81; Psalm 86; Tu as tout seul; Fantasia chromatica; Von der fortuna.]

Netherlands Chamber Choir (De Nobel). Philips WS PHC 9006
[Psalms 20,68,86,122,134,150. O Domine Jesu Christe; Beati pauperes; Magnificat; Domine Deus meus; Venite exsultemus.]

Neumeyer (hpsi). Harmonia Mundi 30627
[Balletto del Gran Duca; Fantasia Chromatica; Toccata in a; Toccata in C, no.23; (variations): Ich fuhr mich über Rhein; Mein junges Leben; Unter der Linden grüne.]

De profundis:622. Durch Adams Fall:894. Ecce Virgo:473. Echo fantasia:455. Echo fantasia in a minor:795. Echo fantasia in d minor: 867. Est-ce Mars:795,797. Fantasia:867. Hodie Christus natus est: 473,691,694,737,772,783. Malle Sijmen:867. Marchan qui traversez: 844. Mein junges Leben:797. O lux beata trinitas:795. Pavana Philippi:826. Ricercare brevis:797. Tes beaux yeux:828. Toccata:797. Toccata no.29, a minor:844. Toccata in a minor:795. Toccata in G major:867. Tu as tout seul:828. Venite exultemus Domino:694. Von der fortuna:637,641,826,867. Wo Gott der Herr nicht bei uns hält:795.

SZADEK, TOMASZ (ca.1550-ca.1611)
Dies est laetitia:753 (Kyrie, Sanctus, Benedictus).

TABOUROT, JEHAN (THOINOT ARBEAU) (1519-1595)
Telemann Society (Schulze). Turnabout TV 4008
[Orchésographie (about 30 selections).]

Allemande:577. Belle qui tiens ma vie:515,577. Gavotte:577. Jouissance vous donnerai:577. Moresca:577. Tourdions:577. Volta:577.

Taeggio, Rognoni. See ROGNONI TAEGGIO, GIOVANNI DOMENICO
TAFALLA, PEDRO DE (17th century)
   810
TALLIS, THOMAS (ca.1505-1585)
   BBC Chorus (Melville).   Pye/Virtuoso TPLS 13019
      12 (verso: Vaughan Williams)

   Cantores in Ecclesia (Howard).   L'Oiseau-Lyre SOL 311/3
      SOL 311: 1,18,27,30,31,38
      SOL 312: 3,5,8,38 (2nd setting),40,44,49
      SOL 313: 17,28,42 (verso: Byrd)

   Deller Consort; Elliott (org).   Harmonia Mundi 30 704; DR 208
      6,7,10,19,20,21,24,38,40,44

   King's College Choir, Cambridge (Willcocks).   Argo RG 479; ZRG 5479
      24,33,39,48

   *King's College Choir, Cambridge; Cambridge University Musical Society;
   Langdon, Davis (org). (Willcocks)*   Argo RG 436; ZRG 5436
      5,10,17,18,30,38,41,44,47

   St. John's College Choir, Cambridge; White (org). (Guest)
      2,4,11,17,21,43 (verso: Weelkes)   Argo RG 237; ZRG 5237

   1. Absterge Domine. 2. Audivi vocem:612,792. 3. Candidi facti sunt.
   4. Clarifica me pater:643. 5. Derelinquat impius. 6. Deus tuorum
   militum. 7. Domine. 8. Dum transisset Sabbatum. 9. Ecce tempus:583.
   10. Ex more docti mistico:552. 11. Fantasy. 12. Gaude gloriosa Dei
   Mater. 13. Gloria:887. 14. Gloria tibi Trinitatis:582,607,727.
   15. Heare the voyce and prayer of thy servants:881. 16. If you love
   me:848,887. 17. In jejunio et fletu. 18. In manus tuas. 19. Iste
   confessor:661. 20. Jam Christus astra. 21. Jam lucis orto sidere.
   22. Jerusalem:805. 23. Jesu salvator:583. 24. Lamentations of
   Jeremiah. 25. Like as the doleful dove:727. 26. Magnificat:714.
   27. Mihi autem nimis. 28. Miserere nostri Domine. 29. Nunc dimittis:
   714. 30. O nata lux de lumine:472,537,714. 31. O sacrum convivium:
   706,879. 32. O ye tender babes:737. 33. Organ lesson. 34. Per haec
   nos:661. 35. A point:643,661. 36. Psalm tune III:731. 37. Remember
   not, O Lord:661. 38. Salvator mundi:537,804. 39. Sancte Deus.
   40. Sermone blando. 41. Spem in alium:582. 42. Suscipe quaeso
   Domine. 43. Te Deum:607. 44. Te lucis ante terminum:804. 45. This
   is my commandment:714. 46. Veni creator Spiritus:804. 47. Veni
   redemptor:643. 48. Videte miraculum. 49. Virtus honor et potestas.
   50. Wherewithal shall a young man cleanse his way:883.
TAPISSIER, JEAN (15th century)
   Eya dulcis / Vale placens:563.
TARRAGONA. MONASTERY SCALA DEI. MS.: 457
TASSIN (13th century)
   Chose Tassin I:844. Chose Tassin II:844.

TAVERNER, JOHN (ca.1495-1545)
King's College Choir, Cambridge (Willcocks). Argo RG 316; ZRG 5316
[Christe Jesu pastor bone; Dum transisset Sabbatum; Kyrie Le roy;
Mater Christi; Mass The western wind.]

Pro Musica Sacra (Turner). (Ger.) Schwann AMS 34
[Missa Gloria tibi Trinitas; Responsorium in pace in idipsum.]

Christe Jesu:537,714. In nomine:551,714. Kyrie Le roy:537. Mass
The western wynde:611 (Benedictus). Sanctus:887. The western wynde
611.
Teramo, Zacharia de. See ZACHARIA DE TERAMO
TERANO
Rosetta:570.
TERTRE, ESTIENNE DU (16th century)
Bransles:625. Bransles d'Ecosses:178,560. Galliarde:625. Pavane:625.
Pavane d'Angleterre:178.
TESSIER, CHARLES (b. ca.1550)
Amants qui vous plaignez:446. Au joli bois:491,495,587. In a grove:729.
THESAURUS HARMONICUS: 707
THIBAUT IV, KING OF NAVARRE (1201-1253)
Aussi comme unicorne sui:535. Danse:575. Pour mal temps:886.
TINCTORIS, JOHANNES (ca.1435-1511)
Blanchard Instrumental and Vocal Ensemble. Nonesuch H 1048
[Missa Trium vocum.]
TISDALL, WILLIAM (16th century)
Mrs. Katherin:539. Pavana chromatica:539,564.
TITELOUZE, JEAN (1563-1633)
Darasse (org). (Ger.) Vox STV 34126
[Ad coenam; Ave maris stella; Exsultet caelum; Urbs Hierusalem.]
(verso: Attaingnant)

Göttsche (org). 10" Da Camera SOL 3202
[Magnificat IV toni; Pange lingua gloriosi.]

Organ verses to Benedictus:705.
TOLAR, JAN KŘTITEL (17th century)
868
TOMAS DE SANTA MARIA, FRAY (d.1570)
Clausulas de I tono:743. Fantasias:641,775,796.
TOMKINS, THOMAS (ca.1575-1656)
Elizabethan Singers. HMV HQM 1040; HQS 1040
[O let me live for true love; Oyez! has any found a lad; Weep no more
thou sorry boy; Yet again, as soon as revived; Was ever wretch
tormented; Too much I once lamented; Adieu, ye city-prisoning
towers; Oft did I marle; Fusca in thy starry eyes; Love, cease
tormenting; When David heard; See, see the shepherd's queen.]

URREDA, JUAN (15th century)
De vos is de mi:750. Muy triste será mi vida:750. Nunca fue pena mayor:
750.

VACQUERAS, BERTRAND (BELTRAME) (15th-16th centuries)
Kyrie:683.
VAET, JACOPUS (1529-1567)
Continuo lacrimas:831. Ecce apparebit:830.
VAILLANT, JEAN (14th century)
Par maintes foys:586,717,724.
VALDERRABANO, ENRIQUE (16th century)
De dondé venis, amore:861. Diferencias sobre Guardame las vacas:612.
Fantasias:600,710. Pavanas:773,807,844. Señora, si te olvidare:861.
VALENCIANO, MIGUEL MARTI (fl.1650)
744
VALENTE, ANTONIO (16th century)
Le ballo dell'intorcia:556. La romanesca:743.
VALLET, NICOLAS (b.1583)
Variations on Les pantalons:446.
Vaqueiras, Raimbaut de. See RAIMBAUT DE VAQUEIRAS
Vaqueras, Bertrand. See VACQUERAS, BERTRAND
VAROTER, FRANCESCO (15th century)
Voi che passate:670.
VASQUEZ, JUAN (16th century)
En la fuente del rosel:600. Morenica, dame un beso:861. Naome firays,
madre:666. Ojos morenos:771.
VAUTOR, THOMAS (16th-17th centuries)
Ah sweet, whose beauty:544. Lock up, fair lids:534. Mother I will
have a husband:542,655,738. Never did any more delight:534. Sweet
Suffolk owl:546. Shepherds and nymphs:545. Weep, weep mine eyes:
553.
VECCHI, HORATIO (ca.1550-1605)
Il Nuovo Madrigaletto Italiano (Grani).   Turnabout TV 4067; 34067 S
[Il convito musicale.]   (verso: Banchieri)

Wenzinger Consort; Deller Consort.
[L'Amfiparnaso.]   Harmonia Mundi 30628/29; Orpheus OR 360

Il bianco e dolce cigno:510. Boscareccia pastorale:896. Con voce dai
sospiri interrotta:851. Cruda mia tiranniella:851. Es sang ein Vöglein:
521. Fa una canzone:454,495,498. Fantasia:779. Leva la man di qui:
851. Quando mirai la bella faccia d'oro:851. Saltavan ninfe:745. So
ben mi ch'a bon tempo:851. Tiridola, non dormire:486,555,618,626.
VEGGIO (CLAUDIO?)
Canone a l'unisono:896.
Venetus, Adam de Antiquis. See ADAM DE ANTIQUIS VENETUS

Ventadour, Bernard de. See BERNARD DE VENTADOUR
VENTO, IVO DE (d.1575)
   Ich bin elend:767. Ich weiss ein Maidlein:767. Vor etlich wenig Tagen:
   767.
VERDELOT, PHILIPPE (16th century)
   Madonna il tuo bel viso:586,629.
VERDONCK, JEAN (16th-17th centuries)
   Alle mijn ghepeys:492.
VERMONT, PIERRE, L'AINÉ (d.1532)
   Ave virgo gloriosa:494.
VIADANA, LODOVICO GROSSI (ca.1564-1645)
   Canzon La padovana:825. Exsultate justi:660. O sacrum convivium:
   598. Salve Regina:759. La venetiana:635.
VIC MS.: 457
VICTORIA, TOMAS LUIS DE (ca.1540-1611)
       Caillard Vocal Ensemble.   Musical Heritage MHS 612; 612-S;
                 (Ger.) Christophorus CGLP 75847; SCGLP 75848
       21,36,39,43,45,60,65

       Carmelite Priory Choir, London (McCarthy).
       6,21,27,30 (verso: Palestrina)   L'Oiseau-Lyre OL 283; SOL 283

       Carmelite Priory Choir, London (McCarthy).
       35,36,63,64   L'Oiseau-Lyre OL 270; SOL 270

       Dessoff Choirs (Boepple).   Fantasy 5011; 8035
       15,31,35,67

       Montreal Bach Choir (Little).   Vox DL 1090; STDL 501090
       14,17,21,23,39,44,50,51,52,62

       New College Choir, Oxford (Lumsden).   Abbey S 629
       36,64 (verso: Byrd)

       Prague Madrigal Choir (Venhoda).
       6,18,19,35,67   Barenreiter MB 441; MB 941; Valois MB 741

       Regensburger Domchor (Schrems).   DG ARC 2533051
       66, plus 7 motets

       Roger Wagner Chorale.   Angel S 36022
       12,35,59 (verso: Palestrina)

       St. John's College Choir, Cambridge (Guest).   Argo ZRG 570
       4,6,15,35,68

       St. John's College Choir, Cambridge (Guest).   Argo ZRG 620
       14,16,20,29,30,36,58,64

       St. Mary of the Angels Choir, Wellington, N.Z. (Fernie).   Kiwi LD 5
       6,9,35,36,43 (verso: Palestrina)

       Schola Cantorum de la Universidad Pontificia de Comillas (Prieto).
       2,3,8,9,12,23,24,39,46,54,55,57   Pax P 378

Schola Cantorum de la Universidad Pontificia de Comillas (Prieto).
41,42   Pax P 379

*Schola du Grand Scholasticat des Pères du Saint-Esprit de Chevilly
(Deiss); Chorale Saint-Jordi du Barcelone (Martorell).*
6,11,37,39,65   Music Guild MG 143; MG 41; S 41

Scuola di Chiesa (Hoban).   Pye Virtuoso TPLS 13015
Tenebrae responsories (presumably same contents as RG 149 --
see below)

Scuola di Chiesa (Hoban).   Pye Virtuoso TPLS 13007; 13008
8,26,34,43,44,53,59   I Classici della Musica Classica SXPY 4137

Treviso Cathedral Chapel Choir (d'Alessi).   Period 756; 2756
6,9,33,43,54,59 (verso: Palestrina)

Westminster Cathedral Choir (Malcolm).
                    Argo RG 149; ZRG 5149; (Ger.) Decca SAWD 9954-A
Tenebrae responsories (1,2,3,5,9,12,13,23,24,39,46,49,50,52,54,55,
56,57

(motets, etc.): 1. Aestimatus sum. 2. Amicus meus. 3. Animam meam:
696. 4. Ascendens Christus. 5. Astiterunt reges. 6. Ave Maria:473,772,
804,824. 7. Beati immaculati:460. 8. Benedictus (Canticum Zacharius).
9. Caligaverunt oculi:638,696,703,824. 10. Domine, non sum dignus:
810. 11. Duo Seraphim:660,667. 12. Ecce quomodo. 13. Eram quasi
agnus. 14. Estote fortes:805. 15. Gaudent in coelis. 16. Hic vir.
17. Hosanna Filio David. 18. In ascensione Domini. 19. In nativitate
Domini. 20. Iste sanctus. 21. Jesu dulcis memoria:598. 22. Jesu
redemptor omnium:808. 23. Jesum tradidit impius:835. 24. Judas
mercator. 25. Laetatus sum:713. 26. Lamentations of Jeremiah.
27. Lauda Sion. 28. Libera me, Domine:806. 29. Litaniae de beata
Virgine. 30. Magnificat I toni:496. 31. Magnificat VI toni. 32. Ne
timeas, Maria:743,830. 33. O crux ave. 34. O Domine Jesu Christe.
35. O magnum mysterium:454,498,505,606,691,737,743,783,789,
808,830. 36. O quam gloriosum:74,900. 37. O regem caeli. 38. O sacrum
convivium:810. 39. O vos omnes:506,606,613,663,667,693. 40. Pange
lingua:810. 41. Passion (St. John). 42. Passion (St. Matthew).
43. Popule meus (Improperia):809. 44. Pueri Hebraeorum:703.
45. Quem vidistis pastores. 46. Recessit pastor noster:835. 47. Sancta
Maria:811. 48. Senex puerum portabat:783. 49. Seniores populi:835.
50. Sepulto Domino. 51. Sitientes venite ad aquas. 52. Tamquam ad
latronem. 53. Tantum ergo. 54. Tenebrae factae sunt:703,843,849.
55. Tradiderunt me. 56. Una hora. 57. Unus ex discipulis. 58. Veni
sponsa Christi. 59. Vere languores:484,809. 60. Vexilla regis.
61. Victimae Paschali:852.

(masses): 62. Alma redemptoris. 63. O magnum mysterium. 64. O
quam gloriosam:769 (Kyrie, Sanctus). 65. Quarti toni. 66. Vidi

VICTORIA, TOMAS LUIS DE (ca.1540-1611) (Continued)
speciosam. 67. Officium defunctorum, 1603. 68. Requiem mass[1]:472.
(From unspec. masses): Gloria, Sanctus, Benedictus:696. Sanctus,
Benedictus:660.

VIDAL, PEIRE (d. ca.1217)
Baron de mon dan covit:489. Pois tornatz sui en Proensa:478.

VIDE, JACOBUS (15th century)
Il m'est si grief:535. Las j'ay perdu mon espincel:488.

VILCHES
Ya cantan los gallos:841.

VILLALAR, ANDRES DE (16th century)
Regina coeli laetare:811.

VINDERS, HIERONYMOUS (16th century)
O mors inevitabilis:831.

Vinier, Guillaume le. See GUILLAUME LE VINIER

Vitry, Philippe de. See PHILIPPE DE VITRY

VIVANCO, SEBASTIAN DE (ca.1550-1622)
De lamentatione Jeremiae prophetae:809. Stabat Mater:811.

Vodňanský, Jan. See CAMPANUS, JOANNES VODNIANUS

Vogelweide, Walther von der. See WALTHER VON DER VOGELWEIDE

VOIT, HANS (16th century)
Für all ich krön:650,760.

VULPIUS, MELCHIOR (ca.1560-1615)
Westfälische Kantorei (Ehmann).   Cantate 650239
[Also wird euch mein himmlischer Vater; Gehe aus auf die Landstrasse;
Die Hochzeit; Mein Freund; Der Same ist das Wort Gottes; Sammelt
zuvor das Unkraut; Und der Herr lobete; Vater Abraham.]

Westfälische Kantorei (Ehmann).   Cantate 658216
[Der Sämann; Das Unkraut; Vom ungerechten Haushalter; Das grosse
Abendmahl; Dir Arbeiter im Weinberg; Der Schalksknecht; Von
reichen Mann und armen Lazarus; Die königliche Hochzeit.]

Jesaja dem Propheten:527. Und als bald war da:448.

WACLAW Z SZAMOTUL (d. ca.1567)
Nunc scio vere:782.

WAELRANT, HUBERT (1517-1595)
Als ick un vinde:585,839. Musiciens qui chantez à plaisir:789.

WAISSEL (WAISSELIUS), MATTHIAS (16th century)
Polish dances:812.

WALHOUT (same as Waelrant?)
Musiciens qui chantez à plaisir:826.

---

[1] Not clear whether by this is meant the Missa pro defunctis (1583) or the
Officium defunctorum (1605).

WALTHER, JOHANN (1496-1570)
>*Westfälische Kantorei (Ehmann).* Cantate 640203
>[Liedmesse in Sätzen der Reformationszeit: Gloria, Credo, Sanctus, Te Deum.]

>*Westfälische Kantorei (Ehmann).* Cantate 72469
>[Kyrie, Gott Vater in Ewigkeit; Allein Gott in der Höh sei Ehr; Wir glauben all'; Jesaja dem Propheten; Christe, du Lamm Gottes; Herr Gott, dich loben wir; Verleih uns Frieden gnädiglich.]

>Aus tiefer Not:611. Christ lag in Todesbanden:888. Ein feste Burg:844. Gelobet seist du, Jesus Christ:447,616,617,847. In dulci jubilo:617. Josef lieber, Josef mein:580,599,787,822. Komm Gott Schöpfer, heilger Geist:881. Mit Fried' und Freud':527. Nun freut euch:709. Nun komm der Heiden Heiland:897. St. Michael:524. Wach auf, du deutsches Land:524,527,590. Wär Gott nicht mit uns diese Zeit:527. Wir glauben all':523.

WALTHER VON CHATILLON
>Ecce torpet:482.

WALTHER VON DER VOGELWEIDE (12th century)
>Mir hat her Gerhart atze:681. Nu alerst leb ich (Palestinalied):615,672, 681,772,886. Under der Linden:681. Wie sol ich den gemynen:672.

WANNEMACHER, JOHANNES (d.1551)
>Aus tiefer Not:838. Min Gmüt und Blüt:838.

WARD, JOHN (16th-17th centuries)
>Ayre:643. Fantasias:466,571,643. Hope of my heart:534. In nomine: 623. Out from the vale:847. Retire, my troubled soul:546,847. Upon a bank:847. Williams his love:623.

WARSAW MUSIC SOCIETY TABLATURE: 813

WECK
>Ein ander dancz / Hopper dancz:652. Spanyöler Tanz:610,741.

WEELKES, THOMAS (ca.1575-1623)
>*St. John's College Choir, Cambridge; White (org). (Guest)*
>2,14,19,29,46,47 (verso: Tallis) Argo RG 237; ZRG 5237

>*Wilbye Consort (Pears).* (Br.) Decca SXL 6384
>3,5,7,8,9,16,17,18,21,23,27,30,33,36,38,40,41,42,43,44,45,49

>1. All people clap:732. 2. Alleluia:732. 3. The Andalusian merchant: 547. 4. The ape, the monkey, and the baboon:721. 5. As Vesta was from Latmos Hill:587,711,734,885. 6. As wanton birds:475,547. 7. Ay me, alas. 8. Cease now delight. 9. Cease sorrows now:542,547, 571,732. 10. Cold winter's ice is fled:544. 11. Come sirrah Jack:747. 12. The cryes of London:553. 13. Death has deprived me:475,547. 14. Give ear O Lord. 15. Gloria in excelsis Deo:783,883,887. 16. Hark all ye lovely saints:492,545,567,725,738,747,828,832. 17. Hark, I hear some dancing. 18. Hence care, thou art too cruel:547,661. 19. Hosanna to the Son of David:654,663,693,783,894. 20. In pride

WEELKES, THOMAS (ca.1575-1623) (Continued)
of May:475. 21. Lady, the birds right fairly:732. 22. Lady, your eye
my love enforced:534. 23. Like two proud armies. 24. Lo, country
sports:655. 25. Lord to thee I make my moan:732. 26. Lord, when I
think:547. 27. My Phyllis bids me pack away:534. 28. The nightingale:
666,709. 29. Nunc dimittis. 30. O care thou wilt despatch me:475,547,
661. 31. O how amiable:732. 32. O Lord, grant the King a long life:
706. 33. On the plains, fairy trains. 34. Our country swains:655.
35. Pavan no.3:732. 36. Say, dear, when will your frowning leave:545,
546. 37. Since Robin Hood:553. 38. Sing we at pleasure:534,544,583.
39. Sit down and sing:475. 40. Strike it up, Tabor:845. 41. Sweet
love. 42. Ta ra ra cries Mars. 43. Though my carriage. 44. Those
sweet delightful lilies. 45. Thule, the period of cosmography:547,
553,732. 46. Voluntaries (organ). 47. When David heard:627.
48. Whilst youthful sports are lasting:655. 49. Why are you ladies staying.

WEERBEKE, GASPAR VAN (15th-16th centuries)
Panis angelicus:777.

WERT, GLACHES DE (1535-1596)
*Accademia Monteverdiana Consort; Jaye Consort of Viols; Ambrosian
Singers (Stevens).*　　　Vanguard VCS 10083; Philips Vanguard 6584 007
[Tis pyri pyr edamasse; Cara la vita mia; Misera! non crede; Fantasia
a 4; J'ai trouvé ce matin; Kyrie eleison (Mass Transeunte Domino);
Felice piume; Datemi pace; De que sirven ojos morenos; Donna, tu
sei si bella; Vaghi boschetti; Ecco ch'un altra volta; In qual parte.]

Cara la vita:613. Non è si denso velo:841. Un jour je m'en allai:618,
841. Vezzosi augelli:629,688,841.

WHITE, ROBERT (ca.1530-1574)
Scuola di Chiesa (Hoban).　　　Pye/Virtuoso TPLS 13008
[Christe qui lux; Lamentations of Jeremiah; Magnificat I toni.]

O praise God:887. In nomine:643,714.

WHYTHORNE, THOMAS (b. ca.1528)
Buy new broom:512,725. Such as in love:587. Thou shalt soon see:587.
When Cupid had:587.

WIDMANN, ERASMUS (1572-1634)
Collegium Terpsichore.　　　ARC 3153; 73153
[Musicalischer Tugendspiel, 1613 (nos.3,4,12,13,15,16).]
(verso: Praetorius, Schein)

Denmark Concentus Musicus (Mathiesen).　　　Nonesuch 1064; 71064
[Dances and galliards: Johanna, Margaretha; Christina; Anna;
Regina; Felicitas; Sophia.] (verso: Demantius. Also Fasch, Händel,
Loeillet)

Kommt her Studenten frei:665. Schneiderlied:519. Wer Lust und Lieb
zur Musik hat:665. Wohlauf, ihr Gäste:486,819. Wohlauf Soldatenblut:
665. Also 651.

WILSON, JOHN (1595-1674)
  Take, O take those lips away:845.
WIPO (ca.1000-1050)
  Victimae paschali laudes:615.
WITHEFELDE
  The English hunt's up:668.
WIZLAW III, PRINCE OF RÜGEN (d.1325)
  Ich warne dich:681. Loybere risen:681,886. We ich han gedacht:886.
WOLFENBÜTTEL 677 (W1): 462,615
WOLFENBÜTTEL 1099 (W2): 462,685
WOLKENSTEIN, OSWALD VON (ca.1377-1455)
  Choral and Instrumental Ensemble (Wolf-Matthäus).
                                        10" (Ger.) DGA 13042 AP
  [Ave Mater; Es fuegt sich; Gelück und hail; Ich klag ein engel; Der Mai
  mit lieber zal; Mit günstlichem herzen; Nu huss; Sag an, herzlieb; Stand
  auf, Maredell; Wach auff, mein hortl; Wolauff gesell.]

  Es fuegt sich:631. Gar wunniklaich:585. In Suria:585,886. Der May:
  608. Wach auf, mein Hort:772.
WOLTZ ORGAN TABLATURE: 812
WORCESTER FRAGMENTS: 684,844
WRIGHT (THOMAS?)
  Nesciens mater:502.
WÜRZBURG, KONRAD VON
  Des soltu clein geniessen:838.
Wylkynson, Robert. See WILKINSON, ROBERT

XIMENEZ, JOSE (17th century)
  799

YOULL, HENRY (16th-17th centuries)
  Each day of thine:512.
YOUNG (prob. NICHOLAS) (d.1619)
  The shepherd, Arsilius' reply:655.

ZACHARIA DE TERAMO (ANTONIO ZACHARA DA TERAMO)
(14th-15th centuries)
  Madrigale (Faenza):535.
ZANETTI, GASPARO (17th century)
  449
ZANGIUS, NICOLAUS (d. ca.1618)
  599
ZARLINO, GIOSEFFO (1517-1590)
  Canzon a cinque:896.
ZELECHOWSKI, PIOTR (17th century?)
  813

ZIELENSKI, MIKOLAJ (early 17th century)
Capella Bydostiensis; Arion Chorus; Pro Musica Antiqua (Galonski).
Orpheus OR 356
[Four motets from Offertoria totus anni; Magnificat a 12.]

Ave Maria:723.
ZIRLER, STEPHAN (16th century)
Die Sonn, die ist verblichen:591.
ZORITA, NICASIO (16th century)
Pueri Hebraeorum:809.
ZWINGLI, ULRICH (1484-1531)
Herr, nun heb' den wagen selb:862.

ANONYMOUS

A combrais:786. A l'entrada del temps clar:489. A la charté (Montpellier):
886. A la fontenelle:886. A la mode de France:515. A la una yo naci:
493. A la villa voy:476. A madre:615,750. A qui dir'elle sa pensée:509.
A solis:580. A su albedrio:748. A vos, douce debonaire:786. A
vosaltres venim pregar:686. Accede nuntia:813. Ach herzig's Herz:521.
Ach reine zart:650. Ach was will doch:594. Ad honorem regis:458.
Ad mortem festinamus:457,899. Ad novem saltus:782. Ad regnum
epulentum:838. Ad solitum / Ad solitum / Regnat:685. Adieu madame:
760. Adieu mes amours:656. Adorazione dei magi:647. Adorazione
dei pastori:647. Adorazione delle madri:647. Advenit nobis desidera-
bilis:485. Aeterna Christi munera:615,705. Aeterne rerum conditor:
615. Agincourt song (Deo gracias Anglia):533,607,674,675,717,733,
853. Agnus Dei (Barcelona C):726. Agnus Dei (Worcester Add.68):844.
Ah, el novio no quiere dinero:718. Ah, my dear son:528. Ah, silly poor
Joas:742. Ah, the sighs that come fro' the heart:853. Ahimè sospiri:
568. Air:642. Al revuelo de una garza:859. Alia poznanie:813. Aliud
praeambulum:812. All in a garden green:853. All mein gedencken dy
ich hab:572. Alle psallite:462,587,615,707,844. Alleluia:615,687,761.
Alleluia Christus resurgens:697,724. Alleluia in greco:458. Alleluia
panna syna porodila:794. Alleluia, personet nostra iocunda:457.
Alleluia psallat:500,608,792,882. Alleluia / Veni sancte Spiritus:788.
Alleluia / Vocavit Jesus:860. Alleluia, Pascha nostrum immolatus est:
462. Alma redemptoris mater:548,769. Almandes:530,550,566,568,
583,655,833,867,869,876. Alman bruynsmedelijn:530. Almande Est-
ce Mars:745. Alman le pied de cheval:530. Alman prince:530,614,877.
Als ich anschau das frohlich Gsicht:469. Alta:815. Alta reina:811.
Alta trinità beata:646,677. Altissima luce col grande splendore:646.
L'alto prense arcangelo lucente:646. Amor dolze senza pare:646. Amor
potest conqueri:724. Amor potest / Ad amorem:676,754. L'amour de

moy:577,656. Angelus ad Virginem:483,502,890. Angelus Domini:615. Anglia tibi turbidas:717. Annua gaudia:860. Annunciazione:647. Ans d'entrar en sepultura:686. L'antefana de ser Lorenco:631. The antyck: 877. Appenzeller Kuhreien:838. Aque serven todo los celestiaes:615. Aquel caballero:477. Aquel rey de Francia:718. Aquella boz de Cristo tan sonora:460. Aquesta gran novetat:686. Ascensione:647. Astra solum qui regis:770. Au cuer ai un mal / Je ne m'en repentirai / Jolietement:676,754. Auf rief ein hübsches freuelein:619. Der Auff und Auff:767. Aufzug:767. L'autre jour / Au tens pascour / In seculum:899. Ave Dei genitrix:646. Ave donna santissima:646. Ave generosa:793. Ave gloriosa mater salvatoris:462. Ave gloriosa / Ave virgo regia / Domino:462,881. Ave in caelum:890. Ave miles caelestis curiae:882. Ave Maria:548. Ave Maria (Paris, Bibl. Natl. 15139):844. Ave Maria (Huelgas 156):459. Ave Maria ancilla Trinitatis:793. Ave Maria gracia Dei plena:674. Ave maris stella:865. Ave regina / Alma redemptoris / Alma:685. Ave regina gloriosa:646. Ave rex angelorum:548,674. Ave vergene gaudente:646. Ave verum corpus:619. Ave virgo virginum:462,467,687,838. Avre tu puerta cerrada:493. Axe Phebus aureo:480,482. Ay, luna que reluzes:460, 666,840. Ay me sospiri:464. Ay que non era:477. Ah que non hay: 718. Ay, trista vida corporal:686.

Il bacio di Giuda:647. Badz wiesiola:890. Die Bankelsangerlieder sonata:740. Balaam:576. Ballets:668. La ballette de la Reine d'Avril:721. Barafostus' dream: New York Pro Musica (Greenberg), Everest LPBR 6145/7 (verso: Morley),564,566. Barley brake:533. La bassa castiglya: Musica Reservata (Becket), Philips 6500085 (verso: Dufay). Bassa imperiale:557,708. Basse danse:556,575,577,708. Basse danse variée:509. Ein Bauer sucht:594. Boumgartner:557. Beata progenies: 548. Beati qui esuriunt:793. Beggar boy:532. Belial vocatur:462. La belle au rossignol:886. Ben è crudele e spietoso:646. Benedicamus-Catholicorum concio:459,750. Benedicamus-Resurgentis:459. Benedicamus Domino:615,786. Benedicamus Domino (Paris, Bibl. Natl. Ital.568):844. Benedicamus Domino (Pluteus):462. Benedicamus Domino / Congaudeant catholici (Calixtinus):860. Benedicti, el laudati:646. Benedictus (with organ verses by Titelouze):705. Benešov Hymnbook:794. La bergomesca:532. Bicinium:624. Bien doit avoir joie / In saeculum:445. Blance flour:717. Blanchete comme fleur de lis / Quant je pens / Valare:735. Blazhenna pervovo glasa:723. Blessed be thou, heavenly Queen:483. Boar's head carol:714,787,898. Bogurodzica:890. Le bon vouloir:178. Bona cat:872. La bonnette: 643,657. Bonny sweet robin:832,845. Bonum vinum:723. Bransles: 668,728. Bransles (Attaingnant):577,621,760. Branle (Dublin):530. Branle (Thesaurus harmonicus):707. Branle de Champagne:867. Bransle de St. Nicholas (Fuhrmann):812. Bransle double:178. Branle gay (Attaingnant):556,575,577. Branle Hoboken (Dublin):530,614.

Bransle simple:178. La brosse (basse danse):573,574,648. Bruder
Konrad:844. Brumans est mors:687. Brunswick's toy:664. Budyi
imya gospodnye:723. Bryd one brere:899. Brynge us in goode ale:707.
Buenas noches:493. Bullfinch:664. Il buratto:877. Bussa la porta:568.
By thy holy resurrection:813.

Caballero, si a Francia ideas:748,807. Calabaca no sè:720. Caleno custure
me:845,853. Can shee: New York Pro Musica (Greenberg), Everest
LPBR 6145/7 (verso: Morley),566. Canario:807. Candida virginitas:
615. Cantantibus hodie cunctis:457. Canzona on Psalm XLIII:813.
Canzone à tre:865. Carnival songs:741. The carman's whistle:532.
Carmen (Glogauer):723. Carmen Hercules:465. Carol with burden:483.
Casta catholica:459. Cedit frigus hiemale:457. Celle qui m'a le nom
d'amy donné:178,560. Celum non animum:482. C'est à ce joly mois
de may:488. C'est la fin:615,636,815. C'est la jus / Quia concupivit:
576. C'est quadruble sans reison / N'ai pas fet / Voz n'i dormirès
jamais / Biaus cuers renvoisiés / Fiat:735. Chaconne:807. Chanconetta
tedescha I:681. Chanconetta tedescha II:681. Chanconnète / A la
cheminée / Veritatem:576,761. Chanson:760. Chanson (13th century):
844. Chanson de toile:761. Chants de Noël:505. Chappeau de saulge:
488. La chasse:899. Che debbo far:632. Chi passa per questa strada:
530. Chi vol lo mondo desprezzare:646. Chramer gip:481. Christ ist
erstanden:723,888. Christe redemptor omnium:761. Christi miseration:
459. Christo psallat:607,615. Christum ducem:793. Christus hunc
diem:615. Christus natus est nobis:808,830. Chwala tobie gospodzinie:
890. La chymyse:643. Ciascun che fede sente:646. Ciz chans veult
boire:844. Clangat tuba:709. Clemens servulorum:458. Cloris sighed:
832. Cobbler's jig:853. The cobler:649. Coda di volpe:670. Colenda:
812,813. Come la rosa:718. Concert pour les chevaliers:577. Concordia
laetitia:677. Condicio nature / O nacio / Mane prima sabbati:685.
Conditur alme siderum:882. Conditor fut le nonpareil:787,898.
Congaudeant catholici:458. Conradi:782,872. Conspexit:481. Constans
esto, fili mi:838. Contemplazione de Maria nel presepe:647. Contre le
temps:844. Coreae:872. Coranto:515,556,566,725. Courante:668.
Court dance:737. Coventry carol:172,533. Cracowia civitas:723,890.
Credo (Torino ms.):726. Cristicolis secunditas:890. Cristo è nato et
humanato:646. Cristo riusati in tutti i cuori:677. Crocifissione:647.
Crucifigat omnes:445,480,482. Cuckoo:532. Cum altre uccele:758.
Cuncti simus:457,899. Cunctipotens genitor:615. Cupido:594.
Currant:649. Czayner thancz:872. Czenner greyner:844.

Da ciel venne messo novello:646. Dadme Albricias:581,743,824. Dale si le
das:585,619,720,743,839. Dalling alman:556. Dame qui j'aime / Amors
vaint tot / Au tans d'esté / Et gaudebit:735. Dami conforto, Dio:646.
Dances (Tänze, danze, etc.):556,633,741,872. Danse royale:615,672,
676,754,844. Daphne:602,642,722,725,885. De calamitatibus Galliae:

525. Ich spring an disem ringe:572,585. Ich trau keinm alten:470. Ich var dahin:572. Ich weet een Vrauken:470. Ik zeg adieu:826. Il est de bonne heure:586. Il était un bonhomme:511. Il me suffit:656,877. Ils sont bien pelz:509. Im maien:470. Imhol vayok:749. Imperayritz: 457,899. Imperitante Octaviano:771. In carnevale:839. In dulci jubilo: 865. In eadem quippe carnis:457. In exitu Israel:686. In gedeonis area: 457,481. In hoc anni circulo:787,898. In illo tempore:462. In pro:719. In questo ballo:568. In seculum:615,786. In seculum (Bamberg):445, 576,724. In seculum artifex:619,636,672,815. In seculum d'Amiens longum:724. In seculum longum:881. In seculum viellatoris:445,619,672, 676,754,772. In this valley:787,898. Infantem vidimus:881. Invocazione: 647. Io vorrei fuggir:633. Iove cum Mercurio:481. Irish ho-hoane:540. Istampita Ghaeta:515,569,570,869. Istampita Palamento:674. Italiana: 653. Ite missa est:683. Iteitas:723.

Ja n'amerai autre / In saeculum:445,735. Jácara:744. Jacet granum oppressum palea:576. Das Jaegerhorn:723,839,844,888. J'ai mis toute ma pensée / Je n'en puis / Puerorum:735. J'ai si bien mon cuer / Aucun m'ont par leur envie / Angelus:735. J'ai au cuer / Docebit:676,754. J'ai vu la beauté:886. J'ay prins amour:715. Je cuidoie bien metre:615. Je demeure seule égarée:507. Je gart le bois:844. Je me leve un bel matin: 495. Je n'amerai autre:881. Je ne m'en repentirai / Jolietement:754. Je suis d'Alemagne:586. Je suis trop jeunette:488. Je vois douleur / Fauvel nous a fait:463. Je vous:800. Jesu Cristo glorioso:646. Jesucristo hombre y dios:800. Jesu nostra redemptio:589. Jeszcze marczynye:872. Ihesu clementissime:459. John, come kiss me now:533. Le joli teton:586. Jolietement:676,754. Joseph lieber, Joseph mein:898. Jube domne benedicere-Primo tempore:462. Judea et Jerusalem:462. Julia dic experta meas vires:862. Julieta:861.

Das kalb get seiner narung nach:594. Die Katzenpfote:619. Kehraus:839. Kemps jig:559,583,627,649,845. The king's mistress:669. The king's morisco:722. Komm, heiliger Geist:687,788. Kosakenballett:723. Kunig Rudolf:772. Kyrie (14th century):844. Kyrie (14th century): 844. Kyrie De angelis:589. Kyrie magne Deus potencie:462. Kyrie virginitatis amator:462.

Lachrimae:533. Lamento di Tristan:570,608,636,642,672,719,758,815,844, 869. Lasse qui deviendrai-je:844. Laude:500,535,646,647,677. Lauda anima mea Dominum:615. Lauda di Maria Maddalena:647. Laudabo Deum meum:615. Laudamo la resurrectione:646. Laudar voglio per amore:646,677. Laude della croce:647. Laude novella sia cantata:646, 677. Laudemus Virginem:457,899. Die Libe ist schoen:650. Libera me, Domine:615. Licet eger cum egrotis:482. Der liebe strick:594. Lieblich hat sich gesellet:591,650,760. Light o' love:853. Un lion say: 780. Lo que demanda el romero:535. Lobe den Herren meine Seele:605.

Sacris solemnis:800. Sage, saz ih dirs:481. St. Magnus hymn:792. Saltarello: 489,515,570,586,636,642,657,672,674,708,719,758,759,815,869. Saltarello de megio:764. Saltarello del Re:556. Salutiam divotamente: 646. Saluts, honor e salvament:686. Salve regina princessa:686. Salve, salve virgo pia:646. Salve sancta parens:674,882,890. Salve virgo:786. Salue, uirgo nobilis, Maria / Verbum caro factum est / Verbum:735. Salve virgo / Ave Gloriosa:750. Salve virgo virginum (Arundel):462. Salve virgo virginum / Omnes (Montpellier):462. Samson dux fortissimae: 584,585. San Iovanni, al mond'è nato:646. Sancta Maria:548. Sancte Dei pretiose:882. Sanctus (Huelgas):462. Sanctus (Ivrea):726. Sanctus et Agnus -- Cleri caetus:459. Sanctus & Benedictus:882. Sane per omnia: 459. Sans roche:574,648. Santo Lorenzo:615. Schephczyk ydzye po ulyczy:872. Scot's marche:583. Se do mal q me greis:476. Se je chant: 899. Se mai per meraveglia:632. The second witches dance:669. Seconda chiamata, che va sonata avanti la battaglia:721. La seconde estampie real: 676,754. Sei willekommen:687,842. Sempiterna:723. Los set gotex: 457,899. La sexte estampie real:676,741. Shepherd's hey:664. La shy muse:797. Si amores me han de matar:840. Si de vos mi bien me aparto: 840. Si fortune m'a si bien pourchassé:739. Si je perdu:465. Si j'ay perdu mon ami:511. Si la noche:505,657,840,861. Sia laudato San Francesco:646. Sic mea fata canendo solor:481. Sick tune:711. Since thou art false to me:661. Sing we to this merry company:733. Sir Philip Sidney's lamentation:534,729. Siralmas énékem:749. La sirena: 493. Sit gloria Domini:607,615. Sobre Baça estaba el rey:718. Sok király oknak:749. Sokféle részögösröl:749. Sol eclysim patitur:456. Sol oritur in sydere:615,636,815. S'on me regarde / Prennés i garde / He! mi enfant:445. Song of the ass see Orientis partibus. Sopra il fieno colcato:850. Sorella mia piacente:568. Souvent souspire:741,899. La Spagna: Musica Reservata (Becket), Philips 6500085 (verso: Dufay), 468,557,619,656,733,741. Spagnoletta:507. The Spanish lady:853. Spirito Sancto de servire:646. Spiritu Sancto, dolze amore:646. Spirito Santo glorioso:646. Splendens ceptigera:457,899. Stabat juxta Christi crucem:675. Staines morris dance:515. Stantipes:642,761,869. Stella nuova in fra la gente:646. Stella splendens:457,899. Stomme alegro et lazioso:646. Stond wel, moder:675. The strake to the fields: 721. Strawberry leaves:885. Studentes conuigo:786. Die süss Nachtigall: 636,815. Sumer is icumen in:533,608,675,792. Der Summer:572. Super cathedrum / Presidentes:463. Swatheo Martina:723. Sweet was the song the Virgin sang:725,742.

Der Tag, der ist so freudenreich:687,842. Take heed of time, tune and ear:553. Taniec:753,782. Tant que vivray:573,574,648,867. Tappster, dryngker: 610,717,721. Te Deum:584,585. Te Deum (Attaingnant):672. Te matrem Dei laudamus:800. Tellus flore:482. Tempus est iocundum:482. Tempus transit gelidum:481. Then they for sudden joy did weep:845. Ther is no rose of swych vertu:483,674. This merry, pleasant spring:742. The three ravens:853. Tibi laus, tibi gloria:548. Tickle my toe:515,642,

PART III

Performer Index

Performer Index

AACHENER DOMSINGKNABEN: 762; Palestrina
ABBEY SINGERS: 567,629
ACCADEMIA MONTEVERDIANA: 515,582,583; Gesualdo, Wert
AGRUPACION INSTRUMENTAL DE MUSICA ANTIQUA DE MADRID: 748
Alarius Ensemble. *See* ENSEMBLE ALARIUS
ALESSI, GIOVANNI D' (conductor): Palestrina, Victoria
ALL SAINTS CHORISTERS: 558,787; Davy
ALTMEYER, THEO (tenor): 617,765
AMBROSIAN CONSORT: 496,582,583,590,688,690,771,840; A. Gabrieli,
    Janequin, Willaert
AMBROSIAN SINGERS: 453,454,496,498,512,544,582,583,661,684,703,
    830,841,882,884,887; Dufay, Fayrfax, A. Gabrieli, G. Gabrieli, Machaut,
    Morley, Wert, Willaert
AMERICAN BRASS QUINTET: 701,740
ANCIENT INSTRUMENT ENSEMBLE OF PARIS: 577
ANGELES, VICTORIA DE LOS (soprano): 718,861
Anthologie Sonore Orchestra. *See* ORCHESTRE ANTHOLOGIE SONORE
Antwerp Collegium Musicum. *See* COLLEGIUM MUSICUM ANTWERPEN
Argentan. Nôtre-Dame Abbey. *See* NOTRE-DAME D'ARGENTAN ABBEY
    NUNS' CHOIR
ARION CHORUS: Zielenski
ARMSTRONG, SHEILA (soprano): 742
ARNDT, GÜNTHER (conductor): 525,617,764-768
ARS MUSICAE, BARCELONA: 689,718,861
ATRIUM MUSICAE: 456,457,459
AVELING, VALDA (harpsichord): 614,690; Morley

BAINES, FRANCIS (conductor): 635,728
BANNWART, P. (conductor): 769
BARBANY (singer): 600
Barcelona Ars Musicae. *See* ARS MUSICAE, BARCELONA
BARCELONA MADRIGAL CHOIR: 824
BARCELONA POLYPHONIC ENSEMBLE: 807
Barcelona Quartet Polifonic. *See* QUARTET POLIFONIC DE BARCELONA
Barmen-Gemarke Kantorei. *See* KANTOREI BARMEN-GEMARKE

Performer Index

BROWN, WILFRED (tenor): 725,856
BRUCHEZ, PAUL (conductor): Ingegneri
BRÜCKNER-RÜGGEBURG, FRIEDRICH (tenor): 572
BRÜGGEN, FRANZ (conductor): 551
BRÜGGEN-CONSORT: 551
BRUSSELS VOCAL ENSEMBLE: Willaert
Brussels Vocal Quartet. *See* QUATUOR VOCAL DE BRUXELLES
BUCHAREST MADRIGAL CHOIR: Palestrina
BUETENS LUTE ENSEMBLE: 619
BURGESS, GRAYSTON (conductor): 546,553,558,655,675,680,733,734,
    787,815,877,885,898; Davy, Depres, Dunstable, Machaut
Busto Arsizio. Frati Minori. *See* FRATI MINORI OF BUSTO ARSIZIO
BYRT, JOHN (conductor): 801

CABERO, MANUEL (conductor): 824
Caillard Vocal Ensemble. *See* ENSEMBLE VOCAL PHILIPPE CAILLARD
CAILLAT, STEPHANE (conductor): 446,508,555
Caillat Vocal Ensemble. *See* ENSEMBLE VOCAL CAILLAT
Caillat Vocal Quartet. *See* QUATUOR VOCAL CAILLAT
CAMBRIDGE CONSORT: 656
CAMBRIDGE UNIVERSITY MUSICAL SOCIETY: Tallis
CAMERATA LUTETIENSIS: 757,779
CAMERATA VOCALE, BREMEN: 492,828; Franck
CAMERON, FRANCIS (organ): Bull
CANBY SINGERS: 789
CANBY, EDWARD T. (conductor): 789
CANTORES IN ECCLESIA: Byrd, Tallis
CANZONA ENSEMBLE: 515
CAPE, SAFFORD (conductor): 699
CAPELLA ANTIQUA, MUNICH: 411,462,467,471,480,485,589,650,685,
    687,760,788,831,842,862,866,892; Depres, Dufay, G. Gabrieli, Isaac,
    LaRue, Machaut, Philippe de Vitry, Senfl
CAPELLA ANTIQUA, STUTTGART: 580
CAPELLA BYDGOSTIENSIS PRO MUSICA ANTIQUA: 782,890; Zielenski
CAPELLA CORDINA: 463; Arcadelt, Depres, Dufay, Mouton, Ockeghem
CAPELLA FIDICINIA: 466
CAPELLA LIPSIENSIS: 479,652; Lechner, Obrecht, Ockeghem
CAPELLA MONACENSIS: 839
CAPILLA DEL MISTERIO DE ELCHE: 686
Capilla Musical y Escolania de Santa Cruz del Valle de los Caidos. *See*
    SANTA CRUZ DEL VALLE DE LOS CAIDOS. CAPILLA MUSICAL Y
    ESCOLANIA
CAPPELLA VOCALE, HAMBURG: Gesualdo, Lassus
CARMELITE PRIORY CHOIR, LONDON: 404,804-806; Anerio, Palestrina,
    Victoria

THE CLERKES OF OXENFORD: 502
Clervaux. St. Maurice & St. Maur Abbey Monks' Choir. *See* ST. MAURICE &
ST. MAUR ABBEY MONKS' CHOIR, CLERVAUX
CLEVELAND BRASS ENSEMBLE: G. Gabrieli
COCHEREAU, PIERRE (organ): 506,597; Depres, Janequin
COHEN, JOEL (conductor): 656
Collegeville, Minn. St. John's Abbey Monks' Choir. *See* ST. JOHN'S ABBEY
MONKS' CHOIR, COLLEGEVILLE, MINN.
COLLEGIUM AUREUM: 871
COLLEGIUM CANTORUM, BONN: Isaac
COLLEGIUM MUSICUM ANTWERPEN: Clément
Collegium Musicum of Columbia University. *See* COLUMBIA UNIVERSITY
COLLEGIUM MUSICUM
COLLEGIUM MUSICUM OF RADIO VIENNA: G. Gabrieli
Collegium Musicum of the University of Illinois. *See* ILLINOIS
UNIVERSITY COLLEGIUM MUSICUM
Collegium Musicum of the University of Missouri. *See* MISSOURI
UNIVERSITY COLLEGIUM MUSICUM
COLLEGIUM MUSICUM ST. MARTINI, BREMEN: 523,747,751,753
COLLEGIUM TERPSICHORE, BIELEFELD: Praetorius, Schein, Widmann
COLOMBO, FRA ILLUMINATO (conductor): 395
COLUMBIA UNIVERSITY COLLEGIUM MUSICUM: 563,576,631,683,700,
723,726; Isaac
Comillas, Universidad Pontificia. *See* SCHOLA CANTORUM DE LA
UNIVERSIDAD PONTIFICIA DE COMILLAS
COMPLESSO MADRIGALE DI MOSCA: 505
CONCENTUS MUSICUS OF DENMARK: 669; Demantius, Widmann
CONCENTUS MUSICUS, VIENNA: 465,571,624,625,724
Conrad, Ferdinand. *See* FERDINAND CONRAD INSTRUMENTAL ENSEMBLE
Conservatorio Verdi Chorus. *See* CORO DI CONSERVATORIO VERDI
CONSORTIUM MUSICUM: 617
CONSTANTIN, MARCU (conductor): 818,819; Palestrina
CORBOZ, MICHEL (conductor): 896; Ingegneri
CORO DI CONSERVATORIO VERDI, MILAN: 510
CORO VALLICELLIANO: 696
COROS DE RADIO NACIONAL DE ESPANA, MADRID: 808-811
CORUL MADRIGAL AL CONSERVATORULUI CIPRIAN PORUMBESCU:
818,819
COSTA, OTHMAR (conductor): 592,622
COTTE, ROGER (conductor): 577,672,780
COURVILLE, YVES (conductor): Marenzio, Palestrina
CRAFT, ROBERT (conductor): Gesualdo
CUCKSTON, ALAN (harpsichord): 530
Cuesta, Fernandez de la. *See* FERNANDEZ DE LA CUESTA, P. I.
CZECH PHILHARMONIC CHORUS: 770,794; Palestrina

d'Alessi, Giovanni. *See* ALESSI, GIOVANNI D'
DALLA LIBERA, SANDRO (organ): A. Gabrieli, G. Gabrieli
DANBY, NICHOLAS (organ): 514
DARASSE, XAVIER (organ): Attaingnant, Titelouze
DART, THURSTON (conductor, harpsichord, etc.): 786,834,889; Bull
DAVENPORT, LA NOUE (conductor): 569
DAVIS, A. (organ, harpsichord): 706
DEISS, LUCIEN (conductor): Victoria
Del Farraro, Alfonso. *See* FARRARO, ALFONSO DEL
DELLER CONSORT: 483,500,542,545,644,697,698,724,845,847,854; Byrd,
    Dowland, Gesualdo, Gibbons, Machaut, Morley, Perotinus, Tallis, Vecchi,
    Wilbye
DELLER, ALFRED (conductor, counter-tenor): 500,528,542,662,724,790,
    845,854
DELLER, MARK (counter-tenor): 528
DELMOTTE, ROGER (conductor): A. Gabrieli, Janequin
De los Angeles, Victoria. *See* ANGELES, VICTORIA DE LOS
Denmark Concentus Musicus. *See* CONCENTUS MUSICUS OF DENMARK
De Nobel, Felix. *See* NOBEL, FELIX DE
DESSOFF CHOIRS: Palestrina, Victoria
DETEL, ADOLF (conductor): 874
DEVEVEY, PIERRE (conductor): 513
DEXTER, JOHN (conductor): Certon
DIJON MIXED CHORUS: 484
Distler-Chor. *See* HUGO-DISTLER-CHOR, BERLIN
DOBRODINSKY, JAN MARIA (conductor): Palestrina
DOLMETSCH CONSORT: 725
Dombois, Eugene Müller. *See* MÜLLER-DOMBOIS, EUGENE
DOMCHOR MÜNSTER: 595,763
DORFNER, JOSEF (conductor): 897
DOWLAND CONSORT: 827
DRESDNER KREUZCHOR: 527,694
Düsseldorf Studio fur alte Musik. *See* STUDIO FÜR ALTE MUSIK,
    DÜSSELDORF
DUPRE, DESMOND (lute): 790,845; Dowland, Janequin
DURAND, GUY: 672

EARLY MUSIC CONSORT: 570; Morley
EASTMAN BRASS QUINTET: 475
EASTMAN WIND ENSEMBLE: A. Gabrieli, G. Gabrieli
Edmundite Novices. *See* ST. EDMUND'S NOVITIATE
EDWARD TARR BRASS ENSEMBLE: G. Gabrieli
EHMANN, WILHELM (conductor): 785; Praetorius, Vulpius, Walther
EHRLICH, PAUL (conductor): 673

Einsiedeln. Stiftschor der Benediktiner-Abtei. *See* STIFTSCHOR DER
    BENEDIKTINER-ABTEI EINSIEDELN
ELIZABETHAN CONSORT OF VIOLS: 532,578,655,711,885; Dowland
ELIZABETHAN SINGERS: Byrd, Tomkins
ELLER, J. P. VON (conductor): Sermisy
ELLIOT, ROBERT (organ, harpsichord): 790; Tallis
ELY CATHEDRAL CHOIR: 894
ELY CONSORT: 728
Encalcat. *See* SAINT-BENOIT D'ENCALCAT ABBEY MONKS' CHOIR
ENGLISH, GERALD (tenor): 636,730,731
ENGLISH CONSORT OF VIOLS: 541,742
ENSEMBLE ALARIUS: 777
ENSEMBLE CUIVRES GABRIEL MASSON: A. Gabrieli, Janequin
Ensemble d'Instruments Anciens de Zurich. *See* ZURICH ANCIENT
    INSTRUMENT ENSEMBLE
ENSEMBLE D'ORGUES W. VON KARAJAN: 865
ENSEMBLE GASTON SOUBLETTE: 488,886
Ensemble les Ménestrels. *See* LES MENESTRELS
ENSEMBLE POLYPHONIQUE DE PARIS: 477,509,535,604,621,658,832;
    Bertrand, Janequin, LaRue, Ockeghem
ENSEMBLE VOCAL CAILLAT: 446,508,555; Lejeune
ENSEMBLE VOCAL GRIMBERT: Lejeune
ENSEMBLE VOCAL PASSAQUET: 490; Lassus
ENSEMBLE VOCAL PHILIPPE CAILLARD: 487,491,497,507; Bertrand,
    Depres, Dufay, Janequin, Lassus, Ockeghem, Victoria
ENSEMBLE VOCAL SAINT-PAUL: 497
EPHRIKIAN, ANGELO (conductor): Gesualdo
EPPENDORF BOYS' CHOIR: 874
ERNETTI, PADRE (conductor): 436-439
EWERHART, RUDOLF (organ, conductor): 768; Anerio

FAROLFI, RODOLFO (tenor): Gesualdo
FARRARO, ALFONSO DEL (conductor): 415,677
FARRELL, GERARD (conductor): 399,598
FENNELL, FREDERICK (conductor): A. Gabrieli, G. Gabrieli
FERDINAND CONRAD INSTRUMENTAL ENSEMBLE: Praetorius, Schein
FERNANDEZ DE LA CUESTA, P. I. (conductor): 419,420,458
FERNIE, MAXWELL (conductor): 835; Palestrina, Victoria
FESPERMAN, JOHN (conductor): Gibbons
FICHERMONT DOMINICAN SISTERS: 402
FIELD-HYDE, MARGARET (conductor): 547,711; Dowland
FIGURALCHOR DER GEDÄCHTNISKIRCHE, STUTTGART: 616
FISCHER-DIESKAU, KLAUS (conductor): 591
FISHER, ESTHER (piano): 614
FLEET, E. (conductor): 615

FÖRSTEMANN, M. G. (organ): 897
Fondation Gulbenkian Chorus. *See* GULBENKIAN FOUNDATION CHORUS
FORBES, ELLIOT (conductor): 692
FORSTER, KARL (conductor): G. Gabrieli, Palestrina
FOTI, C. (mezzo-soprano): Gesualdo
FRANZ TENTA CONSORT: 771
FRATI MINORI OF BUSTO ARSIZIO: 395
Frauenchor der Fachschule für Musik Györ. *See* GYÖR MUSIC HIGH SCHOOL
    WOMEN'S CHOIR
FREI, WALTER and SYLVIA: 758,838
FROIDEBISE, PIERRE (organ): 494,712,713
FURTHMOSER, HERMANN (conductor): 665

GABRIELI CONSORT LA FENICE: G. Gabrieli
GÄCHINGER KANTOREI: Lechner
GAJARD, DOM JOSEPH (conductor): 388-392,421-433
GALONSKI, STANISLAV (conductor): 890; Zielenski
GARCIA LLOVERA, JULIO M. (organ): 796
GARDINER, JOHN E. (conductor): 645; Gesualdo
Gavaldá, Miguel Querol. *See* QUEROL GAVALDA, MIGUEL
Gedächtniskirche, Stuttgart, Figural. *See* FIGURALCHOR DER
    GEDÄCHTNISKIRCHE, STUTTGART
GERWIG, WALTER (lute): 447,522,574,633,634,648; Neusiedler
GILCHRIST, ALDEN (conductor): Dufay
GILLESBERGER, HANS (conductor): Depres, Dufay, Obrecht
GIROD (organ): 593
GISPERT, ENRIQUE (conductor): 689,718
GØTTSCHE, H. M. (organ): Titelouze
GOLDEN AGE SINGERS: 547,711; Dowland
GORBY (mezzo-soprano): 493
GOTTI, TITO (conductor): 774
Grand Scholasticat des Pères du Saint-Esprit de Chevilly. *See* SCHOLA DU
    GRAND SCHOLASTICAT DES PERES DU SAINT-ESPRIT DE
    CHEVILLY
GRANI, EMILIO (conductor): Banchieri, Vecchi
GREENBERG, NOAH (conductor): 548,603,623,627,674,820,825,860;
    Banchieri, Franck, Morley, Senfl, anon. (Barafostus' dream)
GREGG SMITH SINGERS: G. Gabrieli
Grimbert Vocal Ensemble. *See* ENSEMBLE VOCAL GRIMBERT
GRISCHKAT, HANS (conductor): 599
GROSSMAN, FERDINAND (conductor): 651
GROUPE D'INSTRUMENTS ANCIENS DE PARIS: 780
GROUPE VOCAL FRITZ HOYOIS: 814
GRUBICH, JOACHIM (organ): 813
GRUSS, HANS (conductor): 466

HUNTER, GEORGE (conductor): Depres, Ockeghem
HURWITZ CHAMBER ENSEMBLE: 706

ILLINOIS UNIVERSITY CHAMBER CHORUS: Depres
ILLINOIS UNIVERSITY COLLEGIUM MUSICUM: Ockeghem
IN NOMINE PLAYERS: 590

JACCOTTET, CHRISTINE (harpsichord): Ortiz
JAYE CONSORT OF VIOLS: 515,553,635,636,728,730,731,734,815;
    Gibbons, Wert
JEANS, SUSI (virginals): Bull
JESSON, ROY (harpsichord): 840; Byrd
JOHANNES KOCH GAMBA CONSORT: Bull
JONES, GERAINT (keyboard): 637
Jones, Philip. See PHILIP JONES BRASS ENSEMBLE
JOUINEAU, JACQUES (conductor): 517
JÜRGENS, JÜRGEN (conductor): 448,618
JULIAN BREAM CONSORT: 559 See also BREAM, JULIAN
JUNGE KANTOREI MANNHEIM: Demantius

KAHLHÖFER, HELMUT (conductor): 599
KAJDASZ, EDMUND (conductor): Leopolita
KAMMERCHOR WALTER VON DER VOGELWEIDE: 592,622
KANN, HANS (organ, harpsichord): 661; Janequin
KANTOREI BARMEN-GEMARKE: 599
KARAJAN, WOLFGANG VON: 865
KAUFBEURER MARTINSFINKEN: 822,828; Depres, Lassus
KEE, PIET (organ): Swelinck
KENTUCKY UNIVERSITY COLLEGIUM MUSICUM: 612,613
KIND, SYLVIA (harpsichord): 554
KINES, TOM (tenor): 853
KING'S COLLEGE CHOIR, CAMBRIDGE: 691,783,900; Byrd, Palestrina,
    Tallis, Taverner
KIPNIS, IGOR (harpsichord): 543
KISSINGER KANTOREI: Ingegneri
KLAGENFURTER MADRIGALCHOR: 486
KLERK, ALBERT DE (organ): 641
KLOOR, WERNER (conductor): 888
KNEIHS, HANS M. (conductor): G. Gabrieli
KNOTHE, DIETRICH (conductor): 479,652; Lechner, Obrecht, Ockeghem
KOCH, HELMUT (conductor): 520,521
Koch, Johannes. See JOHANNES KOCH GAMBA CONSORT
KÖLZ, ERNST (conductor): 869

KOENIG, CHARLES (conductor): Willaert
KOVATS, BARNA (guitar): 601
KRAINIS BAROQUE ENSEMBLE: 562
KRAINIS CONSORT: 562,581,642,722
KREDER ENSEMBLE: Lejeune

LAMANA, JOSE M. (conductor): 861
LANGENBECK, A. (conductor): 518
LATHAM, RICHARD (organ): Batten, Deering
LAUSANNE VOCAL AND INSTRUMENTAL ENSEMBLE: 896
LAUSANNE VOCAL ENSEMBLE: Ingegneri
Lautenquartett Pöhlert. *See* PÖHLERT LAUTENQUARTETT
LAYTON RING RECORDER CONSORT: 532
LEEB, HERMANN (lute): 711; Campion, Dowland
LEIWERING, HUBERT (conductor): 595,763
LEONHARDT, GUSTAV (virginals, harpsichord): 536,538,539,602; Swelinck
LEONHARDT CONSORT: 536
LEPAUW[1] (vièle): 478; Alfonso el Sabio
LEPPARD, RAYMOND (conductor): 727,728,730,731; Dowland
LESTER, HAROLD (harpsichord): 515
LEVITT, RICHARD (conductor): 738
LIEBLING, JOSEPH (conductor): 587
LITAIZE, GASTON (organ): 450
LITTLE, GEORGE (conductor): 714,743; Azzaiolo, Byrd, Dufay, Gesualdo,
    Victoria
LIVERPOOL AND BOOTLE CONSTABULARY BAND BRASS SECTION: 654
LIVERPOOL CATHEDRAL CHOIR: 654
Llovera, Julio M. Garcia. *See* GARCIA LLOVERA, JULIO M.
LOEHRER, EDWIN (conductor): 647
LONDON BRASS ENSEMBLE: 787
LONDON CORNET AND SACKBUT ENSEMBLE: 635
LONDON EARLY MUSIC CONSORT: 741
LONDON GABRIELI BRASS ENSEMBLE: 833
London Pro Arte Antiqua. *See* PRO ARTE ANTIQUA, LONDON
LONDON SACKBUT ENSEMBLE: 885
London Schola Cantorum. *See* SCHOLA CANTORUM LONDINIENSIS
LORANT, SZALMAN (conductor): 499
LORENZEN, JOHANNES (organ): 579
Los Angeles, Victoria de. *See* ANGELES, VICTORIA DE LOS
LOZANO, LUIS (conductor): 457; Alfonso el Sabio
LUCA MARENZIO ENSEMBLE: 630
Luca Marenzio Sextet. *See* SESTETTO ITALIANO LUCA MARENZIO
Lugano Società Cameristica. *See* SOCIETA CAMERISTICA DI LUGANO

---

[1] Cited as Lepaun in Diapason 1967.

Performer Index

MONTEVERDI CHOIR (Gardiner, conductor): 645; Gesualdo
MONTEVERDI CHOIR, HAMBURG: 448,618
Montreal Bach Choir. *See* SOCIETE DE LA CHORALE BACH DE MONTREAL
Montréal Petit Ensemble Vocal. *See* PETIT ENSEMBLE VOCAL, MONTREAL
MONTSERRAT ABBEY CHOIR: 451; Morales
MORGAN, WESLEY K. (conductor): 608-613
MORLEY CONSORT: Morley
MORROW, MICHAEL (conductor): 680,728
MT. ANGEL SEMINARY GREGORIAN CHOIR, ST. BENEDICT, ORE.: 413, 414
MOWREY, BROTHER (conductor): 416-418
MUDDE (conductor): 785
MÜLLER, ELPIDIA (organ): 403
MÜLLER-DOMBOIS, EUGENE (lute): 649,730,731,765; Dowland, Morley
MÜNCHINGER, KARL (conductor): G. Gabrieli
Münster Cathedral Choir. *See* DOMCHOR MÜNSTER
Münster Kirchenmusikalische Schule. *See* CHOR DER KIRCHENMUSIKA-LISCHE SCHULE, MÜNSTER
Munich Capella Antiqua. *See* CAPELLA ANTIQUA, MUNICH
MUNROW, DAVID (conductor): 570,678,741,790; Morley
MUSICA ANTIQUA, VIENNA: 483,500,640,746,794; Depres, Handl, Monte, Ockeghem
MUSICA RESERVATA: 568,676,680,717,719,720,728,733,754,877; Dufay, Morton
MUSICAE ANTIQUAE COLLEGIUM VARSOVIENSE: 781
MUZERELLE, ARSENE (organ): 504

NABOKOV, D. (bass): Gesualdo
NACHTMANN, LUDWIG (conductor): Ingegneri
NATIONAL SHRINE OF THE IMMACULATE CONCEPTION: 443
N.C.R.V. VOCAAL ENSEMBLE, HILVERSUM: 492,822,828; Demantius, Depres, Gesualdo, Isaac, Senfl, Swelinck
NEGRI, VITTORIO (conductor): G. Gabrieli
NESBITT, DENNIS (conductor): 533,578
NETHERLANDS CHAMBER CHOIR: 473; Palestrina, Swelinck
NETHSINGHA, LUCIAN (conductor): 848
NEUMEYER, FRITZ (conductor): Swelinck
NEW COLLEGE CHOIR, OXFORD: Byrd, Victoria
NEW YORK PRO MUSICA: 445,548,569,603,623,627,643,674,744,803,820, 825,860; Banchieri, Franck, Morley, Senfl, anon. (Barafostus' dream)
NEW YORK BRASS QUINTET: 469
Newark, Sacred Heart Cathedral Men's Choir. *See* SACRED HEART CATHEDRAL MEN'S CHOIR, NEWARK
NICHOLSON, DAVID (conductor): 413,414
NIEDERSÄCHSISCHER SINGKREIS: 492,822; Gesualdo, Isaac, Praetorius

ST.-BENOIT D'ENCALCAT ABBEY MONKS' CHOIR: 400
ST. EDMUND'S NOVITIATE, MYSTIC, CONN.: 412
St.-Esprit de Chevilly. *See* SCHOLA DU GRAND SCHOLASTICAT DES
    PERES DU SAINT-ESPRIT DE CHEVILLY
St.-Eustache Singers. *See* CHANTEURS DE ST.-EUSTACHE
St. Francis of Assisi Papal Chapel. *See* PAPAL CHAPEL OF ST. FRANCIS
    OF ASSISI
ST. HEDWIG'S CATHEDRAL CHOIR: G. Gabrieli, Palestrina
ST. JOHN'S ABBEY MONK'S CHOIR, COLLEGEVILLE, MINN.: 399,598
ST. JOHN'S COLLEGE CHOIR, CAMBRIDGE: 537,628; Palestrina, Tallis,
    Victoria, Weelkes
St.-Jordi Chorale. *See* CHORALE SAINT-JORDI, BARCELONA
ST. JOSEPH'S ABBEY CHOIR, SPENCER, MASS.: 434
St.-Lievain d'Anvers College Choir. *See* CHOEUR COLLEGE SAINT-
    LIEVAIN D'ANVERS
St. Martini Collegium Musicum, Bremen. *See* COLLEGIUM MUSICUM ST.
    MARTINI, BREMEN
ST. MARTIN'S ABBEY MONKS' CHOIR, BEURON: 393,394
ST. MARY OF THE ANGELS CHOIR, WELLINGTON, N.Z.: 835;
    Palestrina, Victoria
ST. MAURICE & ST. MAUR ABBEY MONKS' CHOIR, CLERVAUX: 396-398
ST. MICHAEL'S COLLEGE CHOIR, TENBURY: 848
St. Paul Vocal Ensemble. *See* ENSEMBLE VOCAL ST.-PAUL
ST. PETER AD VINCULA WITHIN THE TOWER OF LONDON, CHOIR: 706
ST.-PIERRE DE SOLESMES ABBEY MONKS' CHOIR: 421-433
ST.-ROMBAUT CATHEDRAL CHOIR, MALINES (MECHLIN): 410
ST. THOMAS ABBEY MONKS' CHOIR: 416-418
St. Thomas' Choir, Leipzig. *See* THOMANERCHOR, LEIPZIG
SALTIRE SINGERS: Byrd, Dowland
SALZBURGER TURMBLÄSER: 897
SALZMANN, PIERRE (conductor): 778,816
SAMSON, JOSEPH (conductor): 484
SAN GIORGIO MAGGIORE SCHOLA, VENICE: 436-439
SANDS, JOYCE (violoncello): 853
SANTA CRUZ DEL VALLE DE LOS CAIDOS. CAPILLA MUSICAL Y
    ESCOLANIA: 457; Alfonso el Sabio
SANTA MARIA LA REAL DE LAS HUELGAS, NUNS' CHOIR: 459
SANTINI-KAMMERORCHESTER: Anerio
SANTO DOMINGO DE SILOS ABBEY MONKS' CHOIR: 419,420,458
SAORGIN, RENE (organ): 837
SARACENI, FRANCO MARIA (conductor): 630
SARTI, G. (baritone): Gesualdo
SARTORI, PADRE (conductor): 696
SCHABASSER, JOSEF: 440-442
SCHÄFER, MICHAEL (lute): 573
SCHERCHEN, HERMANN (conductor): G. Gabrieli

SCHLEAN, K. (soprano): Gesualdo
SCHMIDT, GERHARD (conductor): 695
SCHMITZ, FERDINAND (conductor): 880
SCHOLA CANTORUM BASILIENSIS: 725; Dowland, Machaut
SCHOLA CANTORUM DE LA UNIVERSIDAD PONTIFICIA DE COMILLAS:
    Victoria
SCHOLA CANTORUM LONDINIENSIS: 615
SCHOLA CANTORUM OXONIENSIS: 801
SCHOLA DU GRAND SCHOLASTICAT DES PERES DU ST.-ESPRIT DE
    CHEVILLY: Victoria
SCHOONBRODT, HUBERT (organ): 516
SCHREMS, HANS (conductor): 444; Lassus, Palestrina, Victoria
SCHREMS, THEOBALD (conductor): 638; Hassler
SCHRÖDER, HERMANN (conductor): 880,897
SCHUBA, K. P. (organ): 791
SCHULZE, THEODORA (conductor): 664; Gibbons, Tabourot
SCHWÄBISCHE SINGKREIS: 599
SCHWEIZER, ROLF (conductor): Demantius
SCUOLA DI CHIESA: Victoria, White
SEBESTYEN, JANOS (harpsichord, organ): 812
SEGARRA, IRENEU (conductor): 451; Morales
SEIDEMANN, FRITZ (lute): 479
SEINER, JOHN C. (conductor): 443
SERRA, MONTSERRAT (organ): 796
SESTETTO ITALIANO LUCA MARENZIO: Banchieri
SIDWELL, MARTINDALE (organ): 727
SIEMANN (conductor): Isaac
Silos, Santo Domingo de. *See* SANTO DOMINGO DE SILOS
THE SINGERS: 532
SISTERS OF CHARITY NOVITIATE CHOIR & SCHOLA, DUBUQUE, IOWA:
    401
SISTINE CHAPEL CHOIR: 849,850; Palestrina
SLOVAK PHILHARMONIC CHORUS: Palestrina
Smith, Gregg. *See* GREGG SMITH SINGERS
SMITHERS, DON (conductor): 745
SOCIETA CAMERISTICA DI LUGANO: 647
SOCIETE DE LA CHORALE BACH DE MONTREAL: 714,743; Byrd, Victoria
SOCIETE DE MUSIQUE D'AUTREFOIS: 670
Solesmes. *See* ST.-PIERRE DE SOLESMES ABBEY MONKS' CHOIR
SOLISTENVEREINIGUNG DES BERLINER RUNDFUNKS: 520,521
Soublette, Gaston. *See* ENSEMBLE GASTON SOUBLETTE
SOUTHERN ILLINOIS UNIVERSITY COLLEGIUM MUSICUM: 608-612
SPANDAUER KANTOREI: Demantius, Depres, LaRue, Lassus, Lechner,
    Palestrina
SPECKNER, A. B. (harpsichord): 540
SPENCER, ROBERT (lute): 534

Titles in the
Detroit Studies in Music Bibliography
Series:

General Editor:

Bruno Nettl
University of Illinois at Urbana-Champaign

1
Reference Materials in Ethnomusicology, *by Bruno Nettl*
Rev ed 1967   54p   ISBN 911772-21-9 $2.00 paper

2
Sir Arthur Sullivan: An Index to the Texts of His Vocal Works, *compiled by Sirvart Poladian*
1961   91p   ISBN 911772-22-7 $2.75 paper

3
An Index to Beethoven's Conversation Books, *by Donald W. MacArdle*
1962   46p   ISBN 911772-23-5 $2.00 paper

4
General Bibliography for Music Research, *by Keith E. Mixter*
1962   38p   ISBN 911772-24-3 $2.00 paper

5
A Handbook of American Operatic Premieres, 1731-1962, *by Julius Mattfeld*
1963   142p   ISBN 911772-25-1 $3.00 paper

6
Medieval and Renaissance Music on Long-Playing Records, *by James Coover and Richard Colvig*
1964   122p   ISBN 911772-26-X $3.00 paper

7
Rhode Island Music and Musicians, 1733-1850, *by Joyce Ellen Mangler*
1965   90p   ISBN 911772-27-8 $2.75 paper

8

Jean Sibelius: An International Bibliography on the Occasion of the Centennial Celebrations, 1965, *by Fred Blum*
1965   114p   ISBN 911772-28-6 $3.50 paper

9

Bibliography of Theses and Dissertations in Sacred Music, *by Kenneth R. Hartley*
1967   127p   ISBN 911772-29-4 $3.00 paper

10

Checklist of Vocal Chamber Works by Benedetto Marcello, *by Caroline S. Fruchtman*
1967   37p   ISBN 911772-30-8 $2.00 paper

11

An Annotated Bibliography of Woodwind Instruction Books, 1600-1830, *by Thomas E. Warner*
1967   138p   ISBN 911772-31-6 $3.00 paper

12

Works for Solo Voice of Johann Adolf Hasse, 1699-1783, *by Sven Hostrup Hansell*
1968   110p   ISBN 911772-32-4 $3.00 paper

13

A Selected Discography of Solo Song, *by Dorothy Stahl*
1968   90p   ISBN 911772-33-2 $2.50 paper
Supplement, 1968-1969, *by Dorothy Stahl*
1970   95p   ISBN 911772-34-0 $2.50 paper

14

Music Publishing in Chicago before 1871: The Firm of Root & Cady, 1858-1871, *by Dena J. Epstein*
1969   243p   ISBN 911772-36-7 $6.00 paper

15

An Introduction to Certain Mexican Musical Archives, *by Lincoln Spiess and Thomas Stanford*
1969   85+99p   ISBN 911772-37-5 $3.50 paper

16

A Checklist of American Music Periodicals, 1850-1900, *by William J. Weichlein*
1970   103p   ISBN 911772-38-3 $3.00 paper

17

A Checklist of Twentieth-Century Choral Music for Male Voices, *by Kenneth Roberts*
1970   32p   ISBN 911772-39-1 $2.00 paper

18

Published Music for the Viola da Gamba and Other Viols, *by Robin de Smet*
1971   105p   ISBN 911772-40-5 $3.00 paper

19

The Works of Christoph Nichelmann: A Thematic Index, *by Douglas A. Lee*
1971   100p   ISBN 911772-41-3 $3.50 paper

20

The Reed Trio: An Annotated Bibliography of Original Published Works,
by James E. Gillespie, Jr.
1971   84p   ISBN 911772-42-1 $4.75 paper

21

An Index to the Vocal Works of Thomas Augustine Arne and Michael Arne,
by John A. Parkinson
1972   82p   ISBN 911772-45-6 $3.50 paper

22

Bibliotheca Bolduaniana: A Renaissance Music Bibliography, *by D. W. Krummel*
1972   191p   ISBN 911772-46-4 $8.00   paper $6.50

23

Music Publishing in the Middle Western States before the Civil War, *by Ernst C. Krohn*
1972   44p   ISBN 911772-47-2 $4.00 paper

24

A Selected Discography of Solo Song: A Cumulation through 1971, *by Dorothy Stahl*
1972   137p   ISBN 911772-35-9 $6.50   paper $5.00

25

Violin and Violoncello in Duo without Accompaniment, *by Oscar R. Iotti, based on the work of Alexander Feinland*
1973   73p   ISBN 911772-48-0 $5.75   paper $4.25

PUBLICATIONS IN PROGRESS

Solos for Unaccompanied Clarinet: An Annotated Bibliography, *by James E. Gillespie, Jr.*
1973   ISBN 911772-58-8

Bibliography of Literature Concerning Yemenite-Jewish Music, *by Paul F. Marks*
1973   ISBN 911772-57-X

Titles in the
Detroit Monographs in Musicology
Series:

Editorial Committee:

Albert Cohen
State University of New York at Buffalo

Bruno Nettl
University of Illinois at Urbana-Champaign

Albert Seay
Colorado College

Howard Smither
University of North Carolina

1
The Beginnings of Musical Nationalism in Brazil, *by Gerard Behague*
1971   43p   ISBN 911772-50-2 $5.00 paper

2
Daramad of Chahargah: A Study in the Performance Practice of Persian Music,
by Bruno Nettl with Bela Foltin, Jr.
1972   84p   ISBN 911772-51-0 $6.00 paper